ORGAN-STOPS
AND THEIR ARTISTIC
REGISTRATION

CHURCH OF SAINT-OUEN, ROUEN

ORGAN-STOPS
AND THEIR ARTISTIC
REGISTRATION

G. A. AUDSLEY

With an Introduction by
ROLLIN SMITH

DOVER PUBLICATIONS, INC.
Mineola, New York

Copyright

Published in the United Kingdom by David & Charles, Brunel House, Forde Close, Newton Abbot, Devon TQ12 4PU.

Bibliographical Note

This Dover edition, first published in 2002, is an unabridged republication of *Organ-Stops and their Artistic Registration / Names, Forms, Construction, Tonalities, and Offices in Scientific Combination* by George Ashdown Audsley, LL.D., *Ecclesiastical and Organ Architect*, originally published by The H. W. Gray Co., New York, in 1921. Rollin Smith's Introduction to the Dover Edition was prepared specially for this publication.

International Standard Book Number: 0-486-42423-5

Manufactured in the United States of America
Dover Publications, Inc., 31 East 2nd Street, Mineola, N.Y. 11501

INTRODUCTION TO THE DOVER EDITION

Born in the northern Scottish village of Elgin on 6 September 1838, George Ashdown Audsley was trained as an architect, apprenticing in Elgin and, at the age of eighteen, in Liverpool, England. In partnership with his brother, W. J. Audsley, he designed and built several churches, the Liverpool West End Synagogue, Bayswater, and numerous residences. After he emmigrated to the United States, Audsley designed a medieval baptismal font for the church of St. Edward the Confessor in Philadelphia, Pennsylvania; Christ Chapel (a mission chapel of Christ Church, Clinton and Kane Streets) in the Red Hook section of Brooklyn, New York; the Layton Art Gallery, Milwaukee, Wisconsin; and the Bowling Green Offices at No. 9 Broadway, New York City. He also designed some organ cases of which the 1883 Hilborne Roosevelt in the First Congregational Church of Great Barrington, Massachusetts, is an outstanding example.

As an author, Audsley produced some of the most sumptuous books of the late nineteenth century: illuminated books of *The Prisoner of Chillon* and *The Sermon on the Mount; Colour in Dress;* a three-volume *Dictionary of Architecture and the Allied Arts; Guide to the Art of Illuminating on Vellum and Paper; Notes on Japanese Art; Taste versus Fashionable Colours: A Manual for Ladies on Colour in Dress*, and some thirteen books coauthored with his two brothers and two sons on Japanese art, polychromatic decoration, stenciling, illuminating and missal painting, chromolithography, and practical decorating.

It is remarkable that someone so productive in the visual arts also came to be regarded as one of the world's leading authorities on the organ. Audsley's interest began in Liverpool when he attended concerts of the local Philharmonic Society and the weekly organ recitals given by the great William Thomas Best at St. George's Hall. His first writings about the organ were a series of thirty articles published in 1886 in *The English Mechanic and World of Science.* His masterpiece, seven years in the writing, was published in 1905: *The Art of Organ Building,* a work in which the illustrations, scale drawings, literary style, and sheer breadth of subject matter have never been equaled in texts on music. Fourteen years later, Audsley brought out *The Organ of the Twentieth Century,* an extended elucidation of his views on tonal design.

Despite so notable an output and his recognition as an authority on the subject, only three Audsley-designed organs were built. The first and most famous was for the 1904 Louisiana Purchase Centennial in St. Louis (an instrument later incorporated into the great Philadelphia Wanamaker organ). The other two were organs built by Philip Wirsching for Our Lady of Grace Roman Catholic Church in Hoboken, New Jersey, and a 22-stop, two-manual organ for the residence of Eugene C. Clark of Yonkers, New York. Perhaps Audsley was a dreamer and visionary more interested in what the organ could and should become than in creating workable designs. Yet in all of his writings it is apparent that the tonal architect's concern for the instrument was as great as that for the building that housed it.

Audsley detested the separation of the organ's divisions into chambers, insisting that all pipes be encased in a centralized position. He attributed the term "organ chamber" to ignorant and careless church architects—it having "become an abomination . . . to all interested in the artistic development of the Organ and Organ music." He favored positioning the choir in front of the congregation with the organ immediately behind it, all on one level. Further, he advocated enclosing every division in a swell box so that no part of the perfect organ would be unexpressive—but the swell box would close only to achieve a distinct *piano,* particularly avoiding the inartistic "annihilating swell."

Audsley's definite requirements for the disposition of the organ console often met with resistance. In place of "old-fashioned and objectionable" drawknobs arranged vertically on either side of the manuals, he favored centrally-pivoted rocking-tablets (as on Aeolian consoles), or "tinted pendant tablets pivoted at the upper end," familiar on theater organs "notwithstanding [drawknobs] still being favored by many organists and some conservative organ-builders."

Even more controversial was Audsley's attempt to codify organ nomenclature by labeling all stops in Italian—it being the universal language of music. The only organ-builder to adopt this idea was the Aeolian Company—a decision that caused such confusion among its staff and bafflement among its clients that it was abandoned after three years.

Audsley was writing during a time when he considered "the noble Art of Organ-building [to be] suffering a serious decadence under the hands of too many inartistic, know-little, and don't-care tradesmen." Prophetically, he declared that the art required "serious study by all who respect true ecclesiastical music, hallowed by the use of thirteen centuries, and [who] desire to see the instruments, which accompany it, in every way worthy of the high office they have to fulfill."

Audsley had no sympathy for the organist's love of "*musical noise* at any price: [in which] we see the general craze . . . for unenclosed Tubas, Octave couplers on all claviers creating unbalanced noise, and other means of piling sound on sound, regardless of acoustical laws, or, indeed, common sense." His goal was to design organs capable of producing thousands of tonal combinations but on which it would be "impossible to create undesirable noise."

At the time of his death on 21 June 1925, and the publication of his last book, *The Temple of Tone,* Audsley's concept of organ design embraced four distinct instruments, categorized by the purpose for which each was built: concert room, church, Gregorian (intended for Roman Catholic liturgy), and theater. Logically, each would perform specific tasks and therefore had special needs.

The Concert Room Organ was designed to replace the "quasi-church, bastard instruments" previously designed for concert use. This organ was ideally of five manuals: Grand, Accompanimental, Woodwind, Brass-Wind, and Solo; together with several *Ancillary,* or floating, divisions that could be played on any manual: String, Aërial (intended as a sub-division of the Accompanimental Organ), and Fanfare.

The Church Organ was ideally an accompanimental instrument designed "to meet all the demands in the artistic accompaniment of choral and congregational singing and in the rendition of organ music of an ecclesiastical and dignified character." Audsley was particular to state that "provision for the execution of florid music and the display of executive skill on the part of the organist [was] of no importance. Organists will not agree with us in this dictum; but, as they disagree with us in so many other equally important questions, it is of little moment, as time will show."

The Gregorian Organ—following the rulings of the 1903 papal encyclical, *Motu proprio*—was intended "to sympathetically accompany and support Gregorian Chant with an ethos full of repose, grandeur, refinement, and expression, and to provide rich and solemn strains on great feasts" as well as incidental music "of an impressive and elevating character; inducing in the mind religious aspiration." Thus, its three manuals consisted of a general Grand Organ, a perfect Accompaniment, and an efficient Solo.

The Theater Organ was to replace the "unit orchestras" then ubiquitous in all motion picture houses.

Dissenting organists were often justified in their dissent because over time Audsley designed expensive, impractical, "theoretical" instruments that had less and less in common with the traditional organ for which five centuries of music had been composed. Nevertheless, his concern for and interest in the organ gave him an authority and unique perspective when it came to describing individual ranks of pipes and their effective use. This is the great value of the present volume.

In *Organ-Stops and their Artistic Registration,* Audsley not only describes comprehensively each rank of pipes, but indicates its musical

x

purpose and how it can be combined effectively with other ranks. The author divides organ stops into two general categories: unimitative organ tone and imitative orchestral tone. Under the first, he groups Pure Organ Tone (Diapason tone at all octaves and in many partials of the harmonic series); Free Organ Tone (those hybrids such as the Dulciana, Keraulophone, and Gemshorn); Flute Tone; and Viol Tone (Salicionals, Geigenprincipals, and so on). The four Orchestral Tones are String ("the first and most essential of all . . . in the modern Organ"); Flute (only three harmonic flutes at 8', 4', and 2' pitches); Reed (all imitative woodwind stops); and Brass (trumpets at all pitches).

Throughout the Glossary—as he refers to the main section of this book—Audsley classifies each stop under the above headings and also as *labial* (flue) and *lingual* (reed). The various "ancillary organs" refer to those secondary divisions that he intended to be coupled into the main divisions. Entries define the stop, the languages in which it is found, its history, organs in which it is or was found, its construction, and its use in registration.

As in all his writings, Audsley's text is interspersed with strong opinion. After discussing how various organ-builders construct metal-stop bottom octaves of wood or by common-bassing (a soft Aeoline shares the bass of a soft Bourdon), he adds, "None of these money-saving devices should be followed." Under the entry *Diapason,* he declares "the true English diapason-tone is the most lovely; that of the French Montre the most unsatisfactory: yet to French ears, and those satisfied with power rather than refinement of tone, it seems agreeable."

Opiniated, expert, and wise, George Audsley's commentaries are as valid today as when they were written, adding new dimensions to an acknowledged classic of our time.

ROLLIN SMITH
Spring 2002

FOREWORD

An attempt has been made in the present work to furnish the organist, and especially the organ student, with a work of ready reference respecting the numerous Stops which have been and now are introduced in the Organ: giving, so far as is practicable in a necessarily brief and condensed form, their various names in different languages, peculiarities of formation, tonal characteristics, and value and office in scientific and artistic combination and artistic registration.

It is hoped that the work will be accepted as a text-book in Organ Schools and Conservatories of Music, leading toward, and lending help to, a branch of study of the greatest value and importance to the organ student; but one which, in too many quarters, has been seriously neglected. That a thorough knowledge of the tonal forces of the Organ and their varied powers in scientific and artistic combination and registration, for the production of special and expressive qualities of both compound, unimitative organ, and imitative orchestral tones, is essential to the accomplished organist, admits of no question. Accordingly, it is highly desirable that the student should leave the organ school with, at least, a foundation laid for that thorough knowledge. It is with the earnest desire to contribute effectively to the laying of that foundation that the present work is placed at the command of both teachers and pupils.

In another direction, and one of great importance at the present time, this work, if properly understood, will prove of considerable value; namely, in giving reliable advice and assistance in the preparation of stop appointments and apportionments for new Organs. It will lead away, if read aright, from the present systemless, insufficient, and largely retrograde prevailing method of stop appointment, toward a logical, scientific, and definite artistic system, in which compound tone production in all its desirable forms can be carried out in accordance with the natural laws of sound.

Care has been taken to render correctly all stop-names in the different languages in which they originated and are employed to-day: reference to which will prevent the use of the incorrect names, either wrongly spelt or improperly compounded of words in different languages, which are so commonly found on English and American organ-builders' draw-stop knobs or tablets.   With such a Glossary as is provided in the present work, there need be no mistakes made or incorrect renderings of stop-names perpetrated in new organ consoles.

Certain stop-names introduced by organ-builders have been omitted from the Glossary on account of their absurd or meaningless character.   These are names which have no relation to anything connected with either the formation or tonality of the pipes forming the stops.   All such meaningless names should be condemned by every organist and lover of the Monarch of all Instruments.

GEORGE ASHDOWN AUDSLEY.

BLOOMFIELD, NEW JERSEY,
JANUARY, 1921.

PLATES

ORGAN-STOPS
AND THEIR ARTISTIC
REGISTRATION

ORGAN-STOPS

THEIR ARTISTIC REGISTRATION

"Without the least hyperbole it may be said, that *cæteris paribus*, the man who is capable of being affected by sweet sounds, is a being *more perfectly organized*, than he who is insensible to, or offended by them."

DR. CHARLES BURNEY.

In Organ-stop Registration, as in artistic orchestration, "there is no royal road to learning." Natural musical taste and appreciation of the beautiful in musical sounds may go far in the education of the organist; but earnest studies along scientific and artistic lines are in all cases necessary for the complete command of tonal coloring, by means of registration and the knowledge of the tonal values of the multitudinous and varied voices of the Organ. As Dr. Burney truly says: "The science of musical sounds, though it may have been deprecated, as appealing only to the ear, affording nothing more than a momentary and fugitive delight, may be with justice considered as the art that unites corporal with intellectual pleasure by a species of enjoyment which gratifies sense without weakening reason; and which, therefore, the Great may cultivate without debasement and the Good enjoy without depravation."*

Let the organ student realize, once for all, if he is to become an artist, that haphazard methods of registration must be shunned, and dependence placed on knowledge acquired by study, observation, and experience. The earnest study of artistic registration and the tonal value of organ-stops, singly and in combination, should accompany all lessons on, and the practice of, the technical branch of organ playing: but how seldom, in organ schools, is a student's attention specially directed to the all-important matter of tonal coloring.

* "A General History of Music," by Dr. Charles Burney, London, 1776.

Excellence and precision of manual and pedal technic are, of course, imperative in the satisfactory rendition of an organ composition; but technic is not the only, or, perhaps, the most important, factor. It may be said to be the skeleton which has to be clothed with the flesh and nervous power of beautiful and expressive sounds —alone secured by scientific combination and artistic registration of appropriate and expressive tonal elements. The most consummate technical skill is altogether insufficient in the presence of a careless and inappropriate registration to produce a truly artistic and expressive rendering of an organ composition.

With the acquisition of manual and pedal technic should go a serious study of the tonal forces of the Organ, their combination, and effective registration; for it is appropriate tonal coloring which gives the spirit and expressiveness to the music, which no single performer save the organist is capable of producing, and for which no instrument save the Organ can furnish the necessary tonal elements—music which can only be surpassed by the united forces of the grand orchestra under the control of an accomplished conductor. The organist is as the conductor; the many and diverse tonal forces of the Organ are his instrumentalists: it rests with him to marshal those forces, in ever-changing groups, so as to produce the artistic and life-giving effects his music demands; and for the interpretation of his most refined conceptions. Again, the organist is as the painter before his canvas, brush in hand; the stops of his Organ are the colors of many tints, hues, and shades, spread for his ready use on a serviceable palette; to be combined, at will, in endless variety as the spirit of the tone-picture inspires him. What a wonderful world of tone the organist can live in if he only realizes his birthright—his citizenship in the land of beautiful sound. The organist stands supreme in the musical world—the master of the most stupendous, the most wonderful musical instrument ever conceived by the mind and fabricated by the hand of man. Think of it, O ye Organists, and rise to the level of your birthright!

Before going deeper into our subject, we may here give a few more pertinent words from the able pen of England's great musical historian. Alluding to tonal matters and the Organ of his day, he remarks: "Of Musical Tones the most grateful to the ear are such as are produced by the vocal organs. And next to singing, the most pleasing kinds are those which approach the nearest to vocal; such as can be sustained, swelled, and diminished, at pleasure. Of these, first in rank are such as the most excellent performers produce from the Violin, Flute, and Hautbois. If it were to be asked what instrument is capable of affording the GREATEST EFFECTS? I should answer, the ORGAN, which can not only imitate a number of other instruments, but is so comprehensive as to possess the power of a numerous orchestra. It is, however, very remote from perfection, as it wants expression, and a more perfect intonation." Much of what is said in the concluding sentence is true of the Organ of to-day, greatly superior as the best examples are to the Organ known to Dr. Burney. The Organ still wants full powers of expression combined with tonal flexibility throughout all its divisions. Accordingly, while much has been done of late years in certain directions, still more has to be achieved by the organ-designer and organ-builder before the Organ can be pronounced an instrument for the true artist and inspired virtuoso. Certainly, what has been done during the last seventy years in the direction of imitative orchestral-toned stops, was hardly foreshadowed in Burney's day. The Swell Organ known to him was usually of short compass and very indifferently stop-apportioned. Writing in 1771, this distinguished author remarks:

"It is very extraordinary that the *swell* which has been introduced into the English organ more than fifty years, and which is so capable of expression and of pleasing effects that it may well be said to be the greatest and most important improvement that ever was made on any keyed instrument, should be utterly *unknown* in Italy; and now I am on the subject, I must observe that most of the organs I have met with on the Continent seem to be inferior to ours by Father Smith, Byfield, or Snetzler, in everything but size! As the churches there are very often immense so are the organs; the tone indeed is somewhat softened and refined by space and distance; but when heard near, it is intolerably coarse and noisy; and though the number of stops in these large instruments is very great, they afford but little variety, being for the most part duplicates in unisons and octaves to each other, such as the great and small 12ths, flutes, and 15ths; hence our organs, not only the touch and tone, but the imitative stops are greatly superior to those of any other organs I have met with."*

Alluding to the first swell introduced in a German Organ, which is understood to have been in the Organ, built by Hildebrand, in 1764, for the Church of St. Michael, Hamburg, Burney says: "A swell has been *attempted* in this instrument, but with little effect; only three stops have been put into it, and the power of *crescendo diminuendo* is so small with them, that if I had not been told there was a swell, I should not have discovered it."†

We have introduced the subject of the swell at this early point

---

* "Present State of Music in France and Italy," 1771, p. 375.

† "Present State of Music in Germany, the Netherlands, and United Provinces," 1775. Vol. II., p. 103.

of our brief essay because it has a direct and very important bearing
on the matter of artistic registration. If one examines the stop
appointments of the Organs of Burney's days, or of all the old Organs
in which no swell was introduced; and, indeed, of those, of later
times, which possessed only a single flexible and expressive division,
one cannot avoid being impressed with the very limited opportunities they present for varied registration—artistic registration being
practically out of the question. So few were the useful combinations of the stops in the older Organs that they were commonly
commanded by foot-levers, called "combination pedals." Artistic
registration, as it is understood to-day, was practically unknown in
connection with the old Organs: and it must be acknowledged that
it still continues undesirably difficult in too many of the modern
Organs tonally schemed on old-fashioned lines. Stops properly
chosen and apportioned among the different divisions of the Organ,
under the principles of class grouping, tonal contrast, absolute
flexibility regarding strength of voice, and compound expression, as
long advocated and first practically introduced by us in the Organ,
are the only efficient means by which scientific tonal combination
and truly artistic registration can be carried out to the extreme
extent, now necessary in the proper and effective rendering of the
works of the great and distinguished composers of organ music, and
especially the modern transcriptions of orchestral scores.

The system of stop-apportionment and control which we have
devised and strongly advocate, is widely different from the old-
fashioned and seemingly purposeless method which has so long obtained in organ-building, and may be briefly described here. It
comprises the grouping of stops of different tonalities in the several
manual divisions of an Organ, according to their special offices in
the complete tonal scheme of the instrument, and for the ready
production, without recourse to undesirable coupling, of the numerous and very varied organ and orchestral tonal combinations and
effects, absolutely called for in modern artistic organ playing. To
secure what is essential, each division has a distinct general and
special tonality, contrasting with that of every other division; unnecessary duplication of stops of the same tonality being thereby
avoided. Each division, having its own office to fulfil, is given
special powers of flexibility and expression; those devoted to the
stops representing the "wood-wind" and "brass-wind" forces of
the grand orchestra being divided into two tonally contrasting portions, each of which is given independent powers of flexibility and
expression. The division devoted to the foundation stops and those

properly belonging to the Organ, commonly designated Great Organ, is also divided into two portions, only one of which, comprising special registrational, harmonic-corroborating, and lingual stops, is rendered flexible and expressive; although both subdivisions may be so treated if deemed desirable. The Solo, String, and Ancillary Organs are rendered flexible and expressive, but do not require to be divided.*

On a first and hasty consideration, the introduction of the new principles of divisional and subdivisional tonal contrast and flexibility and expression may not seem to the organist, who has only known the present unsystematic and haphazard method of stop-apportionment (to be observed in every modern organ specification), to be of any great scientific or artistic importance or value. But let him devote sufficient time to the study of those principles, with an open and unprejudiced mind, and he will find that for the convenient and certain production of refined and beautiful tonal combinations and orchestral effects, and for facility in scientific and artistic registration, the combined principles form the greatest and most valuable improvement in the tonal branch of organ-building ever instituted in modern days, since the time we placed—in the year 1870—three independent tonal subdivisions on one manual clavier; two of which are flexible and expressive, being inclosed in separate swell-boxes. This unique step may or may not be considered a small beginning; but, as Burney pertinently remarks: "The feeble beginnings of whatever becomes great or eminent, are interesting to mankind. To Artists, therefore, and to real lovers of art, nothing relative to the object of their employment or pleasure is indifferent."

Let us consider briefly what is possible to be done with a single clavier, tonally appointed in the manner alluded to. Say that it commands sixteen stops of varied and artistically chosen tonalities and pitches; eight of which are inclosed in, say, swell-box A and eight in swell-box B; the stops being divided so as to provide contrasting voices and be practically independent. It also being arranged that either one or both the subdivisions shall be available on the clavier at the pleasure of the performer. Now, for the consideration of registration, we shall confine our remarks to the element of flexibility, neglecting for the present the all-important element of expression, and suppose both the subdivisions to be commanded by the clavier. It can be readily realized that by simply opening either

* For full particulars, see Chapter XI., on the Concert-room Organ, in our work, "The Organ of the Twentieth Century."

swell, more or less, the voices of the inclosed stops can be graduated
to any desirable strength of intonation—an absolutely invaluable
property in refined and artistic registration, multiplying the utility
and combinational effects of the stops at least tenfold. Now suppose
a registration of certain stops of both subdivisions is essayed, the
voices of which are in sharp contrast, the character of the compound
tone produced can be altered, at will, without changing a stop,
either on one side or the other; and the relative strengths of its contrasting elements adjusted through the flexibility imparted to the
voices of the inclosed stops, by the simple opening or closing of the
shutters of the allied swells, commanded by the expression levers.
By the simple touching of these levers any desirable intensity of
tone and effects of light and shade can be imparted to the music
being performed: and this without removing the hands from the
clavier, or having any resort to undesirable coupling, which would
unavoidably cripple the independence of another clavier.

What we have attempted to describe may not appear, on first
impressions, as in any way remarkable to the organist acquainted
only with the one-ply stop-apportionments of the Organs of to-day.
But let us inform him of the fact that the multitudinous and practically inexhaustible tonal effects, colorings, and refined *nuances*,
easy of production, under our system of divisional and subdivisional
stop-apportionment and compound flexibility, on this single clavier,
could not be produced on the claviers of the largest Concert-room
Organ ever constructed up to this year of grace (1920). And let
him try to realize what could be done on an Organ in which three or
four of its manual divisions are equipped in the compound manner
described above. We foolishly essayed the task, and our mind was
quickly baffled in the attempt.

Up to this point we have treated only of the stationary compound tones, produced by registration, under the simple graduation
of strength, effected by the property of flexibility, which merely
called for a set or temporarily fixed adjustment of the shutters of
the swells. We have now to consider the operations of the allied
property of compound expression, which can be exercised in four
different ways. 1.—Expression can be given simultaneously to the
tones of both subdivisions, by operating the expression levers of the
swells (located close together) at the same time. 2.—Expression
can be given to the tones of either subdivision, the tones of the other
subdivision remaining unaffected at the fixed degree of strength
desired; by adjusting one expression lever at any set point, and
operating the other as required. 3.—Expression can be given to the

tones of the subdivisions alternately; by operating the expression levers alternately. 4.—Expression can be given to the tones of the subdivisions simultaneously in contrary directions, one series undergoing a *crescendo* while the other series is undergoing a *decrescendo;* by operating the expression levers, in contrary motion, by both feet (*sans pédale*).

The principles of compound flexibility and expression would be of comparatively little value in the absence of the correlative system of classified stop-apportionment and tonal contrast we have introduced. There are two grand divisions of organ-stops. First, that division embracing those stops essentially of a solo character which imperatively demand the fullest possible powers of expression; but which are practically independent of combination or registration, save for the purpose of accentuation or coloration of tone. Among such stops are those which represent important orchestral instruments such as the Violin, Violoncello, Flute, Oboe, Clarinet, Trumpet, Horn, and Trombone. Secondly, that much larger division composed, for the most part, of organ-toned and unimitative stops, which are largely, and to a considerable extent exclusively, employed in combination and registration, for the production of compound tones of great variety and pronounced colorings. For the full development of these purposes, the system of classified divisional and subdivisional stop-apportionment, under complete control as regards flexibility and expression, we advocate, is absolutely necessary from the simple fact that such essential artistic conditions cannot be met under the aimless and heterogeneous method of stop-appointment followed, practically without variation, in the organ-building world to-day. If this view of the matter is questioned, let anyone, capable of forming an open-minded opinion of a scientific and artistic caliber, take a hundred or more of the so-called specifications of the more important and representative modern Organs and carefully consider their lists of stops and judge for himself.*

There are two classes of labial stops which are of great value in scientific combination and artistic registration; but which have been very unwisely neglected of late years, partly on account of a want of a full knowledge of their great offices in tone-production; but chiefly on the part of those organ-builders who desire to evade the trouble and uncertainty attending their proper formation, artistic voicing,

* It may be helpful to compare any of their tonal schemes with that given for the Concert-room Organ in "The Organ of the Twentieth Century."

and scientific regulation. We allude to the harmonic-corroborating mutation and the compound stops; the latter commonly designated MIXTURES, which, as has been wisely said of other things, "when they're good they're very good, but when they're bad they're horrid." They are usually bad! It is quite easy to understand, in this inartistic and dollar-worshiping epoch, the objection of the organ-builder to the introduction of the necessary amount of harmonic-corroborating work in a large Organ. A MIXTURE, of five or more ranks, requiring three hundred and five or many more pipes, properly composed, scaled, and artistically voiced, and, what is of equal importance, scientifically graduated in tone in strict accordance with the natural laws of compound musical sounds, is a problem very few organ-builders will care to solve. It cannot be satisfactorily essayed in the hurry and noise of the ordinary factory voicing-room. On simple trade grounds, such troublesome and labor-demanding stops are to be omitted in all possible cases; and an examination of the great majority of modern organ stop-appointments clearly show how systematically they are omitted. Alas for Art!

We have before us as we write the lists of the stops of two large and important Organs, which may be accepted as representing the latest and highest achievements in organ-designing, in the direction of stop-appointment. The largest presents upwards of two hundred and seventy complete and independent speaking stops; and in this immense number there are only five MIXTURES, comprising in all only twenty ranks of pipes. The other list presents one hundred and one speaking stops (including derived and borrowed stops); in which there are three MIXTURES, comprising, in all, only eight ranks of pipes.

The most effective criticism we can pass on the insufficient harmonic appointments detailed above, is to give the contrasting appointment of our scheme for the Concert-room Organ, set forth in "The Organ of the Twentieth Century." In this there are two hundred and twenty-three complete and eight derived speaking stops; among which are apportioned fourteen MIXTURES, comprising, in all, sixty-four ranks of pipes. Great as this number may appear, by comparison, we are prepared to prove, on both scientific and artistic grounds, that for such an Organ there is not a rank too many; indeed, had we not introduced the Ancillary Harmonic Organ a larger number of compound harmonic-corroborating stops would have been necessary to meet the demands of artistic and effective registration and tone coloration.

A great injury was done to the tonal structure of the Organ by the false idea, introduced by self-interested parties, that the harmonic-corroborating stops, simple and compound, could be dispensed with, provided certain stops were introduced, the voices of which were naturally rich in harmonic upper partials, such as heavily-blown, small-scaled, string-toned stops; but a greater mistake was never made. Such highly-colored penetrating tonalities are of very little use in artistic registration, generally objectionable, and absolutely valueless in the creation of delicately colored qualities of tone. Such qualities of compound tone are only possible by the use of softly-voiced stops associated with such stops as the scientifically formed and tonally graduated DULCIANA CORNET or HARMONIA ÆTHERIA.

In artistic registration, two distinct classes of musical tones obtain—those due to the Harmony of Analogy and those due to the Harmony of Contrast. The former class is produced by the registration of stops of the same family or of very closely allied families, differing only slightly in strength of voice, or between which a very close affinity exists. The latter class, and much the more effective and important, is produced by the skillful registration of stops of widely different families, of contrasting tonalities, and of pitches far apart. In both classes harmonic-corroborating stops are valuable, and, if properly chosen, enrich without altering to any undesirable degree their characteristic tonalities. Light and shade can be imparted to a compound tone without changing its dominant character; while, on the other hand, very refined colorings can be imparted by introducing compound harmonic timbre-creating stops. Organists will, however, have to wait patiently for these; for organbuilders are at present trying to get rid of, rather than contemplating the introduction of new and more valuable, compound harmonic-corroborating stops: that must be evident to everyone who takes the trouble to critically examine the lists of stops in the so-called specifications of Organs being turned out to-day.

The beauty that perfectly constructed and scientifically balanced compound harmonic-corroborating stops impart to the various tonal groupings characteristic of the Organ is hardly known to the organists of the present time. This is greatly to be regretted; and the knowledge will be very difficult to obtain until some thoroughly scientific artist in compound harmonic tone production furnishes organists with the means of acquiring it.

In scheming the stop-apportionment of every division and subdivision of an Organ, the special value and office of every stop, in solo effects and in artistic combination, should be studiously considered. There should be no combinational stops inserted which would prove of little use. It should be realized that each division and subdivision of an Organ should be devised to occupy a distinct place, and fulfil a special office, in the tonal economy of the entire instrument. As great a degree of tonal independence should be aimed at as general conditions permit of; thereby preventing any undesirable resort to coupling of the claviers. When any two claviers are coupled, one or the other is for the time being crippled tonally, unless under some exceptional conditions. Such coupling should seldom have to be resorted to, unless necessary for the massing of different and contrasting tones and the production of full effects. The more perfectly an Organ is stop-apportioned in its several divisions, the less will the resort to coupling be required, especially in artistic registration for music of an orchestral or symphonic character.

There never has been a more serious blow given to the science and art of organ tonal-appointment than that given when Léonard Dryvers, organ-builder, of Wessel-Loo-Louvain, sprang on the organ-building world his unscientific, inartistic, and pernicious system of stop-appointment, under the appellation "L'Orgue Simplifié." A system founded on trade expedients, and devoid of a single scientific or artistic element in its favor. Had it been confined to its originator and his interested supporter—Couwenbergh —little injury might have accrued. Unfortunately it was espoused by the late Robert Hope-Jones, and is still advocated by some of his followers. On the other hand, and very fortunately for the true art of organ-building, the system (if system it can be called) is condemned by every thoughtful and accomplished organist and leading organ-builder of the present hour. From a purely artistic and common-sense point of view we raise our voice in protest against a system of tonal appointment at variance with all the laws and canons of musical sound.

The Organ, tonally appointed on the Dryvers system, described by H. V. Couwenbergh, of Averbode, in his pamphlet published in 1887, comprises only the following stops: MONTRE, 16 FT.; BOURDON, 16 FT. ("dont le dessus est ouvert en FLÛTE HARMONIQUE"); VIOLON, 16 FT.; and BOMBARDE, 16 FT. From these four stops, of extended compass, are formed no fewer than thirty-one stops of 16 ft., 8 ft., 4 ft., and 2 ft. pitch: the MONTRE furnishing *seven* stops, all of the same quality and strength of tone; the BOURDON furnishing *ten* stops of somewhat irregular quality and strength of tone; the VIOLON furnishing *seven* stops of the same quality and strength of tone; and the Bombarde furnishing also *seven* stops of the same quality and strength of tone: only four qualities of tone, and no mutation and high-pitched harmonic-corroborating ranks, in an instrument presenting—after a fashion—thirty-one speaking stops. Can anyone gifted with musical knowledge and refined taste imagine such a tonal monstrosity anywhere save in a noisy merry-go-round at a seaside resort or a country fair? To conceive it an instrument for the performance of true and refined organ music is impossible: to speak of its stops being capable of scientific combination and artistic registration would be laughable.* Yet the fact remains that instruments—we will not call them Organs—have been constructed on such a systém in this country: but we are not aware of any examples having been perpetrated either in England or France. We sincerely trust that such an outrage on the noble and scientific art of organ-building will not be encouraged.

Only slightly less objectionable and destructive of tonal powers is the present growing system of borrowing stops from certain divisions of an Organ to make up deficiencies in other divisions. This method has the effect of making a poor and badly schemed stop-apportionment look impressive on paper and on the draw-stops of the Organ; and that is all that can be said in its favor. This undesirable and inartistic practice is carried to the extreme in the formation of the Pedal Organ from manual stops; and is necessarily destructive of clavier independence, effective tonal grouping, and artistic registration. To show to what an extent this objectionable practice is now being carried, we may state that lying before us as we write is an organ-builder's Specification for an Organ, showing an ostensible list of sixty speaking stops. The Pedal Organ of twelve stops is entirely borrowed from the manual divisions, with the exception of twenty-four pipes which strictly belong to it. Comment is unnecessary.

Borrowing between manual divisions, if limited in extent and done with well-considered scientific and artistic ends in view, and without having the effect of crippling the independence of the contributing divisions, may be productive of valuable aid in compound tone creation and artistic registration; and, accordingly, may well receive serious attention in scheming the stop-apportionments of the tonal divisions of Organs of moderate dimensions. But unless such borrowing is done with great judgment, care, and a full know-

---

* For further particulars, respecting "L'Orgue Simplifié," and of a larger example of the application of the "nouveau systéme d'orgues," see "The Art of Organ-Building," Vol. II., pp 13–18.

ledge of tone production, the result may be largely destructive of the
musical qualities of the instrument, as past experience has amply
proved.

The great value of Mutation harmonic-corroborating stops in
registration, for the creation of special compound tonalities and
orchestral coloring, must not be overlooked. We desire to impress
this important matter on organists generally, and especially on
those who may have the opportunity of scheming the tonal appointments of Organs. The importance of such stops is little understood
or realized in this country at the present time; simply because they
so seldom appear in the stop-appointments of the Organs that have
been turned out of our workshops.

For proofs of this statement, we may refer to the two large
organ schemes, already commented upon as seriously deficient in
compound harmonic-corroborating stops. They display a still
greater disregard of the important and tonally essential Mutation
stops. In the larger scheme, comprising upwards of two hundred
and seventy speaking stops, there are only three fifth-sounding
stops,—one belonging to the 32 ft. harmonic series; one belonging
to the 16 ft. series; and one belonging to the 8 ft. series. In the
lesser scheme, comprising, ostensibly, one hundred and one speaking stops, there is only one Mutation stop, fifth-sounding, and
belonging to the 16 ft. harmonic series. Not a single one belonging
to the all-important 8 ft. series! We have no desire to be severe in
our comments: but to us it seems very astonishing that the designers of these Organs—intended to represent the latest advance on
old-fashioned tonal appointment—should have so seriously overlooked the important scientific and artistic offices of the Mutation
stops. And the question naturally arises: Did they know, or simply
ignore, the necessity, on both scientific and artistic grounds, of
introducing third-sounding Mutation stops? .

Again, by way of comparison and furnishing an example, we
may refer to the scheme for the Concert-room Organ given in our
work. In the two hundred and thirty-one speaking stops it presents, are included twenty-five Mutation stops, divided as follows:
Of the 64 ft. harmonic series there is one fifth-sounding labial stop;
of the 32 ft. series there are two labial and one lingual fifth-sounding stops; of the 16 ft. series there are seven labial and two lingual
fifth-sounding stops; and of the 8 ft. series there are six fifth-sounding and six third-sounding Mutation stops. The interested student
should note the introduction of the three lingual Mutation stops.
Again we say, large as the number is, there is not a stop too many

to furnish an accomplished performer with adequate means for scientific and artistic registration and orchestral-tone production.

It is to be regretted that no definite rules of universal application can be formulated to direct the organist in the all-important art of registration; because, on the one hand, there are no universally adopted standards of tone in the stops bearing similar names, produced by different makers, at different times, and under different voicing conditions; and because, on the other hand, Organs differ very widely in their stop appointments. So much so, that what may be highly satisfactory and artistic registration on one Organ, may be the reverse on another instrument.

Composers and writers of organ music render great assistance to performers by indicating what to them is desirable and effective registration for their works: but it must be remembered that such registration has been formulated from the tonal material furnished by some special Organ, at the command of the composer, or dominant in his mind. It is, accordingly, questionable to what extent such specific registration will be possible or satisfactory on other Organs of different stop-appointments or stop-tonalities. Marked differences in both directions are almost certain to obtain. It would seem, under such conditions, that special artistic registration, to properly render the composer's intentions, would be absolutely called for on each Organ on which his works are to be performed.

We may close our brief remarks on this introductory branch of our general subject with a few words, which may be of interest to the organ student desirous of acquiring skill in the all-important art of registration. In the first place, it is very desirable that the student should form a clear and comprehensive concept of the tonal structure of the Organ in its fullest scientific and artistic development. This can only be properly arrived at by becoming familiar with the special tonalities, combinational properties, and color-values of all the stops which form that structure; and which are to be found, or are available for introduction, in the Organ of to-day: all of which are more or less fully commented upon in the following pages, under their accepted names. It must be borne in mind, however, that the names given to the stops found in modern Organs do not invariably, or, indeed commonly, indicate their correct or most desirable tonalities. This is simply due to the fact that there are no universally recognized standards of tone in organ-pipes: each organ-builder or voicer invariably adopting his own pipe-scales and system of voicing; thereby producing his own peculiar or preferred quality of tone in each individual stop or family of stops.

This diversity of tonal quality and color-value is very noticeable in even the principal organ-toned stop—the DIAPASON—the voice of which varies, often widely, in Organs by different builders. In the voices of both the labial and lingual imitative stops the difference of tonality is generally very marked. In this class, one seldom hears the same quality of tone in stops of the same name in any two Organs.

Such being the case, it is very important that the student should become thoroughly acquainted with the special tonalities and color-values of all the stops which are comprised in the appointment of the Organ on which he studies and performs: and that he should follow up the knowledge so gained by a study of the tonal effects produced by the combination of the stops of different colorings, strengths of voice, and pitches; carefully noting their mixing qualities and their harmonies of analogy and contrast, until he becomes thoroughly familiar with the tonal resources of his instrument. This somewhat exacting study, requiring time, thoughtful observation, the exercise of memory, and not a little scientific and artistic culture, goes to prove, as we have already said, "there is no royal road to learning."

TONALITY OF ORGAN-STOPS

The stops which are at the disposal of the designers of modern Organs are very numerous, as the present Glossary plainly shows; and their tonalities display a diversity almost as great as that of their names. Certain stops have distinct and pronounced voices, which are either peculiar to them, or which belong to families formed of members having difference of scale, slightly modified voicing, and especially varied pitch. Others, less pronounced in their voices, are more or less derivatives from special or more assertive stops. Further, stops are either unimitative in their voices and strictly belong to the Organ, their tones being unproducible by any other instrument; or they are, in their voices, more or less closely imitative of the tones produced by the string, wood-wind, and brass-wind instruments of the orchestra. Under these conditions, two grand divisions obtain in the tonal forces of the Organ; one formed of stops strictly belonging to the Organ proper, and the other of stops which are imitative and orchestral in their tonalities. In the modern Organ, and especially in the Concert-room Organ, both divisions of the tonal forces must be adequately represented, if the instrument is to be sufficient for the artistic rendition of all classes of organ music.

A careful study of the tonal forces which properly group themselves under the two grand divisions has led us to classify them into eight subdivisions, each of which has a distinctive general tonality: and this system of tonal grouping and subdivision will prove a valuable aid to the organ student in the study of registration and the production of tone-color. The system may be presented in the following form:

FIRST DIVISION	SECOND DIVISION
Organ-Tone	Orchestral-Tone
Unimitative Quality	*Imitative Quality*
1. PURE ORGAN-TONE.	1. ORCHESTRAL STRING-TONE.
2. FREE ORGAN-TONE.	2. ORCHESTRAL FLUTE-TONE.
3. FLUTE ORGAN-TONE.	3. ORCHESTRAL REED-TONE.
4. VIOL ORGAN-TONE.	4. ORCHESTRAL BRASS-TONE.

The eight different qualities of tone thus set forth may be accepted as completely covering the tonal forces of the Organ of to-day in its highest development; and the several classes of stops which yield them may, with advantage, and necessarily briefly, be alluded to here.

It may, in the first place be pointed out that all the stops of the Organ, so far as their formation is concerned, are of two kinds, labial and lingual; the former being constructed of either metal or wood pipes—open, covered, or half-covered—provided with mouths which form their sound-producing portions, hence the term *labial*.* The lingual stops are also constructed of metal and wood pipes, the resonators of which are either open or partially closed; their sounds being produced by tongues, or *languettes*, which vibrate against openings in reeds, or *échalotes*, hence the term *lingual*. Such stops are confined to the production of the imitative orchestral reed- and brass-tones. All other varieties of tone are produced by labial stops.

PURE ORGAN TONE.—This is the foundation tone of the Organ proper. It is *sui generis*, peculiar to the Organ, and cannot be imitated by any other musical instrument. It is yielded in its purity by the true English DIAPASON, 8 FT., formed of full-scaled open

---

* The objectionable term "*flue*" has been hitherto used by English and American organ-parlance: but as the term *flue pipe* is strictly appropriate in connection with a stove or heating apparatus, it certainly should be abandoned, along with other misnomers in organ-building language, in favor of the proper and expressive term *labial*. A labial pipe is literally a *mouthed pipe*; just as a lingual pipe is literally a *longued pipe*.

metal pipes, unslotted, and voiced on a copious supply of wind of moderate pressure   The tone is full, round, and dignified, singularly free from harmonic upper partial tones; the absence of which leaves a simple or pure tone, which, when used alone, is somewhat cloying and unsatisfying to the ear familiar with the complex tonality of orchestral sounds.   Nevertheless, the DIAPASON's tone has always been, and always will be, the unique and special glory of the Organ— a foundation on which to build compound tones of surpassing grandeur and beauty.

In addition to the fundamental DIAPASON, 8 FT., which strictly belongs to the manual department, and especially to the Great Organ, there is the DIAPASON, 16 FT., which furnishes the true foundation tone of the Pedal Organ.   This is, in its correct form, an open metal stop, of large scale, constructed similar to the manual DIAPASON, and, like it, yielding pure organ-tone.   Under the name DOUBLE DIAPASON, 16 FT., a similar stop, but of much smaller scale and less powerful voice, is introduced in the manual department, and, properly, in the First or Great Organ.   This important stop also yields pure organ-tone.

The early organ-builders found that unison stops alone, however massed, produced tones of too monotonous and unsatisfying a character; and to obtain relief and desirable variety they resorted to the formation of ranks of pipes yielding higher and concordant tones. This proceeding led to the early and the mediæval Organs becoming great MIXTURES of several unison-, octave-, fifth-, and third-sounding ranks.   The original introducers of this system of stop-appointment had no clear knowledge of the science of compound musical sounds or their natural harmonic constituents: they simply realized the tonal value of the concordant ranks, and were content with their introduction, unscientifically voiced as they were, and the musical effects they produced.   Since their introduction, such octave and mutation harmonic-corroborating stops have never been omitted from the appointment of the Organ.   While the old European organ-builders certainly introduced high-pitched harmonic-corroborating stops and MIXTURES to excess, and voiced them unscientifically and undesirably loud;* it does not follow that their formation and introduction in the Organs of to-day should be neglected, in the manner in which they are, by the unscientific organ-designers and

---

* An example may be given of this excess. In the Organ in the Monastic Church, at Weingarten, Swabia, built by Gabler, of Ravensburg, in 1750, there are sixty-six speaking stops, having 6,666 pipes, and of this number there are ten compound harmonic-corroborating stops, having a total of 95 ranks and 4,797 pipes. While these numbers are given on authority, the number of pipes are probably not quite accurate.

labor-saving organ-builders of the present time; with a serious loss to the musical resources and beauty of the modern Organ; and a very undesirable narrowing of the opportunity for a wide exercise of artistic and expressive registration, and the production of varied tonal colorings which are unproducible in their absence.

The harmonic-corroborating stops, alluded to, directly associated with the DIAPASONS, are, like them, formed of open metal pipes, yielding pure organ-tones of graduated degrees of assertiveness, becoming perceptibly softer in tone as they rise in pitch, in accordance with the natural laws of compound musical sounds. These stops, accordingly, require to be properly scaled with reference to the scale of the fundamental DIAPASON, 8 FT., and voiced so as to combine with, and be absorbed in, the prime tone; brightening and richly coloring it without asserting undue prominence individually. It has been the neglect of the teachings of the natural laws of compound musical sounds, either through ignorance or carelessness, that has rendered the single and compound harmonic-corroborating stops in so many Organs unsatisfactory and of little value in combination and artistic registration. It is, accordingly, desirable that organists who take any interest in the Organ, beyond merely playing it, should see that in instruments, over the tonal appointment of which they have any control, a sufficient proportion of properly formed and voiced harmonic-corroborating stops be provided.

The more important associated harmonic-corroborating stops are the OCTAVE, 4 FT., TWELFTH, 2⅔ FT., FIFTEENTH, 2 FT., SEVENTEENTH, 1⅗ FT., NINETEENTH, 1⅓ FT., and TWENTY-SECOND, 1 FT. These stops are introduced in separate ranks of full compass, voiced to yield pure organ-tone, and introduce and corroborate the first, second, third, fourth, fifth, and seventh upper partial tones of the foundation unisons, represented by the DIAPASON, 8 FT. To complete the harmonic series it is desirable to add the FLAT TWENTY-FIRST 1¹/₇ FT., corroborating the sixth upper partial tone. This stop is almost unknown, in a complete form, in English Organs, although it has been used in certain breaks of rare MIXTURES. Under the name SEPTIÈME, it appears as a separate and complete stop in certain French Organs. In the Grand Organ in the Cathedral of Notre-Dame, Paris, constructed by Cavaillé-Coll, there is a SEPTIÈME, 1¹/₇ FT., in the Grand-Chœur, belonging to the foundation-work; a SEPTIÈME, 2²/₇ FT., in the Bombardes, belonging to the 16 ft. harmonic series; and a SEPTIÈME, 4⁴/₇ FT., in the Pédale, belonging to the 32 ft. harmonic series. We have not found an instance of the SEPTIÈME being introduced in a French MIXTURE. The higher-pitched harmonic-corroborating stops, owing to the smallness of their pipes, cannot be carried throughout the compass of the manual clavier without a break; accordingly, they appear only in broken ranks of MIXTURES. These stops are the TWENTY-FOURTH, 4/5 FT., TWENTY-SIXTH, 2/3 FT., TWENTY-NINTH, 1/2 FT., THIRTY-THIRD, 1/3 FT., and THIRTY-SIXTH, 1/4 FT., corroborating the ninth, eleventh, fifteenth, twenty-third, and thirty-first upper partial tones of the foundation unisons.

There are, in addition to the stops already named, certain others, properly pure organ-toned, which belong to the series founded on the DIAPASON, 16 FT., of the Pedal Organ. These are the OCTAVE, 8 FT., which is practically a DIAPASON, the TWELFTH, 5 1/3 FT., and the SUPER-OCTAVE, 4 FT., introducing and corroborating the first, second, and third upper partial tones of the 16 ft. harmonic series. Harmonic-corroborating stops of higher pitch are introduced in the MIXTURES sometimes inserted in the Pedal Organ.

The stops, complete and incomplete, enumerated above are all that practically belong to the foundation-work of the Organ; and all should be present in a completely appointed instrument. They are necessary for the production of the entire range of pure organ-tones; and are essential in effective tonal coloration and artistic registration.

FREE ORGAN-TONE.—The few stops which may be properly classed as yielding free organ-tone are strictly of mediate or transitional character; that is, in addition to a foundation of pure organ-tone they encroach, more or less, as it were, upon tones of some distinctive character; producing voices of different shades of tonal coloring, never pronounced, and on this account of extreme value in artistic registration. While the compound voices of such stops cannot be classed as belonging to any special tonality, for they differ greatly, they are invaluable in building-up and delicately tinting other distinctive voices, by means of which the artist organist is painting his musical picture.

Between pure organ-tone, as previously defined, and what must be recognized as free or impure organ-tone, there is a very fine line of demarkation. Immediately on this line stands the beautiful English DULCIANA, 8 FT., the tone of which is only distinguishable from pure organ-tone by its delicate, silvery, singing quality, due to the presence of almost imperceptible harmonic over-tones. Like the foundation DIAPASON, the DULCIANA is properly attended by its family of harmonic-corroborating stops, forming very lovely compound tones, the delight of the tonal colorist. The most useful of these stops are the OCTAVE DULCIANA, 4 FT.; DULCIANA TWELFTH, 2⅔ FT.; SUPER-OCTAVE DULCIANA, 2 FT.; and DULCIANA CORNET.

There are several other stops yielding free organ-tones of a more pronounced mediant character, in which pure organ-tone is more absorbed and a richer coloring imparted. Among these may be named the DOLCAN, yielding a voice of a refined and somewhat plaintive character; and the KERAULOPHONE, yielding a richer tone, which, in good examples, approaches a horn-like quality, extremely valuable in the production of rich and quiet colorings. This fine stop is rarely introduced in Organs built to-day. Still more pronounced in tone are the stops known as the HORN DIAPASON and BELL DIAPASON, the voices of which are rich colorings on grounds of pure organ-tone. Certain stops yielding what must be classed as free organ-tone have their voices comparatively rich in harmonic upper partial tones. Prominent among these stops is the GEMSHORN, the pipes of which, Helmholtz says, have the property of rendering some higher partial tones comparatively stronger than the lower; hence its peculiar value in registration in which brightness is desired, without a cutting quality which is so frequently destructive of refinement and repose. Perhaps such terms as these are rarely used in speaking of organ registration, but they will be understood by the artist organist and the musician, and their meaning should be grasped by the organ student.

FLUTE ORGAN-TONE.—By the term flute organ-tone is signified that wide and varied range of flute-like tones, produced by several varieties of organ-pipes, which are not strictly imitative of the clear and penetrating voices of the Flutes of the orchestra. Some of these unimitative tones differ widely from those of the orchestral Flutes, while others are so closely allied as to be almost undistinguishable from them. It is in this great range of flute-like voices that the organist finds a richly spread palette for the production of innumerable beautiful tonal colors. The organ-toned FLUTES are not only widely varied in strength and character of voice, but they, of all the stops of the Organ, lend themselves most readily and efficiently to effective registration, combining perfectly with the stops of every other tonality, both labial and lingual.

The stops yielding flute organ-tone may be divided into four families, each of which produces a characteristic tonality. These are formed, respectively, of open, covered, half-covered, and harmonic pipes. The variation of their voices is mainly due to the presence of different groups of harmonic upper partials and their relations to the prime tones. As all the stops just alluded to are described in the Glossary, it is unnecessary to go into particulars of their special voices in this brief essay; but the names of a few of the representative ones may be mentioned. Of the open family, may be named the TIBIA PLENA, HOHLFLÖTE, SPITZFLÖTE, and WALD-FLÖTE; of the covered family, the TIBIA CLAUSA, DOPPELFLÖTE, and LIEBLICHGEDECKT; of the half-covered family, the ROHRFLÖTE and FLÛTE À CHEMINÉE; and of the harmonic family, the French FLÛTE HARMONIQUE.

So numerous and varied are the voices of the unimitative flute-toned stops of the modern Organ, and so valuable are they in artistic registration with the voices of all other tonalities, that the organist should make a careful study of them; acquainting himself with all their coloring properties and their peculiar mixing and separating qualities. It must be observed that certain flute-tones hold themselves distinct and remain assertive; while others become absorbed and completely lose their individuality in the compound tones.

VIOL ORGAN-TONE.—Although the stops yielding unimitative string-tone, which, for the sake of distinction, we have designated viol organ-tone, are comparatively few in number, they occupy an important place in the stop-appointment of the Organ, and a prominent place on the color palette of the organist skilled in artistic registration.

Standing on the border-line between pure organ-tone and viol organ-tone is the refined and beautiful voice of the true SALICIONAL. The most important stop of this tonality is the VIOLIN DIAPASON or GEIGENPRINCIPAL. The tone of this fine stop varies in different examples, according to the taste of the voicer; but it should be dictated by the position it holds in the tonal scheme of the Organ, and how it can be of the greatest value in effective registration. While in this stop the string tonality is, properly, not more than the pure organ-tone, there are others, under different names, in which the string-tone is the more assertive; and these are very desirable, in Organs of large dimensions, for registration with labial and lingual stops of powerful intonation. In the Concert-room Organ, they are required for the building-up of the necessary volumes of string-tone.

There are certain other stops which may be classed as yielding viol organ-tone, but which may claim to be imitative, in so much that they are accepted as reproducing the tones of the obsolete Viola da Gamba and Viola d'Amore. But when their tones are compared with those of the modern stops which imitate so closely

the assertive and complex tones of the Violin, Viola, and Violoncello, their timid voices seem to fall back into what may be correctly
considered viol organ-tone.   When these desirable stops appear in
an Organ they deserve the careful attention of the organist.

ORCHESTRAL STRING-TONE.—This is the first and most essential
of all the orchestral imitative tones of the modern Organ; and may
almost be said to be the foundation of the tonal structure of the
true Concert-room Organ; just as the string forces are the foundation of the grand orchestra.   Obvious as this must have been, one
would think, to every thoughtful musician and accomplished organist, it is truly remarkable that such a self-evident fact remained
unacknowledged and unacted upon in the organ-building world,—
cramped by old-fashioned tradition,—until we instituted a separate
and complete string division, comprising eighteen ranks of string-
toned pipes, including full harmonic elements, and endowed with
full and special powers of expression and flexibility, in our scheme
of the Concert-room Organ installed in the Festival Hall of the
Louisiana Purchase Exposition, St. Louis, Mo., 1904.* We feel very
proud of having been the first in the history of the art of organ-
building to realize the necessity for, and to carry into effect, so important and art-serving a step in advance in tonal appointment; now
becoming tardily acknowledged by organ-builders and organists as
essential in every Organ suitable for recital purposes, and which has
any pretension toward completeness.

The stops are comparatively few which strictly fall under the
class now under consideration, being primarily the VIOLIN, VIOLA,
VIOLONCELLO, and CONTRABASSO, which also pass under other equivalent names.   These stops are, however, attended by certain derivatives which are required in the Organ for the production of well-
known orchestral effects, and for purposes of artistic registration.
The derivatives are those which represent the orchestral instruments played under characteristic conditions; namely, *con sordini*
and *vibrato*.   It is, perhaps, unnecessary to remark that the great
value of the orchestral string stops lies in the closeness and beauty
of their imitative voices and their perfect regulation; but such
artistic perfections are rarely the products of the competitive and
hurried organ-building of to-day.   The cry is for quick production,
not artistic and painstaking work; and no class of stops suffers more

---

* See Specification of this Organ given on pages 503–8; and our scheme for the Ancillary
String Organ, of twenty-three ranks of pipes, in the Concert-room Organ on page 323, of our
work, "The Organ of the Twentieth Century," New York, 1919.

from this than that which forms the orchestral string-tone forces of the Concert-room Organ.

Notwithstanding that the foundation orchestral string-toned stops are in themselves very rich in harmonic upper partials, so much so as to practically require no additions in purely solo work: yet for the production of full orchestral effects, it is necessary to have for registration string organ-toned harmonic-creating and corroborating ranks of pipes, belonging to both the 8 ft. and 16 ft. series, and including an effective OCTAVE VIOL or VIOLETTA, 4 FT. These afford great opportunities for tonal coloring and registration of a high order, leading to the production of volumes of brilliant and expressive tone, hardly dreamt of in the Organ of to-day, and only to be surpassed by the full string forces of the grand orchestra. When will the distinguished and respect-commanding musician arise to teach the thoughtless organist and organ-builder what the Concert-room Organ of the twentieth century must be?

ORCHESTRAL FLUTE-TONE.—Little need be said respecting the tonality of the stops yielding orchestral flute-tone. They are only three in number; namely, the ORCHESTRAL FLUTE or FLAUTO TRAVERSO, 8 FT., the FLAUTO TRAVERSO, 4 FT, and the PICCOLO, 2 FT.; and their voices successfully imitate, especially in the finer examples, those of the Flutes and Piccolo of the orchestra, and ably represent them in the tonal appointment of the Organ. Their voices are refined and penetrating having few assertive upper partials except the octaves, naturally subordinated; and they are of extreme value in both solo-work and artistic registration. Seeing the great importance that has been given to the Flute by the great composers, who frequently gave it the leading wind part in their scores, there can be no excuse for the insertion of an indifferent ORCHESTRAL FLUTE in any important Organ. In registration with the orchestral string-toned stops the ORCHESTRAL FLUTES produce beautiful qualities of tone. In general registration, however, they do not stand preëminent, for there are several of the flute organ-toned stops that are equal, if not superior, in imparting effective coloring.

ORCHESTRAL REED-TONE.—The important instruments of the grand orchestra which are more or less closely imitated by the stops of the Organ yielding orchestral reed-tone are the Oboe, Clarinet, Corno di Bassetto, Cor Anglais, Bassoon, and Saxophone. The stops bearing these names, or their equivalents in other languages, are all of unison pitch on the manuals; but the DOUBLE BASSOON or CONTRAFAGOTTO, 16 FT., a stop of great value, is also placed on the manuals in important instruments.

The OBOE appears in two forms, the one commonly introduced not being strongly imitative in its tonality; indeed, it has been found very difficult to imitate the "small acid-sweet voice, having a pastoral character, full of tenderness," as Berlioz cleverly describes it. Certain attempts have been made to imitate this characteristic voice, and results of a fairly satisfactory nature have been obtained from stops of special formation, named ORCHESTRAL OBOES. The Oboe of the orchestra is essentially a melodial instrument, and the ORCHESTRAL OBOE of the Organ must also be accepted as a melodial or solo stop, which is comparatively of little value in registration save for the production of very unusual effects of a pathetic character.

Much more closely imitative is the CLARINET, 8 FT.; indeed, when made by a master-hand, it may be pronounced the best representative of an orchestral reed instrument to be found in the Organ. It is especially satisfactory when associated with a unison covered stop, such as a soft-toned DOPPELFLÖTE or a LIEBLICH-GEDECKT, 8 FT. These voices impart the full and somewhat hollow tonality of the orchestral instrument in its best register. The tube of the orchestral Clarinet is of the nature of a covered pipe, producing, in addition to the prime tone, the second, fourth, sixth, and higher even upper partial tones. Such being the case, it can be realized that the tone of the lingual CLARINET derives considerable richness and increase of character by combination with the tone of a covered stop, which has in its voice the same progression of harmonic upper partials. This affords a simple lesson in scientific combination. The peculiar quality of the tone of the CLARINET renders it a valuable addition to the voices of almost all the labial stops of medium power, producing compound tones of rich and varied colorings: accordingly, in registration, the stop deserves greater attention than seems to have been hitherto bestowed upon it.

More effective and fuller in tone-creation is the CORNO DI BASSETTO, 8 FT., which belongs to the CLARINET family. The orchestral instrument from which it derives its name, and of which it is the organ representative, is practically a Tenor Clarinet having the compass from FF to c³. The voice of the Corno di Bassetto is fuller and more reedy than that of the Alto Clarinet; and, accordingly, the tone of CORNO DI BASSETTO is bolder and richer than that of the

CLARINET, 8 FT. Properly made and voiced by a master-hand, the CORNO DI BASSETTO is of greater value than the CLARINET in effective registration. Unfortunately it is a stop rarely found even in large Organs. While it is properly of 8 ft. pitch, the insertion of a CORNO DI BASSETTO, 16 FT. is greatly to be desired in the expressive "wood-wind" division of the Concert-room Organ; where it would, ir combination with the unison CORNO DI BASSETTO and other wood-wind stops of the Organ, be productive of compound tones absolutely unknown in the old-fashioned tonal-appointments of the Organs of to-day.

The Bassoon of the orchestra is a double-reed instrument like the Oboe, of which it is considered to furnish the proper bass. Its representative in the Organ, the BASSOON or FAGOTTO, 8 FT., fails like the OBOE, in yielding a perfectly satisfactory imitative voice. Nevertheless, the tone of a really good example is extremely valuable in artistic registration and tonal coloration; so much so, that no Concert-room Organ can be considered complete in which the stop does not appear in the manual department. Its proper place is in the "wood-wind" division of the instrument.* The orchestral Bassoon has a conical bore of about eight feet in length, regularly increasing in diameter from $\frac{3}{16}$ inch at the reed end to $1\frac{3}{4}$ inches at the open end. This form of tube generates or favors the production of the uneven upper partials (natural to an open organ-pipe), and, accordingly, yields a compound tone essentially different from that of the Clarinet, while it partakes of that of the Oboe. The voice of the BASSOON, 8 FT., while it closely resembles that of the orchestral instrument, has the advantage of being more uniform in color throughout its compass, and in being entirely free from the grotesqueness which characterizes certain of its lower notes.

The tonal value of the Double Bassoon or Contrafagotto has long been recognized by the great composers; Beethoven, Haydn, Mozart, and Mendelssohn having introduced it in their great works. As Dr. W. H. Stone remarks: "In all cases it forms a grand bass to the reed band, completing the 16-foot octave with the six lowest notes wanting on three-stringed Double Basses." These facts are enough to show the value of, and the necessity for, the DOUBLE BASSOON or CONTRAFAGOTTO, 16 FT., which represents the orchestral instrument in a properly-appointed Organ. Its presence in an important Church Organ is highly desirable; while in a Concert-room Organ it is imperative. The value of its voice in tonal coloration,

---

* See "The Organ of the Twentieth Century," Pages 307 and 505.

and in the registration of grave tones is so great, that in the Concert-room Organ it may, with advantage, be introduced in more than one manual division; preferably in the expressive subdivision of the First or Great Organ, and in the Organ containing the stops representing the wood-wind instruments of the orchestra. In the latter it may be of the more assertive variety, distinguished by the name FAGOTTONE, 16 FT. It is never desirable to have two stops of precisely similar tones in an Organ, however large it may be. Variety of tone is an essential element in artistic registration.

When properly made and artistically voiced, the DOUBLE BASSOON yields a tone of the same quality as that of the BASSOON, 8 FT., but of rather a greater body. Accordingly, if the tone of the middle c^1 (4 ft.) pipe of the former is carefully compared with that of the tenor C (4 ft.) of the unison stop, it will be observed that while they are of the same pitch and character, they are different in tonal value, the unison being somewhat lighter and brighter—the voicing having properly generated one or two higher harmonic upper partials. The true orchestral relationship is thereby established.

Judging from what one observes in the unscientific and inartistic competitive organ-building of to-day, organ-builders certainly will, and many organists probably will, consider such refinements as have been advocated in the preceding remarks quite unnecessary. Certainly they will call for scientific and artistic culture and a high sense of duty on the part of the former; and for a keen appreciation of tonal values on the part of the latter. But the obvious absence of such tonal refinements only goes to prove that the culture alluded to is much to be desired on both sides.

It is unnecessary to comment at length respecting the tone of the COR ANGLAIS, 8 FT., which in its present state imitates as closely as seems practicable that of the orchestral Cor Anglais; which is in reality an Alto Oboe, bearing about the same relation to the ordinary Oboe as the Corno di Bassetto does to the Clarinet. Regarding the orchestral instrument, Berlioz remarks: "Its quality of tone, less piercing, more veiled, and deeper than that of the Oboe, does not so well as the latter lend itself to the gaiety of rustic strains. . . . It is a melancholy, dreamy, and rather noble voice." The organ COR ANGLAIS, in its best form, yields a tone which has very valuable mixing and coloring properties; and these, combined with its somewhat subdued or "veiled" voice, renders the stop highly suitable for the chief accompanimental divisions of both the Church and Concert-room Organs. In such a position it will prove of the maxi-

mum service in artistic registration. While it would seem to belong
to the "wood-wind" division, the kindred nature of its voice to that
of the OBOE renders its presence there unnecessary. In an accompanimental division it is most desirable to have a considerable range
of different tonalities, so that by skillful registration expressive
accompaniments of all tones and colors may be formed.

The latest addition to the orchestral reed-tone forces of the
Organ is the SAXOPHONE, 8 FT., a fine stop of the CLARINET family.
The Saxophones of the orchestra are single-reed instruments, having
wooden mouthpieces, similar to those of the Clarinets, attached to
conical tubes of brass. They are of several keys, covering a compass
of from BBB to c^3, one octave short of the present full manual
compass of the Organ. The lingual SAXOPHONES made up to the
present time have only been moderately successful in their imitative
tones, while otherwise fine stops. The most satisfactory imitative
stop hitherto produced, so far as our knowledge extends, is a labial
one formed of wood. The character and value of its voice may be
in some way realized from the following description by Berlioz of
the tones of the orchestral Saxophones, which he states as possessing, "Most rare and precious qualities. Soft and penetrating in the
higher part, full and rich in the lower part, their medium has something profoundly expressive. It is, in short, a quality *sui generis*,
presenting vague analogies with the sounds of the Violoncello, of the
Clarinet, and Corno Inglese, and invested with a brazen tinge
which imparts a quite peculiar accent." Dr. Stone comments on the
peculiar Violoncello quality of the tone; he says: "It reproduces on a
magnified scale something of the Violoncello quality, and gives great
sustaining power to the full chorus of brass instruments, by introducing a mass of harmonic overtones." From these particulars it
can be readily realized how valuable such a compound tone must
prove in the Organ, and, at the same time, how difficult its production must prove from a single lingual stop. The prominence of the
Violoncello quality clearly points to the labial stop formation in
which a string-tone can, with skillful voicing, be produced accompanied by a pronounced reedy quality.

ORCHESTRAL BRASS-TONE.—The lingual stops of the Organ,
which produce tones imitative, more or less closely, of those of the
brass wind-instruments of the orchestra and band, are not numerous
but of very great importance. To them are added brass-toned stops
which belong exclusively to the Organ, and which have tonal powers
and compasses beyond those possible in instruments blown by the

human breath; and these impart an element of impressiveness and grandeur, when properly used, which alone is sufficient to stamp the Organ the Monarch of all Instruments.

The brass instruments of the orchestra which have representatives in the Organ are the Trumpet, Horn, Trombone, and Ophicleide. Of these the Horn is the instrument of which a satisfactory tonal equivalent is most desirable in the Organ; but which it has been found, up to the present time, practically impossible to produce. Berlioz calls the Horn a "noble and melancholy instrument," and its peculiar tonality supports that description. Although its tones are produced from a large brass instrument, sounded by the lips and a cupped mouthpiece, they have properly no trace of clang and brassiness. The Horn has two series of sounds, known as the *open* and *closed;* and it is the imitation of the latter, also called the "*hand notes,*" which the pipe-voicer has found the *crux*, in the production of the organ HORN, 8 FT. Certain painstaking organ-builders have produced stops which, though not strictly imitative in all respects, are fine tonally, and extremely valuable in refined registration with string-toned stops. The HORN properly belongs to the "brass-wind" division of the true Concert-room Organ; where it is useful as a solo and combinational stop. Every exertion should be made by the organ-designer to obtain a satisfactory HORN; for it is absolutely essential in the artistic rendition of orchestral scores.

The brass wind-instrument of the orchestra most commonly represented in Organs of all classes is the Trumpet, and its normal tone is more satisfactorily imitated by a lingual stop than that of any other brass instrument. The desirable tone for the ORCHESTRAL TRUMPET, 8 FT., is that of the Trumpet played *mezzo forte*, yielding a bright silvery voice with just sufficient brassiness to give it true character. This tone under expression is valuable in solo effects and in general registration, mixing perfectly with tones of all classes. The stop to be preferred for the Solo Organ is the more powerful HARMONIC TRUMPET, which represents the orchestral Trumpet played *fortissimo*. This powerful and penetrating stop must be placed under perfect control. A TRUMPET should never be placed *en chamade*, as in the Organ in the Church of Saint-Ouen, Rouen, and in several large Spanish Organs. To imagine any orchestral instrument, or its organ representative, played without expression, could only be possible in the brain of a musical ignoramus.

The Trombone of the orchestra is a member of the Trumpet family, and, indeed, it may be properly considered as furnishing the bass to the orchestral Slide Trumpet. Its tone is, accordingly, an enlargement of that of the Trumpet, capable, on account of the important size of the instrument which produces it, of great power, brilliancy, and brazen clang. The three Trombones—alto, tenor, and bass—along with the Trumpet, form the only complete enharmonic wind quartet in the orchestra. These instruments are perfectly true in their intonation; in this respect rivaling the stringed and bowed instruments.

The organ representatives—the TROMBONE, 8 FT., and CONTRA TROMBONE, 16 FT.,—are fine and valuable stops when voiced by master-hands; but they cannot be considered perfectly satisfactory tonal equivalents of the orchestral instruments. There is great difficulty in producing the characteristic brazen clang in lingual pipes, without objectionable coarseness and reedy clatter; but, perhaps, this is not to be regretted, for the more desirable tones of the orchestral Trombones are those in which this extreme clang is absent. The TROMBONES of the Organ are of great importance, especially in the Concert-room Organ, and their tonalities and strengths of voice should in all cases be dictated by the places they occupy and the offices they have to fulfill in the tonal economy of the Organ. Although the use of the TROMBONES is somewhat limited in artistic registration, their employment is of supreme value in the proper rendition of certain classes of orchestral music, and in the production of impressive effects and in full organ passages. The proper position of the TROMBONES in the properly stop-apportioned Concert-room Organ is in the expressive division chiefly devoted to the representatives of the "brass-wind" forces of the grand orchestra.*

The Ophicleide of the orchestra is a large key instrument of the Bugle family, being practically the bass correlative of the Key or Kent Bugle. The usual Ophicleide is of 8 ft. pitch, extending only one semitone below the compass of the Violoncello: but as a "Contrabass Ophicleide" has been used in the orchestra (at the Musical Festival in Westminster Abbey and the Birmingham Festival, both in 1834), there is good authority for a representative of this impressive instrument, of 16 ft. pitch, finding a place in the Concert-room Organ of the twentieth century. The tone of the Ophicleide is broad and dignified, so much so, that Wagner found it necessary to fill its place in the orchestra by the Bass and Contra Tubas. Mendelssohn introduces the Ophicleide freely in the scores of his important works, notably in the "Elijah" and the "Midsummer Night's Dream" music.

---

* See "The Organ of the Twentieth Century," Pages 311–14 and 506.

As the Ophicleide has for many years disappeared from the orchestra, it is practically impossible for voicers of to-day to realize the tone they are called upon to reproduce in the organ representative. Some idea may, however, be gathered from the tonality of the substitutes Wagner adopted. The Tuba is a large bass instrument of the Saxhorn family, the tone of which is smooth and rich when produced by a master. It is such a tone, not too assertive, and entirely free from brassiness, that is required in the OPHICLEIDE employed in the performance of orchestral scores. The OPHICLEIDE, 8 FT., of the ordinary modern Organ is a widely different class of stop, yielding a powerful and strident tone. It is voiced on wind of high pressure, as in the representative example in the Solo of the Organ in St. George's Hall, Liverpool, which speaks on wind of 22 inches: and as this dominating stop has very foolishly been planted on an uninclosed wind-chest, and is, accordingly, devoid of powers of flexibility and expression, it is valueless in artistic registration.

Of the tones of the band brass instruments—the Cornopean, Euphonium, and Tuba—and their organ representatives; and of those of the several brass-toned stops which are practically unimitative, and strictly belong to the Organ, it is unnecessary to enlarge here: all useful particulars will be found, under their respective names, in the following Glossary.

DO MATERIALS AFFECT THE TONE OF ORGAN-PIPES?

A question of no little importance has frequently been asked, but never, so far as we are aware, has it been satisfactorily answered. The question is: Does the material of which an organ-pipe is constructed affect the quality of its tone? We have, by long observation of the behavior of organ-pipes, and some special experimentation, given the question careful and thoughtful consideration; yet we are far from being prepared to be dogmatic upon it. The only answer would seem to be this paradoxical one: It does and it does not.

We know that the old German, Dutch, and French organ-builders were very careful about the metals and woods they used for their pipes; and that their finest qualities are very rarely employed in modern organ-building: but whether they were selected on account of their value in tone production, or on the score of their durability only, it is impossible to decide. We do know, on the one hand, that their durability has been remarkable; and, on the other

hand, that the tones of the pipes formed of them are very beautiful.
Take for example the Organ in the Cathedral of Haarlem, built in
1738. All its displayed pipe-work including the Pedal SUB PRINCI-
PAL, 32 FT., is of pure Cornish tin; while all the rest of the metal
pipes in the instrument are of an alloy of equal parts, by weight, of
Cornish tin and pure lead. All these pipes—one hundred and
eighty-two years old—are as good as the day they were made. For
extreme purity and beauty of tone we have only to go to the Silbermann Organs in the Cathedral and churches of Strasbourg, the
pipes of which are formed of similar high-class materials. We
know, from examination of existing pipes of wood and metal, that
the English organ-builders of the seventeenth century used Cornish
tin and fine woods in their fabrication. Bernard Smith seems to
have invariably used wainscot for his STOPPED DIAPASONS and
GEDACKTS, as specified for his Temple Church Organ (1688).*
Examples of these which have been preserved to our time are characterized by great beauty of tone. Even in quite recent times we
find, in the construction of the Organs in the Cathedral and St.
Pauls-Kirche, Schwerin, the organ-builders Ladegast and Friese
using oak, maple, pear-tree, and mahogany in the formation of their
pipe-work. While it is quite reasonable to suppose that these celebrated builders used these special woods on account of their durability, and to favor perfect workmanship, it is still more reasonable
to suppose that they were employed for a still higher reason, namely,
that they were found to be conducive to the perfection of voicing
and the production of beautiful tones. Where do we find such fine
woods used in the pipes made for our organs to-day?

It is well known that the column of air within a pipe, while
speaking, is in a state of extreme pulsation or tremor, especially so
in pipes blown by winds of high pressures; and it is obvious that this
tremor must be conveyed to, and properly resisted by, the walls of
the pipe, be it of metal or wood. By careful observation we have
found that the maximum effect of this pulsation is on the sides of a
pipe, not on its front in which the mouth is formed, or back. This
would point to the necessity of specially fortifying the sides of wood

---

* Dr. Burney, speaking of this master, says: "I have been assured by Snetzler, and by the
immediate descendants of those who have conversed with Father Smith, and seen him work,
that he was so particularly careful in the choice of his wood, as never to use any that had the
least knot or flaw in it; and so tender of his reputation, as never to waste his time in trying to
mend a bad pipe, either of wood or metal, so that when he came to voice a pipe, if it had any
radical defect, he instantly threw it away, and made another. This, in a great measure, accounts
for the equality and sweetness of his stops, as well as the soundness of his pipes to this
day."—"History of Music."

pipes, and imparting a sufficient power of resistance to the walls of metal pipes. The former requirement would be met by the use of a hard wood of sufficient thickness: and for perfection in voicing, and the production of pure and beautiful tones, a close-grained hard wood should be used for the mouth fronts of pipes of moderate size, and for the mouths of large pipes. In the case of a metal pipe, a metal or alloy of a firm body and sufficient thickness to withstand the pulsation of the internal column of air is absolutely necessary for the production of a satisfactory tone. Tin has been found to be suitable in all respects, being much firmer and more resisting than the usual alloys, cast in sheets in the ordinary way which leaves them soft and undesirably open in structure; but tin is much too expensive for general use; and the same may be said of the high-grade alloys of tin and lead. What has long been wanted is a pipe-metal having all the good qualities of tin, without its prohibitive cost; and this has at last appeared in the Hoyt Two-ply Pipe-metal —a product, not of the open casting-table, but of the rolling-mill. The body of this compound pipe-metal is, in its perfected form, an alloy of pure lead, tin, and copper, on which is laid a substantial layer of pure tin. The combination is rolled, under great pressure, into sheets, perfectly uniform in thickness, remarkably tough, and of great resisting properties. These sheets are furnished in twenty-two standard thicknesses, regularly graduated from 0.015 to 0.120 of an inch. Both surfaces are perfectly smooth and polished, giving the interior of a pipe the surface most conducive to the production of refined intonation. From severe tests we have made of its several properties, we have no hesitation in saying it is superior to the ordinary cast spotted-metal so long used in high-class pipe-work. It has everything in its favor, including a moderate price.*

Beyond what has already been said regarding the importance of using fine hard woods and firm and tremor-resisting metals in pipe formation, little seems to have been decided respecting their more direct influence on tone-production: and the deeper one goes into the question the more complex it seems to become. We must admit that we have heard tones in every way satisfactory yielded by pipes formed of nearly all classes of pipe metal,—from the deadest alloys of lead and antimony to the richest alloys of tin and lead, and even tin itself,—and have been compelled to acknowledge that, after all is said, it would appear that the skill of the voicer was the dominating factor. As we have said elsewhere: although in general practice

* For further particulars and Table of standard thicknesses and weights of the Hoyt Two-ply Pipe-metal, see "The Organ of the Twentieth Century," pp. 345, 346.

certain classes of pipes appear to be most satisfactory in tone when formed of tin or high-class spotted-metal, their tonal character and excellence depends chiefly on their correct scaling, proper thickness of material, perfection of formation, the pressures of wind used, and, above all, on their skillful and artistic voicing. It is largely on the score of strength, rigidity, and durability that high-class materials are essential in organ-pipe construction.

GLOSSARY OF ORGAN-STOPS

A

ACUTA.—Vox Acuta (from Lat. *acutus*—sharp). Ger., Akuta, Scharf. Dtch., Scherp.—A compound harmonic-corroborating stop, composed of three or more ranks of open metal labial pipes, preferably of small scales. All the ranks are high-pitched and voiced to yield bright and penetrating tones—hence the name of the stop. When in its best form it has a third-sounding rank which adds greatly to its acute tonality. As the pipes forming the stop are necessarily very small, the ranks will have to break three or four times in the manual compass of five octaves. The following are examples of the composition of stops of three and four ranks:—

ACUTA—III. RANKS.

CC to B	22——24——26.
c^1 to b^1	17——19——22.
c^2 to b^2	15——17——19.
c^3 to c^4	12——15——17.

ACUTA—IV. RANKS.

CC to BB	24——26——29——33.
C to B	22——24——26——29.
c^1 to b^2	19——22——24——26.
c^3 to c^4	12——15——17——19.

In compound stops of the CORNET class, in which third-sounding ranks are introduced, it is desirable to subdue such ranks so as to be less assertive than the octave- and fifth-sounding ranks; but the same practice should not be followed in voicing and regulating the ACUTA, because the sharpness given by the third-sounding rank is an important element in its characteristic tonality. The standard rule which dictates that all compound harmonic-corroborating stops must be gradually softened in tone as they rise in pitch has to be observed in the regulation of the ACUTA.

The Acuta is only required in Concert-room Organs of the first magnitude, and even in them it has been seldom introduced. One of four ranks is in the Great of the Organ in the Cincinnati Music Hall; but in it there is no third-sounding rank.

Combination and Registration.—As the Acuta, when properly made, is strictly a member of the fundamental unison harmonic structure based on the Diapason, 8 ft., it properly enters into numerous combinations either directly with that stop in full harmonic sequence; or with it and other stops in varied registrations, its presence being desired on account of its special brightness and life-giving character. The Acuta is specially valuable in registration with full-toned lingual stops such as are properly inserted in the First or Great Organ. With the Trumpet alone or with the Trumpet and Clarion it is valuable, imparting great brilliancy and a singular orchestral coloring to the brass-tones, by powerfully corroborating the higher harmonics present to some extent in the voices of the lingual stops.

ÆOLINE.—Lat., Æolina. Ger., Äoline. Fr., Éoline. Ital., Eolina.—The name employed by different organ-builders to designate extremely soft-toned stops both lingual and labial. Seidel describes it as a lingual stop voiced in imitation of the Æolian Harp. He adds: "The bodies of the pipes are very small and of a narrow measure. . . . The stop cannot be used by itself, but only in combination with some soft 8ft. covered or open stop of narrow measure, such as the Gamba." This definition is supported by Hamel, who remarks:

"C'est un jeu d'anches libres qui, ainsi que son nom l'indique, doit imiter le murmure de la harpe æolienne, et qui, par conséquent, doit avoir une intonation extremement tendre et aérienne. Le corps des tuyaux qui sonnent quelquefois le seize pieds, sont tres-petits et d'un diapason tres-étroit. On trouve ce jeu disposé avec des huit pieds dans le nouvel orgue de Sainte-Marie à Wismar."*

The Æoline of the old builders was evidently a free-reed stop furnished with small resonators. Töpfer describes it as a free-reed stop of 16 ft. and 8 ft. pitch, either like the Physharmonica or furnished with small conical tubes or resonators. Walcker has placed on the Second Manual of his Organ in Riga Cathedral an Ælodicon, 16 ft., a lingual stop of the Æoline class; and on the Fourth Manual an Æoline, 8ft., a labial stop of tin, with the bass octave of wood, as in the Third Manual of his Organ in St. Petri-Kirche in Hamburg. Speaking of the Æoline, Carl Locher, of Berne, re-

* "Manuel Complet du Facteur d'Orgues."

marks: "It is of a soft string-toned character, occurring in Germany and Switzerland on almost all large and small Organs as an 8-ft. solo stop. It is considered the most delicate of all string-toned stops."*

FORMATION.—The ÆOLINE, properly of eight feet pitch, in its most approved modern form may be classed in the SALICIONAL family, of which it forms the softest-toned member. If voiced to yield a more decided string-tone, it may be considered an ECHO VIOLA DA GAMBA. The stop is formed of small-scale cylindrical pipes, preferably of tin or Hoyt two-ply, hard-rolled, pipe-metal. The mouths, which are about one-fifth the circumference of the pipes, are cut low and sharp, furnished with ears, and voiced with either some form of *frein harmonique* or harmonic-bridge, and on a wind between 1½ inches and 2½ inches. The scale may vary according to the class of Organ in which the stop is placed, and its position in the Organ; but a suitable one, which may be accepted as normal, in the ratio of 1 : 2.519, gives the CC pipe a diameter of 2.51 inches; the C pipe a diameter of 1.54 iuches; and the middle c¹ pipe a diameter of 0.94 inches. Locher says: "The ÆOLINA was originally a metal stop throughout, but as the art of intonation in modern organ-building is capable of making the transition from metal to wood quite imperceptible, it is permissible to construct the lower notes of wood in this and other stops." As before mentioned, Walcker, of Ludwigsburg, has used wood basses for this stop. A certain English organ-builder has used a bass octave of stopped wood pipes, and even gone farther by grooving the ÆOLINE to a soft covered stop. None of these money-saving devices should be followed.

COMBINATION AND REGISTRATION.—The extreme softness of the voice of the ÆOLINE renders its value in combination and registration, comparatively speaking, very limited; yet it has a delicate timbre-creating property which is worthy of the organist's study. For instance, it combines well with such a stop as the FLAUTO D'AMORE, 8 FT., creating a compound tone of peculiar charm. It also combines in an effective manner with the MELODIA, HARMONICA, and other flute-toned stops, provided they are not too loudly voiced to be tonally affected. In simple registration it will be found of value as a solo stop; its delicate singing string-tone rendering it very fascinating to the lover of refined organ music. The ÆOLINE is frequently drawn with the VOIX CÉLESTE.

ÆLODICON, Grk.—The name originally used to designate a keyboard, free-reed instrument and the precursor of the Harmonium. As an organ-stop it is a variant of the free-reed ÆOLINE. An example, under the name ALODICON, 16 FT., by Walcker, of Ludwigburg, occupies a place in the Second Manual Division of the Organ in the Cathedral of Riga, where it is a soft-toned lingual stop. As

---

* "Aeoline 16' und 8', ein zartes Rohrwerk von schönwirkendem, sanftem, säuselndem Tone, mit freischwingenden Zungen und Kurzem Schalltrichter." "Die Orgel," F. Zimmer.

such its presence, in this age of noisy, high-pressure stops, would, indeed, be most welcome.

ÆQUALPRINZIPAL, Ger.—The term which has been used by German organ-builders to designate the principal manual unison stop. In early times of the art in Germany the simple term ÆQUAL or ÄQUAL was deemed sufficient. The term, signifying unison, was sometimes applied to other stops.

AMOROSA, Lat.—The name that has been used by Steinmeyer and other German organ-builders to designate a wood FLUTE, 8 FT., of small scale and soft and pleasing tone, resembling that of the FLAUTO D'AMORE. The extended term VOX AMOROSA has occasionally been used.

ANGENEHMGEDECKT, Ger.—The term which has occasionally been used by German organ-builders, instead of the usual term LIEBLICHGEDECKT, to designate a small-scaled covered stop yielding a refined tone. It is formed from the word *angenehm*—pleasant.

ANTHROPOGLOSSA, Grk.—The name that has been given by old German organ-builders to the lingual stop yielding a tone somewhat resembling the human voice; now designated VOX HUMANA.

APFELREGAL, Ger.—Eng., APPLE-REGAL.—An obsolete lingual stop which must now be classed among the curiosities of German organ-building. The stop received its peculiar name from the shape of its resonators; which were formed of very short cylindrical portions surmounted by apple-shaped heads, perforated with numerous small holes for the emission of wind and sound—the latter necessarily muffled. Seidel tells us that the cylindrical portion of the largest resonator was only about 4 inches long. The stop was also called KNOPFREGAL; and was made of both 8 ft. and 4 ft. tone. See REGAL.

ASSAT.—The term occasionally met with in the stop-lists of old Organs. It is obviously a corruption of the proper term NASAT.

B

BAJONCILLO, Span.—Port., BAIXONILHO.—A lingual stop found in Spanish and Portuguese Organs; the tones of which resemble those of the orchestral Bassoon, which, however, they do not imitate very closely. The stop is of 8 ft. pitch. BAJON or BAIXO being the stop of 16 ft. pitch.

BARDUEN.—The name used by Prætorius to designate a covered stop in all essentials similar to that now known as the BOURDON. He gives the stop as of 8 ft. pitch.

BARDONE, Ital.—The term that has occasionally been employed to designate the stop commonly known as the BOURDON. There was an old bass stringed instrument called Viola di Bardone, which may have suggested the term. It is now rendered, more in keeping with modern nomenclature, BORDONE.

BAREM, Ger.—The name given to a covered wood stop of 16 ft. and 8 ft. pitch, voiced to yield a pure and soft tone. The term is derived from the old German word *baren*—to sing. The stop is practically identical with that commonly known as the STILLGEDECKT.

BÄRPFEIFE, Ger.—Dtch., BAARPYP.—An old lingual stop, the resonators of which assume very peculiar forms. The most common seems to be that of two cones joined together at their bases, and both truncated; the lower one soldered to the reed-block and the upper one open at top, the opening being comparatively small so as to subdue the tone. The illustration given by Seidel shows these double cones surmounted by a third truncated cone, forming a bell to the resonator. The tone of the stop is described by Wolfram* as of a soft growling character. The stop was made of both 16 ft. and 8 ft. pitch. A BAARPYP, 8 FT., is to be found in the Echo of the Organ in the Cathedral of St. Bavon, Haarlem, and in several Organs in Holland and Germany. See REGAL.

BARYTON, (Grk. βαρύτονος—deep-toned).—Ital., BARITONO. Span., VARITONO.—The name given by certain organ-builders to a lingual stop of 8 ft. pitch, properly yielding a singularly rich and full tone of medium strength when voiced on wind of moderate pressure. Under the name BARITONE, 8 FT., a stop of this class exists in the Solo of the Roosevelt Organ in the Cathedral of the Incarnation, Garden City, Long Island. Another example, of 16 ft., obtains in the Organ in the Royal Albert Hall, London, built by Willis in 1871.

FORMATION.—For the production of the desirable tone, the reeds should be the "closed" variety, and the tongues somewhat light and finely curved so as to avoid all brassiness. The resonators to be inverted conical in form, and shaded for fine regulation.

* "Anleitung zur Kenntniss, Beurtheilung und Erhaltung der Orgeln." J. Christian Wolfram, Gotha, 18:5.

COMBINATION AND REGISTRATION.—A lingual stop of this class, having a refined and sympathetic voice, should be placed in one of the accompanimental manual divisions of every important Organ. Its value in artistic registration could not well be overrated. Its rich and full tone would combine with those of the flute-toned and string-toned stops, producing numerous beautiful lights and shades of tonal coloring, not possible with the usual and assertive lingual stops. The day is coming, we feel sure, when the value of soft normal or unimitative lingual stops will be realized in refined and artistic registration.

BASSET-HORN.—Fr., COR DE BASSET. Ger., BASSETHORN. Ital., CORNO DI BASSETTO.—A lingual stop of 8 ft. pitch, voiced to yield a tone resembling that of the orchestral instrument of the same name. See CORNO DI BASSETTO. Locher says the German BASSET-HORN, 8 FT., and the SERPENT, 16 FT., "measured on the same foundation, are smooth-toned, free-reed, Pedal Organ stops, as a rule without resonators, like the PHYSHARMONICA. They represent the smooth reed-tone on the Zweites Pedal of the Ulm Cathedral Organ."

BASS FLUTE.—Ger., BASSFLÖTE.—An open labial stop, of 8 ft. pitch, formed commonly of wood but sometimes of metal, voiced to yield a powerful unimitative flute-tone. This stop properly belongs to the Pedal Organ, where it is frequently derived from the DIAPASON, 16 FT., by means of an extra octave of pipes and an octave coupler. For the purpose of combination and artistic registration it is very desirable that it should be an independent stop of distinctive strength and character of tone; and for this purpose it should be made of metal. The German name FLÖTENBASS is sometimes given to this independent stop.

BASSONELL.—Described by Wolfram as a lingual stop of 8 ft. and 4 ft. pitch, made of metal. Its tone was, in all probability, that of a soft Bassoon character. This is seemingly the stop referred to by Hamel under the Italian name BASSANELLO—"BASSANELLI. Ce sont des instruments à vent du siècle dernier [xviiie]; ils resemblent beaucoup au chalumeau. Dans l'orgue, ils ont été imités par des jeux d'anches particuliers de huit et de quatre pieds."

BASSOON.—Ital., FAGOTTO. Fr., BASSON. Ger., FAGOTT. Span., BAJON.—A small-scaled lingual stop, voiced to imitate as closely as practicable the tone of the orchestral instrument of the same name. As a manual stop of 8 ft. pitch, it is sometimes, and correctly, associated with the OBOE or HAUTBOY; being labeled

OBOE & FAGOTTO or HAUTBOY & BASSOON. It is preferable that, in the modern Organ, the BASSOON, 8 FT., should be introduced as a complete and independent stop. This is very desirable, to facilitate artistic registration. As a stop of 16 ft. pitch, the BASSOON frequently appears in the Pedal Organ, and occasionally in a manual division. When of this grave pitch it is more expressively called DOUBLE BASSOON or CONTRAFAGOTTO. A BASSON, 16 FT., appears in the pedal department of the Grand Organ in the Church of Saint-Sulpice, Paris; and a CONTRA-FAGOTTO, 16 FT., is placed in the Solo of the Organ in St. George's Hall, Liverpool. It seems, however, to have been left to Walcker, of Ludwigsburg, to realize the true value of this important stop. In his original Organ in the Cathedral of Ulm were the following stops: A CONTRA-FAGOTT, 16 FT., and a FAGOTT-DISCANT, 16 FT., in the Hauptwerk (First Clavier); a FAGOTT, 8 FT., on the Zweites Clavier; a CONTRA-FAGOTT, 16 FT., a SECUND-FAGOTT, 16 FT., and a FAGOTT, 8 FT., on the Viertes Clavier; and a FAGOTTBASS, 16 FT., on the Erstes Pedal. In all, seven important stops of the BASSOON family in an Organ of 113 speaking stops. What an opportunity here for unique registration!

FORMATION.—The BASSOON, when in its best form as a striking reed, has resonators of the inverted conical form and small scale. The manual stop of 8 ft. pitch may be constructed entirely of metal, or the resonators of its bass octave may be made of some suitable hard wood, so as not to require undesirable thickness. The same remark applies to the two lower octaves of the DOUBLE BASSOON, 16 FT. The resonators of the Pedal Organ stop may be of wood throughout. For fine regulation the resonators should be shaded, or both shaded and slotted. Satisfactory tonal results have been obtained from metal resonators, closed at top and slotted or perforated in some manner near their closed ends. The wooden resonators are square in transverse section, their lower ends being rounded externally so as to fit into metal socket pieces soldered to the reed-blocks; and they must be bored vertically with holes corresponding with the size of the reeds below. These holes must be continued until they open clearly into the interior of the resonators. In Fig. 1, Plate 1, is shown a CC BASSOON pipe of metal, the resonator of which is closed and slotted. Fig. 2 shows a corresponding pipe with a resonator of wood, shaded with an adjustable plate of thick pipe-metal. The illustrations are drawn to scale. The reeds are of the closed variety, and the tongues are narrow and specially curved so as to produce the characteristic Bassoon tone.

Continental organ-builders have largely resorted to free-reeds in the formation of their FAGOTTS, probably finding their style of striking-reed work productive of too much clang and brassiness; altogether foreign to the tone of the orchestral Bassoon. They have used for the free-reeds comparatively short resonators, formed of two truncated cones, soldered together at their bases, the upper one having a small opening for the emission of the wind and sound. Seidel, however, gives an illustration of a BASSOON pipe having a slender cylindrical resonator, like that now used for the CLARINET.

COMBINATION AND REGISTRATION.—The orchestral Bassoon furnishes the proper bass to the Oboe. Both are double-reed instruments. The value of a good imitation of its peculiar voice in the
Organ may be realized from what Berlioz says: "The Bassoon is of
the greatest use in the orchestra on numerous occasions. Its sonorousness is not very great, and its quality of tone, absolutely devoid
of brilliancy or nobleness, has a tendency toward the grotesque—
which should be always kept in mind when bringing it forward into
prominence. Its low tones form excellent basses to the whole group
of wooden wind instruments. . . . The character of its high notes
is somewhat painful, suffering,—even, I may say, miserable,—
which may be sometimes introduced into either a slow melody, or
passages of accompaniment, with most surprising effect." Even
when voiced by an artist, the organ BASSOON, 8 FT., is only moderately imitative; and on this account it may be recognized as being
more generally useful than if its voice were absolutely imitative.
An artistically made and voiced BASSOON is a stop of the greatest
value in an Organ, combining with all the medium- and softly-voiced
labial stops, producing dual or fuller tonalities of great beauty. In
combination with the OBOE or CLARINET it produces reed-tones of
singular fullness and charm. These facts go to prove that registration in which the BASSOON enters deserves the artist organist's
careful study. Unfortunately, the stop is very rarely introduced in
the ordinary Organs of to-day. In the wood-wind division or subdivision of the Concert-room Organ, its presence, as a complete stop,
is imperative. For remarks on the DOUBLE BASSOON, see CONTRA-
FAGOTTO.

BASSPOSAUNE, Ger.—Eng., BASS TROMBONE.—The Pedal
Organ lingual stop of 32 ft. pitch, also termed CONTRAPOSAUNE, as
in the Organ in Christ Church, at Hirschberg. It appears in several
important German Organs, termed POSAUNE, 32 FT.; as in the Organ
in St. Peter's Church, Berlin. It also appears, under the same name,
as a free-reed stop, in the Pedal of the Organ in the Cathedral of
Merseburg, built by Ladegast in 1855; and also as a free-reed stop
in the Pedal of the Organ in the Cathedral of Gothenburg, built by
Marcussen in 1849. See CONTRAPOSAUNE.

BASS TUBA.—Ger., BASSTUBA.—A powerfully-voiced lingual
stop, the tones of which are supposed to represent in the Organ those
of the Bass Tuba of the modern orchestra as constituted by Wagner
and others. See CONTRA-TUBA.

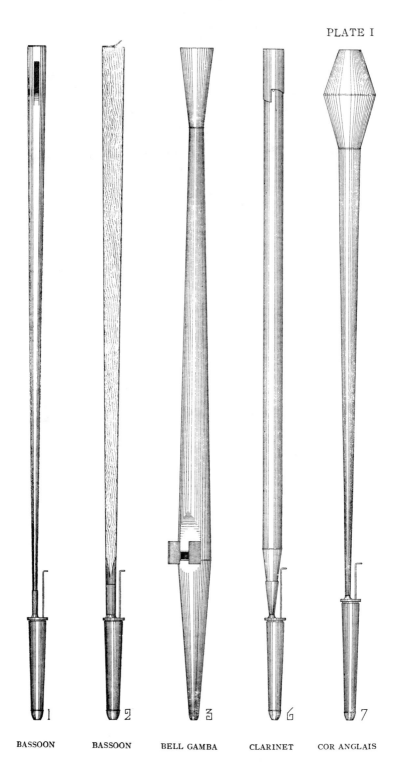

PLATE I

1	2	3	6	7
BASSOON	BASSOON	BELL GAMBA	CLARINET	COR ANGLAIS

BASS VIOL.—An appropriate name for an organ stop of 8 ft. pitch, formed of metal and voiced to yield a string-tone less pronounced than that of the ORCHESTRAL VIOLONCELLO, 8 FT. Its tone may be accepted as representing in the Organ that of the old Bass Viol, the largest of the four instruments in the old English "Chest of Viols." This stop, if voiced to yield a bright, singing string-tone, would be invaluable in refined and artistic registration. In combination with all the softer stops of pure organ-tone, flute-tone, and reed-tone, it would impart to their different voices a delicate coloring without destroying their individuality, adding, at the same time, volume to their voices.

BAUERFLÖTE, BAUERPFEIFE, Ger.—Literally *Peasant Flute.* A covered stop of small scale, commonly made of wood, and of 8 ft., 4 ft., 2 ft., and 1 ft. pitch. The stops of 8 ft. and 4 ft. pitch have clear fluty tones; while those of 2 ft. and 1 ft. have whistling tones resembling those of the human mouth. An example of 8 ft. pitch, under the name BAUERPFEIFE, appears in the Choir of the Organ in the Church of St. Jacobi, Hamburg. The stop in its high pitches has been commonly, and strangely we may add, introduced in Pedal Organs; one of 2 ft. is to be found in the Pedal of the Organ in the Church of SS. Peter and Paul, at Goerlitz, and one of 1 ft. pitch in the Pedal of the Church of St. Dominico, at Prague. Wolfram gives the terms BAUERNFLÖTE and BAUERNFLÖTENBASS. The stop has been made with perforated stoppers, and called BAUERNROHRFLÖTE.

BEARDED GAMBA.—An open metal labial stop of medium scale, producing an unimitative string-tone. The name is given on account of the peculiar treatment of the mouths of its pipes. Each mouth is provided, in addition to its projecting ears, with a projecting plate, soldered to the lower lip and attached to the ears. While this beard exercises an influence on the tone, it must not be confounded with the harmonic-bridge or the *frein harmonique.* The stop is not of much importance and has fallen into disuse.

BELL DIAPASON.—Fr., FLÛTE À PAVILLON.—This stop was invented in France, and introduced into England at the London Exhibition of 1851. For some time it was much esteemed by English builders, but for certain reasons it is no longer made. The English name is not appropriate, while the French name conveys the proper classification of the stop tonally, as well as the distinguishing feature in the formation of its pipes, technically termed the *pavillon.* Tonally the stop belongs to the flute-work of the Organ, and not to the foundation- or diapason work. For further particulars, see FLÛTE À PAVILLON.

BELL GAMBA.—Ger., GLOCKENGAMBA.—A metal labial stop of 8 ft. pitch; the pipes of which have their bodies of a conical form, and of medium scale, surmounted by a slender *pavillon* or bell, in the manner shown in Fig. 3, Plate I. The name was used to distinguish the stop from the ordinary German GAMBA, which has pipes of plain cylindrical form. The stop has very rarely been carried below tenor C in its characteristic form, the bass octave either being omitted or inserted in cylindrical pipes. As the form of the BELL GAMBA does not allow of its being tuned at top in the ordinary manner, its mouth is furnished with large, projecting, flexible ears, as shown in Fig. 3, which flatten or sharpen the tone as they are bent toward or away from the mouth. This stop was usually made of tin or high-class alloy; and when artistically voiced yielded a string-tone of great delicacy and charm, strongly resembling that of the old orchestral Viola da Gamba. The trouble attending its construction, voicing, and perfect regulation has led to its disappearance from the Organs of to-day. See VIOLA DA GAMBA.

BIFARA, Ger.—Lat., TIBIA BIFARIS or BIFARIUS.—This term has been employed by certain old German organ-builders to designate two different labial stops, both of which were double-toned, and one positively dual in formation. Seidel, who one must recognize as an authority on old German organ-building, says: the BIFARA "is a fine but scarce labial stop in the manual, eight or four feet, open, of PRINCIPAL scale. Every pipe has, like those of the DOPPLFLÖTE, two mouths, one of which stands a little higher than the other, whereby a pleasant sort of vibration is caused, similar to that of the UNDA MARIS. To obtain from this stop a very soft and agreeable tone, the feet of the pipes are but partly open, so as to admit only a small amount of wind. The BIFARA is also produced in another way; namely, by giving one tone to two pipes, one of which is tuned a little higher than the other. A BIFARA of tin, of two ranks, first rank a GEDECKT, 8 ft., second rank open pipes of 4 ft., of a soft string-tone, stands on the Third Manual of the colossal Organ built by Walcker, of Ludwigsburg, in St. Peter's Church, St. Petersburg."

The BIFARA is extremely interesting as the first step toward the artistic formation of dual stops, for the production of compound tones, impossible to be produced from single stops, or even two stops not specially combined.* For many years we have pleaded for attention to be given to tone-coloring in this direction, but in this, as in other matters, our appeal has fallen on deaf ears. Dollars and don't-careism have blocked the way

BLOCKFLÖTE, Ger.—Lat., TIBIA VULGARIS. Eng., BLOCK-FLUTE.—The name given to an open metal labial stop of the ordinary cylindrical form, of very large scale, and usually of 4 ft. pitch. The tone of this stop was of a normal flute character, which varied in power in different examples. Respecting the original German versions of the stop, Seidel remarks: "It is of Flute-work, sometimes open, sometimes stopped, and now and then made of conical pipes. It is made of tin or pipe-metal, of 16 ft., 8 ft., 4 ft., and 2 ft. tone. It imitates the tone of the Flute into which the wind is blown at the end." In the concluding remark, allusion is evidently made to the old Flûte à Bec, or Direct Flute. "Father Smith" introduced the BLOCKFLÖTE in his Durham Cathedral Organ (1683), and in that he built for St. Paul's Cathedral, London (1697).

BOMBARDE, Fr.—A lingual stop of 16 ft. pitch and powerful intonation. The BOMBARDE is commonly found in important French Organs; for instance in the Organ in Saint-Sulpice, Paris, built by Cavaillé-Coll, there are four BOMBARDES; and in his Organ in the Cathedral of Notre-Dame there are also four— a CONTRE-BOMBARDE, 32 FT., and three BOMBARDES, 16 FT. In his notable scheme for the "Orgue Monumental" to be erected in St. Peter's, at Rome, we find in the Pedal Organ a CONTRE-BOMBARDE, 32 FT.; a BOMBARDE, 16 FT.; and a QUINTE BOMBARDE, $10\frac{2}{3}$ FT. The tonal effect of these three commanding voices in combination, heard in such a building as St. Peter's, is beyond one's power to imagine. This important stop gives a name to a manual division in large French Organs; namely, "Clavier des Bombardes." The resonators of the BOMBARDE are of the inverted conical form, constructed of stout metal and to a large scale.

There was an old lingual stop sometimes called BOMBARD, but more commonly BOMMER or BÄRBOMMER, evidently deriving its name from *Bombardo*—a mediæval reed instrument of large size and

---

* "La BIFARA (de bifaris) est donc une autre espèce de flûte à deux tuyaux ouverts, de moyenne taille, de huit-pieds, et en étain. Ses deux bouches, étroitement pincées, mais dont l'une est plus haute que l'autre, n'aspirent que peu de vent un seul pied, et rendent une harmonie plus ou moins agréable. On la fait encore de deux tuyaux séparés, ayant chacun leur pied; l'un des deux tuyaux ayant un peu plus hauteur que l'autre, et par conséquent de rondeur de son."—Regnier.

coarse intonation, and probably the precursor of the Fagotto. The old instrument, or some modification of it, was called Pommer, and led to the formation of a family of six instruments under the name.[*] According to Wolfram (1815), the old BOMMER, BOMBARD, or BÄR-BOMMER, was a Pedal Organ stop of 16 ft. and 8 ft. pitch, having resonators of wood, which were sometimes partly covered to soften the tone.

BOMBARDON, Fr.—Ital., BOMBARDONE.—A Pedal Organ lingual stop, full-toned, and of 32 ft. and 16 ft. pitch. It derives its appellation from the large brass instrument of the same name, the powerful and grave tones of which it is designed to imitate so far as its compass extends. The accepted compass of the Bombardon is from FFF to d¹, but five notes lower—to CCC—can, with difficulty, be produced by a skillful performer. The BOMBARDON has been confounded with the BOMBARDE, but they are properly two distinct stops tonally. The voice of the BOMBARDON should be between the voices of the BOMBARDE and the BASSOON, while partaking of the character of both, hence the value of such a stop in Pedal Organ registration. A BOMBARDON, 32 FT., exists in the Pedal of the Organ in the Cathedral of Ulm.

BORDUNALFLÖTE, Ger.—The name given to an open wood stop of 8 ft. and 4 ft. pitch, the pipes of which are properly of inverted conical form, and slightly oblong in transverse section. The pipes are voiced to yield a smooth fluty-tone, having, owing to the creation of certain upper partials, a trace of string quality. An example, of 8 ft. pitch, made of pine and pear-tree, by the celebrated organ-builder, Ladegast, exists on the Second Manual of the Organ in the Cathedral of Schwerin. Another, by the same builder, exists on the Second Manual of the Organ in the Nicolaikirche, Leipzig. The stop deserves consideration for introduction in important Organs; but, owing to more than ordinary labor being required in its forma-tion, it is not likely to be favored by organ-builders to-day. The stop has been frequently, but less correctly labeled PORTUNALFLÖTE.

BOURDON, Fr.—Ital., BORDONE. Ger., BORDUN, BRUMMBASS, BASSBRUMMER.—In English and American Organs the BOURDON may be said to invariably appear in the form of a covered, labial wood stop, of large scale and 16 ft. pitch. Its characteristic tone has a somewhat dull droning quality, which is well expressed by the old

---

* The entire family of Pommers is shown in the Crosby Brown Collection of Musical Instru-ments in The Metropolitan Museum of Art, New York City.

German synonyms BRUMMBASS and BASSBRUMMER (from *brummen*— to hum or drone).

The BOURDON, 16 FT., most frequently appears, in English and American instruments of moderate dimensions, in the Pedal Organ; while in small Organs it is too frequently the only pedal stop. In large instruments it is introduced in one or more of the manual divisions, and commonly in the Swell Organ. In the Concert-room Organ in the Town Hall of Leeds, England, the BOURDON, 16 FT., is introduced in the Great, Swell, and Echo Organs. As might be expected, the manual stops are made of a smaller scale than those introduced in the Pedal Organ. In German instruments the BOURDON, 16 FT., may be said to be a manual stop, although it sometimes appears in the Pedal Organ. In important instruments it is found on the manuals of 32 ft. and 16 ft. pitch. In the Organ in the Cathedral of Bremen, built by Schulze in 1850, we find in the Hauptwerk BORDUNS of 32 ft. and 16 ft., and in the Unterwerk BORDUNS of 32 ft. and 16 ft.; but no stop under the name in the Pedal. It occasionally appears of 8 ft. pitch, as on the First Clavier of the Organ in St. Peter's Church, Hamburg. In French instruments the BOURDON is introduced in the manual divisions of 16 ft. and 8 ft. pitch. In the Organ in the Cathedral of Notre-Dame, Paris, there are no fewer than five manual BOURDONS—two of 16 ft. and three of 8 ft. pitch. In some rare instances the French organ-builders have applied the name to a covered metal stop of large scale and of 4 ft. pitch.

FORMATION.—In modern English and American Organs the true BOURDON, 16 FT., is invariably and properly made of wood; but we are told in Dr. Burney's "History of Music" that the old English builders sometimes constructed it of metal. Speaking of Snetzler's Organ in St. Margaret's Church, Lynn Regis, he says: "One of the metal stops of this instrument, called the Bourdon, is an octave below the Open Diapason, and has the effect of a double bass in the chorus." In all probability the quint was somewhat prominent in the tone of this covered metal stop, imparting to it a similarity to that of the orchestral Double Bass. Both the French and German organ-builders use metal pipes in the higher octaves of their manual BOURDONS, especially in those of 8 ft. pitch. In the Great of the celebrated Haarlem Organ, the BOURDON, 16 FT., is of metal throughout the compass of the manual.

The pipes of the BOURDON, like those of all quadrangular wood stops, are formed of four boards, glued together at their edges and at one end to a block, or, in large pipes, to two cross-pieces of wood, which assume the position and function of the block. The large scale of the pipes renders the use of solid blocks undesirable save in the upper octaves. The block or upper cross-piece should be faced with hard wood, as its upper edge forms the lower lip of the mouth, which is cut in the front board of the pipe. In the accompanying illustration, Fig. 4, is shown the construction of the lower part of a CCC pipe, and the formation of the mouth according to the German and English methods. The former is shown in

Diagram A, in which will be observed the depression of the upper cross-piece, and its front edge beveled and cut so as to form the wind-way of the mouth, and placed level with the upper edge of the cap. In Diagram B is given the corresponding Section of the English mouth, showing the horizontal upper cross-piece, and

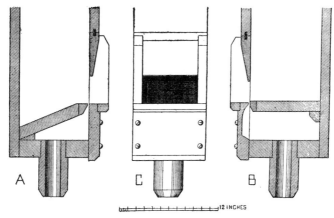

A   C   B

12 INCHES

FIG. 4

the adjustment of the hollowed cap,—in which is formed the wind-way,—slightly below the lower lip of the mouth. Both these treatments have an influence on the tonality of the pipes. In Diagram C is given a Front View of the lower portion of the pipe showing the German mouth.

SCALE.—The scale of the BOURDON—pedal or manual—is a matter of considerable importance, as it affects both the power and tonality of the stop, and, accordingly, its value in combination and registration. It should be dictated by the general character of the Organ, and specially with regard to the tonality of the other stops of the division in which it is placed. It would seem, from the many examples we have examined, that this matter has not been fully considered by the builders of many Organs. Inordinate scales are not uncommon. The BOURDON, in its normal form, varies greatly in scale, chiefly because it is inserted in both the pedal and manual departments of the Organ, and in its different manual divisions. The most suitable scales for the Pedal Organ stops range from a width of $5\frac{3}{4}$ inches by a depth of 8 inches to a width of $8\frac{1}{2}$ inches by a depth of 10 inches—internal measurement—for the CCC pipe; all scales having the ratio $1 : \sqrt{8}$, halving on the seventeenth pipe. The former scale has been adopted by Schulze for the stop in the Pedal Organ of his fine instrument in St. Peter's Church, Hindley, England; the CCC pipe of which has a mouth 4 inches high. The scale of 6.60 inches by 8.56 inches is ample for all ordinary Church Organs which have properly apportioned pedal departments: while the scale of 4.10 inches by 5.56 inches is suitable for a small Church or a Chamber Organ. Larger scales than the maximum given above have been used by English builders, but with no advantage in any direction.

The scales of the manual BOURDON, 16 FT., may range from a width of 3.76 inches by a depth of 5.10 inches, to a width of 5.10 inches by a depth of 7.20 inches. Schulze's effective BOURDON in the Great of the Hindley Organ has its largest pipe measuring 3⅞ inches in width by 6⅜ inches in depth. This scale is noteworthy on account of its proportionate depth, which is unusual. This pipe has its mouth 3⅛ inches in height.

TONALITY.—The tones of the BOURDON vary almost as greatly as its scales. Those which have characterized so many of the stops made and voiced by the older English builders are the least satisfactory; due to largeness of scale, lowness of mouth, and undue thinness of the upper lip. The tones of such stops being tubby and often unmusical in the extreme. The BOURDONS usually made by English organ-builders have mouths seldom over half their width in height, and often less than one-third. Blown by wind of moderate pressure, these stops yield tones in which the twelfth, or first harmonic of a stopped pipe, is more or less prominent in combination with a somewhat dull prime tone, sometimes approaching the tone of the QUINTATEN. In certain tonal apportionments it may be desirable to introduce a BOURDON with this compound voice. The BOURDONS of the German organ-builders, usually of moderate scale, and copiously blown by wind of moderate pressure, have their mouths cut up very high; rising from about two-thirds their width to a height exceeding their width, as exemplified by the stop in the Swell of the Hindley Organ,—labeled LIEBLICHBOURDON, 16 FT.,—the largest pipe of which measures 3⅜ inches in width by 5 inches in depth, and has a mouth 3¾ inches in height. This beautiful stop yields almost a pure organ-tone of singular fullness and sweetness—a perfect stop for artistic registration.

The tones yielded by small-scaled and high-mouthed BOURDONS are fuller and purer than those produced by the large-scaled and low-mouthed English stops; and on this account, combined with the comparatively small standing room they require on the wind-chest, they are most suitable for insertion in the manual divisions of the Organ, and especially those inclosed in swell-boxes. The tone of the BOURDON pipe is affected to a considerable extent by the thickness and finish of its upper lip. These facts were realized by the late T. C. Lewis, one of England's most artistic and accomplished organ-builders. The largest pipe of the fine BOURDON, 16 FT., in the Great of his Organ in the Public Halls, Glasgow, measures 5⅛ inches in width by 6⅜ inches in depth, having a mouth 3 7/8 inches in height, with a square-cut upper lip $\frac{11}{16}$ inch in thickness. The tone of the BOURDON pipe is also affected by the shape given to the upper lip of the mouth, which may vary from the straight line, as shown in Fig. 4, to an arch approaching a semicircle. To produce the desirable ground-tone from pipes so voiced, a copious flow of wind, at a moderate pressure, is absolutely necessary.

While the tones yielded by the different types of BOURDON are somewhat indeterminate and difficult to classify, it is certain the stop belongs to the flute-work of the Organ. It has been considered the bass to the so-called STOPPED DIAPASON, 8 FT.; but it is just as little allied to the DIAPASON proper as the unison stop, which also belongs to the unimitative flute-work.

COMBINATION AND REGISTRATION.—The BOURDON, when properly scaled and voiced, is a valuable stop in artistic registration; combining in a highly satisfactory manner with both labial and lingual stops of almost all pitches. Combined with stops of unison (8 feet) pitch, it adds gravity without prominently affecting their characteristic timbres: this is due to the indeterminate or neutral nature of its tonality, which is, perhaps, its greatest virtue. The true tone of the BOURDON gives firmness and body to the softer lingual stops, and a certain fullness and orchestral richness to such lingual stops as the DOUBLE TRUMPET, CONTRAFAGOTTO, and TROMBONE, 16 FT.; losing itself in their assertive voices so far as their individuality is concerned.

The indeterminate character of the BOURDON tones renders it impracticable to form such a family as one finds in the LIEBLICH-GEDECKTS, but that is not a matter for regret, for little is gained by massing neutral tones.

We strongly recommend the organist who has the command of an Organ which contains a good BOURDON in any of its manual divisions to carefully study what may be called the Registration of the BOURDON. He will be repaid if only education of the ear is the result, rendering it sensitive to the perception of compound tones on a 16 ft. foundation.

BOURDON DOUX, Fr.—The name given by French organ-builders to a soft-toned covered stop of wood and metal, somewhat resembling in formation and tone the German LIEBLICHGEDECKT. This is a very desirable stop in registration, with the more refined labial and lingual stops, on the 16 ft. base.

BOURDONECHO—Ger., BORDONECHO.—The term which has been employed to designate a BOURDON of small scale and of a soft humming tone, differing widely from the covered tone of the LIEB-LICHGEDECKT. The pipes, made on the BOURDON model, should be of wood in the three lower octaves. This stop should be voiced on a wind-pressure not exceeding 3 inches, but preferably lower.

The value of a 16 ft. stop of this class, which would bear about the same relationship to the BOURDON as the DULCIANA does to the DIAPASON, would unquestionably be great in a soft-toned manual division in which an unassertive double voice would prove highly effective in a wide range of artistic registration, in which an assertive double voice would be inadmissible.

BUCCINA, Lat.—The name originally given to an instrument formed from the horn of an ox, blown by a shepherd to gather his flock. It is understood to be derived from *bucca*—the cheek puffed out. Subsequently used by the old organ-builders to designate a POSAUNE. The term is now obsolete in organ nomenclature.

BUZAIN, Dtch.—The name commonly used by the Dutch organ-builders to designate a stop generally known as the POSAUNE. It is applied without any qualification to the stop in its different pitches. In the Pedal Organs of the large instruments in the Cathedrals of Haarlem and Rotterdam it appears of both 32 ft. and 16 ft. pitch.

C

CAMPANA, Ital.—Ger., GLÖCKLEIN. Lat., TONUS FABRI.— The exact nature of the stop to which this name is strictly applicable has not been decided. That its voice shall resemble the sound of bells, or the clang of metal against metal, is evidently implied. Seidel, under the term GLÖCKLEIN-TON (Tonus fabri), describes it as a stop of a large scale and high pitch, the tone of which resembles the clang of hammers beating on a sonorous anvil; an example of which is to be found, of 2 ft. pitch, in the Oberwerk of the Organ in St. Peter's, at Göerlitz. The term has also been applied to a stop of 1 ft. or 6 in. pitch, which, on account of the smallness of its pipes and tonal reasons, consists of similar octaves, repeating at every

octave throughout the compass of the manual clavier. It was introduced, of 1 ft. pitch, in the Organ in the Church of St. Paul, at
Rusthale, Kent, built by Bryceson Brothers, in 1876. It was inserted in the Swell Organ, in which, in certain registrations, it produced bell-like tones. There is an idea suggested by the tonal effects
of this probably unique stop well worth consideration. We are of
opinion, after some study of the subject from a scientific point of
view, that some remarkable tonal effects could be produced in registration, in which a small-scaled and softly-voiced octave-repeat-
ing stop, of 1 ft. or 6 in. pitch throughout, would be introduced along
with both labial and lingual voices. The capabilities of organ-stops
of a refined nature are by no means exhausted.

CARILLON, Fr.—Ger., GLOCKENSPEIL.—The term used to
designate a timbre-creating compound stop, formed of two, three, or
four ranks of medium-scaled open metal pipes, the clang-like tones
of which somewhat resemble the sounds of bells. The characteristic
features of the labial CARILLON lie in the scales and voicing of its
pipes, and in its composition presenting octave-, third-, and fifth-
sounding ranks. The following is an example of a three-rank stop,
in which a third-sounding rank appears throughout its compass.

CARILLON—III. RANKS.

CC to E	. . . .	17——19——22.
F to e¹	. . . .	15——17——19.
f¹ to e²	. . . .	12——15——17.
f² to c⁴	. . . .	10——12——15.

In the regulation of the stop, the third-sounding rank has to be
kept bright and slightly prominent, as on it largely depends the
clang and bell-like effect. Good examples are to be found in some of
the important Organs constructed by Cavaillé-Coll. The CARILLON
in his Organ in the Town Hall of Manchester has a fifth-sounding
rank only from CC to F♯, and a fifth-, a third-, and an octave-sounding rank from G to c⁴. On examining this effective stop, we found
the pipes of large scale, having wide and low mouths, and languids
finely and closely nicked. It would appear that Cavaillé-Coll considered it unnecessary to carry the bell effect below G. There is a
four-rank stop of this class, under the name GLOCKENSPIEL, in the
Echo of the Organ in the Centennial Hall, Sydney, N. S. W. The
CARILLON is to be found in certain old Dutch Organs, as in that in
the Church of St. John the Baptist, at Gouda, built in 1736. The
stop is in the Choir, and is divided and labeled Discant III. ranks
and Bass II. ranks; the third-sounding rank being confined to the

Discant. The stop has been introduced in some German Organs, but we have not been able to find it in the stop-lists of any important modern instruments made by German organ-builders. For particulars respecting the percussion stops, see GLOCKENSPIEL.

COMBINATION AND REGISTRATION.—As the compound labial CARILLON is both harmonic-corroborating and timbre-creating, it can readily be understood that it would enter into numerous tonal combinations with both labial and lingual stops, and produce, in artistic registration, many very effective tonalities. The effects produced in registration in which labial stops are combined with a bell-toned percussion stop are now fairly well known; but the more legitimate organ effects, produced by the employment of the labial CARILLON in registration is almost unknown—in this country entirely so we think. We have heard them and can speak very strongly in their favor. In our study of registration for the production of uncommon tonal effects we struck one, in the Cavaillé-Coll Organ in the Albert Hall, Sheffield, worthy of note. When the combination, in the Solo Organ, of the FLÛTE HARMONIQUE, 8 FT., the DOUBLETTE 2 FT., and the TIERCE, 1⅗ FT., was drawn and played *staccato*, the most remarkable bell-like effect was produced. This would seem to point to a type of registration not commonly adopted or understood: but it might be studied with advantage.

CELESTA.—A percussion stop of recent introduction in the Organ. In its best form it consists of a series of metal plates, of graduated dimensions, adjusted over resonators; all of which being accurately tuned produce pure and agreeable tones which combine well, when in strict accord, with the voices of the softer labial stops.

CÉLESTE, Fr.—A stop formed of small-scaled open labial pipes, preferably of tin, voiced to yield a singing tone, inclining in good examples to a string quality. It is tuned slightly sharp, so as to produce when drawn with another stop of similar tonality and of standard pitch a delicate undulating effect, supposed to imitate a celestial voice. See VOIX CÉLESTE.

CELESTINA.—The name given by English organ-builders to stops of different forms and tonalities. The name appears to have been introduced by William Hill, of London, and given to a small-scaled and softly-toned wood FLUTE of 4 ft. pitch, invented by him. A stop of this name and pitch, and, doubtless, of the same character, is introduced in the Choir of Hill's great Organ in the Centennial Hall, Sydney, N. S. W. A CELESTINA formed of metal pipes, yielding a louder tone differing from that of the original stop, is to be found in the Willis Organ in the Royal Albert Hall, London.

COMBINATION AND REGISTRATION.—In the present school of organ-building in this country, with its craze for high wind-pressures, too little attention is paid to stops of the CELESTINA class and octave pitch: yet anyone who has studied registration must realize the great value of their voices in giving a certain brightness and life to unison combinations, without in any way disturbing their pitch. From a scientific point of view, one must look upon the introduction of such an octave stop as merely corroborating the first harmonic of the open unison stop or stops, while it may, at the same time, introduce a new element into the timbre of the tonal combination. Hence the value of the CELESTINA, 4 FT., in artistic and scientific registration. See CŒLESTINA.

CHALUMEAU, Fr.—Ger., SCHALMEI. Ital., SCIALUMÒ. Eng., SHAWM.—The name given to a soft-toned lingual stop, commonly of 8 ft. pitch, the voice of which is supposed to imitate that of the obsolete instrument called the Schalmei or Shawm, the precursor of the Clarinet. So far as reed instruments are concerned, the term Chalumeau is applied now only to the low register of the Clarinet.

Describing the old SCHALMEI, Seidel says: "It is a soft, agreeable reed stop, in imitation of the instrument of the same name used by the shepherds of Southern Europe. It is of 8 ft. and 4 ft. on the manuals, and 16 ft. in the Pedal Organ, when it is termed SCHALMEIBASS. The tubes are generally funnel-shaped, and of a larger scale than those of the TRUMPET. Sometimes they were closed with the exception of a few sound-holes. The tone of the stop varies as greatly as the form of its pipes." Examples of the stop are to be found in several German Organs, but it is no longer in favor. It appears, of 8 ft. pitch, in the Oberwerk of Ladegast's Organ in the Cathedral of Merseburg, built in 1855. Stops labeled CHALMEAUX, of 8 ft. tone, were inserted by Silbermann in the Choirs of his fine Organs in the Catholic Church and the Marienkirche, at Berlin. In Schulze & Son's notable Organ in the Marienkirche, at Lübeck, there is a SCHALMEI, 4 FT., in the Erste Pedal, thus described: "Von engercr Mcnsur und schönem singenden Ton, vortrefflich zur Führung des Cantus firmus geeignet." In the Great of the Organ built by Elliot & Hill for York Minster there was a SHAWM, 8 FT. There is a SCHALMEI, 16 FT., the resonators of which are cylindrical terminating in a partly covered bell, in the Organ in the Colston Hall, Bristol, built by Norman & Beard. The tone of this stop is rich; partaking, as might be expected, of the tones of the CLARINET and the COR ANGLAIS in effective combination. A Pedal Organ stop of this description would be a valuable addition to a large Organ. Softly-voiced lingual stops are much called for in Pedal Organs to-day. They are conspicuous by their absence.

CHAMADE, Fr.—The term affixed by French organ-builders to the name of a lingual stop, to indicate that its resonators are disposed in, or near to, a horizontal position, and so displayed as to send their sounds perfectly unobstructed to the ear. In the description of the Organ erected by Cavaillé-Coll in the grand Church of Saint-Ouen, at Ruen, we find in the Grand-Orgue, TROMPETTE EN CHAMADE and CLAIRON EN CHAMADE. These are projected, in fan-form, from the lateral divisions of the case, and free of the advanced Positif. See Frontispiece. This treatment is so common in Spain that it may be considered a characteristic of the important Organs of that country. It is to be condemned on all musical grounds; for the powerful lingual stops so disposed should be inclosed in swell-boxes, and so endowed with powers of flexibility and expression. Uncontrollable lingual stops are an abomination from every musical point of view.

CHIMNEY FLUTE.—Fr., FLÛTE À CHEMINÉE.—The names given by English and French organ-builders to the half-covered labial stop more appropriately called in German nomenclature ROHRFLÖTE (REED-FLUTE). See ROHRFLÖTE.

CHORALBASSET, Ger.—Described by Wolfram (1815) as an open labial stop of 2 ft. pitch introduced in the Pedal Organ. The stop is also called CHORALBASS. The term CHORAL has been prefixed to several loud-toned stops to indicate their special suitability for giving out the melody of a Choral. With this meaning, we meet with such stop-names as CHORALPRINZIPAL, CHORALPRÄS-TANT, and CHORALFLÖTE. According to Seidel, the Pedal Organ CHORALBASSET has been made of large-scaled pipes of 4 ft., 2 ft., and 1 ft. pitch: the manual stops, CHORALPRINZIPAL and CHORAL-PRÄSTANT, being of 8 ft. and 4 ft. pitch.

CINQ, Dtch.—The name given to a lingual stop, of 2 ft. pitch, inserted in the Pedals of the Organs in the Cathedrals of St. Bavon, Haarlem, and St. Lawrence, Rotterdam; and churches in Delft and Utrecht. The introduction of high-pitched stops is a characteristic of Dutch Pedal Organs; desirable on account of their brightening effects, and much to be desired in the Pedal Organs of to-day.

CLAIRON, Fr.—A lingual stop of large scale and 4 ft. pitch, commonly attending the TROMPETTE wherever it is introduced, as in the pedal and four manual divisions of the Grand Organ in Notre-Dame, Paris. See CLARION.

CLAIRON-DOUBLETTE, Fr.—Eng., OCTAVE CLARION.—A very uncommon lingual stop, of 2 ft. pitch; an example of which exists in the Grand-Chœur of the Organ in the Church of Saint-Sulpice, Paris. As this high-pitched stop cannot well be carried in lingual pipes of its true pitch above treble c², the two higher octaves may either be duplications of the treble octave, or be formed of large-scaled and loudly-voiced labial pipes. The value of such a stop is very questionable; so much so that the example alluded to is the only one we have found in an Organ. Regnier does not mention the stop.

CLARABELLA.—Ger., OFFENFLÖTE.—The name given to an open wood stop of 8 ft. pitch, which, in its original form, was invented by J. C. Bishop, of London. It became a great favorite of

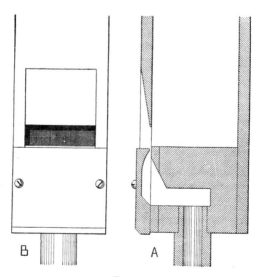

FIG. 5

the English organ-builders; and during the latter half of the last century was inserted in the majority of the organs then constructed. A fine example of the stop exists in the Great of the Bishop Organ in the Church of St. Mary, Nottingham. The CLARABELLA, in its original and most desirable form, has of late years been comparatively seldom made, a fact to be regretted.

FORMATION.—The CLARABELLA was devised by J. C. Bishop to take the place of the higher octaves of the STOPPED DIAPASON, 8 FT., which he found insufficient in volume of tone to cope with the increase of power being given to the OPEN DIAPASON and other stops of the Great Organ. At first it occupied the treble octaves from middle c¹ only, but later it was carried down to tenor C, as in the Great of the Organ in St. Mary's, Nottingham; the bass being in covered pipes. The stop has, however, been made with its open pipes throughout, as in the Organ built by Booth, of Wakefield, for the Brunswick Chapel, Leeds. When properly made and voiced the CLARABELLA is an extremely valuable stop, and in an important Organ it should be carried throughout the manual compass in its open pipes.

The CLARABELLA pipe is of the usual quadrangular form and construction, as shown in the accompanying illustration, Fig. 5. It has the direct, English mouth, usually about one-quarter its width in height, having the upper lip somewhat thin and carefully rounded. It requires no ears; and its cap is hollowed for the windway, level on top, and without a beard, as indicated in Section A. The proportions of the mouth are shown in Front View B. The scale of the stop should vary according to the volume and the strength of the tone required; but as a rule it has been made to what may be considered a large scale for an 8 ft. open wood stop. The following scales, to different ratios, may be accepted as normal:

CLARABELLA SCALE—IN INCHES—RATIO 1:2.66

PIPES	CC	C	c¹	c²	c³	c⁴
WIDTH	4.26	2.62	1.60	0.98	0.60	0.37
DEPTH	5.24	3.21	1.97	1.20	0.74	0.45

CLARABELLA SCALE—IN INCHES—RATIO 1:2.519

PIPES	CC	C	c¹	c²	c³	c⁴
WIDTH	3.79	2.39	1.50	0.95	0.60	0.38
DEPTH	4.96	3.13	1.97	1.24	0.78	0.49

TONALITY.—The tone of the stop as voiced by its inventor was of a full, round fluty quality, naturally brighter and more penetrating than that of the STOPPED DIAPASON pipes it displaced; and, accordingly, it did not join satisfactorily with the tones of the covered tenor and bass octaves, whose harmonics were different. That fact is a strong reason for the formation of the stop with open pipes throughout. The tone of the CLARABELLA, in its best form and when voiced by a master, is beautiful and invaluable in any properly apportioned Great Organ, and whether the stop is inclosed or free. Its tone should be midway between that of the DIAPASON and the full-toned German HOHLFLÖTE, differing from the tone of the wood DIAPASON as made by Schulze. The true tone of the CLARABELLA is clear, singing, and reposeful; making it valuable in every direction in which it may be employed.

COMBINATION AND REGISTRATION.—The CLARABELLA can be used as a solo stop with good effect, especially when strains of a placid nature are desired; when its liquid tones afford an agreeable relief to those of a more assertive and cutting character so commonly resorted to in solo passages. But it is in combination and artistic registration that the chief value of the stop is found. There are very few wood stops which enter so satisfactorily into combination with lingual stops of all classes. When under control, as it should be in a properly appointed Organ, it is a desirable addition to the VOX HUMANA and CLARINET. The true CLARABELLA has the desirable property of building up the tone of almost every unison stop to which it is added without prominently affecting its character. In registration it may be considered an all-round helper. It may, in another important direction, be used as a unison base, on which to build up many beautiful compound tones. For this purpose it may be combined with the softer octave, mutation, and harmonic-corroborating stops. With such a refined stop as the DULCIANA CORNET, V. RANKS (*q. v.*), it produces a charming compound tone,* practically unknown in the Organs of to-day, with their high wind-pressures and MIXTURES of unregulated and screaming voices.

CLARIBEL FLUTE.—An open wood stop of 4 ft. pitch, which in its original form is practically an OCTAVE CLARABELLA, but slightly more fluty in tone. Willis, in his dislike of wood stops,† made his CLARIBEL FLUTES, 8 ft., of metal from middle c^1, and harmonic from g^1. The bass and tenor octaves being of wood pipes.

COMBINATION AND REGISTRATION.—The value of octave stops of varied tonalities has not been fully realized, judging from their sparing introduction even in important Organs. Too much dependence being placed on octave coupling, always to be avoided when possible. The CLARIBEL FLUTE, on account of the good mixing and not too assertive qualities of its tone (when properly voiced on wind of moderate pressure), is a most serviceable stop in registration in both its offices of harmonic-corroborator and timbre-creator. Its best position in the Organ is in the division in which the CLARABELLA is placed; for in combination with that stop it produces a beautiful unimitative tone, upon which string- or reed-tone can be thrown with fine effect.

---

* This tone is well known to us by long experience, for, under the names FLAUTO TEDESCA, 8 FT., and RIPIENO DI CINQUE, both stops were in our Chamber Organ, placed in different swell-boxes, and, accordingly, subject to compound flexibility and expression.

† So great was his dislike that in all the manual divisions of his large Organ in the Royal Albert Hall, London, there are only two wood stops. He assured us, on asking his reason, that he obtained better wood-tones from metal pipes. We questioned it.

CLARIN, Span.—A lingual stop of the TRUMPET class and usually of octave pitch. It is labeled in Spanish Organs with several qualifications as follows: CLARIN REAL, CLARIN DE BATALLA, CLARIN CLARO, CLARIN SORDINO, CLARIN PARDO, CLARIN DE BAJOS, and CLARIN DE ECOS.

CLARINA, Ital.—An open metal labial stop of large scale and 2 ft. pitch, voiced to yield a powerful tone. It is introduced in the Pedal Organ to impart clearness and distinctness to heavy pedal combinations, and especially when they are used in solo passages and fugues. A stop of so high a pitch is very rare in a Pedal Organ. It is desirable in combination. See COMPENSATIONSMIXTUR.

CLARINET.—Fr., CLARINETTE. Ger., CLARINETTE. Ital., CLARINETTO.—The lingual stop formed and voiced to imitate as closely as possible the tones of the orchestral Clarinets. When made by master hands, it is one of the most successful imitative stops in the Organ. It is invariably and correctly of 8 ft. pitch, and has very frequently in English Organs been commenced at tenor C, probably because the orchestral Clarinet in A does not go lower than C♯; but as the Bass Clarinet descends about an octave below this note, the CLARINET of the Organ should be carried, in all cases, throughout the manual compass. The term CLARIONET has been commonly used by English organ-builders, but should never be employed. It has no relation to the English word "clarion" any more than the CLARINET has to the CLARION of the Organ.

FORMATION.—The resonator of the CLARINET pipe is cylindrical throughout save where it is attached, by a short conical piece, to the reed-block: it is entirely open at top, where it should be furnished with an adjustable slide for fine regulation. The form of the complete pipe is shown in Fig. 6, Plate I. It is to this form of resonator that is mainly due the imitative voice of the stop, resembling as it does the cylindrical tube of the orchestral Clarinet. The resonator of the CC pipe, yielding a note of 8 ft. pitch, instead of being, approximately, the true speaking length of 8 ft., is only a little more than 4 ft. in length. Both in length and scale of its resonators the CLARINET differs from all the lingual stops belonging to other families. The reeds of the stop are of medium scale and of sufficient length to receive tongues to speak the unison tone; they are properly of the closed variety, their triangular openings extending directly from the thick discs which cover their lower ends. The tongues are firm and finely curved so as to get rid of brassiness. In German and Swiss Organs the CLARINET is almost invariably a free-reed stop, of a somewhat large scale and generally feeble in tone and far from imitative. Some examples have inverted conical resonators which in no way favor the production of a characteristic Clarinet tone.

TONALITY.—The tones of an artistically voiced CLARINET are extremely pleasing and full of character, and surpass in imitativeness all the other lingual voices of the Organ. From the point of view of uniformity of tone the organ stop may be considered superior to the orchestral instrument. The middle register of the stop—its most valuable portion for solo work—is as satisfactory as the corresponding portion of the Clarinet; but in the low register, the tone does not reach the rich tonality of the chalumeau of the orchestral instrument. The harmonic upper partial tones of the Clarinet are those proper to a covered organ-pipe; and these are present in the imitative tones of the organ CLARINET, secured by the cylindrical form of its resonators and, on account of their half-length, their influence on the motions of the tongues of the reeds. The voicer should do his utmost to impart to the bass and tenor of the stop as much of the chalumeau quality as his skill can accomplish. It is possible that some modification of, or addition to, the resonators would assist in this direction.

COMBINATION AND REGISTRATION.—Although the CLARINET, in both its single and dual form, is *par excellence* a solo stop, it admits of combination and artistic registration with numerous labial stops—both simple and compound—of refined and contrasting tonalities, producing beautiful qualities of tone. It loses too much of its peculiar voice or individuality when combined with loud-toned labial stops; and becomes entirely absorbed when combined with powerful lingual stops. Yet in suitable cases it never fails to be a timbre-creator. With both unison and octave flute-toned stops of the softer varieties it produces compound tones which demonstrate the value of contrasting voices in registration. In combination with the string-toned stops it produces tones strong with orchestral coloring. In these directions the organist will find no little profit in studying what may be designated the Registration of the CLARINET. It is only by means of such studies that the student of the Organ can become a master of the art and science of stop registration. The mere following of registrations marked by the composer or transcriber on a piece of organ music, which have been schemed, as a rule, on some special Organ, and which may or may not be possible or satisfactory on another Organ, will not conduct the student very far in acquiring a personal knowledge and mastery of artistic registration. As we have said elsewhere: In organ-stop registration, as in artistic orchestration, "there is no royal road to learning."

CLARINET FLUTE.—The name which has been given by certain English organ-builders to a half-covered wood stop, of medium scale, and 8 ft. pitch. It is a species of ROHRFLÖTE, differing from that stop in having longer stopper-handles through which larger holes are bored; and also in having much lower mouths—usually under one-quarter their width in height—and voiced with thin upper lips and fine and close nicking. This formation and voicing on a light wind-pressure produces a somewhat reedy tone, so remote from that of the orchestral Clarinet, or the organ stop so-called, as to give no support to the inappropriate name CLARINET FLUTE. Many examples exist in English Organs by different builders, varying in tonality, and commonly labeled CLARIONET FLUTE.

CLARION.—Fr., CLAIRON. Ital., CLARINO.—A lingual stop of 4 ft. pitch, the reeds and resonators of which are similar in all respects to those of the TRUMPET, to which stop it stands in the relation of a true Octave, save in regard to its resonators, which should be somewhat smaller in scale. As an octave stop it should be less assertive in tone than the TRUMPET, or other unison lingual stop with which it may be registered, yet its voice should impart richness and brilliancy to every combination into which it enters. When artistically voiced and finely regulated it becomes a stop of general utility in registration, and a good solo voice on special occasions. More care should be given to the CLARION than is usually bestowed upon it, and organists should give it more attention. Owing to the difficulty of constructing lingual pipes of very high pitch, it has been usual to insert the top octave of the CLARION, 4 FT., in loudly-voiced labial pipes. French organ-builders have frequently formed the top octave of unison or TRUMPET pipes, with a satisfactory result.*

CLARION MIXTURE.—The name given by Walker & Sons to a labial stop, introduced by them to take the place of the lingual CLARION; as in both the Great and Swell of the Organ in Holy Trinity Church, Chelsea; and in the Swell of the Organ in the Church of St. John the Divine, Kennington, London. The stop is

---

* " En France, le CLAIRON a toujours quatre-pieds; en Allemagne, quatre et huit. C'est un régistre d'harmonie mordante et claire, comme l'indique son nom, et destiné à donner de la pointe aux huit-pieds d'anches. Cependant on peut le faire chanter seul, ou mélangé avec les fonds; mais dans ce dernier cas il est bon de ne pas le toucher sur les notes le plus hautes, où il devient d'une grande aigreur. On fait ce régistre d'étain fin et de forme conique. Comme ces tuyaux extrêmes sont fort exigus, on lui donne ordinairement une reprise à la dernière octave; et pour le toucher, on y joint le PRESTANT et la DOUBLETTE, qui dissimulent la reprise en suivent la marche ascendante qu'est censé suivre le CLAIRON. L'habitude de mettre deux clairons au même clavier expose l'ensemble des jeux de ce clavier à être criard et mal d'accord. On met un CLAIRON à chaque clavier complet, même à la pédale; il forme ainsi le sommet d'une pyramide harmonique des jeux d'anches des trois degrés, quatre, huit et seize pieds. A la pédale, son mélange est peut-être plus utile que partout ailleurs; il donne aux huit-pieds d'anches, c'est-à-dire à la TROMPETTE, un vif éclat, de même qu'au mélange de TROMPETTS et BOMBARDES, c'est-à-dire aux huit et seize-pieds. "—Regnier.

composed of an OCTAVE, TWELFTH, and FIFTEENTH, of open metal pipes of full scale, heavily blown, and voiced to yield a powerful tone. The effect of the stop was found, as might be expected, to be unsatisfactory. Like too many screaming compound stops to be found in modern Organs in this country and abroad, the CLARION MIXTURE was valueless in artistic registration.

CLAVÄOLINE, Ger.—In the year 1830 Beyer, an organ-builder of Nürnberg, invented a manual lingual stop, giving it the name CLAVÄOLINE or KLAVÄOLINE, the name being rendered in both forms in old stop-lists. From its name it would seem its inventor considered it to have some relation to the AOLINE, probably in its tone. From the best authority we have been able to find, the stop seems to have been a free-reed something of the nature of the PHYSHARMONIKA (q. v.). The free-reeds appear to have been attached to small blocks of wood standing directly on the wind-chest,—somewhat after the fashion of the reeds of the Harmonium,—and devoid of resonators. The tone under such conditions must be extremely feeble. The CLAVÄOLINE appears in the stop-lists of the Organs in the Town Church of Fulda, placed in the Echo; and in the Church of St. Wenzel, at Naumburg, where it appears in the Swell.*

CLEAR FLUTE.—Ger., HELLFLÖTE.—The stop to which this somewhat indefinite English name was given is said to have been first introduced by Kirtland & Jardine, of Manchester. It is an open wood stop of 4 ft. pitch, yielding a full and clear unimitative flute-tone, but without any particular charm or good mixing quality. The pipes are of medium scale, the CC, 4 ft., pipe measuring $2\frac{5}{8}$ inches by $3\frac{1}{8}$ inches internally; their ratio being $1 : \sqrt{8}$. The chief characteristics of the CLEAR FLUTE pipe are its inverted mouth, sloped block carrying the wind-way, and flat cap. It is voiced on a copious wind supply, necessitating a moderately high mouth. The name can, with equal propriety, be given to any stop producing a clear unimitative flute-tone.

CŒLESTINA, Lat.—An open metal labial stop of 4 ft. pitch, of small scale, and of a soft singing voice. It may be considered the Octave of the true English DULCIANA. An example occurs in the

---

* Alluding to the CLAVÄOLINE, Seidel says: "The Organ in St. Wenzel's, at Naumburg; 52 registers, 3 manuals, 3000 pipes, 7 pairs of bellows. Was first built in 1613 by Joachim Tzchug, and underwent several repairs, the last one by Beyer, on which occasion several alterations were made in the arrangement, in order to obtain a tone as full and pompous as possible. Among the new registers introduced, the TRAVERSFLÖTE, GEMSHORN, 8 FT., and CLAVÄOLINE, 8 FT., are particularly beautiful."

Choir of the Organ in the Centennial Hall, Sydney, N. S. W. The stop has been less correctly labeled CELESTINA and CELESTIANA.

COMBINATION AND REGISTRATION.—The value of such a stop in artistic and refined registration cannot well be overrated; and it is much too seldom that OCTAVES of the nature of the CŒLESTINA are introduced in even large Organs in which some unison stops are inserted which are, comparatively, of less general use in effective registration. It is not very generally realized, even among good organists, that the tonal value and beauty of many a unison voice are never fully developed until a suitable octave tone is combined with it. This is according to the natural law of musical sound in respect to the tones produced by open pipes, to which the octave gives an effective reinforcement to the first and most important upper partial. But, on the other hand, when the OCTAVE is associated with a covered stop, it introduces a foreign element into the unison tone, which, in its nature, does not contain the octave in its harmonic upper partials. Accordingly, a new tonality is created often of a very beautiful character, and one probably impossible in the absence of such a stop as the CŒLESTINA, 4 FT. These considerations would lead to the conclusion that a larger number and a greater variety of OCTAVES should be provided in Concert-room Organs and other important instruments.

COMPENSATIONSMIXTUR, Ger.—Eng., COMPENSATING MIXTURE.—The stop to which the name was originally given is a Pedal Organ compound stop of a harmonic-corroborating character, invented by Musickdirecktor Wilke, of Neu-Ruppin, and first installed in the Organ in the Church of St. Catherine, at Salzwedel. Its purpose was not only to give to the lower pedal notes the most distinct speech possible, but to impart to the Pedal Organ throughout such an even tone that rapid passages could be rendered with the same roundness and clearness from the lowest to the highest note of the clavier. According to Seidel, all experts who tested the stop agreed that it fulfilled its mission. Notwithstanding such approval the invention did not receive the consideration it deserved by the conservative and slow-going organ-builders of Germany. Wilke's stop was of very short compass, extending only to ten notes. It was composed, according to Seidel, of five ranks, as follows:

I. TIERCE, $3\frac{1}{5}$ FT.—CCC to GGG, eight pipes; the tone of which is gradually reduced from DDD until almost inaudible at GGG.

II. QUINT, $2\frac{2}{3}$ FT.—CCC to AAA, ten pipes; the tone of which is reduced from EEE in like manner.

III. Octave, 2 ft.—CCC to GGG ♯, nine pipes; the tone of which is reduced from DDD in like manner.

IV. Quint, 1⅓ ft.—CCC to FFF ♯, seven pipes, the tone of which is reduced from CCC ♯ in like manner.

V. Sifflöte, 1 ft.—CCC to FFF, six pipes; the tone of which is reduced from CCC ♯ in like manner.

It is difficult to conceive on what principle Wilke designed the stop, for it is both insufficient and inartistic. While it may have ameliorated the lower ten notes of the heavy Pedal Organ of the Salzwedel instrument, it certainly could do nothing to impart an "even tone" throughout its compass. The stop, however, suggested an artistic development which we decided to test practically, with tonal results that proved eminently satisfactory. We included a Compensating Mixture, VI. ranks, in our scheme for the Pedal of the Concert-room Organ installed in the Festival Hall of the Louisiana Purchase Exposition, St. Louis, 1904. Again, and for the first time in a Church Organ outside Germany, we inserted a Compensating Mixture, III. ranks, in the Pedal of the Grand Organ we designed for the Church of Our Lady of Grace, Hoboken, N. J.*

Formation.—The following particulars and suggestions are necessarily given as results of our own studies and practical tests; for we are not aware of any English or American organ-builder having paid any attention to the stop under consideration. The simple fact that it calls for more than one rank of pipes will deter organ-builders from advocating its adoption. The stop may be composed of from three to six ranks of open metal pipes, of the usual Diapason form, and, preferably, of different scales: all the ranks to commence on CCC and to terminate on different notes, as the judgment of the designer may decide, properly taking into consideration the stop-apportionment of the Pedal Organ. The scale adopted for the first, the longest, and the lowest pitched rank is to determine the smaller scales for the shorter and higher-pitched ranks. No rule has been formulated in this matter, but a regular gradation derived from a complete scale is to be recommended. It is essential that provision be made for a regular decrease in strength of tone, pipe by pipe, in every rank, from the CCC pipe to the top pipe, the tone of which is to be only just clearly audible. To assist in obtaining this diminution of tone, the scales should decrease so as to place the half diameter on the thirteenth pipe. The following is a suggestion for the composition of a stop of three ranks:

Pedal Organ Compensating Mixture—III. ranks.

I. CCC to G   Super-Octave, 4 ft. .   . 32 Notes.
II. CCC to GG♯ Super-octave Quint, 2⅔ ft. 21   "
III. CCC to EE Twenty-second, 2 ft . . 17   "

Should a stop of four ranks be required for an important Pedal Organ, in which

* For a detailed description of this stop, see our work, "The Organ of the Twentieth Century," page 497.

there is a stop of 32 ft. pitch, add to the above, from CCC to D, a TIERCE, 3⅕ FT 27 Notes.

We suggest the following composition for a stop of six ranks, suitable for the Pedal of a Concert-room Organ of the first magnitude:

PEDAL ORGAN COMPENSATING MIXTURE—VI. RANKS.

I.	CCC to G	SUPER-OCTAVE, 4 FT. .	.	32 Notes.
II.	CCC to D	TIERCE, 3⅕ FT. . .	.	27 "
III.	CCC to BB	OCTAVE-QUINT, 2⅔ FT.	.	24 "
IV.	CCC to GG	TWENTY-SECOND, 2 FT. .	.	20 "
V.	CCC to DD♯	TWENTY-SIXTH, 1⅓ FT.	.	16 "
VI.	CCC to BBB	TWENTY-NINTH, 1 FT. .	.	12 "

A five-rank stop may be formed by omitting the fifth rank, which is of the least importance. It is usually desirable to have both the lowest and highest ranks octave-sounding.

TONALITY AND REGISTRATION.—While the stop is devised as a tonal compensating agent, for the purpose of giving clearness and richness of articulation to the lower and somewhat indeterminate notes of the Pedal Organ unison and double stops, gradually decreasing in its effect toward the higher notes where its help is less required,—an office it fulfills in a satisfactory manner—it is, at the same time, a harmonic-corroborating stop of considerable value in registration; and as such it may take the place of an ordinary MIXTURE with advantage to the Pedal Organ. The most desirable voice for the stop is pure organ-tone, for that will prove most useful in Pedal Organ registration. As has already been remarked, the tone of each rank must be uniformly reduced in strength from that of the first and complete rank; and each rank must be evenly reduced in strength of tone as it ascends the scale, until at its highest note its voice is only just clearly audible. The initial strength of tone, or that of the CCC (4 ft.) pipe of the first rank, must be adjusted according to the demands of the foundation unison, 16 ft., of the Pedal Organ, and from it all graduations of tone in its own and the other ranks have to be regulated. In registration, the COMPENSATING MIXTURE will be found extremely valuable, especially when well-marked articulation is necessary, as in Solos, Fugues, and pronounced pedal passages.

We introduced, for the first time in the history of organ-building, a COMPENSATING MIXTURE, V. RANKS, in the String-toned Subdivision of the Third Organ in the Concert-room Organ installed at the Louisiana Purchase Exposition. We strongly recommend the introduction of compound harmonic-corroborating stops of the compensating class in manual divisions in which there are double stops likely to make the bass unduly heavy. The subject is a new one, and we recommend it to the attention of organ and tonal experts.

CONCERT FLUTE.—Ger., CONCERTFLÖTE.—The name occasionally given to an open labial stop, commonly of wood, and of 4 ft. pitch; the tone of which imitates, as closely as practicable, that of orchestral Flute. See ORCHESTRAL FLUTE.

CONE GAMBA.—The name given to an open metal labial stop of 8 ft. pitch, yielding an unimitative string-tone; the pipes of which are conical, being about half the diameter at top of that at the mouth line; hence the name of the stop. The mouth has a width of about one-third or two-sevenths the larger circumference of the pipe, is cut low, and voiced with the harmonic-bridge, held between projecting ears. In some examples a *frein harmonique* takes the place of the bridge and ears. The pipes are of medium scale and should be made of high-grade alloy.

The tone of the CONE GAMBA naturally varies in different examples; but, as a rule, it is, when artistically voiced by a masterhand, of a singing string quality, delicate, and very beautiful. The unison stop suggests the introduction of a complete family of 16 ft., 8 ft., 4 ft., and 2 ft. pitch, which would be of great value in artistic registration, combining admirably with the family of the LIEBLICH-GEDECKTS, the other softer flute-toned stops, and the reed-toned lingual stops. A CONE GAMBA, 16 FT., of full compass, was inserted in the Choir of the Organ erected by Hill, in 1863, in the nave of York Minster. This fine stop was extremely effective in combination. As a timbre-creating and tone-supporting stop the CONE GAMBA, 8 FT., will be found very useful in artistic registration.

CONTRABASS, Ger.—Ital., CONTRABASSO. Fr., CONTRE-BASSE. Eng., DOUBLE BASS.—The name appropriately used to designate an open labial stop of 16 ft. pitch, of wood or metal, voiced to yield a tone imitating, as closely as practicable, that of the Double Bass of the orchestra. In French Organs the CONTRE-BASSE is invariably a Pedal Organ stop, appearing as such in the Organs in the Cathedrals of Paris, Amiens, and Orléans, and the Churches of Saint-Eustache, Saint-Sulpice, and la Madeleine, Paris. French organ-builders and experts do not seem to have realized the possibility of introducing so grave an imitative string-toned stop in a manual division. It does not appear, save in the Pedal, in Cavaillé-Coll's scheme for the Monumental Organ to be installed in St. Peter's,

Rome. But no French organ-builder ever contemplated the desirability of introducing an independent string-toned division in the Organ: indeed, no one seems to have ever done so, until we realized its necessity, and introduced one in the Organ installed in the Festival Hall of the Louisiana Purchase Exposition.*

FORMATION.—The pipes of the CONTRABASS, 16 FT., are in the best examples of wood, and of what may be considered small scales; although metal pipes can be used with satisfactory results, especially in the higher octaves of the manual stop. For the Pedal Organ stop wood is to be preferred, as it aids in producing a tone fuller in character than is commonly yielded by small-scaled metal pipes. The best example of the stop which has been directly examined and tested by us is that labeled VIOLONBASS, 16 FT., in the Pedal of the Organ constructed by Edmund Schulze for the Church of St. Peter, Hindley, Lancashire, England. In this fine stop the pipes are square and of the following measurements: CCC, 16 ft., 5½ ins. by 5½ ins.; width of mouth 5½ ins.; height of mouth 1⅞ ins. CC, 8 ft., 3⅜ ins. by 3⅜ ins.; mouth 3⅜ ins. by 1 in. C, 4 ft., 2 ins. by 2 ins.; mouth 2 ins. by ⅚ in. The pipes have sunk blocks, the German form of mouth, caps hollowed externally, no projecting ears, upper lips cut almost to a sharp edge, and furnished with harmonic bridges of an unusual form.† No wood pipes of imitative string-tone were known in England prior to their appearance in the Organs installed by Schulze in the Parish Church of Doncaster and St. Peter's Hindley. They were first made in this country by Roosevelt, from models furnished by us in 1883. By special voicing with the harmonic-bridge, covered pipes can be made to yield imitative string-tone, the prominence of the upper partial—the Twelfth—contributing to the tone. The covered stop, owing to its moderate dimensions, is most suitable for a manual division in all save an Organ of the first magnitude.

TONALITY AND REGISTRATION.—In tonality, the voicer of the CONTRABASS should aim at the imitation of the peculiar tones of the different strings of the orchestral instrument, giving greater body to the tones of the 8 ft. and higher octaves, so as to differentiate them properly from the corresponding tones of the VIOLONCELLO, 8 FT. This is important when the stop is associated with a VIOLONCELLO in a manual string-toned division, as it should be in a Concert-room Organ. The tones of the VIOLONBASS in the Hindley Organ are so closely imitative, even to the rasp of the bow on the strings, as to be deceptive to the ear. That is as it should be, if such an important voice is to be of full value in the artistic registration of orchestral-toned stops. The building up of a mass of orchestral string-tone in the Organ, which we were the first to render possible, is a matter in registration of the greatest importance in the artistic and proper rendition of orchestral scores or transcriptions. The student of the art of registration will soon discover the value of so effective and colorful a voice as that of the CONTRABASS. When artistically voiced and perfectly regulated it is a beautiful voice for a bass solo; and may for this purpose be combined with the CONTRAFAGOTTO, or with a good VOX HUMANA in sub-octaves. It is to be regretted that so little attention has been paid to the stop by the organ-builders and experts of this country. It must, however, appear in the Organ of the Twentieth Century.

CONTRA-BOURDON, SUB-BOURDON.—Ger., UNTERSATZ. Fr., SOUS-BASSE.—The name given to a covered wood stop of 32 ft. pitch, properly belonging to the stop-apportionment of the Pedal Organ, but occasionally appearing, in an incomplete form, in the First or Great Organ. It is occasionally resorted to as a Pedal Organ stop when either space or funds prevent of the DOUBLE DIAPASON or SUB-PRINCIPAL, 32 FT., being introduced. As a substitute it is anything but satisfactory tonally. The tone of the stop is that common to the ordinary BOURDON, 16 FT., being carried an octave lower, where its voice becomes painfully indeterminate, as might be expected. It appears in Pedal Organs under the following names: UNTERSATZ in the Organs in the Cathedral of Merseburg and the Royal Catholic Church, Dresden. GROSSUNTERSATZ in the Organ in the Church of Waltershausen, Gotha. SUBBASS in the Organ in the Church of St. Michael, Hamburg. GRAND BOURDON in the Pedal of the Organ, by Cavaillé-Coll, in the Church of Saint Vincent de Paul, Paris. CONTRA-BOURDON in the Organs in the Auditorium, Chicago, and the Centennial Hall, Sydney, N. S. W.

When the CONTRA-BOURDON, 32 FT., is introduced in the Great Organ, it commonly is of short compass, not extending below tenor C. It appears under the following names: UNTERSATZ on the First Clavier of the Riga Cathedral Organ. BORDUN, 32 FT., in the Hauptwerk of Merseburg Cathedral Organ, and in the Second Division of the First Organ in the instrument in Schwerin Cathedral. SUB-BOURDON in the Great of the Organs in the Parish Churches of Leeds and Doncaster, England. On tonal grounds we do not advocate the introduction of this incomplete stop in any manual division; while we are of opinion that a pure and soft organ-tone, of 32 ft. pitch, would be valuable in the First Organ of a large Concert-room Organ. See DOLCIANO PROFUNDO.

CONTRA-DULCIANA.—An open metal labial stop of small scale, of 32 ft. pitch in the Pedal Organ and 16 ft. pitch when introduced in a manual division, as in the Choir of the Organ in the

Centennial Hall, Sydney, N. S. W. It is also named DOUBLE DUL-
CIANA (*q. v.*). We have introduced it, in an extended form and for
a double purpose, in the Pedal Organ of our scheme for the Concert-
room Organ of the Twentieth Century.* See DOLCIANO PROFUNDO.

CONTRAFAGOTTO, Ital.—Ger., CONTRAFAGOTT. Eng., DOU-
BLE BASSOON.—A lingual stop, of 16 ft. pitch, the resonators of
which are of small scale and either of wood or metal. In the former
material they are square and cf inverted pyramidal form: when of
metal they are inverted conical in form. When properly scaled,
voiced, and regulated, its tone closely approaches that of the orchestral instrument of the same name. While usually and correctly
placed in the Pedal Organ, where its voice furnishes the true bass to
the manual FAGOTTO and OBOE, its presence is, however, to be
greatly desired in a suitable manual division, where its rich and
quiet tonality would contribute a remarkable coloring to every
effective registration into which it might enter. In our opinion,
there is no lingual stop of 16 ft. pitch so generally useful on the
manual claviers; and we know it to be so important, tonally, that a
series of most effective and refined registrations can be based upon
it. We introduced it, accordingly, in the First Subdivision—expressive—of the Third Organ in the instrument installed in the
Festival Hall of the Louisiana Purchase Exposition; and we also
inserted it in the Second Subdivision—expressive—of the Third
Organ in the Grand Organ in the Church of Our Lady of Grace,
Hoboken, N. J.

CONTRA-GAMBA, Ital.—A labial stop, of 16 ft. pitch. Its
pipes are of medium scale, of metal, cylindrical in form, and open.
It is introduced in both manual and pedal departments of the Organ,
but usually, when it is introduced, it appears in a manual division,
as in the Great of the Willis Organ in the Church of St. Margaret,
Liverpool, and in the Swell of the Walker Organ in the Church of
St. Matthew, Northampton, England. In the latter Organ it has a
covered wood bass, dictated by its position in a swell-box. An
example appears in the Great of the Roosevelt Organ in the Cathedral of the Incarnation, Garden City, L. I. When introduced in the
Pedal Organ, it is of unison pitch, and may be labeled, simply,
GAMBA, 16 FT., as in the Organ in the Centennial Hall, Sydney,
N. S. W. When properly voiced, the CONTRA-GAMBA has a full
string-like tone, but not so pronounced as to be imitative. The

* "The Organ of the Twentieth Century." Pages 291, 297, 317, 319.

stop is less valuable now than it used to be when string-toned stops were few and very little developed in comparison to what they are to-day. VIOLS now take the place of the German GAMBAS, and their prompter English equivalents.

CONTRA-OBOE, Ital.—Eng., CONTRA-HAUTBOY.—A very un-common lingual stop of 16 ft. pitch, the form and tone of which resemble those of the ordinary OBOE, 8 FT. A fine and note-worthy example, voiced by George Willis, exists in the Swell of the Organ in St. George's Hall, Liverpool, labeled CONTRA-HAUTBOY, 16 FT. This valuable stop should find a place in the "wood-wind" division of the Concert-room Organ, where it would be associated with the unison OBOE and, possibly, with the OCTAVE OBOE, 4 FT., forming a complete family.* All would afford valuable voices in artistic registration. While the CONTRAFAGOTTO may be regarded as affording the bass to the OBOE, 8 FT., the CONTRA-OBOE would be found, in many registrations, to produce closer and clearer effects when combined with the unison stop: but, after all is said, much depends on the voicing and tonality of the respective stops.

CONTRAPOSAUNE, Ger.—A powerfully-voiced lingual stop of 32 ft. pitch in the Pedal Organ and 16 ft. pitch on the manuals. It appears under the name in the Pedal of the Organ built by Buch-holz for the Cathedral of Cronstadt. In the generality of German Organs it appears as simply POSAUNE, 32 FT., or 16 FT. An example of the CONTRAPOSAUNE, 16 FT., exists in the Great of the Organ in the Centennial Hall, Sydney, N. S. W.; and a CONTRAPOSAUNE, 32 FT., is inserted in the Pedal of the same Organ, and in that of the Organ in the Parish Church of Doncaster. The pipes of the stops have open-reeds and broad tongues; their resonators being of the usual inverted conical form and of large scale, producing tones in-tended to imitate those of the Bass Trombones of the orchestra played *fortissimo*. The resonators are sometimes constructed of wood, square, and inverted pyramidal in form; but resonators of thick zinc are to be preferred. Sheet iron may be used in the 32 ft. octave.

CONTRAPRINZIPAL, Ger.—The term which has been used to designate the open metal labial stop known in English nomenclature as the OPEN DIAPASON, 32 FT., in the Pedal Organ and of 16 ft. pitch when inserted in a manual division.

* See "The Organ of the Twentieth Century." Pages 307, 308.

CONTRA-SALICIONAL, DOUBLE SALICIONAL.—As the name implies, this is a SALICIONAL of 16 ft. pitch. In material and formation its pipes are in all respects similar to those of the manual unison stop. The stop is valuable in the Pedal Organ, to which it properly belongs, and, accordingly, its tone should be fuller than that of the manual stop, especially if it is inclosed and rendered expressive. See SALICIONAL.

CONTRA-SAXOPHONE.—The stop of 16 ft. pitch, the voice of which furnishes the true bass to the manual SAXOPHONE, 8 FT. It is, when of imitative quality, a valuable voice in the Pedal of a Concert-room Organ, where it should be inclosed and rendered expressive. The stop can be made with either free- or striking-reeds. On account of the smoothness of the tones of the orchestral Saxophones, we are of opinion that their closest imitation is to be obtained from free-reed pipes; but the most favorable form of resonator has yet to be discovered. The tone of the CONTRA-SAXOPHONE should imitate as closely as practicable that of the Double Bass or Bourdon Saxophone. There is a good free-reed example in the Pedal of the Chamber Organ in Ham House, Richmond, Surrey, England. While an almost deceptive imitation of the tones of the Saxophones have been obtained from labial pipes of wood of 8 ft. pitch, we are not aware of any attempt having been made to produce a corresponding labial CONTRA-SAXOPHONE. See SAXOPHONE.

CONTRA-TROMBONE.—A lingual stop of 32 ft. pitch in the Pedal Organ and 16 ft. pitch on the manuals. In formation it is similar to the CONTRAPOSAUNE, but its resonators are of a smaller scale. An example of the CONTRA-TROMBONE, 32 FT., exists in the Pedal of the Walker Organ in York Minster. Another example exists in the Pedal of the Organ in Leeds Parish Church, where it speaks effectively on a wind of only 3½ inches—an eloquent argument in support of our plea for low pressures, now so thoughtlessly neglected by the inartistic lovers of coarse tones and musical noise in this country. A CONTRA-TROMBONE, 16 FT., occurs in the Great of the Concert-room Organ in the Town Hall, Leeds.

The tone of the CONTRA-TROMBONE is intended to imitate that of the Bass Trombone, in G, of the orchestra. The voice of the organ-stop extends far below that of the orchestral instrument, but this is a gain of great value which no authority on the Organ will question. While the tone is similar to that of the CONTRAPOSAUNE, it should not be so brassy and powerful. The value of the CONTRA-

TROMBONE, 16 FT., in the "brass-wind" division of a Concert-room Organ of the first magnitude would, unquestionably, be great, for not only would it enter with great effect into assertive registration, but it would prove a most dignified and impressive solo voice.

Under the name of CONTRA-TROMBONE, Messrs. Hill & Son, of London, have inserted a monster lingual stop, of 64 ft. pitch (if such a pitch can be recognized as obtaining in the range of audible or determinate musical sounds, a proposition we cannot accept), in the Pedal of the Organ in the Centennial Hall, Sydney, N. S. W. We examined this unique stop, and heard it during a recital on the Organ before it left the factory. While its slow and powerful vibrations succeeded in shaking us bodily, its noise did not impress our musical sense. It seemed to support the old saying: "The game is not worth the candle."

CONTRA-TUBA.—The most powerfully-voiced lingual stop of 16 ft. pitch introduced in the Organ. It is commonly voiced on a wind-pressure of between fifteen and thirty inches. Its resonators are of the inverted conical form, and are necessarily made of thick metal, now usually zinc, so as to withstand the extreme vibration; and they are of large scale. An example exists in the Solo of the Organ in the Centennial Hall, Sydney, N. S. W. The tone of the stop is intended to imitate that of the Bass Tuba of the orchestra, but is much more powerful. It is, accordingly, singularly grand and impressive, but of little general use unless it is inclosed and rendered flexible and expressive, which it should invariably be in all properly appointed Organs. In the Sydney Organ neither it nor any of the Solo Organ stops are inclosed and rendered expressive; surely an anomalous absurdity in a Concert-room Organ, showing a want of artistic taste and common-sense.

CONTRA-VIOLONE, Ital.—A labial stop, of 16 ft. pitch, the pipes of which are open and of medium scale, formed of either metal or wood, or of wood in the lower and metal in the higher octaves. The CONTRA-VIOLONE, 16 FT., is strictly a manual stop; the corresponding stop in the Pedal Organ being properly labeled VIOLONE, 16 FT. The tone of the stop should imitate that of orchestral instrument of the same name. While practically identical with the CONTRABASS, 16 FT. (q. v.), its tone should be smoother and somewhat less assertive. A very beautiful example of the class, from the master hand of Edmund Schulze, is to be found in the Great of the Organ in St. Peter's, Hindley, Lancashire. The stop is formed of wood pipes from CC to B, and of metal pipes from c^1 to the top note.

The proper place for the CONTRA-VIOLONE, 16 FT., is in the string-toned division or subdivision of the Concert-room Organ. In registration for the production of massed string effects of an orchestral character it is extremely valuable. The CONTRA-VIOLONE, in its perfect form and tone, is extremely rare; but it can be easily made now by an artistic voicer of string-toned pipes.

CONTRE-BOMBARDE, Fr.—The lingual stop of 32 ft. pitch, introduced in the Pedal of most of the large Organs in French cathedrals and churches. It is to be found in the Organs in the Cathedral of Notre-Dame and the Churches of Saint-Sulpice and Saint-Eustache, Paris, and in the Royal Church, Saint-Denis, and Saint-Ouen, Rouen. It was introduced by Cavaillé-Coll in the Organ in the Albert Hall, Sheffield. The stop has resonators of the usual inverted conical form and of large scale. As common in French lingual stops, the tone of the CONTRA-BOMBARDE is somewhat dry and hard; widely different from the rich, round, and velvety tones of the Willis stops. In its usual exposed position, the use of so grave and powerful a voice is necessarily very limited, and hardly worth its great cost; but inclosed in a swell-chamber, its tonal value would be increased more than tenfold. A *crescendo* on such a voice would have a stupendous effect—one never yet heard on the Organ; but will be when our scheme for the Concert-room Organ of the Twentieth Century is carried into effect.*

COR ANGLAIS, Fr.—Ital., CORNO INGLESE. Eng., ENGLISH HORN.—A lingual stop of 8 ft. pitch. It has been made in two ways; namely, with striking- and free-reeds, and probably the most successful examples, tonally, have been of the latter class. The stop, in its free-reed form, has long been a favorite with the French organ-builders, being introduced in most of their more important instruments, in either its 8 ft. or 16 ft. pitches. Of the former pitch, it was inserted by Merklin in the Positif of the Organ in the Cathedral of Senlis; and in the Clavier de Bombarde of his Grand Organ in the Church of Saint-Eustache, Paris. It was introduced, in the same unison pitch, by Cavaillé-Coll, in the Clavier du Grand Orgue of the Organ in the Royal Church of Saint-Denis. Of 16 ft. pitch, it was inserted by Cavaillé-Coll in the Positif of the Organ in the Church of Saint-Ouen, Rouen; in the Solo Expressif of his scheme for the Monumental Organ in St. Peter's, Rome; and in the Récit Expressif of the Concert-room Organ in the Albert Hall, Sheffield, in which it

* See "The Organ of the Twentieth Century." Pages 273–332.

is a striking-reed. In his later work, Cavaillé-Coll abandoned the free-reed. The COR ANGLAIS, in both its pitches, has been intro-duced in a few English Organs, the pipes having, for the most part, been imported from France. We inserted a CORNO INGLESE, 8 FT., in the Second Organ of the instrument installed in the Festival Hall of the Louisiana Purchase Exposition. It is a free-reed stop im-ported from Germany.

FORMATION.—The pipes of the COR ANGLAIS are invariably made of metal; and, in the most satisfactory examples of the stop, have resonators of a compound form that has been arrived at as most effective after many experiments. The form is that of a slender inverted conical tube, surmounted by an expanded, res-onant chamber formed of two truncated cones soldered together and to the tube, in the manner shown in the drawing of the complete pipe given in Fig. 7, Plate I. The scale and relative proportions of the parts forming the resonator have a great influence not only on the strength but also on the timbre of the tone produced. The reed and tongues, in the best examples, are similar in form and general treat-ment to those of the OBOE. The value of the stop is considerable; but the time and trouble involved in the proper formation of its resonators have largely pre-vented organ-builders from encouraging its introduction. It should, however, find a place in every Concert-room Organ of any pretensions.

TONALITY and REGISTRATION.—The tone of the COR ANGLAIS of the Organ is intended to imitate, as closely as possible, that of the orchestral instrument of the same name, which is, strictly considered, a Tenor Oboe. The Italians call it the Oboe di Caccia as well as Corno Inglese; while the Germans use the name Englisches Horn. Speaking of the instrument, Berlioz remarks: "Its quality of tone, less piercing, more veiled, and deeper than that of the Oboe, does not so well as the latter lend itself to the gaiety of rustic strains. Nor could it give utterance to anguished complainings; accents of keen grief are almost interdicted to its powers. It is a melancholy, dreamy, and rather noble voice, of which the sonorousness has something of vague,—of *remote*,—which renders it superior to all others, in exciting regret, and reviving images and sentiments of the past, when the composer desires to awaken the echo of tender mem-ories." These remarks, by so great an authority on orchestration, ought to enthuse the voicer in the production of the organ COR ANGLAIS, and inspire the organist who finds a sympathetic one in an Organ. A good COR ANGLAIS is a beautiful solo stop, while it is extremely valuable in artistic registration, producing in combina-tion with softly-voiced stops of contrasting and harmonic-corrobor-ating qualities compound voices of remarkable tonalities. At the present time organists and others in this country have little oppor-tunity of judging the merits of the stop. Many attempts have been

made to produce the characteristic voice of the Cor Anglais by registration; for instance, as we are informed, a distinguished organist
succeeded in producing an almost perfect imitation on the Choir of
the Organ in York Minster, by combining the GAMBA, 8 FT., CLARI-
NET, 8 FT., and GEMSHORN, 4 FT. We venture to think a better imitation would have been the result had an OBOE, 8 FT., been introduced instead of the fuller-toned CLARINET; but the Choir Organ
does not contain one; neither, alas for art, is the Choir Organ
expressive.

COR DE BASSET, Fr.—The name employed by French organ-
builders to designate the lingual stop more commonly known under
the Italian name CORNO DI BASSETTO (q. v.).

COR D' HARMONIE, Fr.—This term, associated with HAUT-
BOIS, 8 FT., occurs in the stop apportionment of the Positif of the
Cavaillé-Coll Organ in the Royal Church of Saint-Denis. It would
appear, in this connection, to be applied to the bass extending
downward the tone of the HAUTBOIS, which would properly be of
Bassoon quality, and, accordingly would be furnished by BASSOON
pipes from CC to A, almost two octaves.

CORDEDAIN.—A labial stop of metal and of 4 ft. pitch, which
is inserted in both the Choir and Echo of Silbermann's Organ in the
Church of St. Thomas, at Strasbourg. The tones of the stops are
described of a bright flute quality, almost imitative.

COR DE NUIT, Fr.—Ger., NACHTHORN. Ital., PASTORITA.—
An open or covered stop of metal or wood, and of 8 ft., 4 ft., and 2 ft.
pitch. The tone is a combination of flute and soft horn qualities.
See NACHTHORN.

CORMORNE, Fr.—The name which has occasionally been
given by French organ-builders to a lingual stop of metal and 8 ft.
pitch. It is probably formed from cor—horn, and morne—sombre or
mournful. But as the stop is commonly met with in the Cavaillé-
Coll Organs labeled CROMORNE, the term may be a corruption of the
German name KRUMMHORN. See CROMORNE.

CORNAMUSA, Ital.—Fr., CORNEMEUSE.—This name, which
was originally used to designate an instrument of the Bagpipe
family, has been occasionally applied by Italian and French organ-
builders to a labial stop of 16 ft. pitch. Examples are rare, but one
exists, according to Hopkins, on the second manual of the Organ in

the Church of Santissimo Crocifisso, at Como. It is evidently a covered stop of wood, and probably derived its name from the drone-like character of its tone. Examples of the Cornemeuse, in Bagpipe form, and of eighteenth century date, are to be seen in the Crosby Brown Collection of Musical Instruments in the Metropolitan Museum of Art, New York City.

CORNET.—A compound labial stop of several ranks of metal pipes. There are two distinct varieties of the stop, which may be called the ancient and the modern and which hold different offices in the tonal economy of the Organ—offices varying greatly.

The old and original form comes first in order. It was usually formed of three, four, or five ranks of large-scaled pipes voiced to yield powerful and dominating tones.* Its compass seems never to have descended below tenor C, while it usually, and invariably in old English Organs, commenced at middle c¹. The lowest rank, which was invariably of unison pitch, was, probably on account of the size of its pipes when the stop descended to tenor C, of covered pipes. In French examples it was usually a BOURDON, 8 FT. All the other ranks were of open metal pipes. The stop was much in favor with the old English organ-builders. In Bernard Smith's Organ built, in 1684, for the Temple Church, London, were two CORNETS— one of five ranks in the Great and one of three ranks in the "Ecchos." In the Organ built by John Harris, of London, in 1740, for the Parish Church of Doncaster there were also two CORNETS, of five and three ranks. All these stops extended from middle c¹ to the top note. Sometimes, as the CORNET required considerable space for its accommodation, its pipes were planted on a special wind-chest, elevated above the main wind-chest, and connected thereto by a series of metal tubes or conveyances—one for each note of the CORNET. When disposed in this manner the stop was designated MOUNTED CORNET. A MOUNTED CORNET, of 4 ranks, was inserted in the

---

* "Le CORNET, jeu bruyant, clair et dominateur de l'harmonie entière de l'orgue. Un *Cornet* complet dans sa facture a par note cinq tuyaux de grosse taille, dont chacun porte un nom et un caractère différents. Le premier tuyaux est un *Bourdon* de huit; le second un *Prestant;* le troisième un *Nasard,* quinte supérieure du *Prestant;* le quatrième une *Quarte de Nasard,* octave du *Prestant,* le cinquième enfin est une *Tierce* au-dessus de cette octave. Ainsi, l'*ut* du *Cornet* est à la fois *ut* de huit-pieds en *Bourdon, ut* de quatre en *Prestant, sol* de trois en *Nasard, ut* de deux en *Quarte* enfin mi d'un-pied cinqseptièmes.

"Ainsi, dans toute sa longueur, le *Cornet* appuie chacune de ces notes ou de ses marches, comme on dit, sur cinq notes à la fois; il y a donc cinq tuyaux *sur marche.* Son régistre est donc un ensemble de cinq régistres, cinq rangées de tuyaux au lieu d'une, comme le jeux simples. Mais le *Cornet* n'a pas toujours toute la longueur du clavier; quoique ces cinq rangées soient à l'unisson du *Bourdon,* du *Prestant,* etc., cependant elles en diffèrent par la taille, qui est plus grosse et l'harmonie plus forte."—Regnier.

Great of the Órgan built by Snetzler, in 1777, for the Parish Church of Rotherham, England: and we understand, from a pamphlet in our possession, that the stop still exists in the Organ under that name. Schulze introduced MOUNTED CORNETS in the Great and Swell Organs of the instrument he built for Doncaster Parish Church in 1862. These still remain in the renovated Organ. In Bernard Smith's Organs the CORNET was never mounted.

In all cases the scales of the pipes of the old CORNET were larger than those of the corresponding pipes of the major DIAPASON or PRINCIPAL, and were much more loudly voiced. The compound tone of the CORNET was, on account of the large scale of its pipes, flutey in character: and owing to its highest pitched rank being a Tierce, and uncovered by a fifth- or an octave-sounding rank, the voice of the stop was necessarily somewhat harsh and cutting.

The old CORNET was chiefly used for playing out the melody of the Chorals, its powerful voice rendering it highly effective for such an office.* Being unbroken in its ranks, it was found serviceable in covering the breaks in the screaming MIXTURES of the time. In England the old CORNET was frequently used in the rendition of what were known as Cornet Voluntaries, the chief features of which were runs and figurative passages on the stop by the right hand. The best known of such compositions are those by Stanley, Dupuis, Bluet, and Russell, all of whom wrote between the years 1726 and 1813.

The old, short-compass, and loud-voiced CORNET finds no place in the modern Organ; and the name is now applied to stops of widely different construction and office. At the present time the name is usually given to a compound harmonic-corroborating stop of full compass, composed of five or more ranks of small-scaled and high-pitched pipes, voiced to yield a bright and singing quality of pure organ-tone. But different qualities of tone may be obtained by using flute-toned or string-toned pipes of small scales. Such being

---

* "CORNET, or 'CORNETTO,' is a mixture of a very wide measure, which begins generally at c¹ or at the G below, and goes through the upper octaves of the manual. It has a strong intonation, and a horn-like tone, which is well adapted for filling out. Sometimes, when hymns are to be sung with a melody which is not familiar to the congregation, this register will be found very efficient for the purpose of making the melody prominent, since the right hand plays the melody upon that manual which contains the CORNET, while the left hand plays the accompaniment upon some other manual, for which weaker registers are drawn. This MIXTURE has sometimes five ranks, 8, 4, 2⅔, 2, and 1⅗ feet; sometimes four ranks, 8, 4, 2⅔, and 1⅗ feet; and sometimes three ranks, 4, 2⅔, and 1⅗ feet. In France, the lowest rank of this register is nothing but a ROHRFLÖTE, 8 FT. Wilke deems it best to construct the CORNET with three ranks only, but so that the lowest of them is a fifth, and next an octave, and the last a third,—5⅓ ft., 4 ft., and 3⅕ ft., or 2⅔ ft., 2 ft., and 1⅗ ft. The latter arrangement is better suited for small Organs, the former for large ones."—Seidel.

the case, it will be seen that the modern CORNET is the antithesis in every respect of the loud and harsh stop of the old masters.   It is usual and desirable in labeling the CORNET to qualify the name, so as to convey some idea of its general tonality, accordingly, such terms as DULCIANA CORNET, DOLCE CORNET, VIOL CORNET, etc., are appropriate.   The following is the composition of a five-rank stop, formed of DULCIANA pipes, which has been tested and found highly satisfactory in registration:

DULCIANA CORNET—V. RANKS.

CC to BB	.	.	.	.	19——22——24——26——29.		
C to B	.	.	.	.	12——15——17——19——22.		
c^1 to b^1	.	.	.	.	8——12——17——19——22.		
c^2 to c^4	.	.	.	.	1—— 8——10——12——15.		

It will be observed that the middle rank is third-sounding throughout, and that it is properly covered by the fourth and fifth ranks, while the fifth rank is octave-sounding throughout all its breaks.   It would be difficult to devise a more satisfactory composition for a stop of this beautiful tonality.   In the Swell of the Concert-room Organ in the Music Hall, Cincinnati, there is a CORNET of six ranks of small-scaled pipes, the composition of which is here given:

DOLCE CORNET—VI. RANKS.

CC to BB .	.	.	15——19——22——26——29——36.		
C to B .	.	.	12——15——19——22——26——29.		
c^1 to b^1 .	.	.	8——12——15——19——22——26.		
c^2 to c^4 .	.	.	1—— 5—— 8——10——12——15.		

Artistically voiced and scientifically graduated in strength of tone throughout its ranks and breaks, such a CORNET would prove extremely valuable in registration.   In this direction, it is to be observed that the composition in the lower two octaves—CC to B—points to considerable brilliancy; that in the middle octave—c^1 to b^1—to sufficient richness of tone; while that in the two higher octaves,—c^2 to c^4,—which belongs to the 16 ft. harmonic series, points to great fullness, just where it is most required.

There is another form of modern CORNET which more fully deserves the name, and one we strongly recommend for general introduction in all important Organs: we allude to the form in which all the ranks are carried throughout the compass without a break.   Of this form we introduced two special CORNETS in our scheme for the Organ installed in the Festival Hall of the Louisiana Purchase Exposition.   One of four ranks in the Expressive Subdivision of the

First Organ, composed of a SEVENTEENTH, NINETEENTH, SEPTIÈME, and TWENTY-SECOND: and the other, a VIOL CORNET—IV. RANKS (muted), in the string-toned Expressive Subdivision of the Third Organ, composed of a TWELFTH, FIFTEENTH, NINETEENTH, and TWENTY-SECOND. The pipes are of tin and of small scale. All Pedal Organ MIXTURES which have no breaks or short ranks in their compass are strictly CORNETS. The largest and most remarkable example of this class of compound stop is that in the Pedal of the Organ in the Wanamaker Store in Philadelphia, Pa. It consists of ten complete ranks of open metal pipes, yielding pure organ-tone, the principal rank being a DIAPASON, 16 FT. As a corroborating stop it belongs to the 32 ft. harmonic series, and comprises four octave, two third-, and four fifth-sounding ranks as follows:

PEDAL ORGAN GRAND CORNET—X. RANKS.

1.	DIAPASON	.	Metal.	16	feet	6.	SUPER-OCTAVE	Metal.	4 feet
2.	QUINT	. .	"	$10\frac{2}{3}$	"	7.	OCTAVE TIERCE	"	$3\frac{1}{5}$ "
3.	OCTAVE	.	"	8	"	8.	TWELFTH .	"	$2\frac{2}{3}$ "
4.	TIERCE	.	"	$6\frac{2}{5}$	"	9.	FIFTEENTH .	"	2 "
5.	OCTAVE QUINT		"	$5\frac{1}{3}$	"	10.	NINETEENTH	"	$1\frac{1}{3}$ "

The compound tone of this stupendous CORNET is that of a magnificent lingual stop, and when registered with the DOUBLE DIAPASON, 32 FT., or the CONTRA-BOMBARDE, 32 FT., or with both, it produces a majestic harmonic tonal structure impossible on any other Pedal Organ ever constructed. The only other stop of the same class, in any way approaching that just described, known to us is the one labeled GRAND BOURDON in the Organ in the Cathedral of Riga. It is composed of the following five complete ranks of open wood pipes:—PRINCIPAL, 16 FT.—QUINT, $10\frac{2}{3}$ FT.—OCTAVE, 8 FT.—TIERCE, $6\frac{2}{5}$ FT.—SUPER-OCTAVE, 4 FT.

TONALITY AND REGISTRATION.—The value of the compound harmonic-corroborating CORNET of the DULCIANA or DOLCE class in artistic registration depends entirely on its tonality—the product of its correct composition, the scales of its several ranks, and, above all, of its fine voicing, and the scientific graduation of the tones of all its ranks and their breaks in accordance with the natural laws of musical sounds. Provided the CORNET is correctly constructed along all these lines, it is a stop to be treasured in every Organ in which it is introduced; and will become the delight of the organist in his registrations, forming with stops of all tonalities combinations of rare beauty and charm. From long experience with just such a CORNET we can speak with authority in this direction. We have found it to combine with labial and lingual stops of different pitches, producing numerous very beautiful compound tones which are absolutely unknown to organists who preside at Organs unprovided with such refined tonal aid; and which have only the crude and screaming MIXTURES which characterize the prevailing inartistic and rule-of-thumb methods of organ tonal appointment. Before a truly satisfactory condition of tonality, offering the maximum of opportunity for artistic registration, obtains in the Organ, all the compound stops—CORNETS and MIXTURES—must undergo a radical change in treatment: more art and science must be concentrated on their production, and more time and care must be devoted to their correct regulation and graduation of tone.

CORNET À PAVILLON, Fr.—The name given by Cavaillé-Coll to a lingual stop, of 8 ft. pitch, inserted in the Grand-Orgue of the instrument constructed by him, in 1841, for the Royal Church of Saint-Denis. The name was suggested by the form of the resonators employed, just as in the case of the FLÛTE À PAVILLON, the pipes of which are surmounted by bells. Another example exists in the Organ in the Church of Saint Vincent de Paul, Paris. ·

CORNETTINO, Ital. Ger., ZINK.—A lingual stop of 2 ft. pitch, and necessarily of short compass. This favored its introduction in the Pedal Organ. An example, labeled CORNETTINO, exists in the Erstes Pedal of the Organ in St. Paul's Church, Frankfurt am Main, built by Walcker. Respecting this stop Schlimbach remarks: "CORNETTINO. Ein Rohrwerk, soll das zu den Posaunen gebräuchliche, unter dem Namen Zinken bekannte Discantinstrument nachahmen. Es ist klein, und sollte eigntlich nur durchs halbe Clavier gehen, indem man keine Basszinken hat." See ZINK.

CORNO DI BASSETTO, Ital.—Fr., COR DE BASSET. Ger., BASSETHORN.—A lingual stop of 8 ft. pitch, the pipes of which are formed, in most examples, after the fashion of those of the CLARINET. Töpfer describes the stop as made of labial pipes; but, in its best form, it has always been a lingual stop, made with free- or striking-reeds, preferably the latter. The stop is by no means a common one and few examples are to be found. As a manual stop it is to be found on the third manual of the Organ in the Cathedral of Lund, Sweden. A fine example exists in the Solo of the Organ in St. George's Hall, Liverpool; and we inserted one in the Expressive First Subdivision (Wood-wind) of the Organ installed in the Festival Hall of the Louisiana Purchase Exposition. As a Pedal Organ

PLATE II

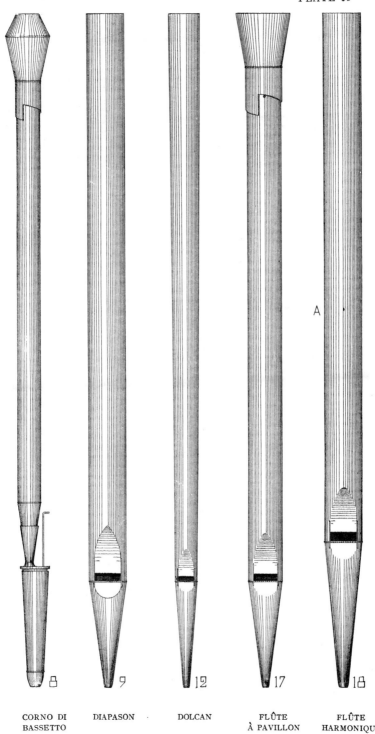

A

| CORNO DI BASSETTO | DIAPASON | DOLCAN | FLÛTE À PAVILLON | FLÛTE HARMONIQUE |

stop of 8 ft. pitch it is introduced in the Organs in the Cathedrals of Ulm and Riga. According to Hopkins, a stop labeled CORNO BASS-ETTO, SOPRANO, 32 FT., was to be found in the Organ in the Cathedral of Como, but regarding the form of this stop we have been unable to obtain information.

FORMATION.—The form of the CORNO DI BASSETTO or BASSETHORN seems to have varied greatly in the hands of different organ-builders in Germany and elsewhere on the Continent. Töpfer describes it as made in the form of a labial stop: while Locher describes it as a smooth-voiced stop made with free-reeds, and, as a rule, without resonators, similar to the PHYSHARMONIKA. In all probability, as their voices are described to be of a "smooth reed-character," the stops in the Ulm and Riga Organs are free-reeds with some form of resonators. But these matters are now of very little practical value.

The CORNO DI BASSETTO, 8 FT., in its best form, as made to-day, is a striking reed, and, being of the CLARINET family, is commonly furnished with plain cylindrical resonators completely open at top, similar to that shown in Fig. 6, Plate I., but properly of a larger scale, so as to develop a fuller tone than that of the CLARINET. With a similar aim, we strongly recommend the addition of a resonant chamber to the top of the cylindrical tube of the form shown in the drawing of the complete pipe, Fig. 8, Plate II. This should have a screw adjustment for regulation, as indicated, and may be further provided with a shade for fine toning. Although organ-builders will not look with much favor on this form of resonator, on account of its troublesome construction, yet every means should be adopted to perfect a stop of such importance. It can be made one of the most beautiful lingual stops in the Organ. While the reeds and their tongues generally resemble those of the CLARINET in form and curvature, they should be slightly larger in all directions, to accord with the larger scale of the resonators. Larger boots are also to be recommended, for they have more influence on tone than is commonly understood; unfortunately large boots cost more than small ones.

Although no authority is furnished by an orchestral instrument, there seems to be no reason why a very valuable voice should not be given to the Concert-room Organ in the form of a CONTRA-CORNO DI BASSETTO or DOUBLE BASSET-HORN, 16 FT. We are strongly in favor of such a stop being introduced in every Concert-room Organ just as it has been in the Organ in the Centennial Hall, Sydney, N. S. W. A beautiful family might be created by the addition of an OCTAVE BASSET-HORN, 4 FT.

TONALITY AND REGISTRATION.—The orchestral Corno di Bassetto is, strictly considered, a Tenor Clarinet with a compass from FF to c^3, but its tone is fuller and of richer reedy quality; and this has to be produced very clearly in the organ stop, so as to differentiate it distinctly from the CLARINET. Voiced by a master-hand and with this aim, the CORNO DI BASSETTO becomes invaluable as a timbre-creator in artistic registration, combining perfectly and producing a beautiful series of tones with all classes of labial stops including such a compound stop as the DULCIANA CORNET (q. v.). The stop should be carefully developed by artistic voicers, and it should find a place in every important Organ. In the properly appointed Concert-room Organ its place is in the division appropriated to the stops representing the wood-wind forces of the grand orchestra. There its voice would be valuable both in tonal massing and as a solo. One has only to turn to the compositions of Mozart and Mendelssohn to realize the high estimation in which these masters held the tones of the Corno di Bassetto.

CORNO DOLCE.—The name given to a stop of 8 ft. pitch, constructed of inverted conical pipes, after those of the DOLCE or DOLCAN. The name is misleading, for the tone of the stop has no horn quality, inclining, on the other hand, to a flute-tone. It is not a common stop, having nothing characteristic to recommend it. A few examples exist in English Organs, as in the Organ in the Free Trade Hall, Manchester.

CORNO FLUTE.—This name has been given to two widely different stops, to neither of which it can be said to be highly appropriate; the two constituents forming it conflicting in a tonal sense. The original CORNO FLUTE is a lingual stop of 8 ft. pitch, formed with resonators of wood, and voiced to yield a quiet tone inclining to an Oboe quality. It was invented by the distinguished London organ-builder, William Hill. An example of this stop exists in the Organ in the Church of St. Olave, Southwark, Surrey.

The second form, of later date, is a metal labial stop of 8 ft. pitch, invented by Herbert Norman, organ-builder, of Norwich. The name, in this instance, seems to have been given to the stop on account of the Horn-like tonality in its tenor portion and the soft fluty character of its higher octaves. We are not surprised at this tonal peculiarity, for we have long been of the opinion that the characteristic tones of the orchestral Horn will be most successfully imitated by labial pipes.*

CORNO INGLESE, Ital.—A lingual stop, of 8 ft. pitch, yielding a reedy tone in imitation of that of the orchestral instrument bearing the same name. For particulars respecting the stop, see COR ANGLAIS.

CORNOPEAN.—A lingual stop of 8 ft. pitch, the tone of which is intended to imitate that of the brass, wind-instrument originally called Cornopean, but now known as the Cornet à Pistons (Fr.).

* The stop in our Chamber Organ, of the KERAULOPHONE class, was named by us CORNO DI CACCIA because of the remarkable imitation of the Horn tones it yielded in its tenor and middle octaves.

Stone describes the instrument as "intermediate between the French Horn, Trumpet, and Bugle"; and this description would point to the quality of tone desirable in the CORNOPEAN of the Organ, but which very rarely attends it.

The CORNOPEAN was invented by the distinguished organ-builder William Hill, of London, and was introduced in several of his organs. The firm placed one in the Swell of the Organ in the Centennial Hall, Sydney, N. S. W. When made and voiced by a master-hand the stop is distinct and agreeable, occupying a place, tonally, between the TRUMPET and the HORN. The resonators of the CORNOPEAN are, like those of the TRUMPET, inverted conical in form, and vary considerably in scale, according to the quality and strength of voice aimed at. The reeds should be of the closed variety; and the tongues should be thick and carefully curved to produce a tone free from the brassy clang of the TRUMPET, but of a firm and singing quality. There is no question respecting the value of a fine lingual stop, having such an intermediate voice, in refined and expressive registration in which the assertive clang of the TRUMPET would be destructive and that of the HORN too dead. In the properly appointed Concert-room Organ the CORNOPEAN should find its place in the division appropriated to the brass-wind stops.

Locher describes the CORNOPEAN as "an 8 ft. labial stop of horn-like tone." Allihn describes it much in the same manner in the following words: "CORNOPEAN (ital.), Päanshorn, ein veraltete Labialstimme von hornartigem Ton. Zu deutsch etwa: Jubelhorn."

COPULA, Lat.—Ger. KOPPEL.—This term is used in two senses in German organ nomenclature. It alludes to the mechanical appliance, commonly known as the coupler, which connects claviers or other portions of an Organ together temporarily. It is also applied to certain labial stops having a tonality which seems to have the property of binding together in a harmonious manner extreme voices of other stops. The KOPPELFLÖTE is an example. See KOPPEL.

CREMONA.—This very meaningless and inappropriate name for an organ stop—labial or lingual—is obviously a corruption. Hawkins, in his "History of Music," says: "The names and descriptions of several musical instruments instruct us as to the nature and design of many Stops in the Organ, and what they are intended to imitate. For instance, in the Krummhorn, the tone of it originally resembled that of a small Cornet, though many organ-makers have corrupted the word into Cremona, supposing it to be an imitation of the Cremona Violin."

Max Allihn gives a more sensible usage of the term in the following words: "Cremona bedeutet eine Labialstimme von streichendem Tone. Die Cremonesergeige wird in Frankreich kurzweg Cremona genannt." Under any conditions, the name of a town must be inappropriate for an organ-stop, although not more so than the name of a person written backwards, which has recently been added to the list of stops. Such a method of naming is ridiculous and should be discontinued. Surely the name of an organ-stop should either indicate tone or some special formation of its pipes.

CROMORNE, Fr.—Ger., Krummhorn.—The name used by French and German organ-builders to designate a lingual stop, the tone of which somewhat resembles that of the Clarinet, but with a smoother and mournful character. It is commonly of 8 ft. pitch. Seidel, in his remarks on the Krummhorn, says: "Properly 'Cormorne,' from cor 'horn' and morne 'mournful, still, soft,' signifying a soft, quiet Horn, is a lingual stop of a delicate intonation, of 8 ft. or 4 ft. pitch, of tin or pipe metal, open or shaded, and sometimes formed of small-scaled cylindrical pipes" (like the Clarinet). This stop has been constructed in imitation of an old instrument, called the Krummhorn (crooked horn), which had six holes, and was, at its lower end, bent in the form of a half circle.

The Cromorne, 8 ft., has long been a favorite stop with the French organ-builders. It appears in the Positif of the Organs in the Royal Church of Saint-Denis; the Cathedral of Chartres; and the Basilique du Sacré-Cœur, Paris: in these Organs there is no Clarinet. It is inserted in the Récit of the Organ in the Church of Saint-Sulpice, Paris, in which there is no Clarinet: and in the Récit, along with the Clarinet, in the Organ in the Conservatoire Royal de Musique, Brussels. It occupies a place, along with the Clarinette-Basse, 16 ft., and Clarinette-Aigue, 4 ft., in the Positif of the Organ in the Cathedral of Notre-Dame, Paris. It is inserted in the Positif of the Concert-room Organ in the Palais du Trocadéro, Paris; and in the Positif Expressif of the Organ in the Albert Hall, Sheffield. We are not aware of any stop under the name Cromorne, or having the characteristic tonality of the French stop, having been inserted in an Organ constructed in England or America. It may be taken for granted that unless the Cromorne had been found valuable in registration by French organists, and held in high estimation by such distinguished organ-builders as Cavaillé-Coll, Merklin, Abbey, and Mutin, it would not have been so systematically inserted in almost all the more important Organs

cònstructed in France. Such being the case it is worthy of consideration as to the desirability of adding such a stop to the tonal appointment of the Organ of the Twentieth Century. To us it would seem
highly desirable.*

CYMBAL.—Fr., CYMBALE. Ger., CYMBEL, ZYMBEL. Ital.,
CIMBALO.—The name used to designate a compound harmonic-
corroborating stop, usually composed of from four to seven ranks
of open, organ-toned pipes, of high pitch, breaking at every octave.
Its ranks are alternately octave- and fifth-sounding. Its name was
suggested by the likeness of its compound tone the clang of the orchestral Cymbals. Such a tone would seem at variance with the
harmonic-corroborating office of the stop; and as noise—even if it is
musical noise—is not desirable in any form of musical instrument,
there would seem to be little in favor of introducing so space-taking
and costly a stop in the Organ. The CYMBALE seems, however, to
have been esteemed for some reason by the great French organ-
builder Cavaillé-Coll. In the Organ in the Royal Church of Saint-
Denis there is a GROSSE CYMBALE, of four ranks, and a CYMBALE,
also of four ranks, in the Grand Orgue; and a CYMBALE, of four
ranks in the Positif. In the Organ in the Church of Saint-Sulpice
there is a CYMBALE of five ranks in the Récit Expressif. In the Concert-room Organ in the Albert Hall, Sheffield, there is a CYMBALE of
four ranks in the Grand Orgue (Premier Clavier). There is a remarkable example, of seven ranks, in the Concert-room Organ in
the Music Hall, Cincinnati; the composition of which is here given:

CYMBAL—VII. RANKS.

CC to BB	. . . .	15—19—22—26—29—33—36.
C to B	. . . .	12—15—19—22—26—29—33.
c¹ to b¹	. . . .	8—12—15—19—22—26—29.
c² to b²	. . . .	1— 5— 8—12—15—19—22.
c³ to c⁴	. . .	DOUBLE— 1— 5— 8—12—15—19.

* "LE CROMORNE (de l'allemand *Krumm-Horn*, Cornu torse), est encore un quatre-pieds qui
en forme huit, en raison de sa forte languette. On conçoit que, n'ayant pas la hauteur de tuyaux que comporte son ton, il rende des sous nécessairement moins forts que la *Trompette*, où la
hauteur et le ton se trouvent d'accord. C'est néanmoins le meilleur des jeux d'anches acces-
soires. Il a le timbre clair, plus nourri que le *Hautbois*, tenant du *Cor anglais* et de la *Clarinette*
avec une teinte plus métallique et une certaine *mollesse gutturale* qui n'est pas sans grâce et qu'on
nomme *cruchement*. La difficulté est d'obtenir cet effet à son point: avec trop de mollesse, le
Cromorne râle; avec trop de raideur, au lieu de crucher, il crache. . . . On peut le placer à tous
les claviers en lui donnant des tailles diverses, mais il ne faut pas les jouer ensemble: leur timbre
est trop saillant et nerveux pour bien s'accorder én se doublant lui-même. Il ne pourrait pas
même se poser en pédale pour appuyer son chant au grand orgue; quoique, en tout autre cas,
isolé en pédale, il puisse faire bon effet, ici évidemment le *Cromorne* en pédale détruira le peu
d'intérêt qu'offre le *Cromorne* manuel. Mêlé à quelques fonds, il perd son âpreté et se prête

The CYMBAL does not appear to have assumed any importance in the practice of the organ-builders of Germany: we have, after a somewhat hurried review, been able to find one instance of its introduction. The stop appears on the Erste Manual of the Organ built by Friedrich Ladegast for the Cathedral of Schwerin in 1871. It is described thus: "CYMBEL 3 fach, 14 löthig; einen halben Ton enger als, Mixtur grösster Chor 2': c¹—g¹—c², repetirt nur einmal."

CYMBELREGAL, Ger.—An obsolete lingual stop, of either 4 ft. or 2 ft. pitch; the tone of which was of a metallic and ringing character. See REGAL.

CYMBELSTERN, Ger.—Literally *Cymbal-star.* This so-called organ-stop, which was merely a mechanical device actuated by the organ-wind, has been properly classed among the several puerilities of old German organ-building. It was in the form of a star, to the points of which small bells or metallic "jingles" were attached. When caused to revolve, at the will of the organist, it gave forth a tinkling sound. A few examples are said to exist; as in the Organs in the Cathedral of Merseburg; the Abbey Church, Weingarten; and the Church of Waltershausen, near Gotha.

D

DECIMA, Ital.—The term used by Italian organ-builders to designate the TIERCE or TENTH, 3⅕ FT. The following terms are used by them for other harmonic-corroborating stops: DECIMA QUINTA—the FIFTEENTH, 2 FT.; DECIMA SETTIMA—the SEVENTEENTH, 1⅗ FT.; and DECIMA NONA—the NINETEENTH, 1⅓ FT.

DIAPASON.—Ger., PRINZIPAL. Ital., PRINCIPALE. Fr., MONTRE.—The word employed by the early English organ-builders, and commonly qualified by the prefix OPEN, to designate the stop yielding the foundation tone of the Organ; and which has been retained, with the same signification, by English-speaking organ-builders to the present day. In the term Diapason Normal it is used in the sense of a standard of pitch. The word is derived from the Greek διαπασῶν, the concord of the first and last tones. In Latin it signifies an octave.

souvent mieux que les grands jeux d'anches à la diversité des expressions. Mélangé avec une *Flûte* ou un *Bourdon* de huit, ses notes supérieures imitent jusqu'à un certain point la *Clarinette;* avec le *Prestant*, ses notes inférieures jouent le *Basson.* Le *Cromorne*, chantant à plusieurs parties, les laisse ressortir toutes; avantage qui manque souvent à la *Trompette*, dont les basses écrasent les dessus; certains organistes l'accouplent à un *Nasard*, pour lui donner plus d'énergie mais seulement dans le cas où il parle avec les fonds."—Regnier.

As a name for an organ-stop the word does not seem highly appropriate, and we much prefer the more expressive one, PRINCIPAL; but it is not likely that the time-honored word will ever be altogether abandoned. Under certain conditions, and for the sake of distinction, tonally, it may be desirable to use both words in the same stop appointment.

PITCH.—The stop appears in the Pedal Organ in two pitches—32 ft. and 16 ft. When of the former pitch it is properly termed DOUBLE DIAPASON, 32 FT.; and when of the latter it may be simply termed DIAPASON, its unison pitch being understood. In the Organs commanded by the manual claviers it also appears in two standard pitches—16 ft. and 8 ft. When of the graver pitch it is correctly termed DOUBLE DIAPASON, 16 FT.; and when of 8 ft. pitch it is simply termed DIAPASON, its unison pitch being understood. In preparing an Organ Specification, the pitches of all the DIAPASONS must be given.

FORMATION.—The pipes of the DIAPASON are cylindrical in form and of large scale, as shown in proper proportions in Fig. 9, Plate II.; and when properly made are of good pipe-metal, of ample thickness to withstand firmly the vibrations of the air within them while speaking. The desire to save money has led to the use of undesirably thin metal, as well as metal of inferior and insufficient quality. Such a practice should be rigorously condemned and guarded against by every one specifying or purchasing an Organ. It is impossible to obtain the necessary full and firm foundation tone, characteristic of the perfect DIAPASON, from pipes constructed of poor or thin metal. The thickness of the upper lip of the mouth, securing perfect rigidity and favoring correct and artistic voicing, is a factor of the greatest importance. Different metals have been and still are being used in the formation of the pipes of this important stop. The old builders used tin almost pure, or very rich alloys of tin and lead; and, accordingly, we find, as in the celebrated Haarlem Organ, pipes one hundred and eighty years old in perfect condition to-day. How many DIAPASONS, constructed of poor, thin pipe-metal or zinc, as commonly placed in modern Organs, will be found in good condition after the lapse of even half that length of time? Whatever the metal or alloy may be, it is essential that it be of ample thickness. This is particularly the case when cast alloys of tin and lead are used, such as the different grades of spotted-metal. Even when hard rolled metals are used, such as zinc or the Hoyt two-ply metal, the matter of adequate thickness must be carefully attended to. Organ-builders, depending upon the firmness of rolled zinc, combined with the desire to save money, have very commonly used it of too thin gauges for DIAPASON pipes, inserting lips of spotted-metal or some such alloy. We strongly advise the disuse of zinc for DIAPASON stops of 8 ft. pitch, but in the 16 ft. octave of the DOUBLE DIAPASON it may be used if of ample thickness. Zinc may, with advantage, be used for the feet of heavy pipes, provided they are properly lipped and toed with good pipe-metal. The following Table may be accepted as a reliable guide, showing the minimum desirable thicknesses of good spotted-metal for DIAPASON pipes. The thicknesses are given in thousandths of an inch, and these are carried through seven octaves, and are calculated on a scale for the CC pipe, 8 feet, not exceeding seven inches in diameter, voiced on a wind-pressure not exceeding six inches.

TABLE SHOWING MINIMUM THICKNESSES OF GOOD SPOTTED-METAL FOR DIAPASON PIPES.

	16′	8′	4′	2′	1′	6″	3″
C	0.110	0.080	0.065	0.055	0.040	0.030	0.025
C♯	0.110	0.080	0.065	0.050	0.040	0.030	0.025
D	0.105	0.080	0.065	0.050	0.040	0.030	0.025
D♯	0.105	0.075	0.060	0.050	0.040	0.030	0.025
E	0.100	0.075	0.060	0.050	0.040	0.030	0.020
F	0.100	0.075	0.060	0.050	0.040	0.030	0.020
F♯	0.095	0.070	0.060	0.045	0.035	0.030	0.020
G	0.095	0.070	0.060	0.045	0.035	0.030	0.020
G♯	0.090	0.070	0.055	0.045	0.035	0.025	0.020
A	0.090	0.070	0.055	0.045	0.035	0.025	0.020
A♯	0.085	0.065	0.055	0.045	0.035	0.025	0.020
B	0.085	0.065	0.055	0.045	0.035	0.025	0.020

If the Hoyt hard-rolled two-ply pipe-metal is used, the Table may be started, for the CC, 8 ft., pipe, at gauge 0.070.

SCALE.—The scaling of the DIAPASONS in Organs of the different classes, and which are to be heard under different conditions, requires the careful consideration of the organ expert. When two or more DIAPASONS are inserted in an Organ, either in one or separate Divisions, they should be scaled differently, so as to aid the voicer in the production of the desirable diversity of tone. Large and inordinate scales have been used by certain organ-builders, apparently with the view of producing great volumes of sound, but the undue preponderance of the bass destroyed their general tonal value. As the true bass of the Organ obtains in the pedal department, the value of the tenor and higher octaves of the manual stops, and of the DIAPASONS in particular, should not be overshadowed by any abnormal development of the bass octave. Even under the most scientific treatment the trebles of the finest DIAPASONS are undesirably weak in proportion to their basses. The tonality of the tenor and middle octaves have to be taken most care of by judicious scaling and artistic voicing. Experience has gone far to prove that nothing is gained by using a larger scale than 7 inches in diameter for the CC, 8 ft., pipe. Indeed, Edmund Schulze, of Paulinzelle, the artist representing the best school of German organ-building of the nineteenth century, and who did much splendid work in England, maintained that for the chief DIAPASON of the largest Church Organ, 6½ inches in diameter was the extreme scale for its CC pipe, provided it was properly voiced. The CC pipe of his superb DIAPASON in the Organ in the Parish Church of Leeds, Yorkshire, is only 6¼ inches in diameter; yet the stop is the grandest of its class known to us. The same scale appears in his celebrated DIAPASON in the Organ in the Church of St. Mary, Tyne Dock. Equal in importance to the measurement of the scale is its ratio. That favored by the great German builders Sauer, Ladegast, Walcker, Reubke, and Schulze, and adopted by the last named for his DIAPASONS in the Leeds and Tyne Dock Organs, is the ratio $1 : \sqrt{8}$, which halves on the sixteenth step or seventeenth pipe. We, however, prefer the ratio $1 : 2.66$, which halves on the eighteenth pipe, favoring a slight increase of tone in the treble, always desirable. The following Tables give desirable scales for DIAPASONS suitable for Concert-room, Church, and Chamber Organs, voiced on winds of proper pressures:

TABLE OF DIAPASON PIPE DIAMETERS IN INCHES, RATIO $1 : \sqrt{8}$.

PIPES	CC	C	c^1	c^2	c^3	c^4
I.—	6.60	3.93	2.33	1.39	0.82	0.49
II.—	6.32	3.76	2.23	1.33	0.79	0.47
III.—	6.06	3.60	2.14	1.27	0.76	0.45
IV.—	5.56	3.30	1.96	1.16	0.69	0.41
V.—	5.10	3.03	1.80	1.07	0.64	0.38

TABLE OF DIAPASON PIPE DIAMETERS IN INCHES, RATIO $1 : 2.66$.

PIPES	CC	C	c^1	c^2	c^3	c^4
I.—	6.68	4.10	2.51	1.54	0.94	0.58
II.—	6.42	3.94	2.41	1.47	0.91	0.55
III.—	6.06	3.78	2.31	1.42	0.87	0.53
IV.—	5.56	3.34	2.05	1.25	0.77	0.47
V.—	5.10	3.08	1.89	1.15	0.71	0.43

TONALITY.—The true tone of the DIAPASON is that which is peculiar to and characteristic of the Organ, and which cannot be produced by any other musical instrument. When at its best, it is singularly pure and simple, being, like the normal tone of the tuning-fork, almost entirely free from harmonic over-tones or upper partials. It is this fact that makes the true DIAPASON ineffective as a melodic stop, played in single notes; while played in full chords its tones are rich and impressive and generally beautiful. If prolonged, however, it becomes cloying and palls upon the ear. It is this simple quality which makes the DIAPASON tone the proper foundation of the tonal structure of the Organ; upon which may be laid tonal combinations of endless variety and beauty.

The following remarks from the pen of Professor R. H. M.
Bosanquet, an authority on tonal matters, are of interest:

"The scales, character, and voicing of the OPEN DIAPASON vary with fashion,
and are different in different countries. We may distinguish three principal types.
The old English DIAPASONS of the days before the introduction of Pedal Organs
into England were characterized by a rich sweet tone, and were not very powerful.
They were generally voiced on a light wind, having a pressure equivalent to that
of a column of water of from 2 to 2½ inches. The scale was in some cases very
large, as in Green's two OPEN DIAPASONS in the old Organ at St. George's, Windsor;
in these the wind was light and the tone very soft. In other cases the scale was
smaller and the voicing bolder, as in Father Smith's original DIAPASONS in St.
Paul's Cathedral. But on the whole the old English DIAPASONS presented a lovely
quality of tone. English travelers of those days, accustomed to these DIAPASONS,
usually found foreign Organs harsh, noisy, and uninteresting. And there are
many still in England who, while recognizing the necessity of a firmer diapason-
tone in view of the introduction of the heavy pedal bass, and the corresponding
strengthening of the upper departments of the organ-tone, lament the disappearance of the old diapason-tone. However, it is possible with care to obtain DIA-
PASONS presenting the sweet characteristics of the old English tone, combined with
sufficient fullness and power to form a sound general foundation. And there can
be no doubt that this should be one of the chief points to be kept in view in organ
design.

"The German DIAPASON was of an entirely different character from the English. The heavy bass of the pedals has been an essential characteristic of the
German Organ for at least two or three centuries, or, as it is said, for four. The
development of the piercing stops of high pitch was equally general. Thus foundation-work of comparatively great power was required to maintain the balance of
tone; the ordinary German DIAPASON was very loud, and we may say coarse, in
its tone when compared with the old English DIAPASON. The German stop was
voiced as a rule on from 3½ to 4 inches of wind, not quite twice the pressure used
in England.

"The French DIAPASON is a modern variety. It may be described as presenting rather the characteristics of a loud GAMBA than of a DIAPASON. In other
words, the tone tends towards a certain quality which may be described as 'tinny'
or metallic; or as approaching to that of a string instrument of rather coarse
character. Some modern English builders appear to aim at the same model, and
not without success.

"The tone of a DIAPASON must be strong enough to assert itself. It is the
foundation of the whole organ tone. It is the voicer's business to satisfy this condition in conjunction with the requirement that the tone shall be full and of agreeable quality."*

That we agree with everything stated by Professor Bosanquet is
proved by every word we have written on the subject during the
past forty years. Unquestionably, to the lover of sweet sounds—
which we claim to be—the true English diapason-tone is the most
lovely; that of the French MONTRE the most unsatisfactory: yet to

* Encyclopædia Britannica: Ninth Edition. "Organ."

French ears, and those satisfied with power rather than refinement of tone, it seems to be agreeable. Different tastes are born and fostered under different conditions.

VOICING AND REGULATING.—As there are various tones produced by stops labeled DIAPASON, so there are different schools of voicing, not only peculiar to different countries but to varied classes of voicers. Such being the case, it is obvious that no standard of diapason- or pure foundation organ-tone has been in any way established, or even suggested, in modern organ-work. Yet it must be admitted that for such an all-important foundation organ-tone a well-defined standard should be set and universally adopted.

At the present time, when wind-pressures of great variety are used at the caprice of organ-builders, it seems a hopeless thing to look for anything approaching a standard diapason-tone. As Professor Bosanquet has pointed out, it has ranged in the past from the refined and beautiful tones of the true English DIAPASONS, on through the loud and coarse tones of the German PRINCIPALS, to the stringy and unsympathetic voices of the French MONTRES. While it is obviously desirable that when two or more DIAPASONS are inserted in an Organ, they should be of different scales, and voiced to produce varied strengths and, within due limits, different tints of true organ-tone; there is certainly no call for them to yield the coarse German quality, on the one hand, or the dry, "tinny," or gambaish tonality favored by the French voicers, on the other hand.

Scale, of course, is a matter of great importance, but it must be conceded that other conditions are of equal, if not of greater, importance in the production of true diapason-tone. These conditions may be embraced under the general term Voicing, which includes wind-pressure, wind-supply, and the artistic treatment of the mouth and top of every pipe. First in order is the proper wind-pressure. Experience has shown that for the production of the pure, smooth, and beautiful tone characteristic of the true English DIAPASON, a moderate wind-pressure is essential, accompanied by a copious supply. The finest DIAPASONS in existence to-day speak on wind of from 3 to 5 inches. For instance, the grandest and most beautiful DIAPASON known to us is the larger of the two, made by Schulze, in the Great of the Organ in the Parish Church of Leeds, already alluded to, which speaks on a copious wind-supply of only 3¾ inches pressure. It is just worth while stating, as a lesson to voicers hit by the high-pressure craze of the present time, the several pressures used in this fine instrument, which owes so much of its grandeur and beauty to the genius of Schulze. All the stops of the Pedal Organ with its 32 ft. and 16 ft. reeds, are on wind of 3¾ inches. The stops of the Great Organ, with the exception of the POSAUNE, are on wind of 3¾ inches; the POSAUNE being on wind of 7 inches. The Swell Organ is on wind of 3 inches; the Choir Organ is on wind of 2½ inches; the Solo Organ, with the exception of the TUBA, is on wind of 5 inches, the TUBA being on wind of 8 inches; and the Echo Organ is on wind of 1½ inches. Although tonally appointed and apportioned in the "good old-fashioned way," this instrument is *par excellence* a Church Organ; dignified and refined in tone, and admirable in its fundamental office—the accompaniment of the musical service. The Organ comprises 77 speaking stops, 11 of which are in the Pedal; having in all 5,060 pipes.

Careful experiment and observation go to prove that in the production of a pure, pervading, and musically perfect normal diapason-tone (or organ-tone) a volume of, and not high-pressure, pipe-wind is the principal factor. The loud and coarse tones which characterize the great majority of the modern DIAPASONS voiced on winds of undue pressures, have nothing like the pervading, traveling, and sympathetic qualities and powers of the stops artistically voiced on a copious supply of low-pressure wind.

It is somewhat surprising that the French voicers have so utterly failed in realizing the value and beauty of the English diapason-tone. They seem to have been satisfied with the cutting, "tinny," tone of their MONTRES. Even the great Cavaillé-Coll apparently did not aim at anything better: and much of the stringy tonality of his stops is due to the practice, he invariably followed, of slotting his pipes at the top, for convenience in tuning. The true English DIAPASON was never slotted; and no DIAPASON ever should be. Let modern voicers take note of these important facts.

A certain method of voicing DIAPASONS has been introduced during recent years, and is now practised by a certain class of voicers —a method which we would never allow to be used in any Organ over the construction of which we had any control. We allude to the leathering of the upper lips of the pipes, with the view of imparting to them the necessary thickness and the desirable roundness and smoothness. It is claimed, by the organ-builders who resort to it, to greatly improve the tones of their pipes. Probably it does in comparison with the tones produced by the unduly thin pipe-metal they may have been accustomed to use. None of the great and truly artistic organ-builders have resorted to this cheap and undesirable expedient. Let the mouths of the pipes be properly formed with lips of sufficient thickness, as in old work and in that of the great builders, and let their upper lips be properly adjusted and smoothly rounded and there will be no necessity for leathering. We presume the question of durability does not trouble the organ-builder who calculates that the leathering will, in all probability,. outlast the rest of his lifetime; but the question is of great importance to the Organ Committee or purchaser of the Organ. In what condition would the DIAPASONS of the celebrated Haarlem Organ be in to-day had its builder used thin metal, and leathered the mouths of their pipes, in the money-saving method now in vogue? We unhesitatingly affirm that the fine work of the past proves that there is not the slightest excuse for leathering the lips of organ-pipes: and the objectionable practice should be discountenanced by every purchaser of an Organ. If a very thick and well-rounded lip is desired, let a strip of pipe-metal be folded—just as the leather is folded—and slipped on the upper lip and soldered in position. This method would be most efficient, but unless imperatively specified there would be no chance of its being adopted by the organ-builder or voicer. Let lips of sufficient thickness be furnished, as in old work, and let a proper school of voicing, on winds of moderate pressures, be instituted, and there will be no need to resort to objectionable and perishable leathering for the production of perfect diapason-tone.

Next in importance to the production of a pure and beautiful diapason-tone is its perfect regulation. This is a matter requiring a sensitive ear and the expenditure of considerable time. Accordingly, it is very seldom that one finds a DIAPASON accurately and artistically regulated throughout its compass. Perfect regulation is essential to the beauty of an Organ; for a few badly regulated stops will go far to destroy that beauty: this will especially be the case if the DIAPASONS are not properly regulated, with due regard to an effective balance of tone in the treble octaves. There is always a tendency to undesirable preponderance of tone in the bass octave; and this should be overcome to as large an extent as possible both in the voicing and regulating. A perfect DIAPASON is a work of science and art that any pipe-maker and voicer may point to with justifiable pride.

COMBINATION AND REGISTRATION.—The diapason-tone is to the tonal structure of the Organ what the solid foundation of a building is to its superstructure. As has already been stated, the pure organ-tone yielded by the true and properly-voiced DIAPASON is simple in its nature: and such being the case, it naturally lends itself to enrichment by the addition of those tones which, by their presence, impart so great a charm and beauty to the compound sounds of the stringed instruments of the orchestra and the cultivated human voice. Accordingly, to the simple prime tone of the DIAPASON must be added a superstructure of upper partials or harmonic over-tones, scientifically graduated in strength in accordance with the natural laws of musical sounds. For this purpose are introduced in the properly-appointed Organ the several derivatives of the DIAPASON —the Octave, Mutation, and compound harmonic-corroborating stops. A deficiency in any one of these classes seriously impairs the desirable range of compound diapason-tones; and, accordingly, divests the Organ proper of much of its usefulness and beauty. This important fact is too largely neglected in the tonal appointment of modern Organs. For the production of the various colors of foundation-tone, not only have greater or lesser proportions of these different harmonic-corroborating stops to be added to the DIAPASON; but greater or lesser strengths in their voices are required. This latter requirement points conclusively to the necessity for their tonal control, through their inclosure in a swell-box. The numerous modes of combining the DIAPASON and its harmonic derivatives alone, may be classed under the term Diapason Registration.

In artistic registration the DIAPASON has a very important rôle; for upon its foundation tone can be built an infinite number of effective and beautiful combinations—the most dignified and impressive the properly-appointed Organ places at the command of the musician. Colorings derived through combinations with flute-, string-, reed-, and brass-toned stops are simply endless in their variety. Indeed, registration on the foundation of the diapason-tone is a study in itself, worthy of the organist's earnest attention; for upon it is based the entire fabric of artistic organ tonal combination. Such registration and the tonal effects it produces belong exclusively to the Organ.

TUNING.—The tuning of DIAPASON pipes deserves the attention of those interested in artistic and good organ-building. The practice of tuning such pipes by means of slotting them near their open ends, so commonly adopted by the French organ-builders, is to be condemned on the ground that such slotting seriously injures the true diapason-tone. Coning, which either expands or contracts the open ends of the pipes,—flattening or sharpening their tones,—has, from old times, been commonly adopted in tuning pipes of the DIAPASON class from tenor C (4 ft.) upwards; but the practice has nothing to recommend it save convenience. It is not desirable on tonal grounds, because in any case of excessive spreading or contracting of the top of a pipe the tone undergoes a certain alteration: and, further, the necessary smart and often heavy blows of the weighty metal cones, frequently repeated, tend to, and ultimately do, seriously injure the top, mouth, or feet of the pipe. The most, and, indeed, only, desirable system of tuning DIAPASON pipes is by means of adjustable slides, which only require to be slightly raised or lowered in tuning; but it is not to be expected that organ-builders will adopt this system unless compelled to do so. Pipes that may be considered too large to be conveniently tuned by slides should be cut a little longer than their correct speaking lengths, and tuned by means of broad tongues, cut in the manner shown in the accompanying illustration, Fig. 10. If the pipes are properly cut to length, only fine tuning will

FIG. 10

be necessary by the easy and slight manipulation of the tongues. No injury need ever be done to the pipes. This method can be carried from the CC to the tenor C pipe, or even farther with advantage. The method will, of course, be carried through the 16 ft. and 8 ft. octaves of the DOUBLE DIAPASON.

DIAPASON, WOOD.—Although German organ-builders have . proved that true diapason-tone can be produced from quadrangular wood pipes, no French, English, or American organ-builder seems to have devoted serious attention to the construction of DIAPASONS of wood throughout. This is to be regretted, for we are convinced, from observation of what has been done by German builders, that, associated with metal DIAPASONS, a wood DIAPASON would be of great value, doing away with all risk of sympathy, while building up a grand volume of tone. Our attention was first directed to the matter when we inspected the fine Organ in the Church of St. Bartholomew, Armley, Yorkshire, constructed by Edmund Schulze.

In this instrument the bass octave of the MAJOR PRINCIPAL, 8 FT., in the Great Organ—a grand stop of pure organ-tone—is carried down in wood pipes in a manner so perfect that the ordinary ear fails to detect the transition from metal to wood. In the accompanying illustration, Fig. 11, is given the Front View and Longitudinal Section of the lower portion of the BB pipe of this stop, drawn to scale. It will be observed that the external slopes of the lower

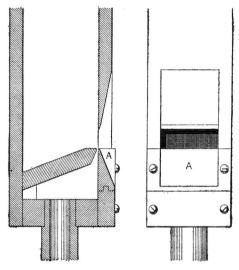

FIG. 11

and upper lips, shown in the Section, closely resemble those of the usual metal DIAPASON. The principal feature here is the recessed and splayed cap A, which is brought almost to a sharp edge where.it forms the lower lip, in this respect resembling the metal lip. The upper lip is thin and cut thin, as shown. As regards scale, the most important dimensions are those of the BB pipe which immediately adjoins the tenor C metal pipe. The tenor C pipe is $3\frac{3}{8}$ inches in diameter, with a mouth 3 inches wide and $\frac{3}{4}$ inch high, and with a wind-hole in the foot $\frac{9}{16}$ inch in diameter. The BB wood pipe measures, internally, $2\frac{13}{16}$ inches in width by $3\frac{3}{4}$ inches in depth, with a mouth $\frac{7}{8}$ inch high. In the same Organ, the SUB-PRINCIPAL, 16 FT., has its two lower octaves of wood; and the MINOR PRINCIPAL, 8 FT., in the Choir Organ, has its bass octave of wood. All are specimens of artistic voicing.

Both the DIAPASON, 16 FT., and DOUBLE DIAPASON, 32 FT., of the Pedal Organ are commonly made of wood; but it is seldom one hears the true diapason-tone produced by such stops as made at the present time. The desire to obtain a powerful intonation, through the use of large scales and wind of undue pressure, goes far to destroy the tone which should always be sought for in such foundation stops, and especially in those of the refined Church Organ. The now common practice of applying the harmonic-bridge, with the view of securing promptness and a certain clearness of speech, imparts a stringy quality to the tone, in itself by no means disagreeable, and which may, perhaps, be considered desirable in this age of borrowed and poverty-stricken Pedal Organs. If properly voiced on a copious flow of wind of a pressure not exceeding 6 inches, scales between 8 inches by 10 inches and 12 inches by 14½ inches for the CCC (16 ft.) pipe will be ample. The German and other Continental builders, in their appreciation of the true nature and office of the Pedal Organ, and also of its adequate stop-apportionment, never, so far as we have been able to learn, used inordinate scales. The largest scale known to us in a German Organ is 12 inches by 14 inches; while the majority of Pedal Organ PRINCIPALS, 16 FT., rarely exceed 9 inches by 11 inches. The late W. T. Best, of Liverpool, the best judge of organ-tone in his day, invariably specified the scale of 10 inches by 12 inches. We have conclusively proved the scale of 8 inches by 10 inches to be perfectly suitable for a Chamber Organ, voiced even on the low pressure of 2⅜ inches. On a higher pressure—say 4 inches—it would be sufficient for a Church Organ of ordinary size. It must be borne in mind that this stop has to provide a properly balanced bass to the Great Organ DIAPASON, 8 FT.

The most satisfactory scales for the DOUBLE DIAPASON, 32 FT., are not proportionately so large as those desirable for the DIAPASON, 16 FT. It is undesirable, on the ground of scientific and artistic tonal balance, that the sub-octave pitch should be as assertive as that of the fundamental unison.

The most suitable minimum scale is 11 inches by 13½ inches for the CCCC pipe, halving on the eighteenth pipe: while the maximum scale may be that adopted by Schulze for the fine stop in the Organ in St. Bartholomew's Church, Armley; namely, 14¼ inches by 18¼ inches. This scale is larger than that adopted by the same builder for his DOUBLE PRINCIPALS, in the Organs in Bremen Cathedral and St. Mary's Church, Wismar, which measure only 12 inches by 15 inches. The equally celebrated builder, Ladegast, uses a still smaller scale—11⅛ inches by 14⅛ inches—for the CCCC pipe of the

Double Principal, 32 ft., in his celebrated Organ in Schwerin Cathedral.

DIAPASON PHONON.—The name introduced during late years to designate a metal labial stop of 8 ft. and 16 ft. pitch, and large scale, voiced to yield a powerful and pure organ-tone. The pipes of the stop are of the same form and construction as those of the standard Diapason. The stop and its name were introduced by Hope-Jones, who adopted the cheap method of forming thick and smoothly rounded upper lips to the mouths of its pipes—so desirable in all pipes of the Diapason class—by covering the thin metal with perishable leather. For further remarks on this practice, see Diapason. The Diapason Phonon will, naturally, be favored by those who love loud sounds; and who advocate the construction of brick-and-mortar or reinforced-concrete swell-boxes.

DIAPASON, STOPPED.—This name is an example of loose terminology: the stop so named does not belong to the class yielding pure organ-tone, and is not a Diapason in any sense of the word. The so-called Stopped Diapason belongs to the Covered Flute-work of the Organ. Long usage, however, is likely to prevail; and in all probability, as there is no English equivalent for the German term Gedeckt, it will be retained by English and American organ-builders, in organ-stop nomenclature, for many years to come. For form and other particulars, see Stopped Diapason.

DIAPHONE.—The name of a stop invented by Hope-Jones. It is of peculiar construction. The tone of the Diaphone pipe is created by pulses or vibrations generated in its resonator by the rapid motions of a pallet actuated by compressed air (pipe-wind) that enters the boot, which contains the mechanical portion of the pipe. The pallet simply closes and opens the lower orifice of the resonator so many times in a second, according to the size and pitch of the pipe, acting much in the same manner as the striking tongue in an ordinary lingual pipe. As the vibrating column of air in the resonator controls the action of the pallet, when adjusted, the pitch of the pipe is not affected by a change in the wind-pressure, while the strength and quality of the tone are altered. The tone produced by the best examples is full and commanding; but owing to the complex character of the mechanical portion of the pipes, and the difficulty of regulating the action of the same, it is almost impossible to secure uniformity throughout even the short compass of the Pedal Organ. There are also very grave questions regarding the durability of the stop. These facts will effectually militate against anything approaching a free introduction of the DIAPHONE. In all probability it is destined to swell the ranks of the curiosities of organ-building.*

DIVINARE.—The somewhat inappropriate term used to designate a covered stop of 4 ft. pitch, belonging to the Covered Flutework, the tone of which is singularly soft and singing.† Such a stop is very desirable in the Choir of a Church Organ, in a Chamber Organ, and in the Echo or Ancillary Aërial Organ of a Concertroom instrument. Its presence would be productive of many charming effects in refined registration. The stop is made of both wood and metal: when of wood, the pipes are of small scale, and made narrow and deep so as to secure small mouths. Low-pressure wind is desirable.

DOIFLÖTE, DUIFLÖTE, Ger.—Names used to designate the covered, flute-toned stop, the pipes of which have double mouths, commonly called DOPPELFLÖTE (q. v.).

DOLCAN.—The name given to an open labial stop of 8 ft. pitch, the pipes of which are of metal—in the best examples tin—the bodies of which are in the form of a slender, inverted truncated cone, as shown in Fig. 12, Plate II., which depicts a CC pipe in correct proportions. The bass octave has been formed of inverted pyramidal pipes of wood, but the metal ones are to be preferred. The scale of the DOLCAN varies, as in other labial stops, according to the volume and quality of the tone desired. The following scales in the ratio of 1:2.519—halving on the nineteenth pipe—may be accepted as productive of satisfactory tones:

DOLCAN PIPE DIAMETERS IN INCHES—RATIO 1:2.519.

PIPES	CC	C	c^1	c^2	c^3	c^4
AT MOUTH	3.38	2.13	1.34	0.84	0.53	0.33
AT TOP	4.96	3.13	1.97	1.24	0.78	0.49
AT MOUTH	3.25	2.05	1.29	0.81	0.51	0.32
AT TOP	5.16	3.25	2.05	1.29	0.81	0.51

* Particulars respecting the origin of the DIAPHONE, its forms and construction, accompanied by fully detailed illustrations, are given in our work, "The Art of Organ-Building," Vol. I., pp. 399–400. Vol. II., pp. 619–622.

† "DIVINARE, flûte de bourdon de quatre-pieds, flûte divine, est une singulière traduction de ce mot, et c'est la seule indiquée pour exprimer la qualité divinement supérieure de cette flûte . . . à peu près inconnue.—Regnier.

"DIVINARE (vom Lat. divinus, göttlich), sondern es gedecktes Flötenwerk zu 4′. Die Intonation dieser Stimme muss dem Namen nach sehr schön sein."—Seidel.

The width of the mouth may be two-ninths or one-fifth the internal circumference of the pipe at its mouth-line, according to the strength of tone required; and its height may vary from one-fifth to one-fourth its width, subject to the wind-pressure employed and the tone aimed at by the voicer. When a very delicate tone is required, on a low pressure of wind,—say 2½ inches,—a mouth of one-fifth the circumference should be adopted, having a height about one-quarter its width; and the languid should be finely nicked. The upper lip should be of good substance, cut straight, and smoothly rounded.

TONE AND REGISTRATION.—When properly formed and artist-ically voiced, the DOLCAN yields a tone which is freer or more open in quality than that of the true English DULCIANA, having a some-what plaintive and singing character, which is highly effective in soft accompanimental music, and extremely valuable in the more delicate and refined school of registration. The tone combines in the most satisfactory manner with all the varieties of flute-tones, giving them a peculiar charm; and also with the voices of the softer lingual stops. The DOLCAN's place is in the softer accompanimental division of the Organ, where it need not displace the DULCIANA.

DOLCE, Ital.—This name has been used to designate stops of different formation and tone; but, as the name implies, all being similar in one important direction—the possession of *sweetness* of voice. The stop is introduced in important German Organs in both 8 ft. and 4 ft. pitch, as in the instrument in the Cathedral of Ulm.* The DOLCE has been made by German organ-builders of both wood and metal, and of both cylindrical and inverted conical pipes, after the fashion of those of the DOLCAN (Fig. 12, Plate II.). A beautiful example of this latter form, made by Edmund Schulze, exists in the Echo of the Organ in the Parish Church of Leeds, England. It is of small scale and its pipes are slightly conical, yielding a tone of a quiet nasal quality; and, being on wind of only 1½ inches pressure, has a tendency to be slow, imparting a peculiar intonation to its speech. In certain German examples the tones are inclined to be stringy; but it is questionable if this is desirable. In our opinion, a smooth, extremely soft, and horn-like tonality is to be preferred, differentiating it from that of the DOLCAN and DULCIANA. The DOLCE, formed of inverted conical pipes, seems to have been intro-

---

* "DOLCE 8′ von Metall, ist eine Stimme, welche im 2ten Manual der neuen Orgel in der Peterskirche zu Petersburg disponiert ist und einen äusserst weichen Toncharakter hat. Im 3ten Manual steht dasselbe Register von Zinn zu 4′. Auch häufiger in Sauerschen Orgeln finden." —Seidel.

duced at an early date in English Organs; for it is stated on good authority that John Snetzler inserted one in the Organ he built, in 1741, for the Parish Church of Chesterfield, Derbyshire.

It is to be regretted that the DOLCE, in its proper form, has not been more frequently introduced in important Organs: but it would seem that the space it requires on the wind-chest, and the additional metal and labor its construction calls for beyond what a small-scaled cylindrical stop, such as the kindred DULCIANA, demands, have militated against its more general adoption by organ-builders. There are, however, several good examples to be found in English Organs constructed by leading English builders. A fine one exists in the Organ in Emmanuel Church, Leicester. A DOLCE, 16 FT., of very beautiful tone—voiced by the artist, W. Thynne—is to be found in the Chapel of St. Katherine's Convent, London. A DOLCE, 8 FT., is inserted in the Swell of the Organ in the Centennial Hall, Sydney, N. S. W. Roosevelt inserted a DOLCE, 8 FT., in the Swell of the fine Organ he built for the First Congregational Church, Great Barrington, Mass. The proper place for the DOLCE in the Organ would seem to be quite undecided by organists and organ-builders, as the following particulars show; yet, in artistic tonal apportionment, it has its proper and logical position. In the Great of the Organ in the Second Church, West Newton, Mass. In the Swell of the Gallery Organ in Emmanuel Church, Boston, Mass. In the Choir of the Concert-room Organ in the Carnegie Music Hall, Pittsburgh, Pa. In the Echo of the Organ in St. Peter's Episcopal Church, St. Louis, Mo.

The scale of the DOLCE, 8 FT., varies in different examples, though not to a large extent. The following scale of a representative stop may be accepted as satisfactory, with low wind-pressures:

DOLCE PIPE DIAMETERS IN INCHES—RATIO 1:2.66.

PIPES	CC	C	c^1	c^2	c^3	c^4
AT MOUTH	3.08	1.89	1.15	0.71	0.43	0.27
AT TOP	4.10	2.51	1.54	0.94	0.58	0.35

The width of the mouth should not exceed one-fifth of the internal circumference of the pipe at its mouth line; and its height need not exceed one-fourth its width unless a leaning toward a flute-tone is desired.

DOLCE CORNET.—This stop, as the name implies, is compound, harmonic-corroborating, and sweet-voiced. It is properly formed of several ranks of very small-scaled open metal pipes, yielding a soft, singing quality of tone. When extreme softness is required, the ranks should be octave- and fifth-sounding only: but when a more assertive tone is desired, a third-sounding rank should appear in every break, as in the following example of five ranks:

DOLCE CORNET—V. RANKS.

CC to f¹	.		.	.	12*—15 —17*—19 —22.
f♯¹ to f²	.	.	.	.	8 —12*—15 —17*—19.
f♯² to b³	.	.	.	.	1 — 8 —12*—15 —17*.
c³ to c⁴	.	.	.	.	1 — 8 —10 —12 —15.

It will be observed that the introduction of the SEVENTEENTH makes the stop a SESQUIALTERA in all save the top octave. Artistically voiced and scientifically graduated in tone this CORNET would be extremely valuable in refined registration. The following is a satisfactory composition for a CORNET of four ranks, octave- and fifth-sounding:

DOLCE CORNET—IV. RANKS.

CC to BB	.	.	.	.	15——19——22——26.
C to B	.	.	.	.	12——15——19——22.
c¹ to g³	.	.	.	.	8——12——15——19.
g♯³ to c⁴	.	.	.	.	1—— 8——12——15.

A DOLCE GRAND CORNET composed of complete, through ranks of true DOLCE pipes, of small scale, would be of great value in any of the softer toned divisions or subdivisions, expressive, of the Concert-room Organ, in which its presence would tend to complete the harmonic structure. It may be composed of an OCTAVE, 4 FT.; a TWELFTH, 2⅔ FT.; a FIFTEENTH, 2 FT.; a SEVENTEENTH, 1⅗ FT.; and a NINETEENTH, 1⅓ FT. The SEVENTEENTH may be omitted if considered too harsh in tone.

DOLCE FLUTE.—A softly-voiced stop of unimitative flute-tone, more commonly known by the Italian name FLAUTO DOLCE (*q. v.*).

DOLCETTE.—The term, as a diminutive, properly applied to designate the OCTAVE DOLCE, 4 FT. This is a valuable stop in refined registration, corroborating the first upper partial tone of all soft-voiced unison open stops, and imparting a foreign element to the voices of the softly-toned covered stops, such as the LIEBLICH-GEDECKTS, FLÛTE A CHEMINÉE, COR DE NUIT, etc.

DOLCIANO PROFUNDO.—The distinctive name we have suggested for a CONTRA-DULCIANA, 32 FT., when such a stop is commanded by a manual clavier. We have shown, in our tonal scheme for the Concert-room Organ of the Twentieth Century, how this grave and most desirable soft-toned, open metal stop, of 32 ft. pitch, can be derived from the Pedal Organ CONTRA-DULCIANA, adequately extended in compass, and be commanded, as an auxiliary stop, by the First or Great Organ Clavier.*

DOLCISSIMO, Ital.—The term appropriately used to designate the softest flute-toned stop made. The extended term, FLAUTO DOLCISSIMO, will, however, be found more expressive, especially if the stop is voiced to yield an imitative tone—that of the orchestral Flute played *pianissimo*. In its best form, the DOLCISSIMO is of 8 ft. pitch, constructed of small-scaled hard wood pipes, having very narrow inverted mouths. It should be voiced on wind of low pressure, not exceeding 2½ inches, preferably of 1½ inches. It is an ideal stop for a refined Chamber Organ; and for the Choir or Echo of a Church Organ, and the Ancillary Aërial Organ or other very softly-toned division of a Concert-room instrument. In registration, the DOLCISSIMO, 8 FT., will be found extremely valuable in imparting a beautiful effect and a desirable firmness and body to the VOX HUMANA and all the other softer-toned lingual stops, without destroying their characteristic tonalities, which a loud-voiced FLUTE, 8 FT., would certainly do in combination.†

DOLZFLÖTE, DULZFLÖTE, Ger.—The name given by old German organ-builders to an open wood stop of 8 ft. and 4 ft. pitch, the pipes of which are of medium scale, yielding a soft and sweet unimitative flute-tone. Seidel describes the stop thus:

"DOLZFLÖTE, DULZFLÖTE, Flauto dulcis (süsse Flöte), auch Tibia angusta, ist eine eng mensurierte offene Flötenstimme von Holtz zu 4′ und 8′, von ausnehmend lieblichem und angenehmem Tone. Im Pedal soll diese Stimme zu 16′ unter dem Namen Flautone vorkomen." See FLAUTO DOLCE.

DOPPELFLÖTE, Ger.—The term commonly used to designate a covered wood stop of 8 ft. pitch, the pipes of which have two mouths placed directly opposite each other, hence the name. As usual with stops that require unusual conditions for their accommodation on the wind-chest, and which call for special skill and more than ordinary labor in their construction, the DOPPELFLÖTE has never been a favorite with English and American organ-builders;

---

* See "The Organ of the Twentieth Century." Chap. XI., pp. 297 and 319.
† See the Aërial Organ in "The Organ of the Twentieth Century," pp. 329–331.

while its great tonal value seems to have been unrealized by the organists of both countries. One, assuming to be an authority on organ-stops, writing on the DOPPELFLÖTE, displays a strange ignorance of its tonal character and value in registration. So far as we have been able to learn, the first DOPPELFLÖTE that appeared in an English Organ was the one we inserted, in 1883, in our own Chamber Organ, under the Italian name, FLAUTO PRIMO, 8 FT. It occupied a prominent position in the Second Expressive Subdivision of the First Organ.* This beautiful stop was presented to us by the late Hilborne L. Roosevelt, of New York. A few examples have since appeared in English Organs, for the most part made by Continental builders. Roosevelt held the DOPPELFLÖTE in high estimation and invariably placed one in the Great of all his important Organs. It is to be regretted that so few examples appear in even large Organs constructed in this country during the present period. One has been wisely inserted in the Great of the Organ in the Carnegie Music Hall, Pittsburgh, Pa.

FORMATION.—The DOPPELFLÖTE, 8 FT., is usually formed of pipes of two different scales and treatments, those from CC to BB being medium-scaled GE-DECKT pipes with single mouths, voiced to yield a full, round tone to carry down, as closely as practicable, the characteristic quality of the principal portion of the stop. From tenor C to the top, each pipe has two mouths, placed on the opposite and narrower sides of a block in which a semicircular depression has been cut, leaving two thin lower lips to the mouths. The mouths and caps are of the English form, the lower lips being somewhat widely nicked, and the upper lips arched and carefully formed and rounded. These and all other details are correctly shown in the accompanying illustration, Fig. 13. In the Drawing 1, is given a Longitudinal Section of a pipe, cut through the mouths, at A, and showing the forms of the block, cap, and wind-ways. Above, at B, is given a section of the stopper, edged with cork and covered with soft leather. A Front View of one of the mouths is given in Drawing 2, showing its height, the arching of the upper lip, the nicking of the lower lip, and the lateral splays. In the Drawing 3 is given a Transverse Section through the mouths, showing the depression in the block, the lower nicked lips, the windways, and the upper edges of the caps. All the parts are drawn in correct proportion and to scale. It would seem to have been the practice of the German organ-builders to use different woods in the formation of their DOPPEL-FLÖTES. In that on the Third Manual of the Organ built by Ladegast for the Cathedral of Schwerin the pipes are of pine fronted with oak: and in that on the First Manual of the Organ of St. Paul's Church, in the same city, the pipes are of pine fronted with oak and mahogany. In the Roosevelt DOPPELFLÖTE, to which allusion has been made, the pipes have sides of sugar-pine and fronts and caps of close-grained mahogany. These are examples of fine pipe-making.

* We may here record the fact that, for the first time in the history of organ-building, three independent tonal subdivisions were placed on a single clavier—that of the First Organ; namely, one unexpressive and two independently expressive. So far as we know this remarkable and beautiful arrangement of tonal apportionment remains unique to-day (1920). See "The Organ of the Twentieth Century," p. 334.

SCALE.—The pipes of the DOPPELFLÖTE, having double mouths, require a scale providing a considerable depth in proportion to width. This is exemplified by the following internal measurements taken from the Roosevelt standard scale: Tenor C pipe $2\frac{1}{4}$ inches in width by $3\frac{7}{16}$ inches in depth; middle c¹ pipe $1\frac{3}{8}$ inches in width by $2\frac{3}{16}$ inches in depth; c² pipe $\frac{3}{4}$ inch in width by $1\frac{7}{16}$ inches in depth.

This is an example of an irregular scale, arrived at by experience. It will be observed that the proportions of depth to width vary as the scale ascends; the C pipe being a little over one and a half its width in depth; while the c² pipe is a little under twice its width in depth. The height of the mouth at the spring of its arched upper lip ranges between one-third and one-half its width, according to the wind-pressure and the volume of tone required. The arching and thickness of the upper lip are also important factors in tone production that the voicer must decide.

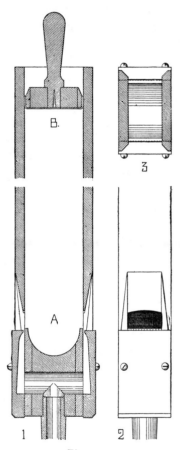

Fig. 13

TONE AND REGISTRATION.— The DOPPELFLÖTE, when properly scaled and artistically voiced, yields a singularly full and pure unimitative flute-tone, having more filling-up power and better mixing quality than any other unison covered stop of medium power in the Organ. It is especially this mixing quality that gives the stop its great value in refined registration. Owing to the rarity of the stop, organists have few opportunities of learning its importance in tonal coloring. But having a beautiful DOPPELFLÖTE in our own Organ, and having carefully observed the use made of it in registration by a large number of distinguished English, French, and American Organists, during a period of eight years, supplemented by our own studies, we have been able to learn the great value of the stop as, perhaps, no other man has done. The DOPPELFLÖTE is specially effective in combination with the softer-toned lingual stops of all classes, imparting to their voices firmness and fullness, and in some cases considerable richness, without injuring their characteristic tonalities. In this direction, however, the DOPPELROHRGEDECKT or DOPPELROHRFLÖTE may be preferred (*q. v.*).

DOPPELFLÖTENBASS, Ger.—A medium-scaled covered wood stop of 16 ft. pitch, formed with double mouths. This stop, which furnishes the true bass to the DOPPELFLÖTE, 8 FT., has its proper place in the Pedal Organ, where its full and smooth fluty voice is of great value for accompaniment and in combination with the lingual stops. A fine example of this uncommon stop exists in the Second Pedal Organ of Schulze's important instrument in the Marienkirche, at Lübeck. It is described thus:

"DOPPELFLÖTENBASS 16'. Holz. Eine weite, gedeckt Stimme mit doppelten Labien. Der Ton ist etwas voller und runder, als der des SUBBASS, und bildet zu den sanften Stimme der Orgel den schonsten Bass."

DOPPELGEDECKT, Ger.—The name given to a covered wood stop of 8 ft. and 16 ft. pitch, the pipes of which are of large scale, and made, after the fashion of the DOPPELFLÖTE, with two mouths: the scale, however, differs from that of the DOPPELFLÖTE, in not having so great a depth in proportion to width. The tone is fuller and richer than that of the ordinary single-mouthed GEDECKT, 8 FT., or BOURDON, 16 FT.

DOPPELROHRFLÖTE, Ger.—A labial stop of 8 ft. and 4 ft. pitch, which, as the name implies, is a modification of the DOPPEL-FLÖTE in so much as it is what is known as a half-covered stop, while the DOPPELFLÖTE is a wholly-covered one. It is properly made of wood throughout when of 8 ft. pitch; and when of 4 ft. pitch, of wood save in its top octave, which is properly of metal, the pipes there being too small to be conveniently made of wood. The wood pipes are constructed in all essentials similar to those of the DOPPEL-FLÖTE (Fig. 13), with the exception of the stopper, which is perforated as in the normal ROHRFLÖTE (*q. v.*).

TONE AND REGISTRATION.—Owing to the perforation of the stoppers of its pipes, the tone of the DOPPELROHRFLÖTE is brighter, lighter, and more open than that of the DOPPELFLÖTE; and on this account is better adapted for combination with the tones of the softer lingual stops. This fact should incline the designer of a Concert-room Organ to place the DOPPELROHRFLÖTE in the division devoted to the stops representing the wood-wind forces of the orchestra. Placing the stop there, he will properly insert the fuller-toned DOPPELFLÖTE in the First or Great Organ, where its good mixing voice will prove valuable in registration. The position of the stop, of either of its pitches, in the Church Organ will properly depend on the general tonal apportionment of the instrument. Examples of the DOPPELROHRFLÖTE of both 8 ft. and 4 ft. pitches are to be found in the Great of Müller's Organ (1843) in the Catholic Church, at Katcher. Other examples, of both pitches, are inserted in the Echo of the Grand Organ in the Cathedral of St. John, Breslau.* The DOPPELROHRFLÖTE, 4 FT., is an octave stop having all the properties which render a labial stop of that pitch valuable in refined registration. It is both a good harmonic-corroborating and timbre-creating stop, the latter on account of its clear fluty voice. It can be properly associated with the DOPPELFLÖTE, 8 FT., in any suitable division of the Organ; or, as in the instances given, with the unison stop of its own class.

DOPPELROHRGEDECKT, Ger.—While this term may be accepted as another name for the DOPPELROHRFLÖTE (q. v.), the stops alluded to being similar in general formation while differing somewhat in scale proportion, the term may be properly applied to a stop, of 8 ft. pitch, yielding a fuller tone than either that stop or the DOPPELFLÖTE. To produce this more assertive voice, the scale of the DOPPELROHRGEDECKT is larger than, and not so deep in proportion to width as are the scales of the other stops alluded to. In preference to duplicating the DOPPELFLÖTE, it may, on the leading principle of tonal variety, be desirable to introduce the DOPPEL-ROHRGEDECKT, 8 FT., along with the DOPPELROHRFLÖTE, 4 FT., in a contrasting division of the Organ.

DOPPELSPITZFLÖTE, Ger.—As the name implies, this stop is a variation of the SPITZFLÖTE (q. v.), its pipes having double mouths. It has been made of metal and wood and of 8 ft. and 4 ft. pitch. An example, of the latter pitch and of wood, exists in the Echo of the Grand Organ in the Church of St. Mary Magdalene,

---

* In our remarks on the formation of the DOPPELFLÖTE, we mentioned the use of different hard woods in the construction of its pipes as displaying conscientious care on the part of German organ-builders. Here, again, we have similar evidence of this care, and examples of fine pipe-making. The DOPPELROHRFLÖTES in the Organ in the Catholic Church, at Katcher, are chiefly of oak, pine being used only in the treble of the 8 ft. stop. In the same stops in the Organ in the Cathedral of Breslau all the pipes are made of maple. When will such a commendable practice be followed by the organ-builders of this country?

Breslau. Wood was, in all probability, used on account of the convenience it afforded, in the quadrangular pipes, for the formation of the double mouths. It is also probable that, as in the case of the other double-mouthed wood stops, the pipes of the DOPPELSPITZ-FLÖTE were made of greater depth than width; a treatment which could not be applied to metal pipes. We are of opinion that very beautiful and valuable voices could be added to the Organ by stops of 16 ft. and 8 ft. pitch, of wood, of medium scale, and constructed in the pyramidal form of the DOPPELSPITZFLÖTE. But we are afraid that the time and trouble such stops would entail, beyond what the construction and voicing of ordinary straight and single-mouthed wood stops call for, will effectually prevent organ-builders advocating their introduction.

DOUBLE BASSOON.—The lingual stop of 16 ft. pitch, the tone of which imitates as closely as practicable that of the Double Bassoon of the orchestra, the compass of which extends from BBB♭ to F, and, accordingly, covers the compass of the Pedal Organ, with the exception of the two top notes, to which department of the Organ the stop may be considered to properly belong. See BASSOON and CONTRAFAGOTTO.

DOUBLE CLARINET.—A lingual stop of 16 ft. pitch, the pipes of which are similar in formation to those of the unison CLARINET (q. v.). The stop was, so far as we can learn, first made by Wedlake, organ-builder, of London, in 1863, and inserted in an important Chamber Organ. Artistically voiced, and placed in an expressive division, the DOUBLE CLARINET would prove a valuable voice in the Concert-room Organ, affording a different tonal coloring from that of the DOUBLE BASSOON, 16 FT. It would also be valuable as a Pedal Organ stop, carrying down the manual CLARINETS.

DOUBLE DIAPASON.—The stop formed of large-scaled open cylindrical metal, or quadrangular wood, pipes, voiced to yield pure organ-tone. When introduced in a manual Organ it is of 16 ft. pitch, and when placed in the Pedal Organ it is of 32 ft. pitch. In almost all satisfactory examples of the manual stop the pipes are formed of metal throughout their compass. In all the finest existing examples the pipes are of tin or high-class alloy; their larger pipes being displayed in the cases, forming salient towers or other effective features. A notable exception to this general and desirable rule is to be found in the remarkably fine stop, labeled SUB-PRINCI-PAL, 16 FT., in the Great of the Organ in St. Bartholomew's Church,

Armley, Yorkshire, which is formed of open wood pipes from CC to B, and of metal from c¹ to the top note. Though perfectly successful in this instance, such a method should not be ventured upon by any one less skilled than the master who made and voiced the Armley stop.

The manual DOUBLE DIAPASON, 16 FT., has its pipes formed in all respects similar to those of the manual DIAPASON, 8 FT. (q. v.), while its relative scale should be smaller; its tenor C (8 ft.) pipe being from two to four pipes less in scale than the CC (8 ft.) pipe of the unison stop. The voices of the respective stops should follow the same relative proportions. The tone of the double stop should never dominate that of the foundation unison stop.

The DOUBLE DIAPASON, 32 FT., as introduced in the Pedal Organ, is formed throughout of either metal or wood; but on account of its great cost metal has been comparatively seldom used. In Organs of the first magnitude the stop exists in both materials complete, as in the Concert-room Organs in St. George's Hall, Liverpool, and the Centennial Hall, Sydney, N. S. W. The DOUBLE DIAPASON scale varies greatly in different metal stops: for instance, the CCCC pipe in the Liverpool Organ measures 25 inches in diameter; that in the Organ built by Walcker for the Music Hall, Boston, Mass., in 1863, was 22⅝ inches in diameter; that in the Organ in the Monastery Church, at Weingarten, is about 15½ inches in diameter; and that in the celebrated Haarlem Organ is 15 inches in diameter. In the last named three Organs English tin was used for all the displayed pipes of the stop including those of which the diameters are given. The bottom octave of the stop in the Liverpool Organ is of thick zinc. Several stops having scales ranging between those just quoted are to be found in other important Organs. While it is not possible or desirable to lay down a hard and fast rule for general adoption in the scaling of this exceptional stop, we can strongly recommend the use of the moderate scales favored by the most advanced German and other Continental organ-builders. It is, however, quite safe to say that with proper voicing and a copious winding there can be no necessity to exceed the scale of the SUB-PRINCIPAL, 32 FT., of the Haarlem Organ.

The Pedal Organ DOUBLE DIAPASON, 32 FT., formed of wood throughout is the prevailing form, and when properly scaled and voiced is all that can be desired in so grave a stop. It must be borne in mind that its office is not to disturb the unison fundamental tone of the Pedal Organ, but to enrich it by harmonic creation. As in the case of the metal stop, inordinate scales have been adopted with

no appreciable advantage. One extreme example may be given: the
DOUBLE DIAPASON, 32 FT., in the Organ in the Wanamaker Store in
Philadelphia, Pa., has its CCCC pipe measuring internally 22¾
inches in width by 27¾ inches in depth.* The Scales adopted by
two of the most celebrated German builders may be safely accepted
as the most desirable maximum and minimum ones for general use.
The fine stop in the Organ, by Schulze, in St. Bartholomew's, Armley, measures 14¼ inches in width by 18¼ inches in depth. This
scale is larger than that adopted by the same builder for his DOUBLE
PRINCIPALS in the Organs in Bremen Cathedral and St. Mary's
Church, Wismar, which measure 12 inches in width by 15 inches in
depth. The equally distinguished builder Ladegast used a still

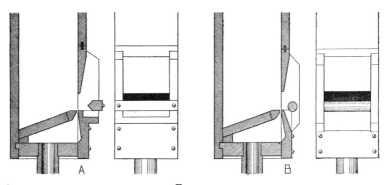

FIG. 14

smaller scale—11⅛ inches in width by 14⅛ inches in depth—for the
32 ft. stop in his Organ in the Cathedral of Schwerin. We can speak
from experience of the satisfactory character of a stop of a similar
small scale in an Organ constructed to our Specification. As it is of
more importance in so large and grave a stop that it should speak
promptly and distinctly than that its exact timbre should be considered, steps were taken by the German builders to secure this desirable result by the most effective means at their disposal, leading
to the application of the harmonic-bridge. Different forms of the
bridge were employed, which, by creating harmonic upper partial
tones, added greatly to the clearness of speech and tonal value of
the stop. The unique method in which the bridge was applied by
Schulze, is shown at A in Fig. 14, which is a Section through the

* This monster pipe called for in its construction over one thousand square feet of 3 inch
sugar pine. It weighs 1,735 lbs.

mouth of the largest pipe of the DOUBLE PRINCIPAL, 32 FT., in his Armley Organ. In Section B is shown the usual form and manner of applying the harmonic-bridge. The bridge imparts not only prompter speech to the pipes but a string quality to their tones. This must have been sufficiently marked in the stop in the Schwerin Organ to decide Ladegast to label it VIOLON, 32 FT.

In German Organs the DOUBLE DIAPASONS bear the more appropriate names PRINZIPAL, 16 FT., PRINZIPALBASS, 16 FT. In the Pedal Organ they appear under the names PRINZIPALBASS, 32 FT., GROSS-PRINZIPAL, 32 FT., and GROSSPRINZIPALBASS, 32 FT. In French Organs the stops appear as: MONTRE, 16 FT. (when mounted in the case), PRINCIPAL BASSE, 16 FT. and 32 FT., CONTREBASSE, 16 FT., FLÛTE OUVERTE, 16 FT. and 32 FT., and simply FLÛTE, 32 FT. In Italian Organs the stops are commonly named PRINCIPALE BASSO, 16 FT. and 32 FT. In Spanish Organs the usual name is FLAUTADO.

DOUBLE DULCIANA—The name properly employed to designate a manual stop of 16 ft. pitch, formed in all respects similar to the unison DULCIANA. When correctly made and artistically voiced by a master-hand it yields a pure organ-tone of extreme beauty and refinement. It is greatly to be regretted that voices of this class are so much neglected by organ-builders and so little desired by organists; but these facts may be accounted for by the modern and present craze for loud tones and high wind-pressures. Purity, refinement, and delicacy of intonation seem to be at a discount in the organ-building of to-day. The DOUBLE DULCIANA forms a perfect Double for the Choir Organ, especially should it be in an uninclosed division; and it is the most beautiful open stop of 16 ft. for the Chamber Organ. On account of its small scale, it furnishes desirable display pipes, while its soft and beautiful tone favors such an exposed disposition. When inserted in the Pedal Organ, it is correctly labeled DULCIANA, 16 FT., being simply a unison stop in that department. In the Pedal Organ, a DOUBLE DULCIANA would be a small-scaled open metal stop of 32 ft. A DOUBLE DULCIANA, 16 FT., exists in the Swell of the Organ in St. Mark's Church, St. John's Wood, London. For further particulars see CONTRA-DUL-CIANA and DULCIANA.

DOUBLE MELODIA—An open wood stop, of medium scale and of 16 ft. pitch, belonging to the manual department of the Organ. On account of the great length of the pipes in its lower octave, and especially when height is limited for its accommodation, the stop is usually formed of open pipes from tenor C (8 ft.) to the top note; the bass octave being in LIEBLICHGEDECKT or some suitable form of covered pipes, of soft tone, voiced to carry down as closely as possible that of the open pipes. The open pipes, like those of the unison MELODIA, have inverted mouths. A fine example of the DOUBLE MELODIA, 16 FT., exists in the Great (tower section) of the Organ in the Cathedral of the Incarnation, Garden City, Long Island, N. Y. See MELODIA.

DOUBLE TROMBONE.—The Pedal Organ lingual stop of 32 ft. pitch, similar in all respects to the CONTRA-TROMBONE, 32 FT. (*q. v.*).

DOUBLE TRUMPET.—The manual lingual stop of 16 ft. pitch, formed of metal pipes of the same construction, and voiced in the same manner, as the pipes of the unison TRUMPET, 8 FT., of which stop it is the true Sub-octave. It is the most appropriate and generally useful lingual stop of 16 ft. pitch for the Great Organ; forming with the TRUMPET, 8 FT., and CLARION, 4 FT., the complete family of the Trumpet-toned stops. To be of full value in combination, the voice of the DOUBLE TRUMPET must be markedly subordinate to that of the unison stop, so that it can be freely used without destroying the dominance of the unison tone of the TRUMPET. This subordination also renders the DOUBLE TRUMPET extremely valuable in general registration with the foundation stops of the Great Organ, and especially so if it is inclosed so as to be flexible and expressive. It may be accepted as an axiom that in proper organ-building and tonal appointment every lingual stop must be endowed with powers of flexibility and expression. Without such powers, lingual stops are practically valueless in solos and in refined and artistic registration. For particulars of formation, see TRUMPET.

DOUBLETTE, Fr.—In French Organs the DOUBLETTE is an open cylindrical metal stop of 2 ft. pitch, belonging to the harmonic-corroborating series of the manual foundation-work, properly yielding pure organ-tone.* The term is used by German and English

---

* The following particulars, from the pen of a distinguished French authority on the Organ will be read with interest and profit by the Organist:

"La DOUBLETTE, ou simplement le *deux-pieds*, car c'est le ton de son plus grand tuyau, est par cette raison même la *double octave* du huit-pieds pris pour base générale du ton d'orgue, puisque le huit-pieds, avons-nous dit, est à l'unisson de la voix commune de l'homme. La doublette est donc l'octave du prestant, ouverte comme lui, de taille médiocre comme lui, et comme lui d'étain fin. Cependant, la finesse de l'étain est généralement négligée, parce que l'exiguité de diamètre et de hauteur compense, ou est censée compenser le tranchant que donne la finesse du métal.

"Elle embrasse toute l'étendue du clavier, parce que son harmonie sert de liaison entre les jeux de mutation et les fonds, et donne aux jeux d'anches mélangés de jeux de fond un degré

organ-builders to designate a stop composed of two ranks of open metal pipes of different pitches. In the Organ in the Cathedral of Merseburg, a DOUBLETTE of 4 ft. and 2 ft. ranks is inserted in the Hauptwerk: and in the same Division of the Organ in the Reformirten Kirche, Elberfeld, there is one of 2⅔ ft. and 2 ft. The DOUBLETTE is not a common stop in English Organs, but examples, of 2 ft. and 1 ft. ranks, exist in the Great and Swell of the Organ in St. George's Hall, Liverpool. We are strongly in favor of DOUBLETTES being made timbre-creating by their ranks being formed of pipes of contrasting tonalities: they would then belong to the tonal appointment of the entire Organ, not specially to its foundation-work.

DRUMS.—Ital., TIMPANI.   Ger., PAUKEN.—Drums were introduced in many old Organs, and were, in some cases, mounted on the case and mechanically beaten by figures of angels. After having long been classed among the curiosities of the organ-builders' art, Drums are again being introduced in Theater Organs and in a certain type of Concert-room Organ. To what extent such accessories are desirable may be left to individual opinion: we would rather see them remain as obsolete curiosities.

DUIFLÖTE, Ger.—The old and practically obsolete name for the double-mouthed, covered wood stop now known as the DOPPEL-FLÖTE (q. v.).

DULCET.—An open metal labial stop of 4 ft. pitch. In its proper and most desirable form it is a DULCIANA OCTAVE, and has been sometimes called DULCIANA PRINCIPAL in English organ nomenclature. The pipes are of small scale, and formed and voiced in all respects similar to those of the unison DULCIANA, 8 FT. Its scale may properly vary according to the tonal apportionment of the division of the Organ in which it is placed: but when associated with the DULCIANA in any manual division its scale should be two or three pipes less, accordingly, the CC pipe of the DULCET, 4 FT.,

d'acuité particulière, Cependant, quoique placée aux claviers de grand orgue et de positif, elle ne se trouve guère sur celui de *récit*, où ne figurent que des jeux de solo, ni sur le clavier connu à Paris surtout) sous le nom de *clavier de bombardes*. La doublette ne s'emploie guère seule que par exemple, pour imiter l'effet d'un sifflet adouci. Unie à la quarte de Nazard, qui est son unisson, elle siffle avec une grande vigueur. Mélangée aux fonds de quatre-pieds, elle y produit l'effet semblable; mais sitôt qu'on la mêle aux huit-pieds, surtout sans y joindre comme transition le quatre-pieds, elle crie, siffle ou gémit désagréablement et fait perdre toute noblesse aux régistres de fonds. Cependant, j'ai ouï souvent la doublette, accouplée à un seul bourdon de seize, produire sous des doigts habiles et dans certains passages un effet singulier, que je n'oserais dire agréable, de peur de donner aux organistes mediocres l'idée de l'essayer; l'effet ne serait pas le même."—Regnier.

would be of the same diameter as the D or D♯ pipe of the unison DULCIANA. The most desirable material for the stop is tin, and next to that Hoyt's Two-ply Pipe Metal, which lend themselves to the delicate manipulation necessary for the production of the light and singing "silvery tone," characteristic of the stop. The DULCET, 4 FT., was introduced by Samuel Green (probably between 1780 and 1790), when soft and refined organ-tones were appreciated by music lovers, and was used by him, in association with the DULCIANA, in certain of his Swell Organs under the name DULCIANA PRINCIPAL.

Octave and Super-octave stops of the DULCET class are practically unknown in modern Organs; the prevailing craze for high wind-pressures and the crude taste (or want of taste) for musical noise, having swept away such beautiful and winning voices. Organists have to learn what tonal wonders lie in refined registration into which such voices enter with tonal effects absolutely unknown to them on the noisy Organs of to-day.

DULCIAN, DOLCIAN, Ger.—The name given to a lingual stop yielding a soft tone, resembling that of the BASSOON, and of 8 ft. and 16 ft. pitch. It is formed with striking- and free-reeds, and with slender inverted conical and pyramidal resonators of metal and wood. Examples are found, in either of the pitches, in different divisions of the Organ. The DULCIAN, 8 FT., exists in the Echo of the celebrated Haarlem Organ; and in the Pedal of the Organ in the Evangelical Church, Münster. The DULCIAN, 16 FT., is introduced in the Oberwerk of the Organ in the Cathedral of Königsberg; in the Fernwerk (Third Clavier) of the Organ in St. Petri-Kirche, Berlin; in the Rückpositiv of the Organ in St. Catherine's Church, Hamburg; as a free-reed stop, in the Pedal of the Organ in the Cathedral of Merseburg; and in the Piano Pedal of the Organ in the Cathedral of Schwerin, where it is a free-reed furnished with resonators of wood.

DULCIANA.—A stop formed of open labial pipes of cylindrical form and small scale, of 8 ft. pitch in the manual Organs and 16 ft. pitch in the Pedal Organ. The stop appears to have been introduced for the first time by John Snetzler in the Organ he built in 1754, under the direction of the distinguished Dr. Burney, for the Church of St. Margaret, Lynn Regis, Norfolk. Ever since then the DULCIANA has been a great favorite with English organ-builders, and numerous beautiful examples exist in English Organs. We have not been able to find the DULCIANA, 8 FT., in its true form in any French Organ; and neither it, nor any equivalent under another name, is mentioned by Regnier. We find a DOLCIANE, 8 FT., in the

Récit of the Chamber Organ built for the late Alexandre Guilmant by Mutin, of Paris: this was in all probability suggested by the English stop, with which M. Guilmant was familiar. On the other hand, however, we find an octave stop, labeled DULCIANA, 4 FT., in several important Organs; for instance, in the Récit of the Organ in the Church of Saint-Sulpice, and in the Bombarde of the Organ in the Church of Saint-Eustache, Paris. We have not been able to find any trace of the DULCIANA in connection with old German Organs; but it appears, invariably on the First Clavier (Hauptwerk), in several of Walcker's large Organs, as in those in the Cathedral of Riga, and St. Petrikirche, Lübeck.

FORMATION AND SCALE—The pipes of the DULCIANA are cylindrical and formed similar to those of the DIAPASON, 8 FT., of which it is, strictly considered, the proper diminutive. Its scale being small and its voice having to be extremely clear and perfectly uniform in tone, the pipes must be carefully made of tin or high-class metal. The scale of the true DULCIANA, 8 FT., varies slightly, according to the class of Organ for which it is designed, the position it is to occupy in the Organ, and the acoustical conditions under which it has to be heard. In so delicate and sensitive a stop as the true English DULCIANA every condition should be carefully considered affecting its scaling and voicing. The following scales, in two desirable ratios, will be found, with careful formation and artistic voicing of the pipes, to produce satisfactory results under favorable conditions:

DULCIANA PIPE DIAMETERS IN INCHES, RATIO 1:2.519.

PIPES	CC	C	c^1	c^2	c^3	c^4
I.	3.25	2.05	1.29	0.81	0.51	0.32
II.	3.38	2.13	1.34	0.84	0.53	0.33

DULCIANA PIPE DIAMETERS IN INCHES, RATIO 1:2.66.

PIPES	CC	C	c^1	c^2	c^3	c^4
I.	3.34	2.05	1.25	0.77	0.47	0.29
II.	3.48	2.13	1.31	0.80	0.49	0.30

The smaller scales to the ratio 1:2.519 give a comparatively full treble; while those to the quicker ratio 1:2.66 keep the lower octaves comparatively full toned. The selection made by the tonal artist will, or should, depend on the special stop-appointment of the division of the Organ in which the DULCIANA is to be placed. In the tradesman organ-building of to-day, and the general don't-careism on the part of organists, such considerations of tonal propriety and refinement are either not realized or are ignored. When will the organist arise who will gloat over the beauties of his glorious instrument, as the violinist gloats over the wonders of his Stradivarius? The width of the mouth of the DULCIANA pipe should not exceed one-fifth the internal circumference, while, except in a stop intended for a true Chamber Organ, it should rarely be less. The height of the mouth may vary from one-fifth to one-third its width, according to the method of the voicer, the wind-pressure employed, and the character of the tone desired. The mouths of all the pipes, except, perhaps, those of the top octave, should be furnished with ears of slight projection, aiding clean articulation. On no account are the pipes to be slotted for tuning if the true tone of the DULCIANA is desired. The larger pipes should be furnished with tuning-slides, as recommended for the DIAPASON. This expedient will prevent the pipes being injured by repeated tuning with the cones; and will secure uniformity in their voices, their open tops remaining at all times of the correct internal diameters. Such matters as these should be attended to by the organ expert in his Specifications.

TONE AND REGISTRATION.—The true English DULCIANA has a pure organ-tone of a sweet singing, silvery, quality—a tone seldom heard in Organs built during late years. To ears vitiated by constant association with powerful and more or less coarse musical sounds—the product of inordinate wind-pressures—such refined tones as those of the DULCIANA, in their purity, seem poor and insipid; accordingly, voicers proceed to *improve* the stop by what they call *giving it color;* removing it from its proper and time-honored place in the tonal appointment of the Organ, and throwing it among the SALICIONALS and quasi string-toned stops. The DULCIANA is either a DULCIANA or it is not one; and every voicer should be requested to remember that important fact, and, at the same time, asked to improve his overblown labial and lingual stops, leaving the DULCIANA queen of the soft organ-toned *cantabile* group.

The place for the DULCIANA, 8 FT., is in the Choir or chief accompanimental division of the Church Organ; certainly not in the Great (or Hauptwerk) where Walcker has invariably placed it. In the Concert-room Organ its proper position is in the softest-toned division, whatever it may be. In such approved situations it will prove most valuable in registration, furnishing a foundation or background for numerous combinations of tone-colors. Its reposeful and *cantabile* voice renders it of great use in quiet solo effects; and in giving body to combinations of special tones without in any marked manner affecting their normal character. In registration with soft-toned open, covered, and half-covered FLUTES, 8 ft. and 4 ft. pitch; with delicately voiced string-toned stops; with the more refined lingual stops; and with its Octave, the CŒLESTINA, 4 FT., and such a compound stop as DULCIANA CORNET, or, better still, the HARMONIA-ÆTHERIA, the DULCIANA contributes to the production of numerous compound tones of great beauty, refinement, and charm. Let not the true DULCIANA disappear from the Organ.

DULCIANA CORNET.—The compound harmonic-corroborating stop, commonly formed of five ranks of high-pitched DULCIANA pipes; yielding delicate silvery tones, representing the higher upper partials of the prime unison, suitable for combination with the softer labial and lingual voices of the Organ, and, accordingly, entering into countless tonal combinations into which the ordinary full-toned MIXTURES could not possibly be introduced. The stop has been formed of octave- and fifth-sounding ranks, and also of octave-, third-, and fifth-sounding ranks, in all cases, owing to their high pitch, requiring several breaks in their compass. The following is the composition of an example of proved excellence under all tests in combination and artistic registration:

DULCIANA CORNET—V. RANKS.

CC to BB	19——22——24——26——29.
C to B	12——15——17——19——22.
c^1 to b^1	8——12——17——19——22.
c^2 to c^4	1—— 8——10——12——15.

This stop carefully regulated and graduated in tone in strict accordance with the natural laws of compound musical sounds, becomes one of the most useful agents in the building up of expressive tonal structures of a refined and fascinating character. It is so sympathetic that it can be used with a single DULCIANA or any soft unison stop in the Organ. The DULCIANA CORNET or some equivalent, should be introduced in every Organ of any importance; and it should be the only compound stop in the true Chamber Organ.

DULCIANA PRINCIPAL.—The term employed by Samuel Green, organ-builder to King George the Third (1780–1796), to designate, according to the English nomenclature, a stop of 4 ft. pitch and of the DULCIANA class: what would now be more correctly called DULCIANA OCTAVE. It has been said: "The organs built by Green are characterized by a peculiar sweetness and delicacy of tone, entirely original; and, probably, in this respect he has never been excelled." It is to be hoped that the mantle of Green will some day fall on the shoulders of one of the aspiring organ-builders of the twentieth century.

DULCIMER.—The name given by Thomas Schwarbrook to a stop, composed of metal strings, inserted in the Organ erected by him, in 1733, in the Church of St. Michael, Coventry. It was, in all probability, sounded by a hammer action, as the real Dulcimer was played. Respecting this notable Organ, Dr. Rimbault remarks: "This noble instrument (Schwarbrook's masterpiece) cost £1400. It originally contained three remarkable stops—the HARP, LUTE, and DULCIMER; but, in consequence of the 'difficulty of keeping the *strings* in tune,' they were removed in 1763."

DUOPHONE.—The name given by G. W. Till, of Philadelphia, to an open labial stop, of 8 ft. pitch, recently invented by him; the pipes of which are of wood, having inclined sides, and mouths furnished with metal upper lips and cylindrical harmonic-bridges.* The tone of the stop is dual, the prime tone and its first upper partial being produced in almost equal volume, and is remarkable on account of its penetrating and traveling quality without undesirable loudness.

E

ECHO BOURDON.—A BOURDON, 16 FT., of small scale and soft intonation, the pipes of which are of wood, preferably of oak or maple, finished as thin as conditions will permit, and otherwise constructed like the ordinary BOURDON. This stop differs from the LIEBLICHGEDECKT in its tone, chiefly on account of the different proportions and treatment of the mouths of its pipes, and, accordingly, in a special style of voicing. The best tone is obtained on wind of low pressure, between $1\frac{1}{2}$ and $2\frac{1}{2}$ inches. The stop may be considered the English equivalent of the German BOURDONECHO, and is an ideal stop for the true Chamber Organ.

ECHO DIAPASON.—The appropriate name for a pure organ-toned unison stop, the scale of which is midway between that of the full-toned DIAPASON, 8 FT., and that of the true DULCIANA, and the voice of which is also a medium one. Such a medium stop is extremely valuable in certain divisional tonal apportionments, furnishing foundation organ-tone commensurate with the requirements of the divisions.

The pipes of the ECHO DIAPASON are formed precisely as those of the foundation DIAPASON; their only difference lying in the subdued character of their tones largely due to their being voiced on wind of low pressure—not exceeding $2\frac{1}{2}$ inches, but preferably less. The following scale is suitable for the stop:

ECHO DIAPASON PIPE DIAMETERS IN INCHES, RATIO 1:2.66.

PIPES	CC	C	c^1	c^2	c^3	c^4
	4.82	2.95	1.81	1.11	0.68	0.42

The mouth, in width, should not exceed two-ninths of the inter-

---

* For full particulars and drawings of this stop, See " The Organ of the Twentieth Century." Pages 109, 451-2.

nal circumference of the pipe, and should be cut up only sufficient to produce the pure organ-tone required. The upper lip must not be leathered; and the pipes must not be slotted for tuning.

TONE AND REGISTRATION.—Like all unison stops yielding pure organ-tone, the ECHO DIAPASON furnishes a foundation or background for fine effects of tonal coloring, to which it gives richness and neutral body. The delicate tone of this stop is extremely receptive and lends itself to the most refined *nuances* and effects of tonal light and shade. It combines perfectly with all the softer tonal colors that can be thrown upon it by the contrasting voices of labial and lingual stops; in this direction resembling the still softer and equally pure-voiced DULCIANA (*q. v.*).

ECHO DULCIANA.—A small-scaled, open, metal stop, of 8 ft. pitch, the pipes of which are formed similar in all respects to those of the English DULCIANA, of which stop it is the proper diminutive in scale and tone. It may be said to occupy an intermediate position between the DULCIANA and the VOX ANGELICA, 8 FT., when these stops are properly related. It should have a pure organ-tone of a *cantabile* character, rendering it peculiarly suitable for the softest division of the true Chamber Organ. The following scale may be accepted as suitable for the stop, relative to the scales given for the DULCIANA (*q. v.*), ratio 1 : 2.66:

ECHO DULCIANA PIPE DIAMETERS IN INCHES, RATIO 1 : 2.66.

PIPES	CC	C	c^1	c^2	c^3	c^4
	2.84	1.74	1.06	0.65	0.40	0.24

The width of the mouth should not exceed one-fifth the internal circumference of the pipe; while its height may vary from one-fifth to one-third its width, according to the wind-pressure employed, the volume of the tone desired, and the special method of voicing followed.

REGISTRATION.—As the ECHO DULCIANA yields a tone which is properly a diminutive of that of the DULCIANA, its offices in registration are practically similar with regard to the stops of soft tonality suitable for combination, and, accordingly, reference may be made to the remarks under DULCIANA. As a single echo voice this stop is the most desirable in the Organ. It completes the family, which stands thus: DULCIANA, 8 FT.; ECHO DULCIANA, 8 FT.; DULCET, 4 FT.; and DULCIANA CORNET, V. RANKS.

ECHOFLÖTE, Ger.—The name that has been used to designate an extremely soft flute-toned stop of 8 ft. or 4 ft. pitch, commonly

of wood and covered or half-covered, made still softer by inclosure
in a box. Sometimes the stop has been simply labeled ECHO; and
Locher remarks: "When this word alone appears on a draw-stop
knob, it indicates an exceedingly soft, flute-like stop, which is often
placed in a swell-box, separate from the main body of the Organ."
On the same single term, Seidel says: "A simple Echo consists of a
single flute-toned register of soft intonation which stands behind the
Organ, and receives its wind through long conveyances. A compound Echo consists of several stops, standing behind the Organ in a
separate box, the inside of which is lined with felt or cloth, so that
if this Echo-work is played upon, the tones will seem to come from
without the church. The Echo often contains also a MIXTURE, for
instance a CORNETT, which is then called the ECHO-CORNETT."

ECHO GAMBA.—The name found in certain English Organs,
designating a stop of the GAMBA class yielding a soft and somewhat
cold string-tone. An example, of 8 ft. pitch, exists in the Swell of
the Organ in York Minster. It is usually made of small-scaled metal
pipes from tenor C, the bass octave being added, very inappro-
priately, in covered wood pipes, as in the Organs in St. Saviour's
Church, Eastbourne, and All Saints' Church, Wokingham. In its
original tonality the stop is of little interest or value.

ECHO OBOE.—The name given by Edmund Schulze, organ-
builder, of Paulinzelle, to an open wood labial stop, of 8 ft. pitch,
invented by him, the pipes of which are of small scale and about
twice their width in depth. The mouth is furnished with a small,
sharp-edged harmonic-bridge, which rests on a sunk and sloped
cap; the edge of the cap at the wind-way is thin; and the upper lip
is cut sharp.* The voice of the stop is a peculiar compound of reed-
tone and string-tone, and is singularly delicate and pleasing, though
not highly suggestive of that of the Oboe of the orchestra. A beautiful example, made by Schulze, exists in the Echo of the Organ in
St. Bartholomew's Church, Armley, Yorkshire: it is of tenor C
compass, being grooved into the bass of the VOX ANGELICA, 8 FT.
Another fine example, by Abbott & Smith, of Leeds, exists in the
Echo of the Organ in the Parish Church of Leeds. Both these remarkable stops speak on wind of 1½ inches pressure.

ENGELSTIMME, Ger.—The name originally given to a lingual
stop of the VOX HUMANA class; and subsequently to a stop also

* A full description and drawings of the ECHO OBOE are given in our work, "The Art of Organ-
Building," Vol. II., pp. 481–482.

called Vox Angelica (*q. v.*). Of the stop Seidel remarks: "Angelica (vox), die Engelstimme, ein angenehmes, aber jetzt veraltetes Rohrwerk zu 8'. Es geht nur durch die oberen Oktaven vom eingestr. c̄ an. Dieses Register scheint eine frühere Art der Vox Humana zu sein."

ENGLISH HORN.—Ger., Englisch Horn. Fr., Cor Anglais. Ital., Corno Inglese.—This stop derives its name from the orchestral instrument, which is a reed of the Oboe family, having a compass extending from tenor E two octaves and a fifth. Accordingly, the stop need not be carried below tenor C; but, as incomplete stops are undesirable in a properly appointed Organ, it is proper to insert it, as a stop of 8 ft. pitch, of the full compass. For further particulars see Cor Anglais.

ENGPRINZIPAL, Ger. (from *eng*—narrow).—The name which has been sometimes used by the old German organ-builders to designate a Principal, 8 ft., of small scale and soft intonation, so as to distinguish it from the foundation Principal of full scale and tone.

ERZÄHLER, Ger.—The name given by Ernest M. Skinner, organ-builder, of Boston, to an open metal labial stop, of 8 ft. pitch, introduced by him in 1904. The Erzähler pipe is similar to that of the Gemshorn in being conical in form; but differing from it in having the diameter of its top opening only one-fourth of the diameter at its mouth line, in being slotted near the top, and having a mouth width equal only to one-fifth of the larger circumference of the body.

The tone of the stop is compound and singularly bright; this is due to the octave being distinctly produced in combination with the unison or prime tone. In addition to this there is a peculiarity in the tone which suggested the somewhat fanciful name to the introducer of the stop. Examples exist in several Skinner Organs.

EUPHONE, EUPHONIUM.—Fr., Euphône. Ger., Euphon. —The name derived from the Greek word εὔφωνος, and properly given to a lingual stop, the tone of which is intended to imitate that of the brass instrument of the same name, a member of the Saxhorn family, the compass of which is a little over three octaves from CC. The stop is, accordingly and properly, of 8 ft. pitch, extending, in keeping with the Euphonium, over the richest portion of the manual compass of the Organ, but necessarily carried through the higher two octaves. Fine stops of the same tonality and 16 ft. pitch have been made, and these are, perhaps, the more valuable. A Euphon, 8 ft., exists on the First Manual of the Organ in the Cathedral of Riga: and representative examples of the stop of 16 ft. pitch exist in the Roosevelt Organs in the Cathedral of Garden City, L. I., and the Auditorium, at Chicago. All are free-reed stops.

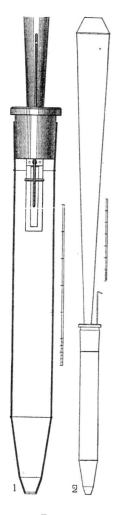

FIG. 15

FORMATION.—The EUPHONE as made by German and French organ-builders are invariably free-reed stops, and their tones are smooth and pleasing. Different forms of resonators have been devised for the purpose of producing the desired tone, some of very peculiar form, but those most approved are either of the plain inverted conical form, shorter and of smaller scale than those used for the TRUMPET, as adopted by Roosevelt; or of the same form surmounted by some contracting or shading device, preferably a short truncated cone, as shown at the top of the resonator in the drawing of the complete pipe, 2, Fig. 15. In other, and less effective, examples the inverted conical resonators are closed at top and slottèd for the emission of wind and sound. The drawings in Fig. 15 are accurately made to scale from a C (4 ft. pitch) pipe constructed by the well-known German organ-pipe maker, August Luakhuff. All free-reed pipes require for their prompt and satisfactory speech large boots; and this is shown in the Section 1, which also shows the free-reed, the block in which it is inserted, and the tuning-wire. The length of the boot is 13¾ inches, while the entire length of the resonator is only 25¾ inches. The largest diameter of the resonator is 2⅞ inches, and that of the opening at top 1½ inches. The length of the tongue is 2.25 inches and its width 0.27 inch.

TONE AND REGISTRATION.—The tones produced by the several stops, of different formation, that have been named EUPHONE have varied greatly. It appears that in the first and earlier forms no attempt was made to imitate the voice of any particular wind instrument. The first stop to which the name appears to have been given was that inserted in the Organ of the Cathedral of Beauvais, in 1829. During the following year, Sebastian Erard inserted a EUPHÔNE, as an expressive free-reed, in the Organ of the Royal Chapel of the Tuileries, Paris. Regarding the tones of these stops nothing is clearly known, but, judging from the peculiar forms of their resonators, which were short, covered, and slotted, their tones must have been somewhat muffled and probably inclining toward the Bassoon quality. The tones of the later examples, such as those made by Roosevelt, Luakhuff, Zimmermann of Paris, and others, are open, smooth, and full; but not strongly resembling those of the Euphonium.*

A soft, full tone, imitative of that of the Euphonium played by a master, is greatly to be desired in the Organ; but, like that of the orchestral Horn, it seems almost impossible to obtain it from lingual pipes. It might, however, be produced by a dual stop, formed by the artistic combination of a labial and a lingual rank of pipes. Such a stop would be very valuable in impressive solos; just as the Euphonium is *par excellence* a solo instrument: and one can easily realize that it would also be extremely valuable in refined registration, especially in its proper 8 ft. pitch. In its 16 ft. pitch it would be an important addition to the expressive forces of the Pedal Organ.

F

FAGOTTO, Ital.—A lingual stop, of small scale, and 8 ft. pitch, voiced to yield a tone imitative of that of the orchestral instrument of the same name. See BASSOON.

FAGOTTONE, Ital.—This term, which has the Italian augmentative ending, has been used to designate a lingual stop of the FAGOTTO family, properly of 32 ft. pitch, and of a full and impressive voice. It is a Pedal Organ stop, and practically carries down the voice of the CONTRAFAGOTTO, 16 FT., an octave lower. It has, however, no equivalent in the orchestra. An example exists in the Organ of the Church of San Alessandro, Milan. The name has also been given to stops of 16 ft. pitch, the scales of which are larger and the voices fuller than those of the imitative CONTRAFAGOTTO. An example exists in the Swell of the principal Organ in the Cathedral of Como.

FELDFLÖTE, FELDPFEIFE, FELDPIPE, Ger.—Lat., FISTULA MILITARIS.—An open labial stop, of a penetrating flute- or fife-tone, hence its names. It has been made by German organbuilders, according to Schneider (Organist of the Cathedral of Merseburg, 1835), of metal and wood, and of 4 ft., 2 ft., and 1 ft.

* The beautiful stop made by Roosevelt for our Chamber Organ, and named by him EUPHONE, had a voice which seemed to incline so much, in its higher compass, to the tone of the Bass Saxophone that we labeled it CONTRA-SAXOPHONE, 16 FT.

pitch. Owing to its very assertive voice, the stop seems never to have been a favorite, and it does not appear in modern German Organs. Organs of every class are better without high-pitched screaming voices; and one can understand the disappearance of the FELDFLÖTES of 2 ft. and 1 ft. pitch.

FERNFLÖTE, Ger.—Literally *Distant* or *Echo Flute.* Properly applied, this name indicates a small-scaled labial stop of 8 ft. and 4 ft. pitch, yielding the softest flute-tone produced by organ-pipes; but the name has been applied to softly-voiced stops of different classes, and both of wood and metal, open and covered. In the Organ in the Church of St. Mary, Tyne Dock, constructed by Edmund Schulze, the FERNFLÖTE, 8 FT., is in the form of an extremely soft SPITZFLÖTE.

FERNHORN, Ger.—Literally *Distant* or *Echo Horn.* The name that has been given to a half-covered labial stop of metal and of 8 ft. pitch. It is practically an ECHO NACHTHORN. The stop would be suitable for the true Chamber Organ, and for a soft ancillary division of a properly appointed Concert-room Organ. It should be voiced on wind of a pressure not exceeding $2\frac{1}{2}$ inches.

FIFE.—Fr., FIFRE. Ger., PFEIFE.—An open metal labial stop of 2 ft. or 1 ft. pitch, yielding a shrill flute-tone, resembling that of the military Fife, the compass of which extends about two octaves from d². As an organ-stop, the FIFE, 2 FT., differs from the PICCOLO, 2 FT., only in the character and loudness of its voice. The latter stop is much to be preferred; accordingly the FIFE is seldom met with. An example of the FIFRE, 1 FT., as made by the French builders, and of comparatively soft tonality, exists in the Postif of the Organ in the Cathedral of Abbeville. It is not a desirable stop for the Organ of to-day.

FIFFARO, Ger.—The name sometimes given by the old German organ-builders to a stop, the voice of which imitated that of the orchestral Flute. Schneider thus briefly describes it: "FIFFARO, QUEERPFEIFE, eine kleine Stimme von 4 oder 2 Fuss." See QUER-FLÖTE.

FIFTEENTH, SUPER-OCTAVE.—The names used to designate open, metal labial stops, yielding pure organ-tone, and sounding two octaves above the unisons. Accordingly, in the manual divisions the FIFTEENTH is of 2 ft. pitch, and in the Pedal Organ of 4 ft. pitch. The stop belongs to the foundation-work of the Organ, representing the third upper partial tone of the prime unison of the department in which it is placed. Its scale is, accordingly and properly, calculated from that of the foundation DIAPASON or PRINCIPAL, 8 ft. or 16 ft., being usually made two or three pipes less in diameter; the voicer taking care of the necessary reduction in the strength of tone. The old English organ-builders, including Bernard Smith, of Temple Church fame (1684), and John Harris, made their FIFTEENTHS only one pipe less in scale than the corresponding pipes of their DIAPASONS, simply voicing them softer than the intermediate OCTAVES, 4 FT. In modern Organs, as a rule, the FIFTEENTH, 2 FT., is made of too large a scale, and voiced much too assertive in tone; builders, desiring to get as much sound as possible out of the pipes, overlooking the scientific side of the matter, and the fact that the true office of the stop is primarily a harmonic-corroborating one, and that it should be treated as such in the tonal appointment of the Organ. In proportionate strength, the tone of the FIFTEENTH should be about 50% that yielded by the fundamental DIAPASON, and be clear and singing in quality.

TONE AND REGISTRATION.—The tone of the FIFTEENTH, 2 FT., being of the pure organ class, as required by its primal office in the tonal structure of the Organ, proves to be of considerable value in registration, especially so when of the proper relative strength, as recommended above. Its pure organ-tone—practically free from harmonics—blends perfectly with every other tone produced by organ-pipes, labial and lingual; imparting the elements of clearness and brilliancy to the heavier and duller tones of many unison and double stops, without sensibly impairing their characteristic voices. This is surely a valuable property and one to be made much use of in artistic registration. Of course, to be of maximum value, the FIFTEENTH must be voiced to the proper strength of tone, as stated above.

FIFTH, QUINT.—Fr. and Ger., QUINTE. Ital., QUINTA.— The name properly applied to a stop the voice of which is at the interval of a perfect fifth above the unison. In the Pedal Organ the FIFTH is of 10⅔ ft. pitch, and in the manual divisions it is of 5⅓ ft. pitch. These stops, under different qualifications, may be of metal or wood, and open, covered, or half-covered. See QUINT.

FLACHFLÖTE, Ger.—The name given to a labial stop of 8 ft., 4 ft., or 2 ft. pitch, the pipes of which are of metal or wood, and either conical or of the same measurement throughout, according to the fancy of the builder and the quality of the tone desired.

According to Wolfram the stop resembles the GEMSHORN and
SPITZFLÖTE.* Seidel describes its tone as somewhat thin but not
disagreeable.† In his illustration, the FLACHFLÖTE pipe is shown
cylindrical, terminating in a truncated cone having a small opening
at top, closely resembling the SPINDEFLÖTE pipe. The mouth is
shown very narrow; but as the illustration is badly drawn this detail
cannot be depended on. Although the stop seems to have usually
been made of metal, there is one, of 4 ft. pitch, made of pear-tree
(Birmbaumholz) in the Organ of the Church of St. Boniface, at
Langensalza. It would seem probable, from the name, which means
Flat Flute, that the original FLACHFLÖTE was made of wood, its pipes
being flat in form, with the mouth on a wider side. Under other
conditions the name would seem meaningless; and German organ-
builders generally had some sensible reasons for naming their stops.
It would be well if such a practice obtained here to-day; for some
names, having no relation to form or tone, which have appeared in
certain stop lists of late, if they were not objectionable in their absurdity, would be only laughable.

FLAGEOLET.—Ger., FLAGEOLETT. Ital., FLAGEOLETTA.
Span., FLAUTIM. Lat., FISTULA MINIMA.—A metal labial stop of
2 ft. and 1 ft. pitch, the pipes of which are cylindrical in form and of
a medium scale. The proper tone of the stop is liquid, clear, and
somewhat penetrating, in imitation of the voice of the old English
Flageolet, the instrument for which it is generally understood Handel wrote the *obbligato* in the song, "O ruddier than the cherry"
("Acis and Galatea"). In some English Organs the FLAGEOLET,
2 FT., is a wood stop, of small scale, and a clear fluty voice. The
metal stop appears in several German and Dutch Organs in both
pitches. Of 2 ft. pitch, the FLAGEOLET exists in the Organs of the
Cathedral of Magdeburg, and the State Church, Triebel: and of 1 ft.
pitch in the Organs in the Marienkirche, Lübeck, and the Church of
St. Stephen, Nymengen. In the celebrated Haarlem Organ the stop
appears in the Echo of 1⅓ ft. pitch. A FLAGEOLET, 2 FT., is inserted
in the Swell of the Roosevelt Organ in the Cathedral of the Incarnation, Garden City, L. I.; but it is rarely inserted in modern Organs.

---

*"FLACHFLÖTE, eine offene sehr angenehme Flötenstimme 4 oder 8 Fuss mit kegelförmigen
Körpern. Sie erhält breite Labien mit engem Aufschnitt, und ist übrigens dem GEMSHORN und
der SPITZFLÖTE ähnlich."—Wolfram.

†"FLACHFLÖTE ist eine Labialstimme, deren Pfeifen nach Art des GEMSHORNS spitz zulaufen
Die Pfeifen haben breite Labien, einen weiten Aufschnitt und Seitenbärte, daher ist der Ton der
Stimme nicht voll, sondern flach, übrigens gerade nicht unangenehm. Sie wird zu 8, 4, 2, und 1'
und zwar konisch und cylindrisch zugleich angetroffen, die 8- und 4 füssige heisst zuweilen
GROSSFLACHFLÖTE."—Seidel.

Tone and Registration.—The position of the Flageolet, in the tonal economy of the Organ, is somewhat undecided; but as a stop of 2 ft. pitch, having a pure flute-tone of less power than that of the Orchestral Piccolo, 2 ft., it would unquestionably prove a valuable addition to an Organ, properly occupying a place in a manual division to which the softer-toned accompanimental stops are apportioned. Voiced to imitate as closely as possible the tone of the true Flageolet, it would become the best stop of super-octave pitch for a solo or an accompanimental *obbligato*, just as the Flageolet was employed by Handel in "Acis and Galatea." In registration, it would be found more generally useful than either the Fifteenth or the Orchestral Piccolo; both of which are too assertive in any combinations save those of full tonality.

FLAGEOLET HARMONIQUE, Fr.—An open metal labial stop, yielding a bright tone, closely resembling that of the true Flageolet. Its pipes are cylindrical, of medium scale, and double the standard speaking length; and have the perforation in their bodies, as usual in harmonic pipes. See Flûte Harmonique. A Flageolet Harmonique, 2 ft., appears in the Postif of the Grand Organ in the Royal Church of Saint-Denis, constructed by MM. Cavaillé-Coll, in 1841.

FLAUTADA, Span.—The name applied by Spanish organ-builders to open lingual stops yielding flute- and organ-tone. Thus: Flautada de 13 signifies a Flute or Principal, 8 ft.; Flautada de 26 signifies a Flute or Double Diapason, 16 ft.; and Flautada de 52, the stop belonging to the Pedal Organ, is in all essentials similar to the Double Diapason, 32 ft. Examples are to be found in the Organs of the Cathedrals of Burgos, Seville, and Valladolid, and also in other important Spanish instruments.

FLAUTINO, Ital.—This word, terminating in the Italian diminutive, *ino*, is employed to designate a flute-toned stop of small size. In its best form, it is an open metal stop of 2 ft. pitch, formed of cylindrical pipes of small scale, voiced to yield a flute-tone softer than that of the proper Flageolet, 2 ft. Examples exist in the Organs in the Cathedral of Milan and the Church of San Gætano, Florence. In the Choir of the Organ in the Jesuit's Church, at Cologne, is a Flautino of 4 ft. pitch. In modern Organs the name should be given only to the stop of 2 ft. pitch. The stop has been frequently and incorrectly labeled Flautina.

Registration.—The Flautino, 2 ft., when properly voiced is

a very valuable stop; and being so closely allied to the FLAGEOLET, of the same pitch, in tonality it can be used instead of that stop in artistic registration. In this direction reference may be made to the remarks under FLAGEOLET.

FLAUTO AMABILE, Ital.—The suggestive name given to a small-scaled labial stop, of either 8 ft. or 4 ft. pitch, properly constructed of open wood pipes, yielding an extremely delicate and sweet unimitative flute-tone. In its best form, its pipes are slender, about one and a half times their width in depth, and have inverted mouths. The pipes should be made of clear spruce, fronted with mahogany or white maple so as to allow their mouths being carefully and accurately formed. Examples of the stop exist in the Organs of the German Church, at Montreux, and the Church of Saint-Martin, at Vevey.

Voiced on wind of low pressure, the FLAUTO AMABILE 4 FT., is an ideal stop for the true Chamber Organ; and of either 8 ft. or 4 ft. pitch it is suitable for insertion in the softest division of a Church or Concert-room Organ.

FLAUTO AMOROSO, Ital.—This name has been employed to designate an open metal stop of small scale and 4 ft. pitch, voiced to yield an extremely soft and singing quality of unimitative flute-tone. A fine FLAUTO AMOROSO, 4 FT., exists in the Echo of the important Organ in the Church of SS. Peter and Paul, Liegnitz, in Silesia, built by Buckow, in the year 1839. Stops of this refined class are held in little esteem by organ-builders of to-day in their craze for high-pressures and loud voicing. When will the musical world protest against such crude and inartistic treatment of the Monarch of all Instruments?

FLAUTO D'AMORE, Ital.—Fr., FLÛTE D'AMOUR.—The name given to special stops formed of small-scaled wood pipes, yielding a peculiarly delicate and fascinating flute-tone. The stop is generally of 4 ft. pitch, which is that most desirable in solo passages and registration; but it has been made of 8 ft. pitch. An example, labeled FLÛTE D'AMOUR, 4 FT., exists in the Choir of the small Organ in the Marienkirche, at Goerlitz, built by Buckow, in the year 1838. It is the only stop of 4 ft. pitch in the Choir formed entirely of soft-voiced stops.

FORMATION.—The pipes of the FLAUTO D'AMORE, 4 FT., have been made of different forms and proportions, according to the fancy of the organ-builder, resulting, of necessity, in slight differences in tonality. The most satisfactory

form, in our estimation, is that here briefly described. The pipes partake of the
character of those of the LIEBLICHGEDECKT and the ROHRFLÖTE; being small in
scale and in general formation like those of the former; and having perforated
stoppers like those of the latter stop. The tone of the FLAUTO D'AMORE is, accordingly, a combination of the voices of the two stops just named, but properly softer
than either. The construction of the FLAUTO D'AMORE pipe is clearly shown in
the accompanying illustration, Fig. 16. In the Longitudinal Section, 1, the formation of all portions of the mouth is correctly delineated; and the manner in
which the stopper, A, is formed and perforat-
ed is shown. It will be observed that the
vertical perforation (Fr. *cheminée*) does not
extend through the entire length of the stopper, but opens into the larger transverse
perforation, B. This is an important expedient. As the perforations of the stoppers affect the quality of the tone of the pipes, their
lengths must, of necessity, be graduated regularly throughout the compass of the stop:
and as this graduation of length would be
difficult, and would make the stoppers in
the higher octaves inconveniently short, if
the perforations were carried through them
and dictated their lengths, the expedient
of the transverse perforation was happily
adopted, rendering correct graduation possible without interfering with the convenient
length of the stoppers. The transverse perforations would not be required in the stoppers of the lower pipes, for they could be perforated throughout and made of the proper
graduated lengths. The diameters of the
vertical perforations may vary according to
the scale of the pipes and the quality of the
tone desired: that of the largest pipe need not
exceed 3/8 inch, while that of the smallest pipe
may be 1/8 inch. The Front View, 2, shows

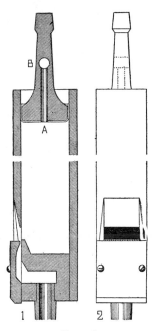

FIG. 16

the desirable proportions of the mouth; but its height may vary according to the
wind-pressure used and the quality of tone desired. For its most characteristic
tones, the FLAUTO D'AMORE should be voiced on wind of from 1½ to 2½ inches.

TONE AND REGISTRATION.—The tone of the FLAUTO D'AMORE,
when correctly made and voiced by a master, is the most beautiful
of those produced by the half-covered stops; occupying a place in
the tonal economy of the Organ that neither the FLÛTE À CHEMINÉE
nor the ROHRFLÖTE can fill. Its extremely delicate and sympathetic
voice fails to recommend it during the present craze for loud and
screaming stops: its appearance will, accordingly, be rare in Organs
in this country—never, probably, voiced on the proper low wind-

pressures.* Its proper place is in the accompanimental division of the Church Organ and in the softest-toned division of the Concert-room Organ, where it will be invaluable, as an octave voice, in refined and artistic registration. It imparts a beautiful tonality, as we have proved, to the Vox Humana, especially for a soprano solo.

FLAUTO DI PAN, Ital.—The name given to an organ-stop, probably on account of the similarity of its tone to the sounds of the time-honored Pandean Pipes—one of the precursors of the Organ. It has been made of 2 ft. and 1 ft. pitch, but is very uncommon in either, having been found, in all probability, to have little to recommend it tonally. As a stop of 2 ft. pitch it appears in the Ober-werk, and as one of 1 ft. pitch in the Pedal of the Organ in the Cathedral of Lund, Sweden. It is likely to be classed among obsolete stops.

FLAUTO DOLCE, Ital.—Fr., FLÛTE DOUCE. Ger., DOLZFLÖTE, DULZFLÖTE.—An open labial stop of small scale, the pipes of which are of metal or wood, and of 8 ft. or 4 ft. pitch. As the name implies, the tone of the stop is soft, and when at its best it resembles that of the orchestral Flute in *piano* passages. Regnier describes it thus:

"FLAUTO DOLCE, la Flûte douce, *Dulzflœte*, que les facteurs de France ont eu tort de confondre avec la flûte allemande beaucoup plus fine et vive, est un régistre également ouvert et de tres-menue taille, mais d'un ton plus rond et eminemment doux."

The FLAUTO DOLCE, in either pitch, is suitable from every point of view for insertion in the Chamber Organ; or in the Choir or Echo of larger Organs when extreme delicacy and refinement of intonation is desired. An example of 8 ft. pitch, of wood, exists in the Choir of the Organ in the Marienkirche, at Goerlitz.† A beautiful example of 4 ft. pitch, of metal, exists in the Echo of the Organ in the Parish Church of Leeds, where it speaks on the appropriate wind

---

* We made one of fine cedar for our own Organ, voiced on wind of 2⅜ inches, and its tone was very delicate and beautiful.

† The Organ in the Marienkirche, at Görlitz, in Silesia, constructed by the celebrated organ-builder, Buckow, in 1838. It is a small instrument, containing only fifteen speaking stops, three of which are given to the Pedal Organ. It is, however, to the stop-apportionment of the Choir Organ that we desire to direct the attention of organists and others interested in refined organ-building. It comprises the following four stops: VIOLA DA GAMBA, 8 FT., metal; DOLCIANO, 8 FT., wood; FLÖTE DOUCE, 8 FT., wood; and FLÖTE D'AMOUR, 4 FT., wood. It requires little imagination on the part of anyone, with some knowledge of organ-stops, to realize the beauty and charm which must characterize the tones of this little Choir: and it, as the work of a distinguished artist, certainly gives a lesson to twentieth-century lovers of musical noise. But it seems hopeless to look for any immediate improvement so long as organists continue to approve of, or remain indifferent toward, the inartistic and tasteless doings in the great majority of voicing-rooms to-day.

pressure of 1½ inches. This fine stop was made by Edmund Schulze.

FLAUTO MAGGIORE, Ital. Ger., Majorflöte.—The term appropriately employed to distinguish the most important or dominating flute-toned stop in the Organ—the stop holding the same commanding position in the flute-work as the Principal or Diapason holds in the foundation-work of the instrument. The Flauto Maggiore is properly an open wood and metal stop of 8 ft. pitch and large scale, voiced to yield a rich unimitative flute-tone of considerable volume. We find the principal flute-toned stop, of 8 ft. pitch, in the Great of the Organ in the Cathedral of Breslau, labeled Majorflöte: and the same name is given to a corresponding stop in the Choir Organ. The term has also been applied to a full-toned covered stop of 8 ft. pitch, in the Great of the Grand Organ in the Church of St. Elizabeth, at Breslau. There is much to recommend the name for general adoption, when confined to a unison stop of dominating unimitative flute-tone, for it clearly denotes its position in a tonal scheme.

FLAUTO MINORE, Ital.—The name appropriately employed to designate an unimitative flute-toned stop of secondary importance as regards strength of tone, placed in any division of the Organ in which a more powerful flute-toned stop, labeled Flauto Maggiore (q. v.), is inserted. The German equivalent—Minorflöte— has been adopted to designate a flute-toned stop of 4 ft. pitch, as in the Organ in the choir of the Cathedral of Breslau. In this latter sense the term is undesirable; for the terms Flauto Maggiore and Flauto Minore should refer to tone,—the only matter of importance to the organist,—not to the sizes of the stops only, which call for other distinguishing names.

FLAUTONE, Ital.—Fr., Flûton.—The name given by the Italian organ-builders to a large-scaled, flute-toned stop, yielding a smooth and somewhat subdued voice. The pipes of this stop are either open or covered, according to the ideas of the builder, or, probably, according to the stop-apportionment of the divisional Organ in which it is placed. The Flautone in the North Organ in the Cathedral of Milan is of metal with a covered wood bass; while that in the Choir of the Organ in the Church of San Gaetano, Florence, is a metal stop of 8 ft. pitch, the pipes of which are apparently open.*

* "A la pédale, les Italiens l'emploient sous le nom de *Flautone*, Flûton, ou grosse flûte douce. Celle de huit-pieds, qui est la plus usitée, chante admirablement les adagios en solo ou en chœur,

FLAUTO TEDESCO, Ital.—The name given by the old Italian organ-builders to an open wood stop, of medium scale, and 8 ft. pitch. The stop resembles, both in the form and tone of its pipes, the English CLARABELLA. Examples are to be found in several Italian Organs; as in the North Organ in the Cathedral of Milan; and in the Organ in the Church of Santa Maria des Vignes, Genoa. It also existed in the old Organ, by Hermann, in the Church of Santa Maria di Carignano, Genoa; but was removed when the present Organ was constructed by Bianchi in 1863.*

FLAUTO TRAVERSO, Ital.—Fr., FLÛTE TRAVERSIÈRE. Ger., TRAVERSFLÖTE, QUERFLÖTE.—The names used by different organ-builders to designate the stop of 8 ft. and 4 ft. pitch, the pipes of which are properly of wood and harmonic, yielding a tone closely imitating that of the orchestral Flute. Ever since the invention of harmonic pipes, this important stop has deservedly become a great favorite, and many fine examples are to be found in well-appointed Organs, notably in those of the great German builders; as in the Ladegast Organ in Schwerin Cathedral. The stop is made of pine and pear-tree, and is thus described by J. Massmann, Grossherzogl, Musikdirector in Wismar:

"FLAUTO TRAVERSO 8', offen aus Tannen- und Birnbaum-holz; hat einen weichen und schönen Ton, der Querflöte des Orchesters sehr ähnlich; die Pfeifen der höchsten Octaven überblasend." See ORCHESTRAL FLUTE.

FLÖTENBASS, Ger.—An open labial stop of 8 ft. pitch, the pipes of which are of wood, of large scale, and yield a powerful un-imitative flute-tone. It is properly a Pedal Organ stop, appearing in that department of the Organs in the Gewandhaus, at Leipzig, and the Domkirche, Lübeck. As a covered stop, an example appears in the Piano Pedal of the Organ in the Cathedral of Schwerin. As a stop of 16 ft. pitch, examples exist in the Walcker Organs in the Cathedrals of Riga and Vienna. The stop is the same as the BASS FLUTE (q. v.) of English and American Organs.

FLÖTENPRINCIPAL, Ger.—The name given by Walcker to the principal unison and the attendant octave stop placed on the Fourth Manual (Echo) of the Organ in the Cathedral of Riga. The

mais seule à la main; il ne faut pourtant pas trop augmenter le nombre des parties, la confusion s'y jetterait, et adieu l'effet instrumental."—Regnier.

* In adopting a consistent Italian stop nomenclature for our own Chamber Organ, we applied the name FLAUTO TEDESCO to what was practically a soft-voiced English CLARABELLA, 8 FT. See " The Organ of the Twentieth Century," pp. 334-5.

stops are of open pipes, yielding flute organ-tone, and are valuable in imparting a distinctive tonality to the division, which is strongly flute-toned throughout. Of its seventeen stops, nine are flute-toned and the most important labial stops in the division. The two stops specially alluded to are labeled respectively FLÖTENPRINCIPAL, 8 FT., and FLÖTENPRINCIPAL, 4 FT.

FLÛTE À BEC, Fr.—The name that has been given to a flute-toned stop of ordinary form the tone of which was supposed to imitate that of the old Flûte à Bec. Engel, speaking of this instrument, says: "The most common *Flûte à bec* was made with six finger holes, and its compass embraced somewhat more than two octaves. . . . There was often a key on this instrument in addition to the finger-holes. This flute was much in favor in England; hence it was called in France 'Flûte d'Angleterre.' The *flageolet*, the smallest *flûte à bec*, was formerly played in England even by ladies." The instrument was also called the Whistle Flute, and was played by a small ivory mouthpiece or beak, hence its French name. The Italians appear to have called this instrument Flauto a Becco or Flauto Suabile.

FLÛTE À CHEMINÉE, Fr.—Eng., CHIMNEY FLUTE. Ger., ROHRFLÖTE.—The stop in its proper form, as constructed by the French organ-builders, is of metal and of large scale; its pipes being furnished with sliding caps, from the centers of which rise small tubes, or so-called chimneys, which give the stop its peculiar name.* The FLÛTE À CHEMINÉE appears in certain French Organs of both 8 ft. and 4 ft. pitch, although it is properly a unison stop. There can be no doubt, however, regarding the value of the octave voice in effective registration. An example of 4 ft. pitch exists in the Choir of the Organ in the Cathedral of Abbeville. For particulars respecting the formation of the pipes of the stop, see ROHRFLÖTE.

---

* La FLÛTE À CHEMINÉE tient le milieu entre les jeux bouchés et les flûtes ouvertes. Si elles étaient tout à fait bouchées, il ne leur faudrait que la demi-hauteur des tuyaux ouverts; mais ouvertes en partie, elles doivent avoir environ les deux tiers de hauteur des fonds ouverts de même ton. Dans cette hauteur des *Rohrflœten*, on comprend celle de la cheminée posée au centre de la calotte. Nous l'avons expliqué: une partie du son se propage par cette ouverture, l'autre par la bouche, après s'être heurtée à la partie couverte du sommet. Le son qui sort par la cheminée demande la même élévation de tuyau que dans les jeux ouverts; et il faudrait bien la lui donner si la partie calottée du sommet où viennent se heurter les vibrations, pour ressortir en partie par les lèvres du tuyau, ne ramenaient pour leur part ce tuyau à l'état de bourdon, et n'en diminuaient par conséquent la hauteur. Pour donner plus de facilité au son de se propager par la bouche, on ouvre celle-ci davantage, on *égueule*, comme on dit, les flûtes à cheminée plus que les flûtes ouvertes et que les simples bourdons. Il va sans dire que plus on les veut sonores, plus on élargit la taille, qu'en général on tient très-grosse. Ces flûtes se font d'étain et à barbes de chaque côté de la bouche, pour en diriger l'intonation et l'accord."—Regnier.

FLÛTE À FUSEAU, Fr.—A metal labial stop, of 8 ft. and 4 ft. pitch, yielding an unimitative flute-tone, the pipes of which are tapered or spindle-shaped, hence its name. An example exists on the Fourth Manual of the Organ in the Church of Saint-Nicholas, at Blois. The FLÛTE À FUSEAU is practically the same as the German SPINDELFLÖTE (*q. v.*).

FLÛTE À PAVILLON, Fr.—The name given by the French organ-builders to a full-scaled metal labial stop, of 8 ft. pitch, the pipes of which have cylindrical bodies surmounted with bells of inverted conical form. Hence the distinctive and appropriate name. It is to be regretted that the labor attending the construction of its pipes, combined with the difficulty of finding proper standing room for them on wind-chests of ordinary dimensions, has seriously interfered with a desirable introduction of this fine stop in important Organs. The FLÛTE À PAVILLON was first brought before the notice of the English organ-builders by Ducroquet, of Paris, in the Organ he sent to the London Exhibition of 1851. It was received with great favor, and several fine examples were made by different builders and pipe-makers, especially by John Courcelle, the celebrated reed voicer, and teacher of George Willis, of equal fame.* So fine were his stops, that in one Organ the name COURCELLINA was given to the stop. An example, under this name, exists in the Organ of the Church of St. John, Portsea. One, under the proper French name, exists in the Back Great of the Concert Organ in the Town Hall, Leeds, Yorkshire; and one, under the English name,—BELL DIAPASON,—in the Great of the Organ in the Oratory, Brompton, London. Notable French examples exist in the Grand Orgue of the Organ in the Church of Saint-Sulpice; and in the same division of the Organ in the Church of Saint-Eustache, Paris. Both in France and England the stop appears to have fallen into disuetude. We introduced a FLÛTE À PAVILLON, 8 FT., in the scheme of the Fourth Organ (Solo) of the Concert-room Organ installed in the Festival Hall of the Louisiana Purchase Exposition, 1904.

FORMATION.—The FLÛTE À PAVILLON pipe comprises two leading portions, a cylindrical body, and a bell (*pavillon*) in the shape of an inverted truncated cone, attached to a short cylindrical portion which slides on the open end of the body for the purpose of tuning, as neither coning nor slotting is admissible for that operation. The cylindrical body is formed in all respects similar to that of the PRINCIPAL or DIAPASON, 8 FT., as shown in Fig. 17, Plate II. The short cylindrical

* In our own Chamber Organ the TROMBA and CLARINETTO were by Courcelle and the OBOE by Willis.

portion, to which the bell is attached, fits closely to the body, its lower edge being diagonally cut, so as to have a screwlike motion against a small projecting button of solder on the body, as indicated. Accordingly, in tuning the pipe it is only necessary to raise or lower the bell by turning it slightly of the right or left. By such a simple method of tuning, the timbre of the pipe will remain constant, and the bell will remain firmly in position: both important matters. The mouth of the FLÛTE À PAVILLON is of the same width as that of a DIAPASON pipe of the same scale, but is cut higher; the height depending largely on the pressure of the wind used and on the volume of tone desired. The pipes should, in all cases, be copiously winded and high pressures avoided. It is questionable if any of the French or English stops were voiced on wind of higher pressure than 3½ inches. The proportions of the bell vary according to the quality of the tone required, but its desirable dimensions are one and·one-half the diameter of the pipe in height, and one and two-thirds the diameter of the pipe in its diameter at top, as shown in Fig. 17. The proportions have been modified by different pipe makers.

TONE AND REGISTRATION.—The stop has been labeled by certain English organ-builders BELL DIAPASON, as by Bishop in the Organ of the Oratory, Brompton; but the term is misleading, for the tone of the stop is not the pure organ-tone of the true DIAPASON. The stop belongs to the flute-work of the Organ, and this fact the French organ-builders recognized when they gave the original name to it. The proper tone of the stop is a combination of pure organ-tone and unimitative flute-tone, characterized by a singular richness and fullness, yet not unduly assertive. It inclines, in certain fine examples, to a horn timbre, which can be intensified, if desired, by slotting or perforating the bell after the fashion of the KERAULO- PHONE tuning-slide. There can be no question as to the tonal value of the FLÛTE À PAVILLON in full registration, in which important lingual stops take prominent part, and call for effective backgrounds of labial tones. Accordingly, while the stop finds a proper place in the Great or Grand Orgue of French and English instruments, its rich compound tone makes it a valuable, and, perhaps, a more valuable, voice in another division of the Organ richer in lingual stops. It was that consideration led us to insert it in the Fourth Organ of the instrument installed at the Louisiana Purchase Exposition, which contained seven very important lingual stops. If the science and art of tonal combination and artistic registration were carefully studied by organ-builders, and better understood by organists than they seem to be in many quarters to-day, a better and more rational system of stop-apportionment would soon appear in new Organs.

FLÛTE À PYRAMIDE, Fr.—The term used to designate an open labial stop of 8 ft. and 4 ft. pitch, the pipes of which are square and inverted pyramidal in form, resembling those of the DOLCAN in being larger at the top than at the mouth-line, and especially in the pipes of the bass octave, which have been made of wood (See Dol-can). The name would be more appropriately applied to a stop the pipes of which are directly pyramidal; that is, square, and larger at the mouth-line than at the top, in this respect resembling the pipes of the Spitzflöte, Gemshorn, and Cone Gamba. We have made wood pipes of this form, having extremely low inverted mouths, which, voiced on wind of $2\frac{3}{8}$ inches, yielded exquisite tones having a rare combination of imitative flute- and string-tones, both of which could be distinctly heard as if fighting for supremacy. There is much to be done in this direction that has not been dreamt of: but the trouble and skill involved in the formation of such pyra-midal pipes will effectively condemn them in the organ-building world.

FLÛTE CONIQUE, Fr.—The name given by Cavaillé-Coll to open stops, of 16 ft. pitch, inserted by him in the Grand-Orgue and Solo of the Organ in the Church of Saint-Sulpice, Paris. The stops are flute-toned, and are practically Double Spitzflötes.

FLÛTE CREUSE, Fr.—The term that has been used by French organ-builders to designate a stop, of full scale, yielding a powerful unimitative flute-tone: it is in all essentials, as the name implies, similar to the German Hohlflöte (q. v.).

FLÛTE DOUCE, Fr.—An open labial stop, of small scale, yielding a soft and pure flute-tone, approaching an imitative quality. An example exists in the Positif of the Organ in the Church of Saint-Sulpice, Paris. Another example is to be found in the same division of the Organ in the Cathedral of Notre-Dame. Both stops are of 4 ft. pitch; evidently the one preferred by the distinguished builder, Cavaillé-Coll, although he introduced one, of 8 ft. pitch, in the Positif of the Organ in the Madeleine, Paris. See Flauto Dolce.

FLÛTE HARMONIQUE, Fr.—Eng., Harmonic Flute.— The principle of formation which obtains in the Flûte Harmonique was long known as applied to wood pipes, the tones of which were more or less imitative of those of the orchestral Flute. The first metal stops to which the principle was applied were constructed by MM. Cavaillé-Coll, of Paris, and inserted in the Organ erected by them, in the year 1841, in the Royal Church of Saint-Denis, near Paris. The series of Harmonic Flutes in the Organ is so note-worthy that the stops which belong to it deserve enumeration here. In the Grand Orgue—Flûte Traversière Harmonique, 8 ft., and

FLÛTE OCTAVIANTE HARMONIQUE, 4 FT. In the Positif—FLÛTE HARMONIQUE, 8 FT., and FLAGEOLET HARMONIQUE, 2 FT. In the Récit-Écho Expressif—FLÛTE HARMONIQUE, 8FT., FLÛTE OCTAVIANTE HARMONIQUE, 4 FT., and FLÛTE OCTAVIN HARMONIQUE, 2 FT. The stop derives its name from the fact that the pipes which form the larger portion of its compass are so formed and voiced as to yield their first harmonic upper partial tones instead of the tones which normally belong to their full lengths; the tones so produced having a distinctive timbre of special tonal value, which has secured the stop universal adoption.

FORMATION.—The FLÛTE HARMONIQUE, properly so-called, is formed of open cylindrical pipes of metal, or straight quadrangular pipes of wood, of large scale. From about the note f¹ the pipes are made of twice the standard speaking length. In the HARMONIC FLÛTE, 4 FT., the harmonic pipes are carried to about G; and the HARMONIC PICCOLO, 2 FT., should be harmonic throughout. Indeed, it is desirable in the unison stop to commence the harmonic pipes on middle c¹. Open pipes of wood or metal of the normal speaking lengths are used for the lower portions of the stops of 8 ft. and 4 ft. pitch; of these, which present no unusual treatment, it is unnecessary to speak here. The FLÛTE HARMONIQUE, 8 FT., we select for description and illustration is that in the Great of the Concert-room Organ by Cavaillé-Coll in the Town Hall of Manchester, a stop we had the opportunity of examining and measuring. The lowest harmonic pipe of this stop is g¹, as shown in correct proportions in Fig. 18, Plate II. The pipe is 2.37 inches in diameter and 29½ inches in effective length from the mouth line. At a distance of 13 inches from the lower lip of the mouth, a hole ⅛ inch in diameter is pierced, as indicated, opposite A, in the illustration. The mouth is 1¾ inches in width and ¹¹⁄₁₆ inch in height, having a straight upper lip, and the languid closely and finely nicked. Through the agency of the small perforation in the body, which prevents the formation of a node in the middle of the internal column of air, and by the pipe being slightly overblown, a note is produced which is about an octave of that which normally belongs to a pipe of the length of 29½ inches. The bass and tenor of this stop are of open wood pipes the CC pipe having the scale of 5.00 inches in width and 6.50 inches in depth. The metal non-harmonic pipe c¹, has a diameter of 2.75 inches, and a speaking length of 22 inches, belonging to a very large scale. Certain organ-builders prefer, and, we think, wisely, to form the HARMONIC FLUTE, 8 FT., entirely of metal, commencing the double-length harmonic pipes at f¹.* For particulars respecting the formation of harmonic pipes of wood, see ORCHESTRAL FLUTE.

TONE AND REGISTRATION.—The tones produced by the harmonic pipes of the FLÛTE HARMONIQUE differ considerably from those yielded by open pipes of the standard speaking lengths: this is due to the large scale allowed by the perforated double-length pipes, which would be excessive and undesirable in pipes of half their length, yielding notes of similar pitch under ordinary conditions;

* For further details respecting formation of harmonic pipes, see "The Organ of the Twentieth Century," page 388.

and also to the prominence of certain upper partial tones, generated by the necessary and special voicing and overblowing of the pipes, which impart a peculiar and characteristic timbre to the compound sounds they produce. Although the tones of the metal FLÛTE HARMONIQUE, as originally and usually formed and voiced, are not strictly imitative they differ considerably from those of the ordinary stops which belong to the flute organ-tone class: they are clearer, more penetrating, and to some extent more valuable in combinations and registration of an assertive character. In artistic registration with all classes of lingual stops, except the VOX HUMANA, the FLÛTE HARMONIQUE, 8 FT., fulfills its highest office; and, accordingly, should find a place in the division of the Organ which is richest in lingual stops. This is especially desirable in a properly stop-apportioned Concert-room Organ, in which provision for the greatest range of tonal contrasts by means of effective and convenient registration should be made.*

FLÛTE OCTAVIANTE, Fr.—The term used by French organ-builders to designate an open flute-toned stop, of either metal or wood, and of octave, or 4 ft. pitch. This stop in its most effective form is constructed of harmonic pipes from tenor F, or better still from tenor C, the lower pipes being of large scale and standard speaking lengths. In this form it is called FLÛTE OCTAVIANTE HARMONIQUE; the first example of which was inserted by MM. Cavaillé-Coll in the Organ erected by them in the Royal Church of Saint-Denis. See FLÛTE HARMONIQUE.

FLÛTE OUVERTE, Fr.—The general name given by French organ-builders to large-scaled open stops, formed of metal or wood, and yielding an indeterminate flute-tone: hence its convenience can be realized. The FLÛTE OUVERTE is of 32 ft., 16 ft., 8 ft., and 4 ft. pitch, as shown by the tonal appointment of the Pedal Organ of the Organ in the Royal Church of Saint-Denis, in which examples of all these four pitches are to be found. In English nomenclature, these four Pedal Organ stops would be labeled DOUBLE DIAPASON, 32 FT., DIAPASON, 16 FT., OCTAVE or FLUTE, 8 FT., and SUPER-OCTAVE, 4 FT.

FLÛTE POINTUE, FLÛTE À POINTE, Fr.—The name given to an open metal stop of 8 ft. and 4 ft. pitch, the pipes of which are conical in form, resembling those of the SPITZFLÖTE. A flute-toned

---

* See the tonal apportionment of the Fourth Organ, in Chapter XI. of "The Organ of the Twentieth Century," page 311.

stop of 4 ft. pitch bearing this uncommon name exists in the Grand
Orgue of the instrument built by Clerinex for the Church of Saint-
Martin, at Liège.

FLUTTUAN, Ger.—The uncommon name given to a short compass manual stop of 16 ft. pitch, the pipes of which are of open
wood. An example, having the compass from middle c^1 to g^3, constructed of pear-tree, exists on the Second Clavier of the Organ in the
Church of Neu-Ruppin. Seidel describes the stop and its tonality
thus:

"FLUTTUAN 16′ steht in der Orgel zu Neu-Ruppin im Mittel-
klavier von c^1 bis g^3 und hat sehr schwache Bretter von Birnbaum-
holz. Diese Stimme ist sehr weit mensuriert, hat engen Aufschnitt,
starke Intonation und einen hornartigen Klang; die Bassoktaven
sind durch Quintatön ergänzt."

FOURNITURE, Fr.—Eng., FURNITURE.—The name given to a
compound harmonic-corroborating stop composed of three or more
ranks of open metal pipes of medium scale, the ranks usually being
alternately octave- and fifth-sounding. With the aim of obtaining
greater assertiveness, a third-sounding rank has sometimes been
added; but this rank will not be called for if there is a SESQUIALTERA
on the same manual. The general pitch of the FOURNITURE is,
properly, higher than that of any other compound stop introduced
in the Organ; and as the pipes composing the stop are of necessity
very small, the ranks have to break at every octave. When properly voiced and scientifically graduated in strength of tone, the
stop adds great richness and brilliancy to all combinations in which
it enters. This fact has been pointedly commented on by Regnier.*
The following examples of FOURNITURES of four and five ranks may
be accepted as representative compositions suitable for insertion in
important Organs. The first, of four ranks, is composed of octave-

* "La FOURNITURE, ou *mixture*, est un jeu multiple, ordinairement quadruple, de menue
taille, fait de l'étain le plus fin et le plus doux. Le plus grand tuyau de la *Fourniture* mesure sa
hauteur sur celle des tuyaux rangés sur le même sommier et correspondant au même clavier.
    "Ainsi le premier *ut* d'une *Fourniture* placé au *grand orgue* d'un seize-pieds y a quatre-pieds,
et deux au positif. L'harmonie de la *Fourniture* est brillante, fine, et destinée à des roulements
rapides. On peut dire que son effet sur l'oreille est comparable en harmonie à celui que ferait
sur la vue une parure d'acier poli et tallé en diamants. On lui donne toute l'étendue du clavier,
trois rangs de tuyaux pour le moins et jusqu'à sept et neuf. Mais son mélange, au lieu de procé-
der comme le *Cornet*, marche par *quinte* et *octave* qui s'arrêtent à peu de distance de leur point de
départ pour reprendre, comme nous allons le voir, la composition de la première note: l'*ut* pour
la *Fourniture* à trois rangs est celle-ci: *ut*¹, *sol*¹, *ut*²: on ajoute le *sol*², si la *Fourniture* a quatre
tuyaux par note: l'*ut*³, si elle en a cinq; le *sol*³, si elle en a six; enfin l'*ut*⁴, si elle en a sept, comme
nos plus grandes orgues. Au positif, on prend la *Fourniture* à l'octave supérieure. Si le positif
n'est qu'un quatre-pieds, on prend la *Fourniture* à la super octave."—Regnier.

and fifth-sounding ranks: the second, of five ranks, is composed of octave-, third-, and fifth-sounding ranks:

FOURNITURE—IV. RANKS.

CC to BB	.	.	.	.	.	.	22——26——29——33.
C to B	.	.	.	.	.	.	19——22——26——29.
c¹ to b¹	.	.	.	.	.	.	15——19——22——26.
c² to b²	.	.	.	.	.	.	12——15——19——22.
c³ to c⁴	.	.	.	.	.	.	8——12——15——19.

FOURNITURE—V. RANKS.

CC to BB	.	.	.	.	24——26——29——33——36.
C to B	.	.	.	.	19——22——24——26——29.
c¹ to b¹	.	.	.	.	15——17——19——22——26.
c² to b²	.	.	.	.	12——15——17——19——22.
c³ to c⁴	.	.	.	.	8——12——15——17——19.

As all the intervals in these examples belong to the 8 ft. harmonic series, both stops are suitable for insertion in any manual division of the Organ in which extreme brightness of harmonic structure is desired: relative strength of tone and perfect regulation being observed in all cases.

The FOURNITURE was introduced by the old English builders in several of their Organs, commonly of few ranks. Renatus Harris, in 1670, introduced one, of three ranks, in the Great of his Organ in the Church of St. Sepulchre, London. John Avery, in 1794, inserted one, of three ranks, in the Choir of his Organ in Croydon Church; and one of two ranks, in the Choir of his Organ in St. Margaret's Church, Westminster. Although, for obvious reasons, the stop has not been a favorite with later builders, Willis inserted FOURNITURES, of five ranks, in the Pedal Organ and the Swell of his instrument in St. George's Hall, Liverpool; and Hill has inserted FOURNITURES, of five ranks, in the Great and Swell of the Organ in the Centennial Hall, Sydney, N. S. W.

The FOURNITURE appears in numerous Organs by French builders. Confining our remarks to instruments constructed by France's greatest organ-builder, Aristide Cavaillé-Coll, we find a GROSSE FOURNITURE, of four ranks, in the Grand-Chœur of the Organ in the Church of Saint-Sulpice, Paris; a FOURNITURE, of five ranks, in the Grand-Orgue of the Organ in the Church of Saint-Sernin, Toulouse; a FOURNITURE, of five ranks, in the Bombarde of the Organ in the Church of Saint-Ouen, Rouen; and a FOURNITURE, of five ranks, in the Grand-Orgue of the Concert-room Organ erected by him in the Albert Hall, Sheffield, England.

FRENCH HORN.—The name commonly given to a lingual stop of 8 ft. pitch, formed and voiced to yield tones imitating as closely as practicable those of the orchestral Horn. It is undesirable to continue this full name; for, as Dr. W. H. Stone points out, "The designation 'French' is commonly added to the name of the orchestral Horn, from the fact that a circular instrument of this nature, without crooks or other appliances, was, and still is, used in France for hunting. Its tones are, "coarse and boisterous, only fit for the open air and for woodland pastimes." For description of the organ-stop see HORN.

FUGARA.—The name that has been used to designate an open stop of metal or wood, commonly of 8 ft. and 4 ft. pitch, the tone of which is somewhat indeterminate in character; in some examples inclining to a cutting string quality, and in others to a combination of string and horn tones. Locher says: "The FUGARA has much in common with the GAMBA, while in quality of tone it stands between it and the GEIGENPRINCIPAL."* The stop appears to have been held in high favor by German organ-builders of the later school. Examples, of 8 ft. pitch, exist in the Organs in the Cathedrals of Ulm, Vienna, Lübeck, Merseburg, and Schwerin; and, of 4 ft. pitch, in the Organs in the Cathedrals of Riga and Schwerin. The FUGARA does not seem to have been valued by the French organ-builders, very seldom appearing in their Organs. One, of 4 ft. pitch, is introduced in the Positif of Merklin's Organ in the Church of Saint-Sulpice, Paris.

FÜLLFLÖTE, Ger.—The name given by German organ-builders to a covered metal stop of large scale, yielding a powerful unimitative flute-tone. It is described by Seidel thus: "FÜLLFLÖTE, 4 Fusston gedeckt, aus 10 löt. Metall, steht im Hauptwerk der von Buckow in Jahren 18⅜⅔ in der Stadtpfarrkirche zu Triebel in der Niederlausitz erbauten Orgel von 25 klangbaren Stimmen."

FULL MIXTURE.—A compound harmonic-corroborating stop, formed of full-scaled open metal pipes, yielding pure organ-tone of

* " La FUGARA est une variété de la longue et incisive famille des régistres étroits et fermes de métal. Elle a plus de clarté et non moins de mordant que la Viole. Malgré sa douceur de voix, elle rappelle plus aussi le son de Violon que la Gambe de huit-pieds. La *Fugara* se fait généralement de huit et de quatre, rarement de seize."—Regnier.

"FUGARA, VOGARA, auch Tibia aperta (offene Flöte), ist ein ziemlich bekanntes offenes Flötenwerk zu 4' und 8' im Manual, von enger Mensur aus Holz oder Zinn, schwerer Ansprache und fast so schneidendem aber hellerem Tone wie die Gamba. Diese Stimme soll', wiewohl sehr selten, auch zu 16' vorkommen."—Seidel.

volume and strength commensurate with the requirements of the tonal appointment of which it forms a part. It belongs to the tonal structure of the foundation-work, and, accordingly, finds its proper place in the First or Great Organ, imparting great richness and fullness to all combinations in which it enters. The following is the composition of an effective stop of five ranks:

FULL MIXTURE—V. RANKS.

CC to G .	.	.	.	.	12——15——19——22——26.
G♯ to f¹ .	.	.	.	.	8——12——15——19——22.
f♯¹ to f² .	.	.	.	.	5—— 8——12——15——19.
f♯² to c⁴ .	.	.	.	.	1—— 5—— 8——12——15.

The intervals in the two higher breaks —f♯¹ to c⁴—belong to the 16 ft. harmonic series, and give great fullness and firmness to this usually weak portion of the compass. A MIXTURE, of four ranks, can be formed by omitting the fifth rank, without seriously impairing the tonal value of the stop which lies in the ranks of lower pitch. This, like all other compound harmonic-corroborating stops, must be graduated in strength of tone as it ascends the manual compass.

FÜLLQUINTE, Ger.—The name used by some German organ-builders to designate the manual QUINT, 5⅓ FT., which belongs to the 16 ft. harmonic series, and should appear only in a tonal division in which there is a stop of 16 ft. pitch. The FÜLLQUINTE may be of wood or metal, and of open or covered pipes. When drawn with a full-toned stop of 8 ft. pitch, it produces the differential 16 ft. tone.

G

GAMBA, Ital.—Fr., GAMBE. Ger., GAMBE.—This term applied alone in stop nomenclature, as it very frequently has been and still is, is senseless; it literally signifies *leg*, and it would seem difficult to apply that term to an organ-stop with any degree of propriety. It is merely a wrong abbreviation of the name Viola da Gamba given to the old instrument which was the precursor of the Violoncello. Long usage, however, has so established the single term GAMBA, that it will probably remain, along with other undesirable terms, for a long time in the modern organ-builder's nomenclature. We strongly recommend the abandonment of the senseless term, and the adoption of the expressive term VIOL in its place.* The stop

---

* Viol was the English generic name of the stringed and bowed instruments which, developed from the mediæval Fiddle, preceded the Violin, and were used in England between the fifteenth

which has passed under the simple name GAMBA has commonly been formed of open cylindrical pipes of metal, of medium scale, and 8 ft. pitch, voiced to yield a more or less pronounced unimitative string-tone. In its original form, as made by German organ-builders, the stop was slow of speech and had a disagreeable "spitting" effect when commencing to speak: these defects have been removed in all later examples. We find the term used alone in the Organ in York Minster, and in the generality of the Organs made by Walker & Sons. The term is frequently used in combination with other terms having reference to the shape of the pipes forming the stop or some peculiarity in its tonality, thus: BELL GAMBA, CONE GAMBA, ECHO GAMBA, CONTRA-GAMBA, 16 FT., etc. Translate these terms into English and realize how absurd they are. See VIOLA DA GAMBA.

GAMBENBASS, Ger.—The labial stop of 16 ft. pitch, formed of open cylindrical metal pipes of medium scale, which furnishes the true Pedal Organ bass to the manual VIOLA DA GAMBA, 8 FT. The stop has been labeled in full, showing this relationship, as stated by Seidel: "Die gewöhnliche Tongrösse der Gamba ist im Manual gewöhnlich 8', selten 4', wo sie im letztern Falle Viola heisst, mit der Altviola oder Bratsche im Einklang steht und der wahre Repräsentant derselben ist, im Pedal kommt sei zu 16' unter dem Namen Viola di Gambenbass oder Gambenbass vor."

GAMBETTE, Fr.—An open metal stop of the VIOL DA GAMBA family, of 4 ft. pitch, the pipes of which are of the same form and tone as those of the unison stop. An example of the GAMBETTE, 4 FT., exists in the Great of the Organ in the Marienkirche, Lübeck. It also exists in the Great of the Organ in the Cathedral of the Incarnation, Garden City, L. I., and other large Roosevelt Organs. In Organs of any importance the GAMBETTE should accompany the VIOLA DA GAMBA, 8 FT., giving desirable aid in tonal grouping and artistic registration.

GEDÄMPFTREGAL, Ger.—The name used to designate an old lingual stop of the REGAL family, characterized by a muted or muffled tone. Both the stop and its name are now obsolete. See REGAL.

century and the end of the eighteenth. The "Chest of Viols" occupied an honored place in almost every lordly mansion. It commonly comprised a Bass Viol, Tenor Viol, Alto Viol, and a Treble Viol. In more important "Chests" these four instruments were duplicated. In some "Chests" the Altos were omitted. The curious can see all these instruments in the Crosby Brown Collection, in The Metropolitan Museum of Art, New York City.

GEDECKT, Ger.—The term is here given in its correct orthography (past participle of *decken*—to cover). The form GEDACKT is frequently used both by German and English-speaking organ-builders, but, being incorrect, should be abandoned in stop nomenclature. The simple term GEDECKT is used generally to indicate a covered stop of wood or metal and of four, eight, sixteen, or thirty-two feet pitch. In the Walcker Organ in the Cathedral of Ulm three GEDECKTS of 8 ft. pitch and two of 16 ft. pitch are so labeled. These five stops have, beyond their pitches, no distinctive tonal coloring, all yielding normal covered flute-tone. The only other stop-name in which the term appears is KLEINGEDECKT, 4 FT. To distinguish the several covered stops, the pipes of which vary either in form or the quality of covered tone they yield, German organ-builders have introduced such compound names as the following: ANGENEHM-GEDECKT, DOPPELGEDECKT, DOPPELROHRGEDECKT, GELINDGEDECKT, GROBGEDECKT, GROSSGEDECKT, HUMANGEDECKT, KLEINGEDECKT, LIEBLICHGEDECKT, MUSICIERGEDECKT, ROHRGEDECKT, STARK-GEDECKT, STILLGEDECKT, and WEITGEDECKT. See these names. The GEDECKTS are made of all pitches from 16 ft. to 2 ft.; but rarely of the last high pitch.

GEDECKTBOMMER, Ger.—The term, rarely used, to designate a covered stop of 8 ft. foundation tone, voiced and overblown so as to sound the harmonic twelfth, if not exclusively, more prominently than the prime tone. A stop of this name and tonality was inserted in the Hauptmanual of the Organ built by Eugenius and Adam Casparini (1703) for the Church of SS. Peter and Paul, Görlitz. It is described by Seidel and other authorities as a QUINT-ATEN.* The name given the stop would seem to imply a disturbed or uncertain tonality, caused by its dual voice. The only covered stop of this class introduced in modern Organs is the ZAUBERFLÖTE (*q. v.*), invented by the late W. Thynne, of London.

GEDECKTFLÖTE, Ger.—A covered wood or metal stop of medium scale and of 8 ft. or 4 ft. pitch, but commonly of the latter. Its tone is of an unimitative flute quality as free from the harmonic Twelfth as possible. Generally its tone resembles that of the DOP-PELFLÖTE, but, necessarily, less full owing to its pipes having single mouths and being smaller in scale.

---

* "GEDACT-POMMER. Pommer soll so viel sein als Bombarda. In der Görlitzer Orgel hingegen soll, wie Adelung anführt, nach Boxbergs Beschreibung, diese Stimme eine starke QUINTA-TÖN gewesen sein."—Schlimbach-Becker, Leipzig, 1843.

Tone and Registration.—Such a voice as that described is valuable in registration, combining well with, and imparting desirable body to, imitative string-toned and lingual stops. As a rule, there are too few stops of 4 ft. pitch introduced in modern Organs for effective tonal combination and artistic registration: too much dependence being placed on octave coupling, which, in its only desirable form, interferes with the independence of the coupled claviers. An octave obtained on any clavier by coupling on itself is inadmissible in tonally correct and artistic registration.

GEDECKTQUINTE, Ger.—A covered harmonic-corroborating stop of 5⅓ ft. pitch, belonging to the 16 feet harmonic series, and, accordingly, suitable for insertion in any division of the Organ in which there are important stops of 16 ft. pitch. When combined with a stop of 8 ft. tone it creates the differential 16 ft. tone. Of 10⅔ ft. pitch it belongs to the 32 ft. harmonic series, and is suitable for the Pedal Organ, where in combination with the Diapason, 16 ft., it generates the differential 32 ft. tone. These differential tones, however, are not so effective as those generated by open stops.

GEIGENOCTAV, Ger.—Eng., Viol Octave.—The appropriate name for the open metal stop of 4 ft. pitch which is the true Octave of the Geigenprincipal, 8 ft. (q. v.). The scale of its pipes should be a little smaller than that of the corresponding pipes of the unison stop. Its voice should be distinctly softer than, while similar in tonal character to, that of the Geigenprincipal, rendering it extremely valuable in artistic registration.

GEIGENPRINCIPAL, GEIGENPRINZIPAL, Ger —Eng., Violin Diapason.—A metal labial stop of 8 ft. pitch, the pipes of which are cylindrical, and of medium scale in the best examples. Its tone is, as the name implies, a combination of organ-tone and string-tone, the former predominating in a decided manner. The German name is to be preferred, for the stop is not, strictly classed, a Diapason. Better English terms, in any case, would be those we have used; namely, Viol Principal, Grand Viol, and Viol Diapason; the last being less appropriate than the others, while, in part, it recognizes old terminology. In form, the pipes of the Geigenprincipal are similar to those of the Principal or Diapason, only being smaller in scale and slightly different in mouth-treatment. The scale of the CC (8 ft.) pipe varies in different examples from 4 inches to 5½ inches in diameter, the mean being the most desirable scale for general adoption. While the Geigenprincipal is rightly a unison manual stop, and invariably appears as such in English and American Organs, German organ-builders have formed it of 16 ft., 8 ft., and 4 ft. pitch, as shown in Walcker's Organ in the Cathedral of Riga. In that important instrument, comprising 116 speaking stops, there is a GEIGENPRINCIPAL, 16 FT., on the Second Manual, and GEIGENPRINCIPALS, 8 FT. and 4 FT., on the Third Manual. It would be more expressive to label the 4 ft. stop GEIGEN-OCTAV. The stop does not seem to have found favor among French organ-builders, for we have not been able to find a single instance of its insertion, or that of an equivalent, in any French Organ. The French organ-builders appear to have been, and indeed are, strangely conservative in all matters of tonal appointment.

TONE AND REGISTRATION.—The tone of the GEIGENPRINCIPAL varies considerably in examples made by different builders; in this as in almost all the other stops, there being no standard studiously worked up to. It is easy to imagine an organist saying: "I have a beautiful GEIGENPRINCIPAL in my Organ which I find very valuable in registration"; while another may, with equal propriety, say: "I rarely use my GEIGENPRINCIPAL, for its tone is neither agreeable alone, nor sympathetic in combination with other stops." This should not be. The proper voice of the stop is a combination of pure organ-tone with a bright string-tone in due subordination; the latter imparting that richness to the foundation tone which has won the stop universal approval among German- and English-speaking organ-builders and organ-lovers. This compound voice, in which certain concordant upper partial tones are present, is extremely valuable in artistic registrations, in which fullness combined with a delicate string quality is called for, and in which so refined a string-tone as that of the VIOLA D'AMORE would be too pronounced. We admit that such tonal refinements are not appreciated by the general class of organists in the noisy craze of to-day.

GEIGENREGAL, Ger.—An old lingual stop, of 8 ft. pitch, the tone of which, from a slight string quality, somewhat resembled that of the Geige or Violin. Both stop and its name are now obsolete. See REGAL.

GELINDGEDECKT, Ger. (from *gelind*—mild).—A covered stop, of 16 ft. or 8 ft. pitch, the pipes of which are of the usual forms, and constructed of wood or partly of wood and partly of metal. As its name implies, the stop, when properly scaled, and voiced under a moderate wind-pressure, yields a soft and refined tone which should be less assertive than that of a LIEBLICHGEDECKT, inserted in the same Organ, and of the same pitch. It is rarely, if ever, desirable to duplicate stops of the same character having the same strength of tone in an Organ, even should they be inserted in different tonal divisions.

TONE AND REGISTRATION.—The GELINDGEDECKT, 8 FT., is a stop of great value in refined registration, specially so when its voice partakes of the tonality of the QUINTATEN. This desirable voice is best obtained from small-scaled wood pipes, voiced on wind of very low pressure: and to be of the greatest value it should occupy a place in the softest tonal division of the Organ.* In such a position it would combine in a charming manner with practically every other stop, labial or lingual, in the division.

GEMSHORN, Ger.—Fr., COR DE CHAMOIS.—The name given to an open labial stop, the pipes of which are conical in form when of metal and pyramidal when made of wood. As a manual stop, it is made of 8 ft., 4 ft., and 2 ft. pitch; and as a Pedal Organ stop it is of 16 ft. pitch, properly designated GEMSHORNBASS (q. v.). The tone of the true GEMSHORN is rich, clear, and penetrating, having a beautiful timbre which may be classed as between a normal reed-tone and a string-tone. This most desirable tone differs according to the tastes of the organ-builders of different countries and the ideas of different voicers.† Of 8 ft. pitch, the stop is inserted in the Hauptwerk (First Manual) of all Walcker's Organs of any importance from that in the Cathedral of Riga, downwards. It is invariably of 8 ft. pitch, and, we presume, of metal throughout, as it should be in all good Organs. In the Choir of the Organ in the Town Church of Fulda it exists as an 8 ft. stop, the bass and tenor octaves of which are of wood and the others of tin. The GEMSHORN, 8 FT., in the Hauptwerk of the Organ in St. Paul's Church, Schwerin, has its bass octave of covered wood pipes, the remainder of the stop being of tin. In the Great of the Organ in the chief Protestant Church of

---

* We have placed the GELINDGEDECKT, in our tonal scheme for the Concert-room Organ of the Twentieth Century, in the Ancillary Aërial Organ, all the nineteen stops of which are on wind of 1½ inches. We give the scale of the CC (8 ft.) pipe 1.78 inches in width by 2.28 inches in depth, the scale ratio being 1: 2.3, halving on the twenty-first pipe. See "The Organ of the Twentieth Century," pp. 329-330.

† "Le COR DE CHAMOIS ou *Gemshorn* est une des jolies flûtes étroites et ouvertes dont l'harmonie suit celle du *Salicional*, mais plus délicate encore. Ses tuyaux, plus pointus que ceux de la *Spitz-Flœte*, les sons clairs mais lointains qui s'échappent de ses lèvres serrées, lui ont sans doute valu le nom qu'il porte. On le fait d'étain ou d'étoffe tant qu'il ne descend pas plus bas que huit-pieds. A seize on peut employer le bois. On le confond, mais à tort, avec deux régistres d'assez semblable timbre, mais à tuyaux bouchés, *Coppel-Flœte, Spielflœte;* enfin, il ne dédaigne pas de figurer comme quinte (*Gemshorn-Quinte* ou *Cylinder-Quinte*) et de produire alors sur une masse de violes un assez curieux effet. Le *Gemshorn* chantant se mélange volontiers avec la *Hohlflœte*, qui lui donne beaucoup de force par son harmonie voilée, mais profonde."—Regnier.

Utrecht GEMSHORNS of both 4 ft. and 2 ft. pitch are inserted. The stop has been made of 16 ft. and several mutation pitches, but these have been seldom resorted to.* As a Pedal Organ stop of 16 ft. pitch it deserves the attention of every artist organ-builder and expert.

FORMATION.—The pipes of the GEMSHORN are invariably of the form of elongated and slender truncated cones; their open tops having diameters equal to one-third of the diameters at their mouth lines. This is a generally recognized rule; but, like all rules in pipe-proportions, it is open to slight modification under artistic treatment and special voicing. The scale of the GEMSHORN like that of all other stops, varies according to the ideas and aims of different organ-builders, and the volume and quality of the tone desired. A scale suitable for a Church or a Concert-room Organ stop, in the ratio 1 : 2.519, gives the CC (8 ft.) pipe a diameter at the mouth line of 4.96 inches, and a diameter at the top of 1.62 inches; the C pipe diameters of 3.13 inches and 1.02 inches; and the c¹ pipe diameters of 1.9 inches and 0.64 inch. The illustration, Fig. 19, Plate III., shows a CC pipe accurately drawn to this scale. For a GEMSHORN placed in a softly-toned division of a large Organ or inserted in a true Chamber Organ a smaller scale should be used.

TONE AND REGISTRATION.—As before stated, the proper tone of the GEMSHORN is rich, clear, and penetrating, having a beautiful timbre which may be classed between a normal unimitative reed-tone and a viol-tone. It is this compound tone, more or less rich in the lower harmonics, which renders the stop, in its different pitches, so valuable in artistic registration. The tone, however, differs under the treatments and ideas of different voicers; and is, of necessity, affected by different scales and the relative proportions of the lower and upper diameters of the pipes. Under all conditions the tone of the true GEMSHORN is so desirable and distinctive that it favors the introduction, when possible, of the entire family of 16 ft., 8 ft., 4 ft., 2⅔ ft., and 2 ft. stops. Such a family would give practically limitless means for effective and refined registration, and, accordingly, the creation of numerous beautiful timbres in combination with labial stops of the FLUTE and VIOL classes, and with all the softer-voiced lingual stops. The great value of gathering families of stops of distinctive tonalities, and placing them in contrasting divisions, is absolutely unrecognized in the organ-building and organ-designing world to-day, which continues to be quite satisfied with the old-

---

*"GEMSHORN ist eine allgemein bekannte, brauchbare und sehr angenehme Flötenstimme welche, mit oben spitzig zulaufenden Pfeifen versehen ist. Dei Pfeifen haben zuweilen Seiten-bärte zu beiden Seiten des Aufschnittes. Man findet dies Register im Manual zu 8′, 4′, 2′ und 1′, zu letzten beiden Grössen zuweilen unter dem Namen SUPER-GEMSHORN und im Pedal zu 16′ wo es GEMSHORNBASS heisst. Als Quintstimme zu 10⅔′, 5⅓′, 2⅔′ und 1⅓′ kommt dieses Register ebenfalls im Pedal und Manual unter dem Namen GEMSHORNQUINTE vor. Die Pfeifen sind gewöhnlich von Zinn oder Metall, bei den 16 füssigen dürfte vielleicht hier und da Holz in Anwendung gebracht werden."—Seidel.

PLATE III

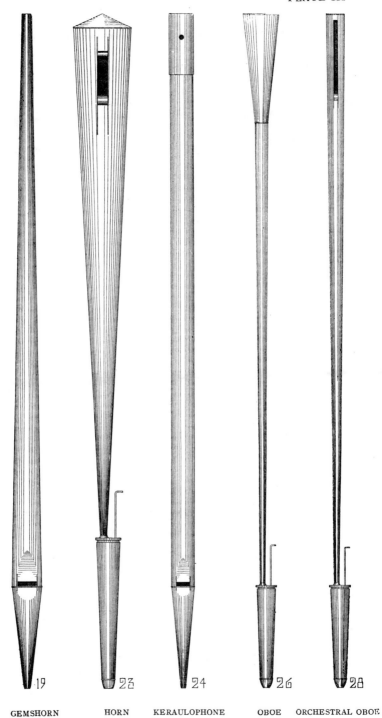

19   23   24   26   28

GEMSHORN   HORN   KERAULOPHONE   OBOE   ORCHESTRAL OBOE

fashioned and systemless manner in which stop-appointments are made.

GEMSHORNBASS, GROSSGEMSHORN, Ger.—The Pedal Organ stop, of 16 ft. pitch, which furnishes the proper bass to the manual GEMSHORN, 8 FT. The pipes of this important and beautiful stop are either made of metal throughout, or of wood and metal, the former material being confined to the 16 ft. octave. This stop should be inserted in every Pedal Organ of the first rank, furnishing a beautiful bass, of a medium weight, to countless manual tonal combinations. By extension to forty-four notes, a very desirable OCTAVE can be derived from it, extremely valuable in Pedal Organ registration. The subject of such registration has not received the attention it deserves; mainly, if not altogether, owing to the generally insufficient and too often miserable tonal appointments of modern Pedal Organs. See GEMSHORN.

GEMSHORNQUINTE, Ger.—An open labial stop, the pipes of which are of metal throughout, or, as in the case of the largest stop, of wood and metal. The pipes are formed in all respects similar to those of the GEMSHORN (q. v.). This stop is fifth-sounding, as its name implies; and, accordingly, is found of $10\frac{2}{3}$ ft., $5\frac{1}{3}$ ft., $2\frac{2}{3}$ ft., and $1\frac{1}{3}$ ft. pitch; the last pitch being rarely used. A GEMSHORN-QUINTE, $10\frac{2}{3}$ FT., of metal throughout, exists in the Pedal of the Grand Organ in the Cathedral of Breslau; one of $5\frac{1}{3}$ ft., also of metal, exists in the Pedal of the Organ in the Church of St. Elizabeth, in the same city; and one of $2\frac{2}{3}$ ft. is introduced on the Second Manual of the Organ in the Cathedral of Schwerin.

GERMAN GAMBA.—The name given by English organ-builders to an unimitative string-toned labial stop made by old German organ-builders, the speech of which was so slow as to render it necessary to draw along with it another quick-speaking stop or KOPPEL (q. v.), commonly in the form of a KOPPELFLÖTE. The GERMAN GAMBA, as made by a German organ-builder, was first introduced into England by Schulze, of Paulinzelle, in the Organ he built for the Parish Church of Doncaster, Yorkshire. The stop, undesirable on account of its tardy speech as well as its peculiar intonation, has properly fallen into desuetude, being interesting only as the precursor of the modern string-toned stops.

GLOCKENSPIEL, Ger.—Fr., CARILLON. Ital., CAMPANELLA, CAMPANETTA.—Correctly considered under its original German name this is a mechanical or percussion stop, of short compass, formed of dish-shaped bells, spiral rods, stee, bars, or bell-metal tubes, sounded by a hammer-action, somewhat resembling that of a pianoforte, actuated by a pneumatic or electro-pneumatic mechanism in the modern Organ. In old Organs the GLOCKENSPIEL was generally little better than a curiosity in organ-building. Examples still exist in some old German Organs, as in those in the Churches of St. Catherine, St. Nicholas, and St. Jacobi, at Hamburg.*

The percussion GLOCKENSPIEL, or what is commonly and appropriately called the CARILLON in its modern form of tubular bells, although it cannot be strictly considered a legitimate organ-stop, has now become a recognized adjunct to the tonal appointment of both Church and Concert-room Organs: and it must be admitted that when artistically used it is not without its claim for recognition, as an effective element in tone production in combination with certain labial stops, and occasionally in solo-effects. Indeed, it might be extended in compass and depth of tone so as to admit of the proper rendition of bell-music, such as that composed and performed by the great carillonneur, Matthias van den Gheyn, of Louvain.

GLÖCKLEINTON, GLOCKENTON, Ger.—An open metal labial stop properly of large scale and 2 ft. pitch, voiced to yield a tone which has a ringing quality suggestive of that of bells. It is described by Seidel thus: "GLÖCKLEINTON (Tonus fabri) ist ein weit mensuriertes Pfeifenregister, welches so klingen soll, als wenn man mit einem Hammer auf einen wohlklingenden Amboss schlägt.

---

*"GLOCKENSPIEL. Carillon. C'est chez les Allemands un jeu composé de clochettes au lieu de l'être ou de tuyaux. Ordinairement, on le place dans l'intérieur derrière le principal en montre; quelquefois il est à l'extérieur où l'on voit des anges placés dans une gloire tenant d'une main une clochette sur laquelle ils frappent avec un marteau qu'ils portent dans l'autre main. . . . Les carillons ne s'éntendent ordinairement que dans les deux octaves supérieures du clavier; cependant, il paraît qu'il s'en trouve de quatre octaves, et que celui de l'église Saint-Michel à Ohrdruff a cette étendue. Il en existe aussi à la pédale. Au lieu de timbres en forme de cloche, on emploie quelquefois des tiges métalliques tournées en spirales et assujéties sur une caisse sonore qui augmente l'intensité de leurs sons. Un des inconvénients des carillons, est de n'être presque jamais d'accord avec l'orgue dont la température fait varier continuellement les jeux de fond dans des proportions qui ne sont point dans le même rapport que celles des variations des métaux. Les marteaux qui frappent les timbres ou les tiges métalliques sont repoussés par un ressort après les avoir mis en vibration, afin de n'en pas arrêter le son."—Hamel.

"GLOCKENSPIEL, Carillon, ist ein Register, welches statt der Pfeifen abgestimmte Glocken hat. Gewöhnlich ist es im Innern der Orgel hinter den Prinzipalpfeifen angebracht, um den Klang recht nahe zu bringen, zuweilen wird es auch von Engeln, welche in einer Glorie angebracht sind und in der einen (beweglichen) Hand ein Hämmerchen, in der andern eine Glocke halten, geschlagen. Manche Glockenspiele sind mit einem Dämpfer von Leder, Tuch u. dergl. versehen, um das Ineinanderschwirren der Töne zu verhindern. Die Glockenspiele gehen gewöhnlich nur durch die zwei oberen Oktaven des Manuals, doch giebt es auch Glockenspiele im Pedal. Da der Glockenton sich auf eine höchst auffallende Art von dem Pfeifenton absondert, und die Glocken nie mit den Pfeifen genau zusammenstimmen, auch die Andacht der Gemeinde durch dieses Klimperwerke gestört wird, so wäre es zu wünschen, dass dergleichen unnütze Register gar nicht mehr verfertigt würden und die hier und da vorhandenen ausser Gebrauch kämen."—Seidel-Kothe.

Diese Stimme steht zu 2' im Oberwerk der Görlitzer Petri-Orgel."

A stop of this class and pitch is hardly to be recommended for insertion in the proper tonal appointment of any Organ constructed to-day. As a SUPER-OCTAVE it would be much too assertive in tone to be used in refined and artistic registration; except, perhaps, in full organ effects, and even in such it might disturb perfect tonal balance.

GRAND BOURDON, GROS BOURDON, Fr.—A covered stop of wood, of large scale, and of 32 ft. pitch, the pipes of which are formed in all respects similar to those of the ordinary BOURDON, 16 FT. (*q. v.*). It appears in the Pedal of the Organ in the Church of Saint-Vincent de Paul, Paris. See CONTRA-BOURDON.

The term GRAND BOURDON has been employed by Walcker to designate a very important Pedal Organ compound harmonic-corroborating stop, of five complete ranks, belonging to the 32 ft. harmonic series. The composition of this stop and the scales of its CCC pipes are as follows:

GRAND BOURDON—V. RANKS.

PRINCIPAL, 16 FT.	Width, 220 mm.		Depth, 280 mm.	
QUINT, 10⅔ FT.	" 110 "		" 153 "	
OCTAVE, 8 FT.	" 108 "		" 131 "	
TIERCE, 6⅖ FT. At mouth, .	" 74 "		" 106 "	
" " At top, . .	" 48 "		" 64 "	
SUPER-OCTAVE, 4 FT. . . .	" 65 "		" 80 "	

It will be observed that all the ranks are formed of wood pipes; and that the TIERCE 6 2/5 FT., is formed of pyramidal pipes of the SPITZFLÖTE type, doubtless with the aim of imparting a lighter and timbre-creating voice to this third-sounding rank; as is always desirable in the third-sounding ranks of compound harmonic-corroborating stops.

GRAND CORNET.—The name properly employed to designate a compound harmonic-corroborating stop, the several ranks of which belong to the 16 ft. harmonic series, and extend throughout the manual compass without a break. An example, of V. ranks, exists in the Bombarde of the Cavaillé-Coll Organ in the Church of Saint-Ouen, Rouen. The stop is desirable only in a tonal division in which there are two or more assertive stops of 16 ft. pitch, preferably lingual. But when the GRAND CORNET is made, as it should be, a timbre-creating stop, its value is great in combination with both labial and lingual stops. An example of such a stop is here given:

TIMBRE-CREATING GRAND CORNET—V. RANKS.

I.	Flûte à Cheminée	. . .	Metal	8 Feet
II.	Spitzquinte	. . . . .	Metal	5⅓ "
III.	Violetta	. . . . .	Tin	4 "
IV.	Gemshorn	. . . . .	Metal	2⅔ "
V.	Piccolo	. . . . .	Metal	2 "

The composition of timbre-creating compound stops will, of necessity, be dictated by the stop-apportionments of the Organs in which they are placed.

GRAND PRINCIPAL, GRAND DIAPASON.—Names that have been employed to individualize the most important unison (8 ft.) stop of pure organ-tone, occupying a place in the foundation-work of an Organ. It was used in the First or Great Organ of the Concert Organ installed at the Louisiana Purchase Exposition, in 1904. The term is desirable when there are three or more Diapasons introduced together in any Organ, indicating the tonal preëminence of one of the series.

GRAND VIOL.—The name employed to individualize the most important unison (8 ft.) stop yielding unimitative viol organ-tone, inserted in an Organ: in this respect occupying a more command-ing position, tonally, than the Geigenprincipal, 8 ft. An example exists in the unexpressive Subdivision of the First or Great Organ of the principal Organ in the Church of Our Lady of Grace, Hoboken, N. J.

The term *grand* has been applied to other stops for the purpose of indicating their relative importance; we, accordingly, find such terms as Grand Flute, Grand Octave, Grand Cornet, and Grand Mixture.

GRAVISSIMA, Lat.—This term, which appears in the tonal schemes of certain important modern Pedal Organs, must not be understood to designate an independent stop. It is simply the acoustical effect, or what is properly designated the differential tone, produced naturally by the combination of tones of 32 ft. and 21⅓ ft. pitch, standing at the interval of a perfect fifth apart, thus:

Generating Tones.		Differential Tone.
CCCC 32 ft.—GGGG 21⅓ ft.	· · ·	CCCCC 64 ft. tone
16 24		8 vibrations

There are three ways of producing what is more expressively termed the Vox Gravissima, varying in effectiveness. 1. By associating with the DOUBLE DIAPASON. 32 FT., an independent SUB-QUINT, 21⅓ FT., tonally the most effective method. 2. By extending the compass of the DOUBLE DIAPASON seven notes, and introducing a Quint coupler acting on the same stop and sounding its notes in fifths. 3. By extending the DIAPASON, 16 FT., downward to GGGG, and coupling it to the DOUBLE DIAPASON, 32 FT. We are in favor of the first method, because it allows the SUB-QUINT or GROSSQUINTENBASS, 21⅓ FT. (*q. v.*), to be used in combination with any other labial or lingual stops of 32 ft. pitch. This arrangement obtains in the Pedal of the Schulze Organ in the Cathedral of Bremen. In the Organ erected by the Hutchins-Votey Organ Company, in Woolsey Hall, Yale University, the GRAVISSIMA was produced by the combination of the open wood DOUBLE DIAPASON, 32 FT., and a QUINT, 21⅓ ft. tone, derived from the CONTRA-BOURDON, 32 FT.

There has not been sufficient experience gained as yet respecting the acoustical effects of the extremely grave differential tones on the proper voices of the Organ for any accurate conclusion to be reached respecting their nature. It is quite evident, however, that they can have no claim to be classed as musical sounds of a 64 ft. octave. When, as Helmholtz states, determinate musical tones cease at that produced by 41.25 vibrations, what can be said of those sounds produced between 8 and 16 vibrations per second? The combination of the two generating stops certainly produces a remarkable acoustic effect, evidently due to the generation of a great series of harmonic over-tones: hence the sole value of the VOX GRAVISSIMA.

GROBGEDECKT, GROSSGEDECKT, Ger.—Lat., PILEATA MAGNA.—The terms signifying "great covered stop," and used by German organ-builders to designate a large-scaled and loud-voiced covered stop of 16 ft. or 8 ft. pitch, commonly inserted in a manual division. A GROSSGEDECKT, 16 FT., exists in the Great of the Organ in the Church of St. Dominic, Prague; and a GROBGEDECKT, 8 FT., is placed on the First Manual of the Walcker Organ in the Synagogue, Berlin.

The word *grobe* has been used as a prefix, for the purpose of indicating strength of tone, in the case of several other stop-names. We accordingly find in old lists such terms as GROBCYMBEL, GROBMIXTUR, GROBPOSAUNE, GROBREGAL, etc.

GROSSDOPPELGEDECKT, Ger.—A covered wood stop of 16 ft. pitch, the pipes of which are properly of large scale, deep in proportion to their width, and have double mouths, after the fashion of the DOPPELFLÖTE (*q. v.*). The stop is suitable for the Pedal Organ or for a manual division in which there are powerful labial or lingual stops of unison (8 ft.) pitch. Carefully made and artistically voiced, this important stop, in combination, would be productive of many fine and uncommon tonal effects in which gravity would be a special element.

GROSSFLÖTE, Ger.—Fr., GROSSE FLÛTE.—An open wood stop of medium scale and properly of 8 ft. pitch; usually placed in a full-toned manual division of the Organ, while it forms a good OCTAVE, 8 FT, for the properly appointed Pedal Organ. In the general form of its pipes it resembles the English CLARABELLA, but it is voiced to yield a more powerful tone of an unimitative flute organ-tone. For this purpose, the mouths are cut high and their upper lips made thick, carefully rounded, and polished with black-lead: this last is seldom done in ordinary trade practice. Leathered lips should be avoided.

TONE AND REGISTRATION.—When the GROSSFLÖTE is properly made and voiced to yield its characteristic tone, it is very valuable in registration in which a background of full unimitative flute-tone is required. It combines in the most effective manner with all the more powerful lingual stops, imparting great body and firmness to their tones without destroying their characteristic voices.

GROSSGEDECKT, Ger.—The term appropriately applied to a large-scaled covered stop, of 16 ft. pitch, yielding a pure covered-tone similar to that of the true LIEBLICHGEDECKT, 16 FT., but of much greater volume and assertiveness. Its place is in a manual division of the Organ, in which there are powerful lingual and other commanding stops, where it will play an important rôle in effective registration.*

GROSSHOHLFLÖTE, Ger.—The Pedal Organ stop of 16 ft. pitch, the open pipes of which are of wood and formed and voiced in all respects similar to those of the manual HOHLFLÖTE, 8 FT. See HOHLFLÖTE.

GROSSNASAT, Ger.—Fr., GROS NASARD, GROSSE QUINTE.— This mutation stop, which is of $10\frac{2}{3}$ ft. pitch in the Pedal Organ and $5\frac{1}{3}$ ft. pitch in the manual divisions, is made of either wood or metal and both in open and covered forms. In the first pitch it belongs to the 32 ft. harmonic series, and in the higher pitch to 16 ft. harmonic series. As GROSSNASAT, $10\frac{2}{3}$ FT., it exists as an

* See " The Organ of the Twentieth Century," pp. 311, 312.

open stop in the Pedal of the Organ in the Cathedral of Halberstadt.
As Grossnasard, 10⅔ ft. of wood, it is inserted in the Pedal of
the Organ in the Cathedral of Merseburg.   It appears as Grosse
Quinte, 10⅔ ft., in the Pédale, and as Grosse Quinte, 5⅓ ft.,
in the Clavier des Bombardes, in the Grand Organ in the Cathedral
of Notre-Dame, Paris.   The stop of 10⅔ ft. pitch was inserted in the
Pedal, and of both 10⅔ ft. and 5⅓ ft. pitch in the First or Great
division of the Concert Organ installed in the Festival Hall of the
Louisiana Purchase Exposition, 1904.

Tone and Registration.—The value of the harmonic-creating
or corroborating tones, such as those of 10⅔ ft. and 5⅓ ft. pitch, in
registration is hardly realized at the present time, owing to the
rarity of their introduction in modern Organs.   In a scheme lying
before us, for a much-divided Organ of 283 speaking stops, there is
only one Pedal Organ stop of 10⅔ ft. pitch, and only one manual
stop of 5⅓ ft. pitch, showing how little attention is paid by the organ-builder of to-day, even in his greatest essays, to the scientific
side of his art; and how little thought or care he bestows on providing the organist with proper material for varied and artistic registration.*   How long are organists to remain content with the results
of incompetency which handicap them at every turn in their essays
in registration?   Surely it is time that science and art are infused
into the tonal appointment of important Organs.

GROSSOCTAV, Ger.—The name given by Walcker to an open
labial stop, of 8 ft. pitch, placed on the First Manual of the Organ
in Paulskirche, Frankurt a. M.   The term is used because, strictly
considered, the manual is of 16 ft. pitch, containing, including the
Principal, three stops of 16 ft. pitch.   In the Pedal of the same
Organ is a stop of 16 ft. pitch labeled Grossoctavbass.

GROSSPOSAUNE, Ger.—The term employed by German organ-
builders to designate the dominating lingual stop, of 32 ft. pitch,
belonging to the Pedal Organ.   It is, as its name implies, similar in
all essentials to the Contra-Trombone, 32 ft. (q. v.).   This grave
stop has not been a favorite with German organ-builders.   In the

---

* If the reader will refer to our scheme for the Concert-room Organ, given in Chapter XI, of
"The Organ of the Twentieth Century," he will find we have provided in the Pedal Organ one
fifth-sounding labial stop of 21 ⅓ ft., one labial stop of 10 ⅔ ft., and one lingual stop of 10 ⅔ ft.
pitch.   Properly distributed in the several manual Organs, are six labial stops of 5 ⅓ ft., and two
lingual stops of 5 ⅓ ft. pitch.   In addition to these important stops, there are six fifth-sounding
stops of 2 ⅔ ft. pitch.   In all, seventeen fifth-sounding stops out of the total number of 230
speaking stops in the entire tonal scheme: yet we know, on both scientific and artistic grounds,
there is not one fifth-sounding stop too many to meet the requirements of artistic registration
and scientific timbre-creation.

Pedal of the Organ in the Nicolaikirche, Leipzig, the stop is labeled POSAUNE, 32 FT. The stop is a free-reed.

GROSSPRINZIPAL, Ger.—Fr., GROS PRINCIPAL.—The name appropriately given to the open labial stops of 16 ft. pitch in the manual divisions and 32 ft. pitch in the Pedal Organ, yielding pure organ-tone, and, accordingly, belonging to the foundation-work of the Organ. It exists, of 32 ft. pitch in the Pedal of the Organ in the Marienkirche, Lübeck. It also exists, as a displayed stop of English tin, of 16 ft. pitch, in the Organ in the Church of Waltershausen. These stops are similar to the English DOUBLE DIAPASONS of corresponding pitches.

GROSSQUINTENBASS, Ger.—This name is given to a covered stop, of $21\frac{1}{3}$ ft. pitch, inserted in the Pedal of the Organ in the Cathedral of Bremen. The stop strictly belongs to the 64 ft. harmonic series, and was evidently introduced with the view of producing the acoustic differential tone which we have termed VOX GRAVISSIMA (see GRAVISSIMA). This fine Organ of 59 speaking stops, was built by Schulze, of Paulinzelle.

GROSSREGAL, Ger.—An old lingual stop of the REGAL family, the only peculiarity of which existed in its grave pitch, which was of 16 ft. The stop is no longer made and its name is obsolete. See REGAL.

GROSSTERZ, Ger.—Fr., GROSSE TIERCE.—This mutation harmonic-corroborating stop is of $6^2/_5$ ft. pitch in the Pedal and $3\frac{1}{5}$ ft. pitch in the manual Organs. In the former it belongs to the 32 ft. harmonic series, and in the latter to the 16 ft. harmonic series; in each case corroborating the fourth upper parial tone of the prime of the corresponding series. A GROSSE TIERCE, $6^2/_5$ FT., is inserted in the Pédale, and a GROSSE TIERCE, $3\frac{1}{5}$ FT., in the Bombardes, in the Grand Organ in the Cathedral of Notre-Dame, Paris.

The stop may be formed of pipes of metal or wood and either open or covered, according to the quality of the tone desired. In any case, the tone should be somewhat subdued, for third-sounding tones are liable to be undesirably assertive and penetrating, and, accordingly, have to be confined to full-toned combinations. When properly subordinated to the fifth-sounding stops, the TIERCES become extremely valuable in artistic registration, imparting distinctive tonal coloring.

GROSSUNTERSATZ, Ger.—A large-scaled covered stop of

wood, and of 32 ft. pitch, belonging to the Pedal Organ. An example, under the name, exists in the Pedal of the Organ in the Church of Waltershausen. The Organ was built by Trost, of Altenburg, in 1730. When of medium scale, the stop has been commonly labeled UNTERSATZ, 32 FT., as in the Pedals of the Organs in the Cathedral of Merseburg and the Nicolaikirche, Leipzig. A stop of the same form and pitch, but of smaller scale, occupies a place on the First Manual of Walcker's Organ in Paulskirche, Frankfurt, a. M., where it is labeled MANUAL-UNTERSATZ, 32 FT.

A covered stop of this grave pitch cannot be pronounced entirely satisfactory, and utterly fails to take the place of an open stop of 32 ft. Cheapness and limitations of space are the only arguments that can be advanced in favor of its introduction, either as a Pedal Organ or a manual stop. If it is made, we strongly advise its being voiced with the harmonic-bridge, so as to generate as great a series of harmonic upper partials as possible: these partials alone give tonal value to the lower octave and a half of the stop; the prime tones of which are not *per se* musical sounds.

H

HALBPRINZIPAL, Ger.—The term sometimes used by the old German organ-builders to designate the half-length PRINCIPAL; namely, the ordinary organ-toned OCTAVE, 4 FT. Schlimbach says: "HALBPRINCIPAL so viel als Principal 4 Fuss, weil das gewöhnliche Hauptprincipal 8 Fuss hat. Zuweilen bedeutet es auch Octav 8 Fuss." The old English organ-builders abbreviated the term, and called the stop, simply and illogically, PRINCIPAL, 4 FT. The correct term, now coming into general use, is OCTAVE, 4 FT.

HARFENPRINZIPAL, Ger.—A manual, open labial stop of 8 ft. pitch, the pipes of which are cylindrical and of small scale. The stop was commonly made of tin, and voiced to yield a delicate compound tone, which, in quick *arpeggio* passages, bore a faint resemblance to those of the orchestral Harp. The effect was secured by the presence of certain upper partial tones which are prominent in the sounds produced by plucked gut strings. Seidel says: "HARFENPRINZIPAL ist ein lieblich intoniertes Prinzipal, welches einen der Harfe ähnlichen schnarrenden Ton haben soll." The stop is disused and the name is obsolete.

HARFENREGAL, Ger.—A soft-toned lingual stop, the tones

of which bore a remote resemblance to the twang of harp strings when roughly plucked. The stop and its name are both obsolete.

HARMONIA ÆTHERIA, Grk.—A compound harmonic-corroborating stop, composed of two or more ranks of very small-scaled and delicately voiced metal pipes. In its most desirable form it is composed of ÆOLINE labial pipes (See ÆOLINE); but in this extremely refined form it is at present practically unknown. The stop has been made in different forms. It appears, under the unusual name "HARMONICA ÆTHERICA," of two ranks, in the Echo of the Organ, built by Schulze, in the Parish Church of Doncaster, Yorkshire. In Walcker's Organ in Riga Cathedral a HARMONIA ÆTHERIA, of three complete ranks—TWELFTH, $2\frac{2}{3}$ FT., FIFTEENTH, 2 FT., and SEVENTEENTH, $1\frac{3}{5}$ FT.,—is placed on the Third Manual. Similar stops are inserted in the Organ in the Gewandhaus, Leipzig, and several other Walcker Organs. The German organ-builders do not seem to have carried the stop beyond three ranks, nor do they appear to have made breaks in the ranks.

FORMATION.—While a stop of through ranks, such as adopted by Walcker and other builders, formed of small-scaled and softly voiced pipes, could not fail to be very useful; a HARMONIA ÆTHERIA, in the form of a MIXTURE, composed of several ranks of high-pitched ÆOLINE or VOX ANGELICA pipes would be extremely valuable as a harmonic-corroborating stop in the softest toned manual division of an artistically appointed Organ. It certainly should find a place in the Organ of the twentieth century. The following is the appropriate composition for a full stop of six ranks:

HARMONIA ÆTHERIA—VI. RANKS.

CC to F♯	. . .	15—17*—19 —22 —26 —29.
G to f♯	. . .	12—15 —17*—19 —22 —26.
g¹ to f♯	. . .	8—12 —15 —17*—19 —22.
g² to c⁴	. . .	1— 8 —12 —15 —17* -19.

Should this composition be considered too full, the third-sounding break* in each rank may be omitted, making a five-rank stop. If the SEVENTEENTH is retained, it should be voiced softer than the octave- and fifth-sounding ranks, for that interval is, otherwise, very liable to be too assertive. This refined harmonic-corroborating stop should speak on wind of $1\frac{1}{2}$ inches to $2\frac{1}{2}$ inches, and be most scientifically regulated. The pipes to be of tin.

TONE AND REGISTRATION.—Properly made and artistically voiced, the HARMONIA ÆTHERIA should yield a singing, silvery, compound tone of great beauty; so delicate that, in registration, it may be employed with any of the softest unison stops in the Organ, string- or flute-toned. As a harmonic-corroborating or timbre-creating stop it would be difficult to overrate its value—a value absolutely unrealized in the present noisy-organ epoch.

HARMONICA, HARMONIKA, Ger.—An open labial stop, usually of 8 ft. pitch, the pipes of which are of wood, of small scale, and voiced to yield a combination of flute-tone and string-tone of a soft and beautiful quality. The stop has long been a favorite with German organ-builders, while it is practically unknown by those of this and other countries: indeed, both in the design and construction of wood stops, generally, the German organ-builders have always taken the lead, surpassing all others. Both French and English organ-builders have favored metal pipes, under the mistaken impression, perhaps, that a better tone could be obtained from them than from wood pipes; but more likely from the fact that metal-pipes are more easily made and voiced. This was the rock Willis split upon in his tonal appointment of the Organ in the Royal Albert Hall, South Kensington, London. In that large Organ there are only two complete wood stops, and the tone of the instrument suffers accordingly.

Fine examples of the HARMONIKA, 8 FT., exist on the Third Manuals of the Organs, by Walcker, in the Cathedrals of Riga and Ulm, and in the Concert Organ in the Gewandhaus, Leipzig. It exists in the Echo of the Organ in the Cathedral of Lund, Sweden, in which it is said to produce "a most beautiful effect." The stop is of wood. Equally good examples, labeled HARMONICA, 8 FT., exist in the Echo of the Schulze Organ in the Parish Church of Doncaster, and in the Choir of the Organ in the Church of St. Bartholomew, Armley, Yorkshire.

FORMATION.—The scale and form of the HARMONICA vary in different examples; and while in the generality of cases its pipes are straight, in some examples they are slightly pyramidal. For the stop of 8 ft. pitch, formed of straight, square pipes, Haas, the distinguished German organ-builder, has recommended the following small scale:

SCALE OF HARMONICA, 8 FT.

CC	C	c^1	c^2	c^3
66 mm.	40 mm.	24 mm.	15 mm.	9 mm.

We are in favor of a slightly larger scale and the slower reduction secured by the ratio 1:2.66, which halves on the eighteenth pipe. The following is our proposed scale, in inches, for square pipes:

SCALE OF HARMONICA, 8 FT.—RATIO 1:2.66.

CC	C	c^1	c^2	c^3	c^4
2.84	1.74	1.06	0.65	0.40	0.25

Some German organ-builders use scales which give the pipes of the HARMONICA a greater depth than width. An example of this treatment obtains in the fine stop in the Armley Organ, in which the pipes from middle c^1 to the top note are about twice their width in depth. Schulze seems to have found this extreme proportion favorable to the production of very soft and refined qualities of tone. The chief peculiarity of the HARMONICA pipe is the formation of its mouth and attendant cap, shown in the accompanying illustration, Fig. 20, which presents a Front View and Sections of the mouth portion of the c^1 pipe of the Armley stop. It will be seen that the mouth is circular, hollowed on the inside of the pipe so as to present

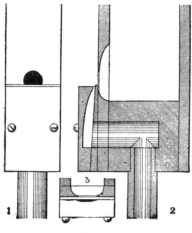

FIG. 20

a thin lip to the wind-stream. The manner in which this is done is shown in the Sections 2 and 3. The size of the circular mouth varies according to the quality and strength of the tone desired, but it should not be less than one-half the internal width of the pipe. It will be observed in Section 2 that the cap is compound, being formed of an inner, wedge-shaped piece, which forms the lower lip of the mouth; and an outer piece, in which the wind-way is carefully cut in the manner shown, in black, in the Transverse Section of the mouth, 3. In the formation of the compound caps extreme care and accuracy must be observed in graduating the thickness and slope of the wedge-piece, and smoothly rounding and polishing with black-lead its upper edge or lip.* The chief difficulty in connection with the voicing of this beautiful stop lies in the adjustment of both parts of the caps with relation to the circular mouths, and the exact proportions of the wind-ways, so as to obtain a perfectly even intonation throughout the compass. As a rule, the cap is adjusted to cover about one-third of the diameter of the mouth, but different

* The dimensions given by Töpfer-Allihn for the outer portion of the cap (Frosch) and the inner wedge-piece (Platte) are of sufficient importance to be given here: "Die Lange der grössten Frösche kann 50 mm betragen und nimmt ab bis zu 36 bis 40 mm. Die Dicke kann für die grösseren Pfeifen 20 mm und für die kleineren zwischen 8 bis 10 mm betragen. Es versteht sich, dass die vordere Dicke der Platte von den höchsten Tönen bis zum tiefsten gleichmässig zunehmen muss, weil ausserdem die Gleichmässigkeit des Tones darunter leiden würde. Man kann diese Dicke für C_0 8 Fuss 5 mm und für c^3 0,2 mm setzen. Bei diesen Annahmen erhält man die vordere Dicke der Platte für c^0 = 2.2 mm; für c^1 = 1 mm; für c^2 = 0.45 mm. Die hintere Dicke nimmt von 8 mm bis zu 3 mm ab."—"Die Theorie und Praxis des Orgelbaues," p. 232.

positions are adopted according to the tonality desired. While pine may be used for the sides and backs of the pipes, it is necessary, with such a form of mouth, for their fronts and caps to be of some close-grained hard wood: preferably beech for the caps.

TONE AND REGISTRATION.—The tone of the HARMONICA in its finest quality is extremely refined, being a combination of flute- and string-tone, in some examples inclining to one and in some to the other tonality. Locher says it "is a very tender 8-ft. string-tone stop, of narrow scale, intonated between the ÆOLINA and SALICIONAL." According to Töpfer-Allihn, "Es ist eine Stimme von ätherischem Charakter, welche bei sanften Altargesängen zum Gemüte des stillen Beters spricht." Although in the case of this stop one cannot speak from actual experience, it is not difficult to arrive at a fairly accurate estimation of its value in refined registration. It has hitherto been, and will continue to be inserted in the softest-toned division of the Organ, where it will be associated with stops—labial and lingual—of varied tonalities and, properly, of equally refined voices, admitting of combinations of great variety and beauty. If the HARMONICA inclines to flute-tone, the most effective registrations will be those with labial stops of string-tone and the lingual stops. It will be specially valuable with the VOX HUMANA, should one be present. On the other hand, if the HARMONICA inclines (as many German examples seem to do) to string-tone, its most effective registrations will be with stops of flute-tone and pure organ-tone, imparting to them a delicate brilliancy and clearness. To the lingual stops it will add firmness and richness. In the registration of stops of soft and refined tonalities the principle of tonal contrast should always be observed. The HARMONICA should speak on wind of 1½ inches to 2½ inches pressure.

HARMONICABASS, Ger.—A Pedal Organ labial stop, of 16 ft. pitch, formed of small-scaled open pipes of wood, voiced on a low-pressure wind, and yielding (like the HARMONICA, 8 FT., to which it is the true bass) a tone in which both refined flute-tone and string-tone are combined. A representative example of this uncommon stop exists in the Pedal of the Organ in the Catholic Church, at Berne, Switzerland. Locher describes this stop as "specially suitable for the accompaniment of soft passages."

The pipes should be constructed and voiced in the same manner as those of the HARMONICA (q. v.); and the following scale will be found suitable. As this stop would be required to furnish the bass to combinations of soft stops, it should be voiced on wind of 2½ or 3 inches.

SCALE OF HARMONICABASS, 16 FT.—RATIO 1: 2.66.

CCC	CC	C	G
4.44	2.73	1.67	1.25

HARMONIC CLARIBEL.—The name given by Thomas Casson, organ-builder, of London, to a HARMONIC FLUTE of a large scale and full intonation, constructed by him. Other English organ-builders have used the name to designate harmonic stops of a similar character. A fine example exists in the Organ constructed by Norman & Beard, of Norwich, in 1905, for the Colston Hall, Bristol. This stop is of 8 ft. pitch, and speaks on high pressure wind. Its pipes have inverted mouths, and are of double standard length and harmonic from c^1 to the top note. Such a treatment is favorable to the augmentation of the treble.

HARMONIC CLARION.—Fr., CLAIRON HARMONIQUE.—This lingual stop is the true Octave of the HARMONIC TRUMPET, 8 FT., and is, accordingly, of 4 ft. pitch. The pipes are formed in all respects similar to those of the unison stop, being of about double the normal speaking lengths, voiced on high-pressure wind to speak the octave pitch. The CLAIRON HARMONIQUE was invented by Aristide Cavaillé-Coll, and introduced for the first time in the Récit-Echo Expressif of the Organ in the Royal Church, Saint-Denis, constructed in 1841.

HARMONIC DIAPASON.—The name used by Bryceson Brothers, organ-builders, of London, to designate a large-scaled labial stop of DIAPASON formation, the pipes of which are, in the more important examples, of double the standard speaking length and harmonic from G or c^1 to the top note. The aim of the builders was to produce a volume of powerful foundation-tone; but, as might be expected on scientific grounds, the result was anything but pure organ-tone. The step was in the wrong direction, and, naturally, the result was a powerful and unpleasant flute-tone. Examples exist in certain Organs by Bryceson Brothers, notably one in the Organ built in 1882 for the Concert Hall, Paisley, Scotland. Such a stop is not a desirable addition to the Organ of to-day, which is over-furnished with unduly assertive voices.

HARMONIC FLUTE.—Fr., FLÛTE HARMONIQUE.—The stop formed of cylindrical metal pipes of 8 ft. and 4 ft. pitch. In the unison stop the pipes from the middle octave to the top note are made of double the normal speaking lengths; and are voiced and so blown as to speak the octaves of the tones properly belonging to the full lengths of the pipes so treated. For full particulars respecting this important stop, see FLÛTE HARMONIQUE. This stop was invented by Cavaillé-Coll, and inserted, for the first time, in the Organ in the Royal Church, Saint-Denis, in the year 1841.

The HARMONIC FLUTE has been very successfully constructed of wood in several forms. For particulars respecting those yielding imitative flute-tone, see ORCHESTRAL FLUTE.

HARMONIC PICCOLO.—Fr., PICCOLO HARMONIQUE.—A cylindrical metal stop, of 2 ft. pitch; the pipes of which are double the standard speaking lengths, and are formed and voiced in all respects similar to those of the harmonic portion of the HARMONIC FLUTE, 8 FT. (q. v.). An example of this stop under the name OCTAVIN HARMONIQUE, 2 FT., was inserted by Cavaillé-Coll in the Récit-Écho Expressif of the Organ in the Royal Church, Saint-Denis, in the year 1841. See FLÛTE HARMONIQUE.

HARMONIC TRUMPET.—Fr., TROMPETTE HARMONIQUE. Ger., HARMONIETROMPETE.—A lingual stop, of 8 ft. pitch, the reeds of which are of special formation, and the resonators of inverted conical form are, for the greater portion of its compass, of greater lengths than those required for the ordinary TRUMPET, 8 FT. The reeds are of the open class and of large scale, and the tongues are thick and well curved, so as to respond properly to the high-pressure wind on which the stop is voiced; producing powerful tones, which are the octaves of those which naturally belong to the lengths of the resonators. Accordingly, the resonator of eight feet in length in the HARMONIC TRUMPET yields a note of the same pitch as that produced by the resonator of four feet long in the ordinary TRUMPET, both stops being of 8 ft. pitch. The double-length resonators usually commence at tenor C.

The TROMPETTE HARMONIQUE was invented by Aristide Cavaillé-Coll, and used for the first time in the Organ erected, in 1841, in the Royal Church, Saint-Denis. One TROMPETTE HARMONIQUE was placed in the Positif; two in the Grand Orgue; and two in the Récit-Écho Expressif; all of 8 ft. pitch.* These stops, voiced on compara-

---

* "La *trompette harmonique* du clavier de récit est, par sa puissance et par l'excellence des sons qu'elle produit, incomparablement supérieure à tout ce que l'on connaît en ce genre. Le caractère tout-à-fait particulier de ses basses, lorsqu'on l'emploie comme partie chantante accompagnée des jeux de fond, est d'un effet admirable. On en peut dire autant des séries de jeux de *flûtes harmoniques* qui donnent à l'ensemble de l'orgue tant de rondeur et de puissance."—J. Adrian de La Page, in Report to the Société des Beaux-Arts, on the Organ in the Royal Church Saint-Denis, 1844.

tively low-pressure wind, were widely different in tone from the corresponding stops subsequently developed by Willis and other leading English organ-builders, who adopted suitable high wind pressures to produce .the rich tone desired.

TONE AND REGISTRATION.—The tone of the HARMONIC TRUM-PET varies considerably, according to the method in which it is voiced and the pressure of the wind on which it speaks. The tones of the French stops are, like the generality of the French striking-reed stops, somewhat hard and brassy, due to the thinness and peculiar curvature of their tongues, combined with wind of moder-ate pressure. On the other hand, the HARMONIC TRUMPETS made by the Willis school of reed-voicers, in which thick tongues are used, beautifully curved so as to strike the *échalote* with a smooth uncurv-ing motion, yield, under high-pressure wind, full rich tones, which, practically free from objectionable brassy clang, are imitative of the tones of the orchestral Slide Trumpet played by a master.

The office of so powerfully-voiced a stop as the HARMONIC TRUM-PET is necessarily limited in artistic registration. Its chief value is in solo passages of an orchestral character, and when suitably accompanied. It is also suitable in very full combinations in which it assumes the dominating tonality, assisted, perhaps, by its true Octave the HARMONIC CLARION, 4 FT., or the TUBA CLARION, 4 FT. Powerful as its voice is and naturally rich in harmonics, it can be effectively colored by the addition of loud-toned harmonic-cor-roborating stops, simple and compound. The HARMONIC TRUMPET should never be placed in an unexpressive division of an Organ.

HARMONIC TUBA.—The most powerful lingual stop, of 8 ft. pitch, inserted in the Organ. Its pipes are of large scale, having resonators of inverted conical shape and double the normal standard length. The reeds are formed similar to, but slightly larger in scale than, those of the HARMONIC TRUMPET (*q. v.*). The stop is voiced on wind of fifteen inches upward, according to the volume and power of the tone required. Reeds with double tongues have been sug-gested for this impressive stop; but they are too troublesome to make, too uncertain in speech, and too difficult to tune, ever to favor their adoption: and it is questionable if they are desirable; for sufficient musical noise can be produced by the single-tongued reeds for all legitimate effects in dignified music.

TONE AND REGISTRATION.—The proper tone of the HARMONIC TUBA is full, sonorous, and commanding; dominating all the voices of the 8 ft. stops, labial and lingual, in the Organ. Its use is, accordingly, limited to rare and very special effects, chiefly of an orchestral character, and to grand climaxes in which a "full organ" burst of sound is called for. The stop is, therefore, only necessary and appropriate in Concert-room Organs of the first magnitude. Although stops of this dominating assertiveness have in several noteworthy cases been thoughtlessly—not to use a stronger expression—planted in exposed and uncontrollable positions, it is surely unnecessary to insist, on both artistic and common-sense grounds, that the HARMONIC TUBA be placed under control and in an expressive division, of the Organ. Its place is either in the Solo Organ or, better still, in the Brass-wind division of the properly schemed Concert-room Organ. Generally, the remarks anent the registration of the HARMONIC TRUMPET apply in the case of the stop under review, although the HARMONIC TRUMPET must be considered to be more generally useful than the more powerful HARMONIC TUBA.

HARMONIC TWELFTH.—A covered labial stop, of $2\frac{2}{3}$ ft. pitch, the pipes of which are of metal, of medium scale, and stopped so as to have speaking lengths equal to one and one-half times the lengths of the standard open pipes of the corresponding pitch. Thus, the CC pipe of the HARMONIC TWELFTH, having a speaking length of 4 ft., yields, on being properly voiced and overblown, a tone of the same pitch as that of an open pipe of $2\frac{2}{3}$ ft. speaking length.

The HARMONIC TWELFTH was introduced by Thomas Casson, and inserted in the Organ installed in the London Organ School and certain other instruments constructed, under his supervision, by the Positive Organ Company, of London. It has been made by some other builders.

TONE AND REGISTRATION.—The tone of the stop is properly full, smooth, and clear; and owing to its having comparatively few upper partial tones of an assertive character it mixes well, and is more agreeable in combination than the open TWELFTH, $2\frac{2}{3}$ FT., which belongs to the foundation harmonic series. It is on this account less prominent, while it is more effective as a timbre-creating stop in combination with both labial and lingual stops of the softer class. It may, accordingly, be considered more valuable in artistic registration than any open-toned TWELFTH. In fact, it can be used in such registration ten times for once that the TWELFTH of the foundation-work can be used. Its proper position is in a soft-toned division of the Organ; and it is specially to be recommended for insertion in the chief accompanimental division of the properly appointed Church Organ.

HARMONIEFLÖTE, Ger.—The name given to an open labial stop, of 8 ft. pitch, the pipes of which are of wood and of small scale, narrow and deep, voiced on wind of low pressure. In the best examples the tone is soft and singing, in character between the voices of the HARMONICA and the MELODIA, while it is less assertive than either. Desirable as a stop of this tonality would be when refinement is aimed at, it is not likely to be favored during the present prevailing craze for loud and crude intonation. Such a flute-toned stop would be ideal for a properly appointed Chamber Organ. We are not aware of a single example obtaining in an English or American Organ.

HARP.—Commonly, in modern Organs, a percussion stop, of 8 ft. pitch, formed of metal or wood plates or bars, suspended over tuned resonators, and struck by a hammer-action, electrically commanded by a manual clavier. The compass of the stop is usually of 49 notes—CC to c^3—but is properly made of the full manual compass, 61 notes. Different opinions obtain respecting the most desirable material for the resonant bars; some maintaining that the Harp tone is better imitated by sonorous wood than metal. The latter, however, is generally used. To produce the desired tone, the hammers have to be very carefully padded, and the action artistically adjusted.

In 1733, Thomas Schwarbrook inserted in his Organ in the Church of St. Michael, Coventry, three remarkable string stops— HARP, LUTE, and DULCIMER. But owing to the difficulty of keeping the strings in tune, the stops were removed in 1763. Some attempts have been made to furnish the modern Organ with a string HARP, sounded by plectra.

HAUTBOIS D'AMOUR, Fr.—Ital., OBOE D'AMORE.—A lingual stop of the OBOE species, the pipes of which have resonators of small scale, partly covered so as to impart to the tone a singular softness and refinement which, in all likelihood, suggested its name.* This stop seems to be no longer made, being displaced, along with other softly-toned stops, by those of more powerful and less beautiful voices. The stop should be revived for insertion in the true Chamber Organ, and in the softest and accompanimental divisions of the Church and Concert-room Organs.

---

* "HAUTBOIS D'AMOUR. Hat mit der vorhergehenden Stimme viel Aehnliches, doch muss sie wie die Vox humana halb gedeckt sein. Man findet sei zu 8 Fusston, und kleiner darf sie ihrer Natur nach auch nicht sein."—Schlimbach, 1843.

HAUTBOY.—Fr., HAUTBOIS.—Ital. and Ger., OBOE.—A lingual stop, of 8 ft. pitch, the tone of which imitates, more or less closely, that of the orchestral instrument of the same name. The resonators of the ordinary HAUTBOY are slender and of standard length, and are surmounted by long inverted conical bells, which are sometimes shaded. The variety of the stop designated the ORCHESTRAL OBOE has been made with resonators of different forms and proportions, with the view of obtaining a close imitation of the tone of the orchestral instrument. In England and America the HAUTBOY is invariably a striking-reed; but in France and Germany the free-reed stop seems to have been preferred. An example exists on the Second Manual of Ladegast's fine Organ in Schwerin Cathedral. For description and illustration of the striking-reed stops, see OBOE and ORCHESTRAL OBOE.

HELLFLÖTE, HELLPFEIFE, Ger.—This name, which signifies *Clear-toned Flute*, has been given by German organ-builders to an open labial stop, of 8 ft. pitch, the pipes of which are of wood and of small scale, voiced to yield a clear semi-imitative flute-tone, of medium strength, and of good mixing quality. Schlimbach does not mention the stop; and Seidel dismisses it in these words: "HELL-PFEIFE, ein offenes Flötenwerk zu 8' von besonders hellum Ton." For description of the corresponding English stop, see CLEAR FLUTE.

HOHLFLÖTE, HOHLPFEIFE, Ger.—Fr., FLÛTE-CREUSE.—Dtch. HOLFLUIT, HOLPIJP.—This name, which means *Hollow-toned Flute*, is used to designate an open labial stop, of 8 ft., 4 ft., and, sometimes, 2 ft. pitch, the pipes of which are of large scale, made, in the most characteristic examples, of wood, and voiced to yield a full, somewhat dull, and hollow tone, which has suggested its name. Examples exist in several of the more important Walcker Organs, including those in Riga Cathedral and the Gewandhaus, Leipzig. In both these Organs they are of 8 ft. pitch. In the Organ in Pauls-kirche, Frankfurt a. M., the HOHLFLÖTE is of 4 FT. pitch. They are all placed on the First Manual—the proper division (the Great) in a Church Organ. In the properly stop-apportioned Concert-room Organ it should find a place in the Wood-wind division, and in the subdivision devoted specially to the FLUTES.*

* "La FLÛTE-CREUSE (*die Hohlflœte*) est une flûte de grosse taille en étoffe et mieux en bois pour répondre à son nom et sonner le creux du sapin par ces lèvres étroitement pincées. On la peut faire de toutes les hauteurs; à seize-pieds, elle est fort originale, mais aussi rare qu'à deux; à huit-pieds, elle chante avec beaucoup de mélancolie; généralement, on ne la mélange qu'avecles jeux effilés et tranchants."—Regnier.

FORMATION.—The HOHLFLÖTE, of wood, is made in different forms; all with the aim of obtaining from pipes of moderate scales the maximum volume of the tone peculiar to the stop, while speaking on a copious supply of wind at a moderate pressure. We cannot do better than describe the formation of the pipes of two representative stops, made and voiced by the distinguished artist, Edmund Schulze, of Paulinzelle. The first stop, from the Organ formerly in the Town Hall of Northampton, was formed of quadrangular pipes of greater width than depth, with the mouth cut on a wide side. The lower portion of a pipe of this stop is shown, in Front View and Longitudinal and Transverse Sections, in Fig. 21. The

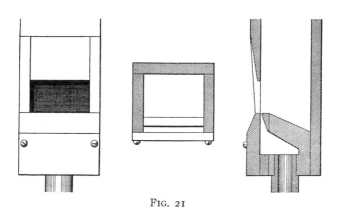

FIG. 21

mouth is of the German form, cut up equal to one-half its width, having a straight upper lip, and its side-pieces and the upper portion of the cap sloped toward the lower lip. The second stop, from the Organ in the Church of St. Peter, Hindley, is formed of triangular pipes of greater depth than width, with the mouth cut on the narrow side. The lower portion of the middle c^1 pipe of this stop is shown in Front View and Longitudinal and Transverse Sections, in Fig. 22. The peculiar formation of the pipe is clearly indicated by the Sections. The internal dimensions are $1\frac{5}{8}$ inches in width at the mouth by $2\frac{1}{8}$ inches in depth.* These measurements give an internal transverse area equal to that of a quadrangular pipe of $1\frac{3}{8}$ inches in width by $1\frac{1}{16}$ inches in depth. The adoption of the triangular form is simply for the purpose of obtaining a mouth large in proportion to the transverse area of the pipe, as in the case of the preceding example. The mouth is $\frac{7}{8}$ inch in height and arched as shown. HOHLFLÖTE pipes have also been made of greater depth than width, as in the stop in the Great of the Organ in the Public Halls, Glasgow, constructed by Lewis, of London. The tenor C pipe of this stop measures $2\frac{1}{8}$ inches in width by $2\frac{11}{16}$ inches in depth. The mouth, formed on the wide way of the pipe, is cut up $1\frac{1}{8}$ inches in height, and its upper lip is thick and carefully rounded, as is generally the case in HOHLFLÖTE pipes. The bass octave of this stop is, as usual, of large-scaled covered pipes. Provision for a copious supply

* In speaking of the width of a pipe, allusion is invariably made to the internal dimension of the side in which the mouth is cut. A pipe may, therefore, be described as having a greater depth than width, or greater width than depth, according to the location of its mouth.

of wind is necessary in the pipes of the HOHLFLÖTE. The stop has in some instances been made of metal; but, in the matter of tone, it cannot be considered the true stop when of that material.

TONE AND REGISTRATION.—The proper full unimitative flute-tone of the HOHLFLÖTE, 8 FT., somewhat dull and hollow in its character, places the stop almost in a class by itself. Its recognized place is in the Great Organ, where its voice is of the most value in combination, imparting great firmness and tonal solidity to the uni-

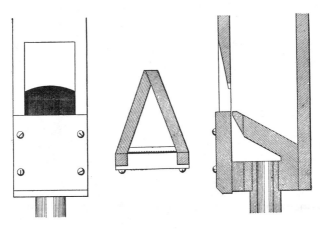

FIG. 22

son foundation tone, and fullness to the voices of the lingual stops belonging to that fundamental division. The tone being deficient in harmonic upper partials of high pitch, and free from any of an assertive character, prevents its assuming the office of a timbre-creator, while it admits of its being freely used in registration as a body-builder. To be of maximum use, the stop should be placed under control and rendered flexible and expressive. By affording tones of different degrees of assertiveness, its value in registration with exposed stops will be greatly increased. In full effects it will largely help in binding the various tonalities and the several pitches together, admitting of a free use of the compound harmonic-corroborating stops at their full tones. In the Second Pedal of the Organ in the Cathedral of Ulm there is a HOHLFLÖTE of two feet pitch. Speaking of this stop, Locher remarks: "As a particularly rare specimen, I found this stop in Ulm Münster, as a 2 ft. pedal stop, where combined with other stops on the Upper Pedal, it gives, without need of any coupler, a power of expression belonging almost exclusively to the manuals. To explain the term 'Upper Pedal,' I must say that at Ulm, as well as in the Church of St. Paul, Frankfurt-on-the-Main, in the Marienkirche, Lübeck, and in the Stifts-kirche, Stuttgart, there are two pedal claviers placed one above the other (like the manuals) instead of the customary single clavier."*

HOHLFLÖTENBASS, Ger.—An open labial stop, of 16 ft. pitch, the pipes of which are of wood, quadrangular in form, and mouthed and voiced similar to those of the HOHLFLÖTE (*q. v.*). It furnishes the proper bass to the manual unison stop, and is, accordingly, a Pedal Organ stop; but rarely introduced in modern Organs.

HOHLQUINTE, Ger.—An open labial stop, of 5⅓ ft., 2⅔ ft., and 1⅓ ft. pitch, the pipes of which, in the two lower pitches, are commonly made of wood, and, in the 1⅓ ft. pitch, of metal. In formation and tone, the stop resembles the unison HOHLFLÖTE. As a tone-building harmonic-corroborating stop it would prove valuable in either the Great or the Solo of a large Church or Concert-room Organ. Its tone not being highly distinctive, the stop lends itself very freely to combinations of both labial and lingual stops. In the Pedal Organ the HOHLQUINTE, 5⅓ FT., finds its most useful place; while those of 2⅔ ft. and 1⅓ ft. belong to the manual department.†

HOHLSCHELLE, Ger.—The term that has been employed by German organ-builders to designate a QUINTATEN. Schlimbach says: "HOHLSCHELLE. Ist ein veralteter Beiname der Quintatön." From the name, which means *Hollow-Bell*, it might be supposed that the tone of the stop resembled that of the HOHLFLÖTE, strongly inclining to that of the HOHLQUINTE—a compound tone that might prove very valuable in artistic registration. Perhaps it is to be re-

---

* In our work, "The Art of Organ-Building," Vol. II., pp. 145, 146, we give a Section and Plan of the double pedal claviers of the Ulm Organ, made from drawings furnished by Messrs. Walcker, of Ludwigsburg, the builders of the Organ.

† "Mais ce qu'il faut bien retenir, comme nous l'avons déjà fait remarquer et comme le prouvent encore les quintes tirées des régistres etroits, c'est qu'à peu près tous les jeux de fonds allemands engendrent leur quinte, et que sa génération par un régistre spécial donne à la quinte tous les caractères de ce régistre, la montre, par exemple, a sa quinte ouverte, et de même mesure qu'elle et de mêmes proportions.

"Cette affection des Allemands pour la quinte est logique; ils ne veulent pas accompagner leurs fonds avec des fonds seulement, parce que c'est un accompagnement sans viguer; ils ne le feront pas non plus avec des timbres éclatants comme les jeux d'anches; la quinte leur offre un renfort tout simple et se marie convenablement avec le chant, qui occupe une part si importante dans leur culte extérieur. Quand la quinte est à cheminée, comme en France, c'est souvent le *Nasard;* elle se nomme *Rohrnasad, Rohrquint;* quand elle ne s'accorde qu'avec les fonds d'un degré supérieur, on l'appelle souvent *Quinta ex octava;* quand elle est à la douzième, on la nomme en Italie *Dodecima,* à la dix-neuvième, *Decima-Nona.*"—Regnier.

gretted that some of the tones due to the skill of the old voicers are no longer heard in the Organ.

HORN, ORCHESTRAL HORN.—Fr., COR D'ORCHESTRE. Ital., CORNO. Ger., HORN.—Stops named HORNS were introduced by some of the old English organ-builders. Renatus Harris, Junr., erected an Organ, in 1724, in St. Dionis Backchurch, in which he inserted a stop labeled FRENCH HORN. In 1730, Richard Bridge inserted a similar stop in the Organ he built for Christ Church, Spitalfields; and another, in 1741, in the instrument he erected in the Church of St. Anne, Limehouse, London. All these stops were doubtless designed to imitate in their tones those of the Horn of the time, which was first used in England, in 1720, at the performance, in London, of Handel's opera "Radamisto." What success attended the organ-builders' imitations can only be surmised.

The orchestral Horn of to-day produces tones—open and hand-closed—which are *sui generis*, and particularly difficult to imitate by organ-pipes, lingual or labial. Yet essays have been made by skillful pipe-makers and voicers, chiefly with lingual pipes, which have been attended with such good results that there are hopes of a satisfactory imitation some day rewarding their labors. The tones of the orchestral Horn are so peculiarly smooth and tender, that we have long held the opinion, supported by effects that have come before our notice, that there is a likelihood of a good imitation of the Horn tones being produced by metal labial pipes. At present, however, no serious attempt has been made in this direction.

Neither the French nor German organ-builders seem to have considered the beautiful tones of the orchestral Horn either capable or worthy of imitation; and, accordingly, have made a great mistake. In all the lists of stops of Walcker Organs we have examined, we have only found HORN, 8 FT., given once, in that of the Concert-room Organ in the Philharmonie, Warschau. In this instrument it is inserted, along with the OBOE, 8 FT., in the soft-toned Third Manual division, where it is expressive. Two HORNS, of 8 ft. pitch, were inserted by the celebrated German organ-builder, Edmund Schulze, in the Organ in the Parish Church of Doncaster, but neither of these can be considered imitative. In the stop-appointments of French Organs we have been unable to find a single instance of the introduction of the imitative HORN or COR D'ORCHESTRE. It, accordingly, seems to have been left to English and American artists in reed-voicing to develop the imitative HORN to a state approaching all that can reasonably be expected of lingual organ-pipes.

FORMATION.—In certain attempts made, during the latter part of the last century, by English organ-builders to produce tones resembling those of the orchestral Horn, lingual pipes were used having resonators of inverted conical form, like those of the TRUMPET, but usually of a larger scale; in which some device of a muting character, such as a perforated disc of metal, was inserted so as to obtain tones having the peculiar tonality of the closed or "hand notes" of the orchestral instrument, which are absolutely free from brassiness or reediness. In other stops, the resonators were shaded to obtain the desired subdued tones. Such expedients proved only partly successful, and merely pointed the way to more effective methods, involving the adoption of resonators of widely different forms and proportions: of these two representative examples will be sufficient, both due to American ingenuity and skill.

The most successful HORN which has come under our notice is that recently produced by the Hook and Hastings Company, organ-builders, of Kendal Green, Mass., through whose courtesy we are able to describe and illustrate the formation of the pipes of the stop. It will be seen, on referring to the illustration, Fig. 23, Plate III., that the resonator employed is mainly of the inverted conical form, but differing from all other resonators of the form, in being closed at top with a conical cap, soldered on, and having a slot, with double adjustment for regulating and tuning, cut close to its upper end, as shown. It can be readily understood that the peculiar cap exerts a considerable mellowing effect on the tone in conjunction with the adjustable slot through which alone the subdued sound finds free egress. The slot is properly placed in a line with the tuning-wire, but it is so placed in the illustration that both it and the wire can be properly shown. The measurements of the pipe are as follows: The length of the resonator, exclusive of the conical cap, is 2 feet $3\frac{3}{4}$ inches; diameter at top $3\frac{3}{8}$ inches; height of cap internally $\frac{5}{8}$ inch. Length of slot (subject to alteration) $2\frac{1}{16}$ inches; width $\frac{9}{16}$ inch; distance from top edge of resonator $1\frac{1}{2}$ inches. The measurements of the sound-producing portions are: The length of the reed (*échalote*) from the under side of the block is $1\frac{3}{4}$ inches, the width of the tongue (*languette*) at its free end is $\frac{11}{32}$ inch, and where it enters the block $\frac{3}{16}$ inch. The reed is of the closed form, its perforation commencing $\frac{5}{16}$ inch from the lower end.

The second noteworthy example is the HORN which Mr. E. M. Skinner, organ-builder of Boston, Mass., added some years ago to the list of imitative stops. The formation and proportions of the pipes of this stop forcibly illustrate by what very dissimilar treatments similar results are obtained. In this case it may be stated that the resonator, instead of being of large scale and after the TRUMPET model, is extremely slender and, accordingly, very slightly tapered. Also unlike that of the other HORN, it is open at top, and has a short cylindrical portion carrying an adjustable slide shaded by a partially attached disc of metal. The measurements of the tenor C pipe are as follows: The length of the resonator is 3 feet $3\frac{1}{2}$ inches (subject to slight alteration), and its internal diameter at top is 1.63 inches. The measurements of the sound-producing portions are: The length of the reed from the under side of the block is $2\frac{3}{16}$ inches; the width of the tongue at its free end is $\frac{7}{16}$ inch, and where it enters the block $\frac{7}{32}$ inch. The reed is of the closed form, its perforation being about $1\frac{3}{16}$ inches long, commencing about $\frac{3}{8}$ inch from the lower end. Of examples of less importance it is unnecessary to speak. As a specially refined tone, entirely free from clang or brassiness, is required, it is necessary that a suitable wind-pressure be adopted for the imitative HORN. This may vary under certain conditions; but, in our opinion, it should never exceed twelve inches. The stop represented by the pipe illustrated in Fig. 23 was wisely voiced on wind of eight inches, which should never be exceeded in a Church Organ HORN.

TONE AND REGISTRATION.—The closer the tone of the organ HORN approaches the tones of the orchestral instrument the greater will its value be in solo work and in registration. But, it may reasonably be asked, to which of the characteristic tones of the orchestral Horn is it most desirable for the tone of the organ stop to approach? The two tones of the Horn are the *open* and *closed;* the latter being also designated the *hand-tones,* because they are formed by inserting the hand, in a special manner, and more or less, into the bell of the instrument while it is being played. These tones are widely different in sonorousness, and call for great skill on the part of the performer to reconcile them.* It would seem most desirable for the voicer of the HORN to aim at obtaining a tone as free from brassy clang as possible in striking-reed pipes, and approaching closely the tender sympathetic tonality of what are known as the "*half-stopped notes*" of the orchestral Horn. Such a tonality would give the HORN, 8 FT., an individuality of peculiar charm and value both in solo effects and in refined registration; separating its voice from the voices of all the other lingual stops in the Organ; and placing itself, as it were, midway between them and the voices of the organ-toned labial stops. With such an intermediate tonality it is not difficult to realize the unique position the imitative HORN would occupy in registration with the more refined and contrasting stops of the Organ. To even such a distinctive stop as the VOX HUMANA it would impart volume and dignity of peculiar value in a tenor solo. In combination with the FLUTES it would create tones of beautiful colorings. In the properly-appointed Concert-room Organ its correct place is in the Brass-wind division; while in the Church Organ its appropriate place is in an expressive accompanimental division.

HORNBÄSSLEIN, Ger.—The name given, according to Schlimbach (1843), to a Pedal Organ stop, of 2 ft. pitch, formed of open metal pipes of medium scale. The stop is represented in the Pedal Organ of Walcker's instrument in the Cathedral of St. Stephen, Vienna, under the name OCTAVBASS, 2 FT. While stops of this high

* Dr. W. H. Stone remarks: "Between the stopped or 'hand notes' and the open notes there is an obvious difference in character and quality which it is impossible wholly to suppress, but which may be sufficiently modified so as not to offend the ear. This object is attained by blowing the open notes softly, so as to reduce the contrast between their sonorousness, and the closed or 'stuffed' (*étouffé*) character of those modified by means of the hand."—Grove's "Dictionary of Music."

pitch are common in German Pedal Organs, they are practically unknown as independent stops in French, English, and American Pedal Organs. They should, however, appear both in the full COMPENSATING MIXTURE, and the Pedal GRAND CORNET.

HORN DIAPASON.—The name that has been used to designate a metal stop, of 8 ft. pitch, the pipes of which resemble in formation and scaling those of the true DIAPASON, but which are modified in tone by being boldly slotted and, necessarily, slightly increased in length. The effect of the slotting is the introduction of certain harmonic upper partials into the pure organ-tone belonging to the normal DIAPASON, changing it into a horny and somewhat stringy quality which fails to satisfy the sensitive musical ear. The value of the tone is, in our opinion, not sufficient to warrant its insertion in any save a Concert-room Organ of the first magnitude, in which it may be valuable in building up a full volume of foundation tone through the absence of tonal sympathy with the pure DIAPASON voices. With this view, it may occupy a place in the First or Great Organ. Messrs. Walker & Sons, organ-builders, of London, appear to favor the stop, having introduced it in several of their important instruments. They inserted a HORN DIAPASON, 8 FT., in the Greats of the Organs in St. Martin's Church, Leicester, and the Church of St. Mary-le-Bow, London; and in the Swells of the Organs in York Minster; and Holy Trinity Church, Chelsea, London. We inserted the stop in the Third Organ, or Wood-wind division, in our scheme for the Organ installed in the Festival Hall of the Louisiana Purchase Exposition, 1904, chiefly on account of its value in contrasting combinations.

HÖRNLEIN, Ger.—The name employed, according to Schlimbach (1843), to designate a manual stop, of 2 ft. pitch, which may be either of the GEMSHORN or the NACHTHORN tonality. Such a stop, both as a harmonic-corroborator and timbre-creator, would be found valuable in artistic registration, furnishing a vivid contrast to the PICCOLO, 2 FT. The term HÖRNLEIN was applied, in the original Organ in the Cathedral of Lucerne, to a soft-toned lingual stop of 8 ft. pitch.

HUMANGEDECKT, Ger.—A covered stop, of 8 ft. pitch, the soft and compound tone of which seemed to imitate a refined human voice.* The pipes were of similar formation to those of the LIEB-

---

* "Human heisst so viel als lieblich, dar HUMANGEDECKT: ein liebliches, angenehmes, gedecktes Register. Man findet es gewöhnlich zu 8 Fusston."—Seidel.

LICHGEDECKT, 8 FT., but of somewhat smaller scale, and voiced on wind of lower pressure.

A stop of this description would be a valuable addition to the tonal forces of the true Chamber Organ, and also to the tonal apportionment of the Choir or chief accompanimental division of the Church Organ, in which great refinement of tone is essential.

J

JEU ÉRARD, Fr.—The name given to a free-reed stop, invented by Érard, of Paris, and inserted by him in the Organ erected in the Tuileries, now destroyed. Like all properly-constructed free-reed stops, the JEU ÉRARD was furnished with very large boots. Its resonators were in the form of a short inverted cone, surmounted by a hemispherical capping, having a perforation, where the two forms joined, for the escape of the condensed air and the emission of the sound. The tone of this stop is stated to have been agreeable but rather muffled, as might be expected from a free-reed under such a resonator. The stop is now obsolete. See REGAL.

JUBALFLÖTE, Ger.—An open labial stop of 8 ft. and 4 ft. pitch, the pipes of which have double mouths, and yield a full unimitative flute-tone.* A JUBALFLÖTE, 8 FT., exists in Walcker's Organ in St. Paul's Church, Frankfurt. It also exists, of both 8 ft. and 4 ft. pitch, in the Pedal of the Organ in the Church of SS. Peter and Paul, Göerlitz. Hopkins gives, in his specification, a third JUBALFLÖTE, of 2 ft. pitch, but we question his accuracy in this small matter.

JULA, Ger.—The name given, according to Schlimbach and Seidel, to the SPITZFLÖTE, 8 FT., but for what reason neither authority gives any information. The term JULAQUINTE has, after the same fashion, been used to designate a similar stop of either $5\frac{1}{3}$ ft. or $2\frac{2}{3}$ ft. pitch.

JUNFERNREGAL, Ger.— An old lingual stop, which was usually made of 8 ft. and 4 ft. pitch; but an example of 16 ft. pitch exists, or did exist about fifty years ago, in the Choir of the Organ in the Church of St. Dominick, Prague. Like all old REGALS, the stop is one of the tonal curiosities of the art of organ-building. See REGAL.

* "JUBALFLÖTE, ein Bezeichnung für ein offenes Flötenwerk 8′ oder 4′, auch mit doppelter Labiierung, kommt im deutschen und amerikanischen Orgelbau vor. Der Name ist entnommen aus I. Mos. 4, 21."—Töpfer-Allihn.

JUNGFERNSTIME, Ger.—Lat., Vox Virgine.—The term which has occasionally been employed by German organ-builders to designate an open labial stop, the pipes of which were cylindrical, of small scale, and properly made of tin in the best examples. The stop, voiced on wind of low pressure, yielded a tone of an extremely refined and delicate character, probably closely resembling that of the Vox Angelica, 8 ft., of to-day. It was usually and properly made of unison (8 ft.) pitch, but an Octave seems to have sometimes been made.

K

KÄLBERREGAL, Ger.—An obsolete lingual stop of the old Regal family, which received its remarkable name from the subdued and lowing character of its voice, which somewhat resembled that of a calf (*Kalb*). See Regal.

KERAULOPHONE, Grk.—This name, compounded from the Greek words κερας—a horn, αὐλός—a pipe or flute, and φωνή—voice or sound, is used to designate an open metal labial stop, of 8 ft. pitch. The stop was originally made by Gray & Davison, organ-builders, of London; and was introduced by them, for the first time, in the Organ they constructed, in 1843, for the Church of St. Paul, Knightsbridge, London. The stop is common in English Organs, but has very seldom been made by Continental builders: an example appears in the Positif of Merklin's Organ in the Church of Saint-Eustache, Paris. We have been unable to find an example in any Organ built by Walcker, Ladegast, or any other great German organ-builder: but Locher states that a Keraulophone was inserted by Steinmeyer, in 1880, in the Organ in the Frauenkirche, Munich. Roosevelt, of New York, showed his wise appreciation of the value of this stop by inserting it in some of his important Organs. He placed it in the Great of his Organ in Grace Church, and in the Solo of the Organ in the Church of St. Thomas, New York City; in the Echo of the Organs in the Auditorium, Chicago; the Cathedral of The Incarnation, Garden City, L. I., and the First Congregational Church, Great Barrington, Mass. English organ-builders are, to-day, very unwisely abandoning the stop.

Although the name of the stop under consideration has commonly been rendered Keraulophon, it seems clear to us that, as its last syllable is derived from the word φωνή, it should be rendered Keraulophone; agreeing with many other words which derive their terminations from the same Greek word—such as EUPHONE, STEN-TORPHONE, DIAPHONE, graphophone, microphone, telephone, etc. The French term is KÉRAULOPHÔNE. Roosevelt invariably used the final E in his stop names.

FORMATION.—The pipes of the KERAULOPHONE are cylindrical in form and of medium scale. The desirable maximum scale in the ratio 1 : 2.66—halving on the eighteenth pipe—gives the CC pipe a diameter of 3.94 inches; the C pipe a diameter of 2.41 inches; the c¹ pipe a diameter of 1.47 inches, and the c⁴ pipe a diameter of 0.34 inches. Smaller scales have been adopted by different builders, and are desirable when the stop is destined for an Echo Organ or a Chamber Organ: but too small a scale will destroy the characteristic tone of the stop, which should be round and rich. The mouth of the KERAULOPHONE pipe should be one-fifth the circumference of the pipe in width, and about one-fourth its width in height. This latter proportion, however, depends upon the wind-pressure—which should not exceed 3½ inches—and the quality of the tone desired. The upper lip is straight and not cut sharp, being smoothly rounded, and the nicking of the languid is moderately fine. The mouth has ears of small projection and without any harmonic attachment. The characteristic feature of the pipe, and that which is the principal factor in the production of its special tone, is its perforated tuning-slide, as shown at A in Fig. 24, Plate III. The length of the slide is about two and a half times its own diameter; and its perforation is made the distance of one diameter from its top edge, as indicated. In the CC pipe the diameter of the perforation should be 0.79 inch; in the C pipe 0.56; and regularly diminishing to 0.14 inch in the c⁴ pipe. The slides must be so accurately fitted to the bodies of the pipes as to firmly retain their position, while they can be easily tapped up or down in the process of tuning. Metal of good substance must be used for this stop; and Hoyt's Two-ply Pipe-Metal is highly suitable, being specially firm at moderate thicknesses.

TONE AND REGISTRATION.—The tone of the KERAULOPHONE when in its true form and artistically voiced is full, smooth, and in the principal portion of its compass so strongly resembling the tone of the " hand notes " of the orchestral Horn as to have suggested its name.* In this respect the KERAULOPHONE may be said to stand alone among labial stops: and its present neglect by English organ-builders goes far to show how little they appreciate refinement of tone, and the great value of timbre-creating voices in the Organ. There is not sufficient roar or scream in the KERAULOPHONE to please the present prevailing want of taste in the organ-building world.

We can speak, from long experience, of the great value of the true English KERAULOPHONE in refined and artistic registration. Its building-up and vivid-coloring properties are remarkable; and in this direction it is specially valuable in association with both open and covered, unimitative, flute-work. It combines admirably with

* In the KERAULOPHONE in our own Chamber Organ this horn-like tone was so pronounced that we labeled it CORNO DI CACCIA. It spoke on wind of 2⅜ inches.

all the softer lingual stops; and would form an effective helper to the
ORCHESTRAL HORN. The proper situation of the stop is in the true
accompanimental divisions of the Church and Concert-room Organs.
It would also be very valuable in the Wood-wind division of the
properly-apportioned Concert-room instrument.

KINURA.—The name, derived from the Greek word κινύρα—
Harp; and given by Hope-Jones to a lingual stop, of 8 ft. pitch,
somewhat resembling a poor OBOE in tone, and, accordingly, having
nothing to recommend it for adoption in any class of Organ. It was,
however, introduced by him in the Organ installed in McEwan Hall,
Edinburgh; and in a few other instruments.

KLEINGEDECKT, Ger.—The name given to a covered stop
of 8 ft. and 4 ft. pitch, of small scale, and yielding a delicate unimitative flute-tone. This stop, according to Regnier, is of metal and of
4 ft. pitch only, and of small scale; but this is not altogether correct,
for in the Choir of the Organ in the Church of St. Michael, Hamburg,
there is a KLEINGEDECKT, 8 FT., of wood—probably a diminutive in
scale and voice of the usual LIEBLICHGEDECKT, 8 FT. Examples, of
4 ft. pitch, exist in the Organs in the Cathedral of Ulm and the Town
Church of Fulda.

The prefix *klein*—small, has been employed by German organ-
builders in the names of other organ-stops; we, accordingly, find the
following: KLEINCIMBEL, KLEINFLÖTE, KLEINFLÖTENBASS, KLEIN-
REGAL, and KLEINTERZ (1⅗ FT.). The prefix is employed to indicate
either octave pitch or small scale.

KLEINPRINZIPAL, Ger.—Literally *Small Principal*. The
term which has occasionally been employed to designate the OCTAVE,
4 FT., of pure organ-tone, the scale of which is adjusted from that of
the MAJORPRINZIPAL, 8 FT. This octave stop is identical with the
old English PRINCIPAL, 4 FT., and the HALBPRINZIPAL of the old
German organ-builders. See OCTAVE.

KLEINREGAL, Ger.—An obsolete stop of the old REGAL
family, which derived its name from the small size of its pipes of 4 ft.
pitch. There seems to have been nothing special about its tone.
See REGAL.

KNOPFREGAL, Ger.—Literally *Knob-Regal*. An obsolete
lingual stop, of 8 ft. pitch, which, as in the case of several other old
REGALS, derived its name from the peculiar form of the resonators
of its pipes. The resonator consisted of a short cylindrical body or
tube surmounted by a globular head, across which a narrow slit or

opening was cut for the escape of the pipe-wind and the emission of the sound. The head in some examples assumed a pear-shape or some other bulbous form. See REGAL.

KOPFREGAL, Ger.—One of the curious and now obsolete lingual stops, which, like several others of the REGAL family, derived its name from the form of the resonators of its pipes. The usual form of the resonator was that of a short body surmounted by a headpiece in the shape of two truncated cones joined together at their bases; a form which, considerably modified, has been followed in the resonators of the free-reed COR ANGLAIS. This form, however, was not invariably adopted in the old KOPFREGAL of the early German organ-builders. See REGAL.

KOPPEL, Ger.—The term employed by old German organ-builders to designate a labial stop, usually of the flute-toned family, and of different pitches; peculiarly suitable, on account of its unpronounced tone and good mixing quality, for combination or coupling with almost any other stop in the Organ. Another somewhat useful office of the KOPPEL was that of a "helper," commonly employed to help or cover the slow speech of certain stops, notably the GERMAN GAMBA (q. v.). This valuable stop in the old Organs was sometimes labeled KOPPELFLÖTE when of 8 ft. pitch, and KOPPEL-OCTAVE or KOPPELOKTAV when of 4 ft. pitch. Seidel remarks: "It is a common labial stop, covered, of 4 ft., 8 ft., or 16 ft. pitch, and in some very few cases it is open, like the HOHLFLÖTE. It belongs to the manual department. The 16 ft. stop is termed GROSS-KOPPEL; the 8 ft. stop is found under the name COPULA MAIOR; and the 4 ft. stop under the name COPULA MINOR. Some call the GEMSHORN a KOPPELFLÖTE. The KOPPEL is sometimes a description of QUINT, 5⅓ ft., 2⅔ ft., and 1⅓ ft., and in this case it is open, like the HOHL-FLÖTE. KOPPEL means also a variety of MIXTURE, of two or three ranks. There is a KOPPEL of three ranks in the Pedal of the Organ in the Church of St. Dominick, Prague, composed of a TWELFTH, 2⅔ FT., a FIFTEENTH, 2 FT., and a SEVENTEENTH, 1⅗ FT."

TONE AND REGISTRATION.—Although such a stop as the German KOPPEL is not required in its office of helper in the Organ of to-day, it is just worth while considering the use of a unison stop, preferably of wood, having a pure organ-tone of medium strength, for the purpose of coupling with, and imparting desirable smoothness and body to certain labial and lingual stops—especially the latter. Such a stop, which might appropriately be called a body-builder, would be extremely valuable in artistic registration, in combination with the

more cutting string-toned stops and such lingual stops as the CLARI-
NET, CORNO DI BASSETTO, FAGOTTO, and VOX HUMANA With the
last-named it would go far to remove the prominence of the objectionable nasal twang so commonly and unfortunately characteristic
of the stop.*

KURZFLÖTE, Ger.—Fr., FLÛTE COURTE.—Literally *Short
Flute.* A cylindrical metal labial stop, of medium scale, and 4 ft.
pitch, yielding an unimitative flute-tone of an agreeable quality.
An example exists in the Echo of the Organ in the Cathedral of
Lund, Sweden.

KÜTZIALFLÖTE, Ger.—This, according to Wolfram (1815), is
a small-scaled, flute-toned stop, of 4 ft. and 2 ft. pitch. According
to both Seidel and Hamel, it is an open stop of 4 ft., 2 ft., and 1 ft.
pitch; while it is sometimes met with of 1⅓ ft. pitch. The pipes of
the KÜTZIALFLÖTE, 4 FT., have been properly made of wood, while
those of the stops of higher pitch are of metal. A KÜTZIALFLÖTE,
1 FT., exists in the Great of the Church of St. Dominick, Prague;
and one, of 1⅓ ft. pitch, in the Organ in Kreuzkirche, Dresden.
Beyond its affording examples of the employment of complete stops
of such high pitches, there is nothing further calling for special
comment.

L

LARIGOT, Fr.—Eng., NINETEENTH. Ital., DECIMA NONA.—
An open cylindrical metal stop, of 1⅓ ft. pitch in the manual department and 2⅔ ft. in the Pedal Organ.† The pipes are properly of
small scale; but, when forming the independent stop, are invariably
voiced too loud and piercing. The fact seems to be ignored that the

---

* While performing on the Organ in St. George's Hall, Liverpool, the great master of the
Organ, the late W. T. Best, invariably used a body-giving stop along with the VOX HUMANA.
† "LARIGOT (from an old French word *l'arigot*, for a small flute or flageolet, now obsolete),
the old name for a rank of small open metal pipes, the longest of which is only 1⅓ ft. speaking
length. . . . It is first met with, in English Organs, in those made by Harris, who passed many
years in France, and who placed one in his instrument in St. Sepulchre's, Snow Hill [London],
erected in 1670."—E. J. H., in "A Dictionary of Music and Musicians."
"Le LARIGOT est la quinte de la *Doublette*, par conséquent l'octave supérieure du *Nasard*, et la
superoctave du *Gros-Nasard*. On le fait, ou plutôt on le faisait de grosse taille et d'étoffe: seize
pouces, ou quarante-trois centimètres, à son premier tuyau. On le plaçait d'ordinaire au positif,
à cause de son peu de hauteur; mais il est tombé en désuétude dans la facture française où l'on
ne s'est pas suffisamment pénétré de la nécessité d'assembler toujours les trois degrés de l'harmonie pour l'avoir complète, quatre, huit et seize-pieds, et dans ceux-ci, les deux et demi, cinq
et dix-pieds. Quand les trois degrés de quinte étaient tirés avec les trois, quatre et cinq degrés de
sons toniques, l'effet à ce qu'il paraît en était si perçant qu'on a encore gardé dans la conversation
l'expression vulgaire de jouer à *Tire-Larigot*, pour signifier un vacarme solennel."—Regnier.

LARIGOT is a mutation stop belonging, in its different pitches, to an 8 ft. or 16 ft. foundation harmonic series; and, to be of true value as a harmonic-corroborating stop should be subordinated in tone to the prime unison tone of the series to which it belongs. The LARIGOT, 1⅓ FT., seldom appears as a complete and independent stop, but examples exist in the Grand Chœur of the Organ of the Cathedral of Notre-Dame, and in the Positif of the Organ in the Church of Saint-Sulpice, Paris. There is much to be said in favor of this practice of introducing the LARIGOT as an independent stop. For further particulars see NINETEENTH.

LIEBLICHFLÖTE, Ger.—The name sometimes used to designate a small-scaled labial stop, formed of either wood or metal. The name refers to the tone only, which, freely rendered, signifies *Lovely-toned Flute*. The pipes are invariably covered, and form the correct OCTAVE LIEBLICHGEDECKT. If properly made and artistically voiced, the wood stop is to be preferred to that of metal, although fine examples in the latter material have been produced. So long as zinc or inferior pipe-metal can be used, the wood stop is not likely to be favored by organ-builders.

TONE AND REGISTRATION.—The true LIEBLICHFLÖTE, 4 FT., yields a soft unimitative flute-tone free from any prominent harmonics: accordingly, as an octave stop it is extremely valuable in registration, brightening and enriching almost all classes of unison (8 ft.) tone, without impairing their individual colorings. As a rule, there are too few stops of 4 ft. pitch introduced in modern Organs; for, as they corroborate the first and principal upper partial tone of all open labial stops of 8 ft. pitch, their value is unquestionable and their importance only second to that of the unison stops. The LIEBLICHFLÖTE should be introduced in the manual division in which the LIEBLICHGEDECKTS of 16 ft. and 8 ft. pitch are placed, practically completing that valuable family of covered stops. It may be remarked, that as the stops of 16 ft. and 8 ft. pitch will properly be made of wood, it may be desirable to secure a somewhat lighter and brighter tone by having the LIEBLICHFLÖTE made of a high-grade alloy or Hoyt's hard-rolled Two-ply Pipe-Metal.

LIEBLICHBORDUN, Ger.—A covered wood stop, of 16 ft. pitch, and small scale; the pipes of which are constructed on the BOURDON model, and voiced, on wind of moderate pressure, to produce a soft and good mixing quality of tone, in which the second upper partial is slightly in evidence. In this respect differing from the purer-toned LIEBLICHGEDECKT. A good example exists in the

Great of the Schulze Organ in the Church of St. Peter, Hindley, Lancashire. The CCC pipe of this stop measures, internally, 3⅜ inches by 5 inches, with a mouth 3¾ inches in height.

LIEBLICHGEDECKT, Ger.—The name appropriately given by the German organ-builders to a covered labial stop, of small scale, and 16 ft. and 8 ft. pitch. The larger stop is usually and properly made of wood throughout; while the stop of 8 ft. pitch, which should, preferably, be made of wood throughout, has in some examples its two or three higher octaves made of metal. On the Fourth Manual of the Ladegast Organ in the Cathedral of Schwerin, the LIEBLICHGEDECKT is formed of metal throughout.* Both the stops belong to the manual divisions of the Organ. Instances of the insertion of the stops of both pitches in the same division obtain on the Second Manuals of the Organs in Christuskirche, Aachen, and Predigerkirche, Erfurt. The stop of 16 ft. pitch is inserted on the Second Manual and that of 8 ft. pitch on the Third Manual of the Organ in St. Petrikirche, Lübeck. We have not been able to find a single instance of the insertion of the LIEBLICHGEDECKT, 16 FT., in the Pedal of a German or other Continental Organ.

It is strange that the value of a soft-toned unison stop in the Pedal Organ has been so systematically overlooked by all Continental organ-builders and organists. It would seem that the desirability for refinement in Pedal Organ tone never entered their brains; yet on artistic grounds alone its necessity must be obvious to everyone endowed with musical sense and taste. It is not too much to say that the presence of such a stop as the LIEBLICHGEDECKT, 16 FT., is imperative in all well-appointed Pedal Organs; unless its insertion is not absolutely necessary through the presence of a DULCIANA, 16 FT. In the Pedal of a Concert-room Organ, or a Church Organ of any pretensions to proper tonal appointment, both stops should certainly be present, and from these, by extension, may be derived valuable OCTAVES, 8 FT.

FORMATION AND SCALE.—In general formation the pipes of the LIEBLICHGE-DECKT differ in no essential from those of the BOURDON, the only distinction lying in scale, proportions of mouth, and treatment in voicing. The LIEBLICHGEDECKTS of different German organ-builders vary in scale and in the proportions of depth to width, the latter, carrying the mouth, being of the most importance. In the softer toned stops the pipes are narrow in proportion to their depth; while in the louder voiced stops the pipes approach the square. The most satisfactory proportion being as two to three. This is practically the proportion adopted by Edmund

* It is described thus: "LIEBLICHGEDECKT 8', aus 12löth, Zinn; Mensur 4½; ebenfalls von zarter Intonation, das schwächste Gedeckt in der Orgel."

Schulze, of Paulinzelle, for the LIEBLICHGEDECKT, 8 FT., in the Choir of his Organ in the Church of St. Peter, Hindley, England, the CC pipe of which measures, internally, 2⅛ inches in width by 3⅛ inches in depth. The following scale, in inches, to the ratio 1 : 2.66—halving on the eighteenth pipe—is practically that adopted by Schulze:

SCALE OF LIEBLICHGEDECKT, 8 FT.—RATIO 1 : 2.66

PIPES	CC	C	c^1	c^2	c^3	c^4
WIDTH	2.13	1.31	0.80	0.49	0.30	0.20
DEPTH	3.08	1.89	1.15	0.71	0.43	0.27

As the pipes in the two high octaves are very small, it will be generally deemed desirable to form them of metal in the usual shape. It is not in these octaves that the individuality of the stop obtains. For insertion in a large Concert-room Organ, the following slightly larger scale may be found desirable:

SCALE OF LIEBLICHGEDECKT, 8 FT.—RATIO 1 : 2.66.

PIPES	CC	C	c^1	c^2	c^3	c^4
WIDTH	2.95	1.81	1.11	0.68	0.45	0.26
DEPTH	3.94	2.41	1.47	0.91	0.55	0.34

Regarding the LIEBLICHGEDECKT, 16 FT., suitable for insertion in a manual division, different opinions obtain among organ-builders on the question of scale. It is certain, however, that a small scale is desirable: and when it is inserted along with the LIEBLICHGEDECKT, 8 FT., in the same division, it should be of a somewhat smaller scale than the unison stop, so as to be voiced slightly subordinate in tone. Dr. Hopkins, in his work, "The Organ," gives a scale for a Choir or Swell LIEBLICHGEDECKT, 16 FT., apparently of German origin. The CCC pipe is 3⅜ inches in width by 5 inches in depth; the CC pipe is 2 3/16 inches in width by 3 inches in depth; and the C pipe is 1⅜ inches in width by 1⅞ inches in depth. The scale is irregular, not being developed on any standard ratio. It approaches most closely to the ratio 1 : 2.519, halving on the nineteenth pipe. The following scale will be suitable for a Pedal Organ stop of 16 ft. pitch:

SCALE OF PEDAL LIEBLICHGEDECKT, 16 FT.,—RATIO 1 : 2.519.

PIPES	CCC	CC	C	G
WIDTH	3.79	2.39	1.50	1.15
DEPTH	5.36	3.38	2.13	1.62

Of equal importance to the scale is the form of the mouth; and that, in its proportions of height to width, differs considerably from the mouths of the generality of wood pipes belonging to other stops of the flute-toned family. The height of the mouth is an important factor in the production of the pure organ flute-tone of the true LIEBLICHGEDECKT. In no case should it be less than half its width in height; while it may with advantage exceed its width in height, as in the stop in the Swell of the Organ in St. Peter's, Hindley, the CC pipe of which has a mouth 2⅛ inches wide and 2¼ inches high. The lower portion of this pipe, in correct proportions, is shown in Front View and Section in the accompanying illustration, Fig. 25. The mouth of the CC pipe of the Choir stop is 2⅛ inches wide and 1½ inches high. In the smaller scales, mouths ranging from three-quarters to their

entire width in height may be used with advantage tonally.   The thickness of the
upper lip is another factor in the production of satisfactory tone.   This may vary,
in the CC pipe, from a quarter to half an inch (the thicker lip producing the
smoother tone), and be cut square or have carefully rounded edges: and the lip
may be straight, as in the illustration, or arched.   Pipes having mouths of so
great a height in proportion to width require a copious supply of wind, desirably
of moderate pressure, for their proper speech.   The manual stop should speak on
wind of $3\frac{1}{2}$ inches and the pedal stop on wind of from 4 inches to 5 inches.

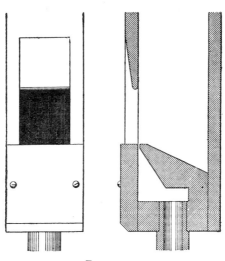

FIG. 25

TONE AND REGISTRATION—The tone of the properly made and
artistically voiced LIEBLICHGEDECKT is very beautiful, being of a
singularly pure organ flute quality almost free from its first upper
partial tone.   It may be accepted as the most refined tone produced
by the covered stops of the Organ; while it is equal to the finest
tones of the half-covered stops.   The purity of its tone renders it
extremely valuable in simple combination and artistic registration,
chiefly on account of its perfect mixing quality, and its forming so
fine a background for the display, so to speak, of pronounced tone-
colors furnished by stops having imitative voices.   The value, from a
registration point of view, of the entire family of the LIEBLICH-
GEDECKTS, 16 ft., 8 ft., $5\frac{1}{3}$ ft., and 4 ft., has not been properly, if at
all, recognized by organ experts and designers; and their special
value when grouped in the same division has been altogether unrealized.   The LIEBLICHGEDECKT, $5\frac{1}{3}$ FT., may be omitted should a
stop of the same pitch and of the flute-toned class be considered

more desirable in the stop apportionment of the division.* But we strongly recommend retaining the complete family.

LIEBLICHGESCHALLT.—The name, derived from the German, given by Hope-Jones to a small-scaled metal LIEBLICHGEDECKT, 8 FT., voiced to yield a very soft tone, as if it was an echo of that of the normal full-toned LIEBLICHGEDECKT. Otherwise of no special interest.

LIEBLICHQUINTE, Ger.—The covered labial stop, of 5⅓ ft. pitch, belonging to the LIEBLICHGEDECKT family; the pipes of which are formed in all respects similar to those of the LIEBLICHGEDECKT (q. v.).

LITICE.—Lat., LITUUS.—"A curved brass trumpet, clarion, used by cavalry" (Nall).—The name that has been used by old German organ-builders to designate a lingual stop yielding a piercing tone. It is described by Seidel: "*Litice* oder Lituus ist einerlei mit Zink, Krummhorn oder Cornett." Schlimbach agrees with this definition. Now obsolete.

LLENO, Span.—The name used by Spanish organ-builders, as a general appellation for all compound harmonic-corroborating stops or MIXTURES.

LUTE.—The name given to an organ-stop formed of strings, in all probability sounded by plectora or "jacks," after the method followed in the Harpsichord. The stop was introduced by Thomas Schwarbrook, organ-builder, of Warwick, in his masterpiece, the Organ in the Church of St. Michael, Coventry, constructed in 1733. Dr. Rimbault says: "This noble instrument cost £1400. It originally contained three remarkable stops—the HARP, LUTE, and DULCIMER; but, in consequence of the 'difficulty of keeping the *strings* in tune,' they were removed in 1763." History is repeating itself: after the lapse of more than a century and a half the HARP stop is again appearing in the Organ, and, perhaps, the Lute and the Dulcimer will find their imitations in the Organ of the Twentieth Century.

M

MAJORBASS, Ger.—The name that has sometimes been used to designate the Pedal Organ covered labial stop, of 32 ft. pitch, as

---

* The stop apportionment here alluded to will be found fully developed in the First Expressive Subdivision of the Second Organ, in our scheme for the tonal appointment of the Concertroom Organ, given in "The Organ of the Twentieth Century," page 303.

in the Organ in the Church of St. Elizabeth, Breslau. The stop has been better known as the UNTERSATZ, 32 FT., as in the Organ in the Cathedral of Schwerin. Walcker has employed the term GRAND BOURDON, 32 FT., in the Organs in the Cathedrals of Ulm and Frankfurt a. M.: and this term is appropriate for the stop in our own Organs to-day. We find the stop under the name CONTRA-BOURDON in certain English and American Organs.

MANUALUNTERSATZ, Ger.—The name to be found in certain important Organs constructed by Walcker, of Ludwigsburg, designating a manual covered labial stop, of 32 ft. pitch. This very grave stop is never carried below tenor C, chiefly on account of the great size of the pipes composing its bottom octave, but also to avoid giving undesirable gravity and dullness to the manual bass. Examples of the MANUALUNTERSATZ, 16 FT., under that name, exist in the First Manual divisions of the Organs in the Cathedrals of Ulm and Vienna. This grave stop has been seldom introduced in English Organs; examples exist in the Greats of the Organs in the Parish Churches of Leeds and Doncaster, labeled SUB-BOURDON, 32 FT. Under the name CONTRA-BOURDON, 32 FT., Hill has inserted it in the Great of the Organ in the Centennial Hall, Sydney, N. S. W. All these stops commence at tenor C. We have not been able to find a single example in a French Organ.

TONE AND REGISTRATION.—It is very questionable if such a stop as the MANUALUNTERSATZ is necessary in any Church Organ, especially if it is of the ordinary BOURDON quality of tone. If, however, it should be deemed desirable in a very large instrument, it should certainly be of the LIEBLICHGEDECKT family. The heavy droning tone of the ordinary BOURDON should be avoided. In the Concert-room Organ of the first magnitude such a stop, in its most desirable form, may be introduced in the foundation division—First or Great Organ—but there an open stop of pure organ-tone is greatly to be preferred. To meet this demand, without entailing the necessity of cumbering the division with a rank of such large pipes, a soft-unison Pedal stop, preferably a DULCIANA, 16 FT., may be borrowed and made to speak on the manual clavier from tenor C. In our scheme for the Concert-room Organ of the Twentieth Century, we have suggested adding an Auxiliary Stop, of full compass, under the name DOLCIANO PROFUNDO, 32 FT., derived from the CONTRA-DULCIANA, 32 FT., of the Pedal Organ, necessarily extended to 61 notes.* It is quite obvious that a stop of this soft and pure organ-

* See "The Organ of the Twentieth Century," pp. 297 and 319.

tone would be productive, in registration with the double and unison foundation stops of the First Organ, of many tonal effects of a dignity and grandeur never yet heard in organ music.

MEERFLÖTE, Ger.—The name that has been given to the stop commonly designated UNDA MARIS (q. v.).

MELODIA.—An open labial stop, of 8 ft. pitch, having an unimitative flute-tone of a smooth and singing quality, in certain examples inclining slightly to a horn-like intonation. This fine stop, in its proper form, may be said to be unknown in English organ-building; its closest representative being the WALDFLÖTE (q. v.), many fine examples of which exist in English Organs. In the soft-toned Fourth Manual of the Walcker Organ in the Cathedral of Riga, the stop exists under the name MELODICA, 8 FT. An example exists in the Choir of the Hook and Hastings Organ in the Music Hall, Cincinnati, O.; the tone of which is described as "round, rich, and mellow." A MELODIA, 8 FT., of a pure and beautiful tone, existed in the Choir of the Organ constructed by the Hutchings-Votey Company for Woolsey Hall, Yale University. The organ-builders who seem at the present time to realize most clearly the value of the MELODIA are MM. Casavant Frères, of St. Hyacinthe, P. Q. Examples exist in the Choirs of their Organs in Emmanuel Church, Boston, and the Second Church of West Newton, Mass.; and in the Positif of the Organ in the Church of Notre-Dame, Montreal, Canada; where it bears the French name MÉLODIE.

FORMATION AND SCALE.—The pipes forming the true MELODIA are of wood and quadrangular: white pine being used for their sides and backs, and some close-grained hard wood, such as mahogany or maple, for their fronts from tenor C to the top note. The pipes of the bass octave may have fronts of pine with hard wood mouth pieces. The mouths are of the inverted form, and are cut up about one-third their width in height. The caps to be of hard wood, hollowed, and the wind-way formed in them, and to be set below the under lip of the mouth just sufficiently to produce perfect intonation. The block is set about half the internal width of the pipe below the under lip. The scale of the stop varies in different examples, but the following may be accepted as suitable:

SCALE OF MELODIA, 8 FT., IN INCHES,—RATIO 1: 2.66.

PIPES	CC	C	c^1	c^2	c^3	c^4
WIDTH	3.34	2.05	1.25	0.77	0.47	0.29
DEPTH	4.44	2.73	1.67	1.02	0.63	0.38

It is a common practice to insert the bass octave in covered pipes, so as to save money; but this practice is contrary to the canons of artistic and correct organ-building, one of which is: *Each stop in the Organ must be carried throughout its compass in pipes of its own class and tonality.*

TONE AND REGISTRATION.—When artistically voiced, on wind of low pressure, the tone of the true MELODIA is very beautiful: as before stated, it is of an unimitative flute quality, smooth and singing, inclining in the tenor and middle octaves to a horn tonality. This latter is largely due to the smooth speech of the pipes; just as in the case of the KERAULOPHONE. The appropriate place for the MELODIA is in the Choir or accompanimental division of the Church Organ, and in the softest-toned division of the Concert-room Organ.* It is a perfect stop for the true Chamber Organ.

It is hardly necessary to point out that a stop of this beautiful and refined tonality is invaluable in artistic registration. Perfect in mixing quality and capable of receiving tonal coloring of any class, it furnishes an admirable foundation for the most delicate labial and lingual combinations. It is a perfect body-giver to the Vox HUMANA, imparting roundness and fullness where it is so greatly required.

MENSCHENSTIMME, Ger.—The term employed by the old German organ-builders to designate a lingual stop which, in its peculiar tone, imitated in some respects the human voice while singing. See VOX HUMANA.

MESSINGREGAL, Ger.—An obsolete lingual stop, the tone of which was strongly suggestive of the clang of brass wind instruments. See REGAL.

MITTELFLÖTE, Ger.—This term, which has neither reference to formation nor tonality, has been employed to designate a FLUTE, of 4 ft. pitch, simply because it occupied a *middle* position between FLUTES of 8 ft. and 2 ft. pitch in the same division of the Organ. This name is a good example of the vagueness and senselessness one too frequently meets with in organ-stop nomenclature.

MITTELGEDECKT, Ger.—The term that has been used by old German organ-builders to indicate a GEDECKT which occupies a middle position between two other stops of the same family, placed in the same division of an Organ. Schlimbach says: "Wenn z. B. auf einen Clavier Gedact 8, 4, und 2 Fusston sich zugleich befindet, so ist das von 4 Fusston das Mittelgedact."

MIXTURE.—Lat., MISCELLA. Ger., MIXTUR. Dtch., MIXTUUR. Ital., RIPIENO. Span. LLENO.—The generic name for all

---

* In our tonal scheme for the Concert-room Organ, the MELODIA, 8 FT., is placed in the Ancillary Aërial Organ, where it speaks on wind of 1½ inches. It is, accordingly, available for registration purposes on any manual clavier. See "The Organ of the Twentieth Century." Pages 329 and 331.

compound harmonic-corroborating stops, applied generally to such stops as are composed of octave- and fifth-sounding ranks of ordinary open metal labial pipes, and to such compound stops as do not call for any special name indicative of peculiar composition, formation, or intonation. The MIXTURE may be composed of two or more ranks of pipes, according to the tonal structure or appointment of the division of the Organ in which it is placed. The different pitches of the separate ranks and their breaks are dictated by that tonal structure, and the number and nature of the single harmonic-corroborating stops that are included in the divisional appointment.

The presence of a MIXTURE, of suitable size and appropriate composition and tonality, is essential in every important division of an Organ—pedal and manual—in which a proper scientific and artistic tonal structure or effective stop apportionment is essayed. This fact has, of late years, been systematically neglected or ignored by unscientific and inartistic organ-builders: and almost completely unrealized or misunderstood by organists, who have been content to accept the opinion of self-interested organ-builders on the subject. It is quite easy to see on what grounds organ-builders hate all compound harmonic-corroborating stops; and it is proper that some light be let in upon the matter.

In the first place, the willingness of musicians to allow the elimination of MIXTURES in the tonal appointment of Organs has been largely, if not entirely, due to the very crude, unscientific, and highly objectionable form in which organ-builders have commonly constructed, voiced, and regulated them. Such stops, producing loud screaming voices, more like the noise of smashing glass than musical sounds, entirely at variance with their scientific and tonal office in the economy of the Temple of Tone, are certainly better absent than present in any Organ. It seems questionable if organists have given sufficient study to the subject to realize the great value, both from a scientific and musical point of view, of a correctly proportioned and artistically voiced and regulated MIXTURE, in effective registration, and in the production of the richest tones the Organ can furnish.

In the second place, organ-builders have, during recent times, strongly advocated the elimination of compound harmonic-corroborating stops, not on any contention based on scientific or musical grounds, which they were in no form able to advance; but because the formation of such complex stops are undesirably troublesome; involving a considerable amount of scientific knowledge, and what to them seems an unprofitable expenditure of high-class skilled labor in their formation, artistic voicing, and scientific tonal graduation. In short, the organ-builder fails to see sufficient remuneration, in dollars, for such stops; and relying on the apathy, if not the want of knowledge, on the part of the organist, he cries, "Away with all MIXTURES!"

In old Organs the introduction of compound stops was carried to an extent altogether unwarranted by either scientific or artistic demands. Two instances may be given: in the Great of the Organ in the Old Church, Amsterdam, finished in 1686, there are eighteen ranks, and also in the Choir eighteen ranks of MIXTURE work; and in the Organ in the Monastery Church, at Weingarten, finished in 1750, there are no fewer than ninety-five ranks of MIXTURE work, two stops alone having twenty and twenty-one ranks, respectively. Such excessive apportionment—out of all reason on any grounds—has naturally led to a swing in the opposite direction, which has ended, as we now see, in a too sparing introduction, or frequently in the entire omission, of MIXTURES; creating a starvation in the true and the most characteristic tones of the Organ, a fact that is greatly to be regretted.

The largest compound harmonic-corroborating stop we have examined and know of in a modern Organ is the HARMONIC MIXTURE, of fourteen ranks (784 pipes), in the Organ in the Edinburgh University. Turning to examples in modern German organ-building, and selecting two representative instruments by Walcker, of Ludwigsburg, we find in the Organ in the Cathedral of Riga—an instrument of 124 speaking stops—on the First Manual, fifteen ranks of MIXTURE work; on the Second Manual, ten ranks; on the Third Manual, four ranks; on the Fourth Manual, three ranks; and in the Pedal Organ, twelve ranks, including the GRAND BOURDON, V. RANKS. In all, forty-four ranks. In the Organ in the Cathedral of Ulm—an instrument of 107 speaking stops—on the First Manual, twenty-one ranks of MIXTURE work; on the Second Manual, eleven ranks; on the Third Manual, five ranks; and in the Pedal Organ, five ranks. In all, forty-two ranks. No such apportionments of MIXTURE work are to be found in modern Organs built in any other country. In the Organs constructed by Cavaillé-Coll we find an adequate amount of MIXTURE work provided: for instance, in the Organ in the Church of Saint-Sulpice, Paris, there are in the Grand-Chœur (portion of the Grand-Orgue), nineteen ranks; in the Positif, six ranks; in the Récit, fourteen ranks; and in the Solo, five ranks. This is the largest apportionment of MIXTURE work we have been able to find in a French Organ.

FORMATION.—The formation of a MIXTURE, properly proportioned to the stop-appointment of the division of the Organ in which it is placed, calls for a certain amount of scientific knowledge and a keen appreciation of the value of musical sounds. The prevailing "rule-of-thumb" methods are invariably attended by failure.

A properly formed MIXTURE comprises different ranks of pipes of high pitches; which, as they cannot be carried complete throughout the compass of the division in which the stop is placed, have to be divided into two or more portions, technically termed *breaks;* each of which, in each rank, commences on a pipe of a lower pitch, so as to allow the stop to be carried throughout the compass of the division. This arrangement is shown in the following example—a MIXTURE, of five ranks, composed of octaves and quints, breaking on each octave of the compass:

MIXTURE—V. RANKS.

		RANKS I.	II.	III.	IV.	V.
BREAK	1. CC to BB	. . 19	—22	—26	—29	—33.
"	2. C to B	. . 15	—19	—22	—26	—29.
"	3. c^1 to b^1	. . 12	—15	—19	—22	—26.
"	4. c^2 to b^2	. . 8	—12	—15	—19	—22.
"	5. c^3 to c^4	. . 1	— 8	—12	—15	—19.

All the sounds produced by the pipes, in the several breaks and ranks, serve to corroborate the harmonic upper partial tones of the unison sounds, with which they combine, throughout the compass of the clavier. Accordingly, to everyone conversant with the phenomena of compound musical sounds, the value of, and, indeed, the necessity for the introduction of compound harmonic-corroborating stops—represented by MIXTURES of proper formation—in the Organ must be evident and incontestable.

It is well known to all who have devoted any serious study to the phenomena of musical sounds, that in those produced by the cultivated human voice and the string instruments of the orchestra, the prime tones are accompanied by a great number of upper partials or harmonic over-tones; and that these sensibly decrease in strength as they rise in pitch, until they become inaudible. This important natural law has to be recognized in the proper voicing and regulating of the MIXTURES and all the harmonic-corroborating stops in the Organ. It is not too much to say, and our extended observation supports the assertion, that this acoustical phenomenon has been seriously, if not altogether, ignored by all organ-builders who have hitherto constructed MIXTURES: and, accordingly, stops so unscientifically constructed have outraged the natural laws of musical sounds, and have destroyed, instead of enriching and beautifying, the voices of the Organ with which they were combined.

TONE AND REGISTRATION.—The tone of the MIXTURE varies according to the nature of the pipes of which it is composed. It may be of pure organ-tone, belonging to the foundation-work, corroborating the harmonic upper partial tones of the prime tones of the DIAPASONS; and infusing into them rich compound tones, so satisfying to the cultivated musical ear. Or the MIXTURE may be so constructed of pipes of special tonalities as to become both harmonic-corroborating and timbre-creating; finding its proper place in different tonal divisions, according to their stop-apportionments.

In artistic registration, a properly constructed, voiced, and regulated MIXTURE is of the greatest value; entering into combinations of infinite variety, either in its office of harmonic corroborator or timbre-creator, and imparting to them elements of singular brilliancy and beauty all but unknown in organ music to-day. We have practically proved that a five-rank MIXTURE can be scaled, voiced, and regulated, so as to become one of the most valuable and generally useful stops in refined and effective registration. We have heard beautiful passages rendered on such a MIXTURE while in combination with a PICCOLO, 2 FT., only; and equally beautiful solo passages when combined with the VOX HUMANA alone. The MIXTURE, in whatever division of the Organ it is placed, should be inclosed and rendered flexible and expressive.

For further particulars respecting MIXTURES, see ACUTA, CARILLON, CLARION MIXTURE, COMPENSATIONSMIXTUR, CORNET, CYMBAL, DOLCE CORNET, DULCIANA CORNET, FOURNITURE, FULL MIXTURE, HARMONIA ÆTHERIA, PLEIN-JEU, SESQUIALTERA, and TERTIAN.

MONTRE, Fr.—The term commonly used by French organ-builders to designate such foundation and organ-toned and highly-finished metal stops as may be mounted and displayed in the *buffet* or case of an Organ. For such a purpose, the MONTRES are usually made of tin, highly burnished, and may be of 32 ft., 16 ft., or 8 ft. speaking lengths, as in the Organ in the Royal Church of Saint-Denis. Sometimes the term is applied to the PRESTANT, 4 FT., when its pipes are mounted and displayed. All the MONTRES are most carefully fashioned, having the boldly-formed French mouth, and being of tin brightly burnished, produce a fine effect in combination with the dark woodwork of the case.*

MOUNTED CORNET.—The name given by the old English

---

* "LA MONTRE. Jeu labial ouvert, le plus ordinairement de moyenne taille, dont tous les tuyaux ou la plupart sont en évidence, en *montre*, comme les plus brillants et les plus parfaits. Le métal, qui est ou doit être d'étain fin, revêt un poli digne de rivaliser avec les métaux d'Ulm ou de l'Escurial. Les bouches de montre sont ordinairement écussonnées, c'est-à-dire que leurs lèvres, au lieu d'être simplement pliées comme dans le tuyau commun, sont formées de deux pièces rapportées, courbées et terminées en forme d'écusson. . . .

" Nos montres françaises ont les trois degrés de ton, seize, huit, et quatre-pieds: à cette dernière dimension, elles prennent le nom de *prestant;* elles vont rarement à trente-deux ou même vingt-quatre-pieds, à cause de la quantité de vent, de métal, et d'espace nécessaire; souvent même la montre de seize n'exhibe pas ses plus gros tuyaux, qui, simplement en bois, cachent leur humble costume à l'intérieur du buffet. D'autres fois, on aperçoit en montre de magnifiques vingt-quatre et trente-deux-pieds qui n'appartiennent qu'à la pédale de l'orgue; mais *la montre s'entend toujours des tuyaux correspondant aux claviers manuels.*"—Regnier.

organ-builders to a compound stop, of short compass, which, to economize room inside the Organ, was mounted, above the main wind-chest, on a small wind-chest designed for its reception alone; the wind to its pipes being conveyed from the grooves of the main chest by conveyances—one for each note of its compass. The Mounted Cornet consisted usually of five ranks of large-scaled open metal pipes, yielding a full dominating tone, though sometimes the unison rank was inserted in covered pipes. Its ranks comprised a Diapason, or a Flûte à Cheminée, and an Octave, Twelfth, Fifteenth, and Seventeenth. In old English Organs its compass never extended below middle c^1; but in German Organs, in which the stop held a more important office, it usually was carried down to tenor C. Hopkins says the Mounted Cornet "was chiefly used for playing out the melody of the chorals upon, and for the performance of an obsolete kind of voluntary: but it is of great use in large Organs in hiding the breaks in the several compound stops, as it proceeds itself without any 'repetitions.' In Father Smith's Organs the Cornet was never 'mounted,' but stood on the sound-board." Schulze introduced a Mounted Cornet, of four ranks and tenor C compass, in both the Great and Swell divisions of the Organ in the Parish Church of Doncaster. There is no call for the Cornet of short compass, in any form, in the Organ of the Twentieth Century.

MUNDFLÖTE, Ger.—Literally *Mouth-Flute.* An open labial stop of metal, and of 2 ft. pitch; similar in all essentials to the French Flûte à Bec (*q. v.*). The stop has no distinctive flute tonality. A stop under the name exists in the Organ in the Cathedral of Königsberg.

MUSETTE, Fr.—Ger., Sackpfeife. —The Musette was a small Bagpipe much used in olden times by the people of different European countries; and the Musette of the Organ is supposed to imitate the characteristic tone of that old instrument. The Musette, as made in France, is a free-reed stop, having resonators of small scale and inverted conical form, made of tin, and yielding a bright and pleasing tone, as might be produced by a small and weak species of Bagpipe.* Examples of the stop have been made with striking-

---

* "La Musette, le Chalumeau (*Sackpfeife, Schalmey*). Jeu d'anche de forme pyramidale, en étain fin comme la plupart des timbres effilés. La *Musette* a quatre-pieds de hauteur et huit de ton. Le timbre, plus faible que celui du *Cromorne*, imite assez bien le chétif instrument dont on lui a donné le nom. Dom Bedos disait de la *Musette:* 'Ce jeu est encore peu connu, dans le royaume.' Il y est tous les jours moins connu, et si dans certaines mélodies populaires et rares, tolérées par l'Église qui se fait toute à tous, il peut paraître utile, il n'est jamais nécessaire."— Regnier.

reeds and slender cylindrical, covered, and perforated resonators, producting refined and characteristic tones. We introduced a free-reed MUSETTE, 4 FT., to serve as an OCTAVE to the free-reed CORNO INGLESE, 8 FT., in the Second Organ of our scheme for the Organ installed in the Festival Hall of the Louisiana Purchase Exposition, 1904. The MUSETTE when of its true and characteristic tonality is a valuable voice in the properly-appointed Concert-room Organ. It mixes well and, accordingly, enters freely into combinations of a soft and distinctive character. It is peculiarly useful in music of a pastoral description.

MUSICIRGEDECKT, Ger.—A name sometimes given by the old German organ-builders to a covered stop, of 8 ft. or 4 ft. pitch, yielding a peculiarly soft and sweet unimitative flute-tone. Schlimbach, a great authority on old stops, describes it thus: "MUSICIR-GEDACKT. Die Bestimmung dieses Gedacts ist: zur Begleitung der Musik gebraucht zu werden. Man findet es zu 8 und 4 Fusston, still intonirt. Man vergleiche Kammerflöte." This stop was probably identical with the later GELINDGEDECKT (q. v.).

N

NACHTHORN, Ger.—Fr., COR DE NUIT. Ital., PASTORITA.— In addition to the name first given, German organ-builders have occasionally employed the term NACHTSCHALL, which signifies *Night-sound.* The stops bearing these names in German and French Organs are formed of covered or open labial pipes, usually of metal but in some examples of wood. It is found of 8 ft. and 4 ft. pitch, and very rarely of 2 ft. pitch. According to Wolfram (1815), the covered NACHTHORN resembles the QUINTATEN both in formation and tone, but its pipes are of larger scale. The open stop has pipes resembling those of the HOHLFLÖTE. The tone of the NACHTHORN is round, soft, and agreeable; and in fine examples has, as its name implies, a combination of flute and horn tones, which imparts individuality to the stop.* Wolfram alludes to this horn-like tonality.

---

* "La PASTORITA ou le NACHTHORN, *cor de nuit.* Cette flûte de bois ou d'étoffe, tantôt bouchée, tantôt ouverte, mais toujours large et trapue, se fait souvent de quatre-pieds et ne descend jamais à plus de profondeur que huit; son timbre est agréable, son harmonie délicate. Ouverte, elle se rapproche de la flûte creuse, mais on tient alors sa taille plus étroite et ses lèvres plus serrées. Bouchée, elle imite le son du cor dans le lointain et dans le silence des nuits, d'où lui vient son nom; à cette fin, on lui donne une plus large taille qu'à un des plus curieux bourdons allemands, le *Quintaton,* si l'on ne veut pas qu'elle lui emprunte son principal effet. Bien des facteurs promettent un *nachthorn* de quatre-pieds, qui ne tiennent pas autre chose que le."— Regnier.

A representative example of the covered NACHTHORN, 8 FT., of large scale, exists in the Positif Expressif of the Cavaillé-Coll Organ in the Albert Hall, Sheffield. One of 4 ft. pitch appears in the Pedal of the Organ in the Garrison Church, Berlin; and one of 2 ft. pitch in the Echo of the celebrated Haarlem Organ. Seidel says: "Im Pedal heisst diese Stimme NACHTHORNBASS, ist sie 2 füssig, so kommt sie zuweilen unter dem Namen NACHTHÖRNCHEN vor."

NASARD, Fr.—Ger., NASAT, NASSART. Ital. and Span., NASARDO.—The name given to a manual labial stop, of 2⅔ ft. pitch, the pipes of which are of metal, and either open or covered. It is the equivalent of the TWELFTH, 2⅔ FT. in English and American Organs, when in its open form, although it differs in tone according to its position in the stop-appointment of the Organ. In all cases it is a harmonic-corroborating stop, representing the 11th upper partial tone of the 32 ft., the 5th upper partial tone of the 16 ft., and the 2nd upper partial tone of the 8 ft. harmonic series. When inserted in the foundation division of the Organ, it is properly formed of open metal pipes, scaled, voiced, and regulated in strength of tone with respect to the MAJOR PRINCIPAL or DIAPASON, 8 FT. (See TWELFTH). When inserted in a soft-toned division of an Organ, it sometimes assumes the form of a FLÛTE À CHEMINÉE. A NASARD, 2⅔ FT., exists in the Récit Expressif of the Organ in the Church of Saint-Sulpice; and others are introduced in the Grand Orgue and the Bombarde of the Organ in the Royal Church, Saint-Denis. The stop frequently appears in French Organs, named QUINTE, 2⅔ FT. NASARDS are to be found on the Third Manual of the Organ in the Cathedral of Ulm, and on the First Manual of the Protestant Church at Mulhausen. A NASAT, 2⅔ FT., exists in the Echo of the Grand Organ, and another in the Choir Organ in the Cathedral of Breslau.

The corresponding stop, of 5⅓ ft., called GROS NASARD, belongs to the harmonic structure of the Pedal Organ. An example exists in the Pedal of the Organ in the Royal Church, Saint-Denis. See GROSSNASAT.

NASARD FLÛTE.—The name given by its introducer, George W. Till, of Philadelphia, Pa., to a labial dual stop, formed of a metal FLÛTE HARMONIQUE, 8 FT., and a metal NASARD HARMONIQUE, 2⅔ FT.; and introduced, for the first time, in the Concert Organ in the Wanamaker Store, in Philadelphia, Pa., where it occupies a place in the Great Organ, speaking on wind of 5 inches. This compound stop is essentially timbre-creating, yielding a tone of a remarkable quality and volume, impossible of production by a stop, however voiced, having only a single rank of pipes. As we have said elsewhere, the existence of such a dual stop multiplies to an undreamt of extent the resources of the flute-toned forces of the Organ, when used in combination. The tone might well earn the stop the name GRAND QUINTATEN, 8 FT.*

NASARD GAMBA.—The name given by its introducer, George W. Till, of Philadelphia, Pa., to a labial dual stop, formed of a metal GAMBA, 8 FT., having the compass of CC to c^5, and a tin NASARD GAMBA, 2⅔ FT., of the same compass. The unison stop is voiced to yield a powerful string-tone, so as to firmly establish the unison pitch. The NASARD is voiced to yield a clear but a decidedly subordinate string-tone. The combined ranks, which speak on wind of 15 inches, produce a tone of wonderful richness and color-value; unlike anything known to be yielded by a single-ranked string-stop. The NASARD GAMBA was designed for, and introduced for the first time in, the Swell of the Concert Organ in the Wanamaker Store, in Philadelphia, Pa.†

NASON.—The name used by the old English organ-builders to designate a covered stop of wood, of 4 ft. pitch, yielding a soft flute-tone, inclining to that of a QUINTATEN. The stop was practically an OCTAVE STOPPED DIAPASON. A NASON, of 1⅓ ft. pitch, was inserted by Casparini in the Echo of the Organ he erected, in 1703, in the Church of SS. Peter and Paul, Görlitz. It is probably still in existence. The name has entirely disappeared from modern nomenclature.

NINETEENTH.—Fr., LARIGOT. Ital., DECIMA NONA.—A mutation, harmonic-corroborating stop, of 1⅓ ft. pitch in the manual department, and 2⅔ ft. pitch in the Pedal Organ. In its proper form, it corroborates the fifth upper partial tone of the unison tone of the department of the Organ in which it is placed. The NINETEENTH is invariably formed of open metal pipes, which should be scaled in proportion to the scale of the principal unison stop with which it is associated. When it appears as a separate stop it is almost invariably voiced much too loud, seriously impairing its tonal value in combination and registration. It, however, seldom appears as a complete and separate stop: but certain old English and

* Full particulars of the formation and scales of this stop are given in "The Organ of the Twentieth Century," pp. 104–5.
† Full particulars of the formation and scales of the NASARD GAMBA are given in "The Organ of the Twentieth Century," pp. 105–6.

modern French organ-builders have favored it in that form.   Under
the name LARIGOT, 1⅓ FT., it appeared as an independent stop in
the Great of the Organ built by Renatus Harris, in 1670, for the
Church of St. Sepulchre, Snow Hill, London.   He also introduced
one in the Organ he built for the Church of St. Peter, Mancroft,
Norwich.   The stop is inserted, in its complete form, in the Grand-
Chœur of the Organ in the Cathedral of Notre-Dame; and in the
Positif of the Organ in the Church of Saint Sulpice, Paris: both by
Cavaillé-Coll.

The NINETEENTH, 1⅓ FT., may form a complete rank in a COR-
NET; but it commonly appears, in a broken form, in the ranks of
MIXTURES.   As a harmonic-corroborating stop, it should, in whatever form it appears, be graduated softer in tone as it rises in pitch,
in accordance with the natural laws of musical sounds.

O

OBOE, Ital.—Eng., HAUTBOY. Fr., HAUTBOIS. Ger., HOBOE.
—A lingual stop, of 8 ft. pitch, which belongs to the manual department of the Organ.   Two varieties of the stop are introduced in the
Organ to-day.   The older and still prevailing form cannot be considered as imitative in tone; but in the finest examples of the strictly
modern forms the tones produced closely resemble those of the
orchestral Oboe.   The former stop is labeled, simply, OBOE; while
the imitative stop is properly labeled ORCHESTRAL OBOE; under
which name it will be found fully described.   The OBOE in its common and unimitative form is best suited for a Church Organ in
which only one is inserted; because, unlike the ORCHESTRAL OBOE
with its somewhat thin and characteristic voice, it is an all-round
useful stop when a soft-toned lingual voice is desirable.   It is generally found in Organs of any pretensions toward completeness; and,
indeed, in most small instruments.

FORMATION.—The resonators of the unimitative OBOE, 8 FT., are approximately of the standard speaking lengths; and are in the form of slender tapered
tubes surmounted by long inverted conical bells, after the fashion of the conical
and belled tube of the orchestral Oboe.   In its best treatment, the resonator has
its bell shaded by a disc of spotted-metal, soldered to its edge so as to allow about
one-half being bent up, to any required extent, in the process of regulating the
tone of the pipe.   Shaded resonators are not invariably used but they are unquestionably the most desirable, for without them artistic toning is practically impossible.   The form of the OBOE pipe just described is shown in Fig. 26, Plate III.,
which represents a pipe of a lower octave of the stop.   As the pipes become shorter,
the relative proportions of their tubes and bells are largely altered; until in the top

octave there is little difference in their respective lengths. The reeds or *échalotes* of this stop are of medium scale and are invariably of the closed class, having small triangular openings which extend from the thick discs which close their lower ends. The tongues or *languettes* are correspondingly slender in form and of medium thickness, and have a slight and finely-formed curve, preventing coarseness or brassiness of intonation.

The formation just described is that of the striking-reed stop, as constructed in this country and in England; but the OBOES of the French and German organbuilders have frequently been made with free-reeds. An example exists on the Second Manual of the Organ, built by Friederich Ladegast, in 1871, for the Cathedral of Schwerin. Of late years, however, the French have adopted the striking-reed. French examples are rare.

TONE AND REGISTRATION.—The tone of the unimitative OBOE varies according to the proportions of its pipes, the pressure of the wind on which it speaks, and the method and musical sense of its voicer: but its most desirable tone is smooth and of medium strength, inclining, in the finer examples, to a plaintive quality, which imparts a certain charm and impressive character to it. With such a voice, the stop becomes extremely valuable both in solo passages and in combination; occupying in a softly-toned division about the same position as that held by the TRUMPET in the Great or fundamental division of the Organ. Under such conditions the OBOE is extremely valuable in artistic registration. It combines perfectly with both open and covered flute-toned stops, imparting to their voices richness and dignity. It also imparts to the keen voices of the stringtoned stops, imitative and unimitative, a fullness and impressiveness highly desirable, without seriously affecting their characteristic voices. It is questionable if there is another lingual stop in the modern Organ more generally useful in refined registration: of course this last remark applies only to the OBOE produced by a masterhand. It is remarkable that so valuable a stop should have been systematically neglected by Cavaillé-Coll. In not one of his Organs have we been able to find an OBOE.

OBOE D'AMORE, Ital.—The orchestral instrument of this name—the French, Hautbois d'Amour—now almost obsolete, has a "tone more veiled and pathetic than that of the ordinary orchestral Oboe." This tone is due to the different form of its bell, which is globular with a somewhat contracted opening, contrasting with the flaring bell of the ordinary Oboe. This fact leads to the construction of an organ-stop, having resonators formed with the slender tubes of the OBOE surmounted by small bells, in the shape of two truncated cones soldered together at their bases, after the fashion of those of the CORNO DI BASSETTO, Fig. 8, Plate II. The addition of a stop producing a quality of tone between that of the unimitative OBOE and the imitative ORCHESTRAL OBOE would be a valuable addition to the tonal forces of the Concert-room Organ.

OBOE-FLUTE.—The name given by William Hill, organ-builder, of London, to an open labial stop, of 4 ft. pitch, and small scale, which yielded a soft flute-tone combined with a slight reedy intonation. He introduced it in the Organ he installed in Worcester Cathedral. It was probably not considered sufficiently distinctive to recommend its general adoption, for it was disused. There is room, however, in the Organ of the present century for a timbre-creating OCTAVE, in the voice of which flute- and reed-tones are in full combination. Ample proof obtains that such a desirable stop could be made, wood pipes being used.

OBOE-HORN.—The name given by Hope-Jones to a stop developed by him from the common unimitative OBOE, by imparting to it a broader and somewhat hornlike intonation. As a compromise between the OBOE and HORN, without the advantage of either, such a stop has very little to recommend it. An example exists in the Organ in Llandaff Cathedral, Wales.

OCARINA.—An open metal labial stop, of 4 ft. pitch, which yields a hollow fluty tone, resembling that of the instruments of the same name.* The special pipes of this purely modern and uncommon stop commence at tenor C and extend to the top note. The pipes have cylindrical bodies surmounted by long and slightly spreading bells, the proportions of which may be realized from the following dimensions of the c^2 pipe. The speaking length of this pipe is $6\frac{1}{8}$ inches; the cylindrical body being $3\frac{1}{8}$ inches long and 1.13 inches in diameter; while the bell is 3 inches long and the diameter of its open end is 1.69 inches. The mouth is $\frac{7}{8}$ inch in width, and about one-fourth its width in height: its upper lip is straight, and the languid is finely nicked. The pipe is tuned by means of a strip cut from a small slot in the bell. We obtained these particulars from the stop in the Choir of the Organ in the Church of St. Mary, Bradford, Yorkshire, constructed by M. C. Annessens, of Gramont, Belgium. There is a stop of the same name in the Positif of the Organ, built by A. Amézua, in 1903, for Seville Cathedral.

* "OCARINE (It.). A series of seven musical instruments [of different pitches] made of terra cotta pierced with small holes [and having whistle-like mouthpieces], invented by a company of performers calling themselves the Mountaineers of the Apennines. With these instruments, which are of a soft and sweet, yet 'traveling' quality of tone, operatic melodies with simply-harmonized accompaniments were given." —"A Dictionary of Musical Terms." Stainer and Barrett.

OCTAVE.—Ger., OCTAV. Ital., OTTAVA. Span., OCTAVA. Dtch., OCTAAF.—The name properly used by German, Italian, Spanish, Dutch, American, and to some extent by English and French organ-builders, to distinguish the chief stop of octave or 4 ft. pitch in a manual division, and of 8 ft. pitch in the Pedal Organ. The French organ-builders commonly use the term PRESTANT for the stop, of 4 ft. pitch, which belongs to the foundation-work; occasionally applying the term OCTAVE, of the same pitch, to some subordinate stop. In this relationship we find both terms in the stop-apportionment of the Grand-Orgue in Cavaillé-Coll's fine instrument in the Cathedral of Notre-Dame, Paris. In the Pédale of the same Organ, we find the term OCTAVE illogically applied to a stop of 4 ft. pitch. In this department such a stop is strictly a SUPER-OCTAVE or FIFTEENTH. But organ-builders are not distinguished for their regard to correct stop nomenclature.

The old English organ-builders invariably used the term PRINCI-PAL, 4 FT.; and the practice has been largely followed up to the present time. Proof of this may be readily found. In a list of specifications of thirty-three Organs, constructed by J. W. Walker & Sons, of London, between the years 1858 and 1904, we find the term PRINCIPAL, 4 FT., used fifty-nine times in the manual divisions, and PRINCIPAL, 8 FT., twelve times in the Pedal Organ: whereas the term OCTAVE occurs only eight times, chiefly in the Organ in York Minster, constructed in 1903. At the present time American organ-builders wisely and almost invariably use the term OCTAVE.

As the OCTAVE, 4 FT., is the leading stop of medium pitch in the manual foundation-work, it is commonly and properly the one first correctly pitched and tuned, the other stops below and above it in pitch being tuned from it. It was probably on this account that the old English builders gave the name PRINCIPAL to the stop. There seems to be no other apology possible for so illogical an appellation.

FORMATION.—The OCTAVE, 4 FT., which strictly belongs to the foundation-work of the Organ, is composed of open cylindrical metal pipes, formed in all respects similar to the pipes of the DIAPASON, to which they are tonally related. In old English work the scale of the CC (4 ft.) pipe was commonly made one pipe smaller than the tenor C (4 ft.) pipe of the DIAPASON, 8 FT. In modern work it has frequently been made two pipes smaller in scale. Unscientifically voiced as the OCTAVE commonly is, a smaller scale would seem desirable. When the DIAPASON scale is of the ratio $1 : 2.66$ (See DIAPASON),—halving on the eighteenth pipe,—it may be desirable to have the scale of the OCTAVE of the ratio $1 : \sqrt{8}$,—halving on the seventeenth pipe.

TONE AND REGISTRATION.—The OCTAVE is essentially and properly a harmonic-corroborating stop, and its chief office is to establish the first and most important upper partial of the tone produced by the fundamental unison. Accordingly, while its voice should be of pure organ-tone, similar to that of the DIAPASON, it must be sufficiently soft to intimately combine with and enrich the unison tone without disturbing its pitch. A properly proportioned OCTAVE is of great importance and value in registration; combining with other labial stops than the DIAPASONS, and also with lingual stops, imparting to their voices clearness and brilliancy.

In a division of the Organ in which there is no DIAPASON, the OCTAVE should partake of the character of the principal labial unison or be suitable for combination with it in artistic registration. In this case the OCTAVE will generally serve as a solo stop, a timbre-creating, and a harmonic-corroborating one.

The term OCTAVE has been frequently applied as a prefix to the names of stops, to indicate their pitch with relation to the unison pitch of the divisions in which they are placed, or with relation to some musical interval calculated from that unison. Accordingly, we find stops bearing the compound names: OCTAVE DULCIANA, OCTAVE FIFTEENTH, I FT., OCTAVE FLUTE, OCTAVE GAMBA, OCTAVE QUINT, 2⅔ FT., OCTAVE TWELFTH, 1⅓ FT., etc.

OCTAVE OBOE.—The lingual stop, of 4 ft. pitch, bearing this name has been inserted in certain important modern Organs. It is the proper OCTAVE of the unimitative OBOE, 8 FT. An example exists on the Second Manual of the Organ in the Cathedral of Riga; and examples exist in the Choir and Solo of the Organ in the Centennial Hall, Sydney, N. S. W. Hutchings inserted one, under the name OBOE CLARION, 4 FT., in the Chancel Swell of the Organ he installed in the Church of St. Bartholomew, New York City. We inserted one in the First Subdivision of the Third Organ—representing the wood-wind forces of the orchestra—in our tonal scheme of the Organ installed in the Festival Hall of the Louisiana Purchase Exposition, 1904.

Although the introduction of such a soft-toned stop as the OCTAVE OBOE is, or should be, is extremely rare, there can be no question regarding the value of its voice in expressive registration. The present prevailing craze for musical noise is not favorable to the introduction of refined voices in the Organ, or to the development of artistic registration.

OCTAVE VIOLA.—An open metal labial stop, of 4 ft. pitch, the tone of which is intended to imitate that of the orchestral Viola.

An example exists in the Swell of the Willis Organ in St. George's Hall, Liverpool. Another, labeled VIOLA, 4-FT., exists in the Great of the same instrument, where it serves as the OCTAVE to the VIOLONCELLO, 8 FT. Neither stop is highly imitative.

Imitative string-toned stops, of 4 ft. pitch, are extremely rare; but their value in tonal-coloring and artistic registration must be evident to everyone who has studied the combinations of organ-stops scientifically and practically. The imitative stop is more appropriately termed VIOLETTA (q. v.). As a harmonic-corroborating and timbre-creating stop it should find a place in every Concert-room Organ; preferably in the String division, ancillary or otherwise, where it forms the most perfect OCTAVE.

OCTAVIN, Fr.—The term sometimes employed by French organ-builders to designate an open metal labial stop, of 2 ft. pitch; equivalent, in all essentials, to the SUPER-OCTAVE or FIFTEENTH in English and American Organs. Examples of the OCTAVIN exist in the Récit Expressif of the Organs in the Cathedral of Notre-Dame and the Church of Saint-Sulpice, Paris.

OCTAVIN HARMONIQUE, Fr.—The name given to an open labial stop, of 2 ft. pitch, all the pipes of which are of double the standard speaking length, and voiced harmonically; examples of which exist in the Récit-Écho Expressif of the Organ in the Royal Church, Saint-Denis, and in the Organ in the Church of Saint-Vincent de Paul, Paris. The stop is flute-toned, and is practically a HARMONIC PICCOLO.

OFFENBASS, Ger.—The name that has been used by certain German organ-builders to designate an open bass stop simply in contradistinction to the covered stop GEDECKTBASS. It is an open appellation, conveying no idea of pitch or tonality. Without the addition of some expressive qualification such a term must be considered practically valueless.

OFFENFLÖTE, Ger.—The name given by German organ-builders to an open wood stop, of 8 ft. or 4 ft. pitch, yielding an unimitative flute-tone closely resembling that of the English CLARABELLA. The stop obtains, under the simple name FLÖTE, in the Organ in the Cathedral of Ulm. We find the German word *offen* used in other compound stop-names, as OFFENQUINTFLÖTE and OFFENFLÖTENQUINTE, meaning *Open flute-toned Quint*.

OPEN DIAPASON.—The term employed by English organ-builders from the middle of the seventeenth century to designate the principal foundation stops both in the manual and pedal departments of the Organ. In the former it is invariably of 8 ft., and in the latter of 16 ft. pitch; these being the standard unison pitches of the respective departments. The prefix *open* was applied to distinguish the stop from the one, of the same pitch, illogically named STOPPED DIAPASON, which is in no sense a DIAPASON, being a covered wood stop, strictly belonging to the Flute-work of the Organ. For full particulars see DIAPASON.

OPHICLEIDE.—Fr., OPHICLÉIDE. Ger., OPHICLEÏD. Ital., OFFICLEIDE.—The name derived from ὄφις—a serpent, and κλείς—a key, and given to a large brass instrument of extensive compass and powerful voice. The organ-stop to which the name is applied is supposed to imitate the tone of the orchestral instrument. It is a striking-reed of large scale and powerful intonation, of 8 ft. pitch in the manual divisions, and 16 ft. pitch in the Pedal Organ. The OPHICLEIDE was first introduced by W. Hill, of London, in the Great of the Organ he erected in the Town Hall of Birmingham. It is labeled GREAT OPHICLEIDE, 8 FT., and speaks on high-pressure wind. In the Organ in St. George's Hall, Liverpool, there are three OPHICLEIDES, of 8 ft. pitch, inserted in the Great, Swell, and Solo divisions, and one, of 16 ft. pitch, in the Pedal Organ. As a proof of the old-fashioned system of tonal appointment pervading this instrument, the only OPHICLEIDE endowed with flexibility and power of expression is that in the Swell Organ.* The stop in the Solo Organ speaks on a wind of 22 inches pressure: it is a superb stop of its class, but its value is unfortunately circumscribed through its voice being beyond artistic control.

FORMATION.—The pipes of the OPHICLEIDE have resonators of inverted conical form, of full speaking length and large scale, made of thick spotted-metal or zinc. Their reeds or *échalotes* are also of large scale and of the open variety. These have tongues or *languettes* of hard rolled brass, thick, and carefully curved, so as to produce a tone full and commanding, but without brassy clang; so as to resemble as closely as practicable the full round tones of the orchestral Ophicleide.

* "Before the recent renovation [1898], the Swell Organ was the only expressive division in the instrument; for in the year 1855 the introduction of more than a single swell-box was neither appreciated nor understood. It is, indeed, remarkable that for upwards of forty years the Solo Organ of fifteen stops, including four high-pressure reeds, remained uninclosed and entirely devoid of flexibility and powers of expression; and, to our mind, it is still more remarkable that when the swell-box was applied to the Solo Organ in 1898, the four high-pressure and very powerful reed stops were left uninclosed. It is not too much to say that had these noisy stops been placed under control their utility and effectiveness would have been increased tenfold. In our opinion, while it was right to inclose the eleven stops of the Solo Organ, it was positively barbarous to leave the very stops which call most loudly for tonal control in the whole Organ absolutely uncontrollable."—"The Art of Organ-Building." Vol. II., p. 730.

REGISTRATION.—Unless used under perfect control and more or less subdued, the OPHICLEIDE is practically valueless in general artistic registration, and even under such control it is only good in exceptional effects. It is occasionally employed as a solo stop when it is expressive; but its principal use and value is in impressive crescendo passages and grand climaxes. Under all circumstances, a lingual stop of so powerful a voice has to be very carefully used; and will always be so when commanded by a true musician and artist. It will, however, be beloved by the lover of musical noise.

ORCHESTRAL BASSOON.—The name properly given to the lingual stop, of 8 ft. pitch, the tones of which successfully imitate those of the orchestral Bassoon. The pipes of the most satisfactory examples of the stop have resonators of wood or metal, conical or pyramidal in form and of very small scale. The true compass of the Bassoon of the orchestra does not extend beyond e♭¹; accordingly, above this note the stop is completed in what are practically ORCHESTRAL OBOE pipes (See ORCHESTRAL OBOE). The tone of the ORCHESTRAL BASSOON should throughout its compass be of greater body than that which characterizes the ORCHESTRAL OBOE, so as to give a marked individuality to the stop. For further and full particulars, see BASSOON.

ORCHESTRAL CLARINET.—The name properly employed to designate the lingual solo stop formed and voiced to yield a tone imitative of that of the orchestral Clarinets. For general particulars respecting the formation, tonality, etc., of the CLARINET, 8 FT., of the Organ, see CLARINET. As it has been found that the CLARINET, in its usual form, is rendered much more closely imitative of the tone of the orchestral instruments, by having a soft-toned labial stop of perfect blending quality combined with it, we would suggest that the term ORCHESTRAL CLARINET be confined to a dual stop so formed. In our experience we have found that a covered wood flute-toned stop—preferably a small-scaled and softly-voiced DOPPEL-FLÖTE, 8 FT.—combines perfectly with the lingual stop, and produces a compound tone of remarkable imitative quality. It is in the imitation of the chalumeau register of the Clarinet of the orchestra that the voicer will meet with the principal difficulty; but this can be largely overcome by skillful voicing, without causing any perceptible break in the tone of the stop.

ORCHESTRAL FLUTE.—Fr., FLÛTE TRAVERSIÈRE. Ital., FLAUTO TRAVERSO. Ger. CONCERTFLÖTE.—The stop to which these names are properly applied yields tones as closely imitative of those of the Flute of the orchestra as are practicable in a rank of organ-pipes, blown by wind of uniform pressure. There are only two Flutes employed in the orchestra, the Flauto Traverso and the Flauto Piccolo; accordingly, the range of tone to be imitated is very limited. Several forms of both metal and wood pipes have been devised, by organ-builders of different nationalities, for the production of satisfactory ORCHESTRAL FLUTES. The most effective examples which have come to our observation are those labeled FLAUTO TRAVERSO, of both 8 ft. and 4 ft. pitch, in the Organ in the Parish Church of Doncaster, Yorkshire, made by Edmund Schulze of Paulinzelle. In these we find cylindrical pipes of wood employed yielding tones almost identical with those of the orchestral instrument. Another beautiful example, by the same artist, of 8 ft. pitch and tenor C compass, exists in the Echo of the Organ in the Parish Church of Leeds, where it speaks on wind of 1½ inches. The stop appears under the names CONCERTFLÖTE, 8 FT., and TRAVERSFLÖTE, 4 FT., on the Second Manual of the Organ in the Cathedral of Lübeck. In its most expressive name, ORCHESTRAL FLUTE, 8 FT., it exists in the Solo of the Organ in the Music Hall of the Carnegie Institute, Pittsburgh: and, of 4 ft. pitch, in the Solo of the Organ in St. George's Hall, Liverpool. Under the name FLAUTO TRAVERSO, of 8 ft., 4 ft., and 2 ft. pitch, it is introduced in the Solo of the Organ in the Centennial Hall, Sydney, N. S. W. The stop of 2 ft. pitch should have been labeled ORCHESTRAL PICCOLO. The stop exists in French Organs under the name FLÛTE TRAVERSIÈRE, 8 FT., as in the Organ in the Church of Saint-Sulpice, Paris; and under the uncommon name FLÛTE D'ORCHESTRE, 8 FT., in the Récit of the Organ in the Cathedral of Albi.

FORMATION.—Three forms have been adopted for the wood pipes of the ORCHESTRAL FLUTE; namely, cylindrical, quadrangular, and triangular; all of which are, in the best examples, harmonic in the principal portion of their compass. In the 8 ft. stop the harmonic pipes should commence on c¹, and in the 4 ft. stop on tenor C.

The pipes which produce tones most closely resembling those of the orchestral Flute are formed of circular tubes of hard wood, having small mouths, placed in relation to their blocked ends just as is the embouchure of the orchestral Flute. Their caps are formed so as to direct the wind-stream across their mouths, just as the wind from the human mouth is directed across the embouchure of the orchestral instrument. The cylindrical pipes are invariably harmonic, and, accordingly, are about double the standard speaking length.* Flutes of this imitative form are

* A full description, accompanied by accurately detailed drawings, of the fine cylindrical stops in the Organs in the Parish Churches of Doncaster and Leeds, made by Schulze, is given in

met with in high-class German work; but we are not aware of one ever having
been made by a French, English, or American organ-builder; their cylindrical
FLUTES being invariably of metal, and, when imitative, harmonic

Very successful ORCHESTRAL FLUTES have been made with quadrangular
harmonic pipes, usually of 4 ft. pitch. These are usually square, though in some
cases slightly deeper than wide. Their mouths are circular and inverted: and
their caps, which cover a small portion of the mouths, are formed so as to direct
the wind-stream in the manner described above.* A good example of the ORCHES-
TRAL FLUTE, 4 FT., formed of harmonic triangular pipes, is furnished by the stop
in the Echo of the Concert-room Organ in the Town Hall of Leeds. The harmonic
pipes commence on the tenor C key and are carried to the top. The bottom octave
is of nonharmonic pipes. The form and construction of the triangular pipes are
shown in Fig. 27, in which are given a Front View and Longitudinal and Transverse Sections of the largest one. The following are the measurements of the three
pipes yielding the 2 ft., 1 ft., and ½ ft. notes, taken in the Organ. C, 2 ft. tone,—
width 2¾ ins.; depth along sides 2 ins.; length from lower lip 3 ft. 10 ins.; distance
of perforation from lower lip 1 ft. 9 ins.; diameter of perforation ¼ in.; width of
mouth 1⅜ ins.; height of mouth $\frac{9}{16}$ in.; and block sunk below lower lip of mouth
¾ inch. Pipe c¹, 1 ft. tone,—width 1⅞ ins.; depth along sides 1⅜ ins.; length
from lower lip 1 ft. 10 ins.; distance of perforation from lower lip 11 ins.; diameter
of perforation $\frac{3}{16}$ in.; width of mouth ⅞ in.; height of mouth $\frac{7}{16}$ in.; and block
sunk below lower lip ⅝ in. Pipe c², ½ ft. tone—width 1⅛ ins.; depth along sides
$\frac{13}{16}$ in.; length from lower lip 10¾ ins.; distance of perforation from lower lip 5$\frac{1}{16}$
ins.; diameter of perforation ⅛ in.; width of mouth ⅝ in.; height of mouth $\frac{7}{32}$ in.;
and block sunk below lower lip $\frac{7}{16}$ in. The wind pressure is 2½ inches; and the
tone is pure and of medium strength. The FLÛTE TRAVERSIÈRE and FLÛTE
D'ORCHESTRE, of the French organ-builders appear to be formed invariably of
metal harmonic pipes of usual shape and treatment.

TONE AND REGISTRATION.—While the strictly imitative voice of
the ORCHESTRAL FLUTE renders the stop essentially a solo one, and
most effective in that capacity, it is extremely valuable in combination and artistic registration. Its pure and singularly liquid intonation, when not undesirably prominent, creates beautiful qualities of
compound tone of an orchestral character, through its decided contrast with the voices of the imitative string-toned and reed-toned
stops, with which it combines perfectly. In both its solo and combinational offices, the ORCHESTRAL FLUTE is valuable in both its
8 ft. and 4 ft. pitches.

ORCHESTRAL HORN.—The name given to the important
lingual stop, the voice of which imitates that of the Horn of the
orchestra. For full particulars respecting formation, tone, etc., see
HORN.

"The Art of Organ-Building," Vol. II., pp. 463–4; and in "The Organ of the Twentieth Century,"
pp. 438–9.
* A fine quadrangular example is described and illustrated in "The Art of Organ-Building,"
Vol. II., pp. 465–7: and in "The Organ of the Twentieth Century," pp. 439–40.

ORCHESTRAL OBOE.—The lingual stop, of 8 ft. pitch, voiced
to imitate the tones of the Oboe of the orchestra.   Both in formation
and tonality it differs from the ordinary unimitative OBOE of the
Organ.   The ORCHESTRAL OBOE, 8 FT., is of comparatively rare
introduction in even the large Organs of to-day; the difficulty of
producing the peculiar voice of
the orchestral instrument being
the principal cause. Speaking of
the Oboe, Berlioz correctly remarks: "It is especially a melodial instrument, having a pastoral character, full of tenderness
—nay, I would even say, of tim-
idity." From such a description
one can readily realize the problem before the pipe-maker and
reed-voicer. The most successful examples of the ORCHESTRAL
OBOE, 8 FT., which have come
under our direct observation are
those constructed by Willis, and
inserted in several of his important Organs, including those in
St. George's Hall, Liverpool; the
Town Hall, Huddersfield; and
the Cathedrals of Durham and
Glasgow.   The ORCHESTRAL
OBOE was invented and first
made by George Willis, brother
of Henry Willis, England's most
distinguished organ-builder.
George voiced all the superb
series of lingual stops in the St.
George's Hall Organ (1855)
founding thereby the unequalled
Willis school of reed-voicing.

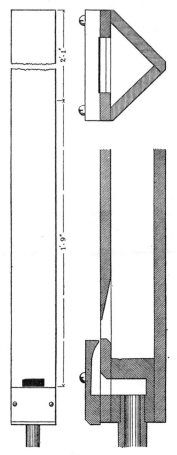

FIG. 27

The stop has been, so far as our observation extends, completely
ignored by French organ builders: we have been unable to find an
example even in their most important Organs.   The stop labeled
BASSON-HAUTBOIS exists in many instruments, but it cannot be considered orchestral in character. Stops labeled ORCHESTRAL OBOE,
8 FT., exist on the First Manual of the Organ in the Cathedral of

Ulm; and on the Third Manual of the Organ in the Synagogue, Berlin.

FORMATION.—In briefly describing the formation of the pipes of the ORCHES TRAL OBOE, one cannot do better than follow that adopted by Willis. The resonators are of an extremely slender inverted conical form, devoid of bells, and having closed upper ends and long and narrow slots adjoining them. This form of resonator is shown in Fig. 28, Plate III., which is drawn from the Willis ORCHESTRAL OBOE in the Organ in the Town Hall, Huddersfield. The reeds or *échalotes* are of very small scale, and have their stopped ends formed at an acute angle upward from the lower edge of their faces. The tongues or *languettes* are very narrow, of good substance, and finely curved, as usual in all Willis reeds. Other makers have adopted resonators of the ordinary OBOE form but of very slender proportions. Others have been content to use plain inverted conical resonators, of extremely small scales, and open at top: these have only cheapness to recommend them—a very strong recommendation in the mind of the pipe-maker.

Up to this point lingual stops have been alluded to, but we have now to briefly describe a labial stop, formed of quadrangular wood pipes, invented by Mr. William E. Haskell, which yields a tone closely imitative of that of the Oboe of the orchestra. It will be more convenient to describe a single pipe, taking the middle c^1 pipe as representative. The stop is of 8 ft. pitch. The pipe measures $\frac{7}{8}$ inch square, internally, at its mouth line; and, while its width remains the same, its depth is gradually reduced to $\frac{11}{16}$ inch at its open top end, the reduction commencing about 12 inches above the mouth and taking a curve inward from that point in the front of the pipe. The block is slightly sunk below the mouth, which is inverted, carefully formed, and furnished with a sloping cap and cylindrical harmonic-bridge. The length of the pipe from the mouth is 1 foot $11\frac{1}{2}$ inches. The stop speaks on wind of $3\frac{1}{2}$ inches pressure.

TONE AND REGISTRATION.—It is somewhat difficult to describe the peculiar tone of the Oboe of the orchestra. In addition to his description, quoted above, Berlioz speaks of its "small acid-sweet voice"—a very happy expression. Judging from the number of compositions written for it, and the place it has always held in orchestral music, it is obvious that the voice of the Oboe was highly esteemed by all the great composers. As the Oboe of the orchestra does not go below tenor B♭, it is obvious that the imitative tones of the ORCHESTRAL OBOE, 8 FT., of the Organ must commence on that note. Below that note the pipes should strictly be of the FAGOTTO class, because the Fagotto provides the proper bass to the Oboe in the orchestra: it is this fact that led the French organ-builders to use the term BASSON-HAUTBOIS. But it is neither necessary nor desirable to break the organ-stop in either its tone or the form of its pipes. In correct Oboe solos, the performer will never be compelled to go below the compass of the instrument; while in general organ playing the complete stop of uniform tone will be extremely valuable in combination and registration. While the ORCHESTRAL OBOE will not be so generally useful in registration as the unimitative OBOE (*q. v.*), it will lend itself to the production of many beautiful compound tones having very marked tonal colorings. In this direction, the stop and its effects are well worthy of the organist's careful study.

ORCHESTRAL PICCOLO.—An open labial stop of metal or wood, sometimes of both; formed, in the finest examples, of harmonic pipes. It is of 2 ft. pitch; and is voiced to yield bright and piercing flute-tones, imitative of those of the orchestral Flauto Piccolo. See PICCOLO.

ORLO, CRO ORLO, Span.—A lingual stop, of 8 ft. pitch, of the MUSETTE or CHALUMEAU character. It exists in certain large Spanish Organs, including those in the Cathedrals of Burgos and Valladolid. In the North Organ in the former Cathedral there are two ORLOS on the First Clavier, probably of different pitches; and on the Second Clavier there are two stops labeled CRO ORLO. The Spanish organ-builders seem to have had a great love for lingual stops, judging from the number introduced in their Organs, and the manner they disposed them, *en chamade*, in their sumptuous cases.

P

PANFLÖTE, Ger.—Ital., FLAUTO DI PAN.—The name that has been given to a very rare Pedal Organ labial stop, of 1 ft. pitch, formed of open metal pipes, yielding acute tones resembling those of the Pan-pipes. An example exists in the Pedal of the Grand Organ in the Cathedral of Lund, Sweden. See FLAUTO DI PAN.

PASTORITA, Ital.—The name that has occasionally been used to designate the labial stop now commonly known as the French COR DE NUIT or the German NACHTHORN (*q. v.*).

PAUKE, Ger.—The stop so called by German organ-builders was one of the curiosities to be found in old Organs. It consisted of two large-scaled and loudly-voiced covered wood pipes, sounding the notes of the proper pitches of the Pauken or Kettle-drums of the orchestra, placed in the Pedal Organ. The loud and thumping sounds produced by these special pipes, when played *staccato*, were supposed to imitate those of the Kettle-drums.

Another curiosity, called PAUKERENGEL, was a mechanical accessory, which took the form of an angel playing the Drum. Two or more of these were mounted on the case, chiefly as ornaments and were actuated by pedal mechanism. Examples are said to have existed in the Organ built by Joachim Wagner in 1725, for the Garrison Church, Berlin.

PERDUNA.—The name which has sometimes been employed by old German organ-builders to designate a covered wood stop, of 16 ft. pitch, and similar in all essentials to the BOURDON.

PFEIFE, Ger.—This term when used alone properly designates an open metal labial stop, of 2 ft. pitch, yielding a bright flute-tone. It is, in the generality of examples, practically identical with the stop named FIFE (*q. v.*). In certain compound names, used by German organ-builders, the terms PFEIFE and FLÖTE seem to be synonymous. An instance of both terms being used in combination is given by Seidel-Kothe: "PFEIFERFLÖTE wird zuweilen NASAT 2⅔′ genannt."

PHILOMELA.—Ital., FILOMELA.—The name, which means *Nightingale (Daulias philomela)*, has been used to designate stops of widely different tonalities—so different, indeed, that one is disposed to ask, so far as organ-builders' terminology is concerned, "What's in a name?" In the first place, it has been applied, appropriately, to a small-scaled wood stop voiced to yield an extremely refined and soft flute-like tone, suggestive of the voice of the Nightingale. Clarke, in his "Structure of the Pipe Organ," describes the PHILOMELA, 8 FT., as a flute-toned stop formed of "Small scale stopped wood pipes, voiced with the sweetest and most delicate quality." In the second place, and with a widely different signification, the name is given to wood stops of large scale and powerful intonation. The PHILOMELA, 8 FT., in the unexpressive Solo of the Organ in the Cincinnati Music Hall, built by Hook & Hastings in 1878, is thus described by the builders: "Open pipes of wood, having two mouths. Tone full, rich, and mellow." This stop speaks on wind of ten inches pressure. As a large-scaled, open, double-mouthed stop, the PHILOMELA has been styled a wood STENTORPHONE. If the name is to be retained in modern stop nomenclature, let it be confined to the stop which, however imperfectly, yields a tone having some resemblance to that of the Nightingale's song.

PHOCINX.—An uncommon term that has been applied, in a few instances, to the German lingual stop usually known as the KRUMMHORN. Fr. CROMORNE (*q. v.*).

PHYSHARMONIKA.—A soft-voiced lingual stop, of 16 ft. and 8 ft. pitch, to be found in several German and Swiss Organs.

It is placed on the Fourth Manual of the Organ in the Cathedral of
Riga; and on the Third Manual of the Organ in the Cathedral of
Ulm. Both stops are of 8 ft. pitch. In the well-known Organ in the
Cathedral of Lucerne, the Physharmonika, 8 ft., is placed in the
Swell. In the Organ in the Cathedral of Fribourg, in Switzerland,
there are Physharmonikas, of 16 ft. and 8 ft. pitch. The stops in
both the Lucerne and Fribourg Organs we personally examined,
accompanied, in Lucerne, by F. Haas, the organ-builder who inserted them: accordingly, we are able to describe the stops. In the
Organ in the Cathedral of Magdeburg there is an 8 ft. stop of similar
description, labeled Harmonium.

Formation.—The best examples of the Physharmonika to be found in
modern European Organs have been made by J. & P. Schiedmayer of Stuttgart,
through whose courtesy we are able to give an illustration showing the formation
of the stop. Fig. 29 is a Transverse Section of the complete appliance in its most
improved form. A is the chamber into which the compressed pipe-wind is con-

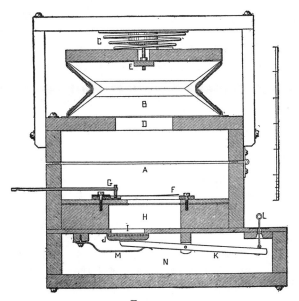

Fig. 29

ducted by a suitable wind-trunk or conveyance. This chamber is connected
through the opening D, with the bellows B, which, together with the chamber A,
forms the compressed-air reservoir. The bellows B is acted on by the spiral spring
C, which properly regulates the wind-pressure at all times on the many tongues.
E is a small escape-valve, held against its port by a light spring. A Longitudinal
Section of a free tongue or vibrator with its brass frame is shown at F; and its

tuning-clip and wire are shown at G. The wire passes air-tight through the side of the chamber A, to enable the tuning to be done from the outside. H is the reed-groove special to the vibrator F, furnished with the pallet-hole I. J is the pallet, covering the hole I, and commanded by the key-action of the Organ through the agency of the rocking-lever K and the pull-wire L. The pallet is held against its seat by the spring M, which is strong enough to resist the downward pressure of the wind on the surface of the pallet. N is the sound-chamber, general to all the reed-grooves: this is properly made much deeper than is shown. It is furnished at its end, or ends, with a pivoted or sliding appliance for *crescendo* and *diminuendo* effects. The free-reeds of the PHYSHARMONIKA are similar in all respects to those used for the ordinary free-reed stops; the only difference lies in the manner in which they are mounted.

The PHYSHARMONIKA, 8 FT., in the Lucerne Organ is, in its sounding portion, similar to that just described, but is inclosed in a special swell-box, in one side of which several heart-shaped openings are cut for the egress of sound; and these are commanded by a sliding shutter in which corresponding perforations are made. The to-and-fro motions of the shutter, under the action of a small expression lever, produce a perfect and gradual *crescendo* and *diminuendo*. In the Fribourg Organ the PHYSHARMONIKAS have their reeds furnished with short resonators. They are inclosed in the same manner as in the Lucerne instrument.

TONE AND REGISTRATION.—The tones of the PHYSHARMONIKA are somewhat indeterminate but generally pleasing, combining in a satisfactory manner with the tones of the labial stops of all tonalities, chiefly in the capacity of timbre-creator. In this direction one tonal difficulty obtains; for, like all free-reed stops, the PHYSHARMONIKA is not affected by changes of temperature in the same manner as are the labial stops; and, accordingly, is not always in perfect tune with them. It, however, can be easily tuned and that difficulty is readily overcome.

Free-reed stops devoid of resonators have recently been intro-duced by certain English organ-builders, with favorable results in tonal combination and registration. In the Organ in Colston Hall, Bristol, built by Norman & Beard in 1905, there are three such free-reed stops, labeled HARP ÆOLONE, KEROPHONE, and SAXOPHONE.

PICCOLO, FLAUTO PICCOLO, Ital.—A labial stop, of 2 ft. pitch, formed of metal, or of wood and metal, the pipes of which are of small scale, and voiced to yield a clear flute-tone. While 2 ft. pitch is obviously the correct and most desirable one, the PICCOLO some-times appears as a stop of 1 ft. pitch, as in the Positif of the Organ in the Church of St. Sulpice, Paris. Under the name HARMONIC PICCOLO, 4 FT., it is inserted in the Solo of the Organ in the Town Hall of Leeds; while in the Great there is a PICCOLO, 2 FT. In the case of a stop like this, which is, or should be, imitative of the orches-tral Piccolo, it is most desirable that organ-builders should adopt a uniform pitch, that of 2 ft. When voiced to closely imitate the voice of the orchestral instrument, it is appropriately called ORCHESTRAL PICCOLO. The French organ-builders usually fashion this imitative stop with harmonic pipes, and label it PICCOLO HARMONIQUE.

TONE AND REGISTRATION.—The PICCOLO, 2 FT., in its proper and most desirable form, may be considered the FIFTEENTH or SUPER-OCTAVE of the Flute-work of the Organ: but, being highly imitative in its voice, it holds a decided position in the orchestral forces; its proper place being in the Wood-wind division, or·in the Solo, of the properly-appointed Concert-room Organ. It is very questionable if·its voice is called for in the legitimate Church Organ. The tone of this imitative stop should be carefully proportioned to those of the ORCHESTRAL FLUTES, 8 FT., and 4 FT., so that whilst it will prove amply sufficient for any solo work, it will not dominate, by its high pitched and necessarily piercing voice, the graver and richer voices of those more important stops. In artistic registration its chief office will be in the production of bright qualities of orchestral tone, in which it will prove invaluable, never, however, losing its identity; in this respect resembling the Piccolo of the orchestra.

PICCOLO D'AMORE, Ital.—The true OCTAVE of the FLAUTO D'AMORE, 4 FT. It is a softly-voiced flute-toned stop of 2 ft. pitch, properly formed of half-covered wood pipes of small scale, from CC to c², and thence to top note in small-scale open metal pipes, preferably of SPITZFLÖTE form. The PICCOLO D'AMORE, 2 FT., is an ideal SUPER-OCTAVE for the true Chamber Organ, or for an Ancillary Aërial Organ.

PIFFERO, Ital.—Literally *Fife*. The name used by Italian organ-builders to designate a stop which is in all essentials similar to the French CHALUMEAU (*q. v.*).

PILEATA, Lat.—Literally *Hooded*. A generic name for labial covered stops, having no direct reference to their tone.* When used alone it simply means a GEDECKT. Combined with other terms, we find PILEATA MAXIMA—a GROSSUNTERSATZ, 32 FT.; PILEATA MAGNA—a GROBGEDECKT, 16 FT.; PILEATA MAJOR—a MITTELGEDECKT, 8 FT.; and PILEATA MINOR—a KLEINGEDECKT, 4 FT.

---

* "VOX-PILEATA, ou simplement PILEATA. C'est encore un de ces noms génériques de jeu bouché, dont la facture allemande abonde même par tradition, puisque les premiers traités de facture furent écrits en latin. Cela veut dire *voix couverte*, ou, mot à mot, *coiffée;* la coiffe est ce que l'on nomme aujourd'hui *calotte* dans les bourdons de métal, et tampon ou bouchon dans ceux de bois. La qualification de *Pileata* se modifie selon la grandeur du régistre; de tous petits régistres bouchés, tels que la *Bauer-Flöte* d'un pied s'appelleront *Pileata-Minima*. Un bourdon de

PLEIN-JEU, Fr.—The name used by French organ-builders to designate a compound harmonic-corroborating stop, of several ranks of medium-scaled open metal pipes, yielding pure organ-tone. A fine example of the stop exists in the Organ in the Town Hall of Manchester, constructed by Cavaillé-Coll. The composition of this stop is here given:

PLEIN-JEU—VII. RANKS.

CC to E	15—19—22—26—29—33—36.
F to e¹	8—12—15—19—22—26—29.
f¹ to e²	1— 8—12—15—19—22—26.
f² to b²	1— 5— 8—12—15—19—22.
c³ to f³	DOUBLE— 1— 5— 8—12—15—19.
f♯³ to c⁴ . . .	DOUBLE—$^{\text{DOUBLE}}_{\text{QUINT}}$—1— 5— 8—12—15.

This PLEIN-JEU has no special feature to distinguish it from an ordinary MIXTURE in which octave- and fifth-sounding ranks only are employed, except in its extreme richness of structure, and the introduction of breaks lower in pitch than the unison of the manual division (Grand-Orgue) in which it is placed. It may be remarked that this division, of fourteen speaking stops, contains three stops of 16 ft. pitch, which fact accounts for the introduction of the DOUBLES and DOUBLE QUINT in the upper breaks of the PLEIN-JEU, and also the fifth-sounding ranks in the three higher breaks which strictly belong to the 16 ft. harmonic series. A PLEIN-JEU of ten ranks is the only compound stop in the Grand-Orgue of the Organ in the Madeleine, Paris. In the Positif of the Organ in Saint Sulpice there is a PLEIN-JEU HARMONIQUE of three and four ranks. Further particulars are given in the appended note.*

---

seize, façonné de manière à prendre un nom quelconque de flûte, ajoutera à ce nom de fantaisie la qualification de *Pileata-Magna* qui empêche l'organiste de l'employer comme jeu ouvert. Enfin *Pileata-Maxima* désignera les bourdons gigantesques de la pédale."—Regnier.

*"LE PLEIN-JEU. Les modernes ont souvent donné le même nom à toute espèce de mixtures; c'est une de ces petites erreurs de détail qui entrainent après elles l'oubli des principes en facture. Ainsi ai-je rencontré souvent dans de petites orgues un régistre appelé *Plein-jeu*, qui n'avait rien de plein, et qui n'était un jeu que dans le sens ridicule du mot. Il y avait de quoi faire prendre en horreur toute espèce de mixture; et j'attribue à ce vol, fait aux vraies conditions du *Plein-jeu* par les facteurs charlatans, la réaction qu'on voit se prononcer contre la vénérable antiquité de cette harmonie. 'Dans un seize-pieds,' dit Dom Bedos, 'le moindre *Plein-jeu* est de neuf tuyaux *sur marche* (ou par note). . . . Si c'est un huit-pieds, le *Plein-jeu* est (au moins) de sept tuyaux sur marche; si l'orgue est un trente-deux-pieds ouvert avec bourdon de trente-deux, on doit mettre *Fourniture* entière et *Cymbale* entière (c'est-à-dire que chacun de ces régistres doit avoir sa plus grande force connue). Pour un positif, si c'est un huit-pieds en montre, on met le *Plein-jeu* de sept tuyaux sur marche. S'il n'y a point de huit-pieds ouverts, le *Plein-jeu* ne sera que de cinq tuyaux sur marche, c'est-à-dire composé des trois dernières rangées de la *Fourniture* et des deux dernières de la *Cymbale*.' (Parce qu'alors un *Plein-jeu* plus fort serait trop dur, n'étant pas soutenu par la force des huit-pieds ouverts.) Dom Bedos donne encore les

PORTUNAL, PORTUNALFLÖTE, Ger.—An open wood stop, of medium scale, and of 8 ft. and 4 ft. pitch. Its pipes are, in the finer examples, of inverted pyramidal form,—after the fashion of the DOLCAN,—yielding a very pleasing fluty tone inclining, in good representative examples, to a Clarinet quality.

POSAUNE, Ger.—A lingual stop, of 8 ft. pitch on the manuals and 16 ft. pitch in the Pedal Organ; the pipes of which have resonators of large scale and inverted conical form. In the manual stop, metal resonators are invariably employed; while in the Pedal stop they are made of either metal or wood; and sometimes of both, wood being used for the lower octave. The tone of the POSAUNE is intended to imitate as closely as possible that of the orchestral Trombone when played *forte* and firmly; it, accordingly, should have more brassiness than the TROMBONE or TRUMPET.

Examples of the POSAUNE, 8 FT., exist in the Greats of the Organs in Westminster Abbey and the Royal Albert Hall, London; and in the Pedal of the Organ in the Cathedral of Riga. Examples of the POSAUNE, 16 FT., are to be found in the Pedals of the Organs in the above-named churches; and in those of the Organs in the Cathedral of Ulm, and the Centennial Hall, Sydney, N. S. W. Under the name POSAUNENBASS, 16 FT., it exists in the Pedals of the Organs in the Cathedral of Lübeck, and the Gewandhaus, Leipzig. See CONTRA-POSAUNE.

PRESTANT, Fr.—The name commonly employed by French organ-builders to designate the principal OCTAVE, 4 FT., in a manual division; yielding pure organ-tone. Its scale is properly derived from, and proportioned to, that of the MONTRE, 8 FT., or chief unison of the division. The PRESTANT occupies the same tonal position and fulfils the same office in a French Organ, as the so-called PRIN-

règles pour un *Plein-jeu* de quatre tuyaux sur marche, mais dans ce cas la maigreur du régistre doit le faire rejeter, car il est déjà trop grinçant, même avec cinq tuyaux seulement. 'Si le *Plein-jeu* est de huit ou de six tuyaux sur marche, on prend la moitié dans la *Fourniture*, et l'autre moitié dans la *Cymbale*: voilà les règles ordinaires. . . .' Dom Bedos ajoute: 'Je ne ferai point remarquer ici toutes les variations de quelques facteurs dans la composition et l'arrangement du *Plein-jeu* (il paraît que dès ce temps-là on cherchait à économiser sur la peine et la dépense qu'occasionne la facture du vrai *Plein-jeu*); mais tous s'accordant à ne mettre que des quintes et des octaves, et jamais de tierces.' Je ne puis omettre ici la citation de l'éloge du *Plein-jeu* par le grand artiste bénédictin; il donne trop d'autorité à ce que nous avons déjà dit: 'Tout ce qu'il y a de plus harmonieux dans l'orgue, au jugement des connaisseurs et de ceux qui ont du goût pour la vraie harmonie, c'est le *Plein-jeu*, lorsqu'il est mélangé avec tous les fonds qui le nourrissent dans une juste proportion; et la raison pour laquelle on met toujours ensemble les fonds de l'orgue avec la *Fourniture* et la *Cymbale*, est que si l'on employait celles-ci seules dans les différentes combinaisons d'accords que fait un organiste, elles formeraient des sons désagréables, qui disparaissent à l'oreille, lorsque le mélange des sons fondamentaux les mettent au rang des sons harmoniques.'"—Regnier.

CIPAL does in an English instrument, and the OCTAVE, 4 FT., in an American and German Organ.* The name PRESTANT, derived from the Latin *Præstare*—to stand in front, was given to the stop because, like the MONTRE, it was commonly displayed in the case-work. See OCTAVE.

PRINZIPAL, Ger.—Ital., PRINCIPALE.—The name appropriately and logically employed by German and Italian organ-builders to designate the *principal* unison stop in both the manual and pedal departments of the Organ—that which is commonly named DIAPASON in English and American Organs, and MONTRE in French Organs. French organ-builders have in some instances used the borrowed terms PRINCIPAL and DIAPASON, as in the Récit and Solo of the Organ in the Church of Saint-Sulpice, Paris. In a manual division the PRINCIPAL is correctly of 8 ft. pitch, and in the Pedal Organ of 16 ft. pitch: but in many German Organs, as in those of the Cathedral of Bremen and the Marienkirche, Lübeck, we find PRINZIPALS of both 8 ft. and 16 ft. pitch in the chief manual division (Hauptwerk), while the foundation unison in the Pedal Organ is labeled PRINZIPALBASS, 16 FT. German organ-builders have applied the term PRINZIPAL alike to the organ-toned foundation stops of 32 ft., 16 ft., 8 ft., and 4 ft. pitch.

English organ-builders have from old times continued to apply the term PRINCIPAL to the open metal stop, of large scale, and 4 ft. pitch, which is the true OCTAVE of the DIAPASON, 8 FT. The term, so applied, is both illogical and undesirable. See OCTAVE.

PRINZIPALDISKANT, DISKANTPRINZIPAL, Ger.— A PRINCIPAL or DIAPASON, 8 FT., of large scale and short compass, which extends throughout the treble octaves of the manual compass,

---

*"Le PRESTANT, c'est la suite de la Montre, dont il a toutes les proportions. Nous avons vu qu'en Allemagne, le prestant allait du seize-pieds au quatre-pieds: en France, le prestant a toujours quatre-pieds à son plus grand tuyau, tellement que souvent les facteurs ne l'appellent que le quatre-pieds. Et lorsqu'ils disent tout court aussi le huit-pieds, ils ne désignent pourtant pas l'octave du prestant, c'est-à-dire la montre de huit, mais bien une flûte qu'on adjoint à la montre et qui, au besoin, la supplée à l'interieur de l'orgue, quand on n'a pas le moyen d'avoir d'autre montre qu'un prestant. Faisant suite à la montre, le prestant est donc, comme elle, ouvert, de moyenne taille, et construit en étain fin. Son harmonie, en rapport avec cette taille élancée et ce métal de choix, est fine et brillante; elle donne un tel éclat, un tel tranchant aux fonds de taille ordinaire et de grosse taille, que son adjonction ou son silence se font vivement sentir. Le prestant parle rarement seul; marié aux flûtes de quatre, il prend un corps dont il n'a que l'ombre dans l'isolement, et devient une flûte éclatante si les timbres sont bien d'accord. Lié aux huit-pieds, il leur donne du brillant; il ne supporte la grave adjonction des seize-pieds que moyennant celle des huit, qui servent de transition. . . . Quelques facteurs intitulent prestant le quatre-pieds de la pédale; ce n'est qu'une flûte de grosse taille en étoffe, qui domine ses deux compagnes ordinaires, flûtes de huit et de seize, surtout quand ces flûtes sont en bois, et même *bouchées.*"—Regnier.

or from middle c¹ to the top note. The stop has very rarely been
carried to tenor C. This short stop was considered of considerable
value by the old German organ-builders, on account of its power of
reinforcing the weaker octaves of the unison foundation-work. This
weakness was so forcibly realized by Christian Muller, that he inserted two pipes to each note in the treble of several of the more
important stops in his noble Organ in the Cathedral of Haarlem.
This matter might, with advantage, receive serious consideration
at the present time; for the natural weakness of the treble in the
Organ still remains one of its tonal short-comings.*

PRINZIPALFLÖTE, Ger.—A powerfully-toned, open metal,
labial stop, of large scale, and 8 ft. and 4 ft. pitch; the voice of which
is a compromise between pure organ-tone and flute-tone. It has
been introduced as a Solo stop; as, by Walcker, in the Organ in St.
Peterskirche, Frankfurt. Such a stop, of unison pitch, would be
valuable as a timbre-creator; and might, with advantage, take the
place of a DIAPASON, 8 FT., when several are introduced. It would
form an admirable foundation stop in the wood-wind division of the
true Concert-room Organ.

PROGRESSIO HARMONICA.—A compound harmonic-corroborating and treble-enriching stop, the ranks of which have no
breaks, but increase in number as the stop progresses upward
through the manual compass. According to Seidel the stop was
invented by Musikdirektor Wilke, of Neu-Ruppin, and recommended by him especially for small Organs. The stop, as originally
devised, begins at CC with two ranks of 1⅗ ft. and 1 ft. pitch, and
at tenor C a third rank of 2 ft. pitch is added. Seidel adds: "The
scale of the stop is between those of the PRINZIPAL and the CORNETT.
The intonation is strong and the effect very fine. The tone of the
Organ becomes by this stop distinct, full, and bright." The PRO-
GRESSIO HARMONICA in the Brustwerk of the Organ in the Cathedral
of Merseburg, in Saxony, built by Ladegast in 1855, commences with
two ranks in the bass and finishes with four ranks in the treble. A
similar stop exists on the Third Manual of his Organ in the Cathedral
of Schwerin. The stop in the Unterwerk of the Organ in St. Peterskirche, Berlin, commences with three ranks and finishes with five
ranks in the treble.

To any one who has given serious consideration to the subject
of compound-tone production in the Organ, the advantages attend-

* See "Weakness and Augmentation of the Treble," Chap. XV., Vol. II., pp. 1-12, of "The
Art of Organ-Building."

ing the introduction of stops of the PROGRESSIO HARMONICA class must be obvious and deserving of careful study. The inventor of the stop was also the inventor of the COMPENSATIONSMIXTUR (q. v.), applied to the Pedal Organ, in which the opposite treatment is adopted; the purpose being to impart distinctness and richness to the lower and somewhat indeterminate notes of that grave department.

PYRAMIDFLÖTE, Ger.—Eng., PYRAMIDAL FLUTE.—A wood stop, of 8 ft. pitch, the pipes of which are square and, as the name implies, are smaller at the top than at the mouth line. The tone differs in stops made by different organ-builders, but in the best examples it is light and clear, resembling a combination of the tones of the MELODIA and the GEMSHORN. A good example exists in the Unterwerk of the Organ in the Church of SS. Peter and Paul, Liegnitz, in Silesia, built by Buckow in 1839. A stop of this class is more suitable for a Chamber Organ than for either a Church or a Concert-room Organ: its tone is refined but without marked individuality.

PYRAMIDON.—The name given to an open wood stop, of 16 ft. pitch, the pipes of which were of inverted pyramidal form and remarkable proportions. It was invented by the Rev. Sir Frederick A. Gore Ouseley, and made by Flight. The peculiarity of the stop, which was applied to the Pedal Organ, lay chiefly in the form and proportions of its pipes, which were covered, the CCC pipe measuring 2 feet 3 inches square at top, 8 inches square at the mouth line, and only 2 feet 6 inches speaking length. The 16 ft. tone produced by this pipe resembled that of a BOURDON, but had nothing special to recommend it. The chief interest of the stop lay in the acoustical problem it presented: its disadvantages were several. It now takes its place among the discarded curiosities of organ-building.

Q

QUARTE DE NASARD, Fr.—The term sometimes employed by French organ-builders to designate the open metal stop, of 2 ft. pitch, belonging to the 8 ft. harmonic series. It is practically identical with the English FIFTEENTH or SUPER-OCTAVE, 2 FT. It derives its name from the fact that its pitch is at the interval of a fourth above that of the NASARD, 2⅔ FT.* An example exists in the Positif of the Organ in the Church of Saint-Remi, Amiens.

---

*"QUARTE. Jeu de l'orgue. Quoique ce jeu soit à l'unisson de la doublette, on lui a donné le nom de quarte, parce qu'en suivant la progression ascendante des jeux du cornet dont il est

QUERFLÖTE, Ger.—The name, which is formed of the words *quer*—cross or athwart—and *Flöte*—Flute, has been frequently used by German organ-builders to designate the stop which, in its voice, imitates, as closely as practicable in organ-pipes, the tone of the Flute of the orchestra. Under the heading QUERFLÖTE, QUER-PFEIFE, Seidel gives the following particulars:

"QUERFLÖTE is a labial stop of a particularly fine tone, imitative of that of the real Flute. Organ-builders, in their endeavor to make this imitation as striking as possible, have essayed with this stop all sorts of shapes and proportions. The pipes are usually made of oak, pear-tree, or maple; and they are either cylindrical or quadrangular, open or stopped. Some organ-builders make the pipes twice as long as they usually appear, and overblow them so as to make them sound the octave higher. Other organ-builders bore out the bodies of the pipes, and provide them with mouths of an oval form, like the embouchure of the real Flute. The QUERFLÖTE made by Müller, of Breslau, for his Organ in the Cathedral of his city, has oval mouths in its pipes, against which the wind is directed sidewise, imitating the method of blowing the real Flute."

A QUERFLÖTE, 8 FT., of the compass of the orchestral Flute, was inserted in the Organ reconstructed by Engelbert Maas, in 1821, for the Cathedral of Cologne. For further particulars see FLAUTO TRAVERSO and ORCHESTRAL FLUTE.

QUINT.—Fr. and Ger., QUINTE. Ital. and Lat., QUINTA.—The stop, correctly termed, which speaks a fifth above the unison pitch of the division of the Organ in which it is placed: it is, accordingly, of $5\frac{1}{3}$ ft. pitch on the manuals, and $10\frac{2}{3}$ ft. pitch in the Pedal Organ. The pipes forming the manual QUINT are properly of open metal, and of medium scale; while those of the Pedal Organ QUINT, though preferably of open metal, may be made of wood. Covered pipes have been used, but they are not to be recommended; they do not satisfactorily fulfil the office for which they are intended.

TONE AND REGISTRATION.—The QUINT, $5\frac{1}{3}$ FT., is a mutation or harmonic-corroborating stop, belonging to the 16 ft. harmonic series, and, as it is strictly a member of the foundation-work of the Organ, its voice should be of pure organ-tone of medium strength, produced by cylindrical metal pipes of the DIAPASON formation. Its presence is not called for in any save the First or Great Organ, and only there

une des parties constituantes, il se trouve à la quarte au-dessus du nasard. Aussi l'appelle-t-on réellement *quarte de nasard*, et ce n'est que par abréviation qu'on dit simplement *quarte.*"—Hamel.

when a DOUBLE DIAPASON, 16 FT., is present. Under certain conditions, however, it may be introduced in the division when no foundation stop of labial character below 8 ft. pitch is present, for the purpose of generating the differential 16 ft. tone, in combination with the DIAPASON, 8 FT. In registration, the QUINT, $5\frac{1}{3}$ FT., may be effectively combined with any lingual stop of 16 ft. pitch, producing beautiful compound tones, not possible of production without it. Much, however, depends on the quality of the voice of the stop and the pipes from which it is produced. To save expense, English organ-builders have commonly used covered pipes, inartistically voiced, producing undesirable thick and dull effects in combination. Better results are obtained by Continental builders, who use open metal and wood pipes, cylindrical, quadrangular, conical, and inverted conical in form; producing various tones, all of which introduce colorings, and affect artistic registration.

The QUINT, $10\frac{2}{3}$ FT., should be introduced, in one form or another, in every important Pedal Organ in which there is no stop of 32 ft. pitch. The stop may be either of metal or wood, and either open or covered—preferably open—according to the stop apportionment of the department. In the Organ built by Schulze, in 1850, for the Cathedral of Bremen, there is a stop labeled QUINTEN-BASS, $10\frac{2}{3}$ FT., and another labeled GROSSQUINTENBASS, $21\frac{1}{3}$ FT. The former is legitimate, corroborating the second upper partial tone of the 32 ft. prime, and in combination with the DIAPASON, 16 FT., corroborating the 32 ft. tone; while the latter could have been introduced solely with the view of generating the differential tone of the 64 ft. pitch, just as it has been employed in other important Organs. See GRAVISSIMA.

QUINTADENA.—Stops bearing this name have been introduced in numerous Organs. The earliest instances of its introduction we have been able to find are those in the Organ in the New Church, Amsterdam. It is an old instrument, enlarged in 1673 by Duyshor van Goor, of Dordrecht. In the Great there is a QUINTA-DENA, 16 FT., and in both the Choir and Echo a QUINTADENA, 8 FT. The stop seems to have been a favorite with the old Dutch organ-builders.

The QUINTADENA is in all essentials similar to the covered stop correctly designated QUINTATEN (q. v.), yielding a compound tone in which the twelfth, or second upper partial tone, is present in a pronounced degree along with the prime or fundamental tone. The stop is formed of covered pipes of metal or wood: as a rule the metal stop is to be preferred, if not too large a scale, and artistically voiced. We find some variations of the prevailing name; namely, QUIN-TADEN, QUINTADENE, and QUINTADEMA. Under the last name, the stop exists in the Swell of the Organ in the Music Hall, Cincinnati. It is formed of covered pipes of tin, of 8 ft. pitch.

QUINTATEN.—The name derived from the Latin words *quintam tenentes* (holding the fifth), and properly applied to covered stops which yield compound tones, in which the second upper partial tone is almost as pronounced as the prime or ground tone. Helmholtz correctly remarks: " Narrow stopped pipes let the twelfth be very distinctly heard at the same time with the prime tone; and have hence been called *Quintaten (quintam tenentes).*"* The term QUITATEN has comparatively seldom appeared in organ specifications or stop-knobs, several corruptions having been substituted according to the caprice of different organ-builders in different countries.   We give these corruptions so that they may be known and avoided in the stop nomenclature of to-day: QUINTATON, QUINTATÖN, QUINTADEN, QUINTADÖN, QUINTADINER, QUINTADÈNE, and QUINTGETÖN.

The QUINTATEN is formed of covered pipes of metal and wood, and of 16 ft., 8 ft., and 4 ft. pitch: all are very valuable in their respective places; and collectively they form a remarkable family, the importance of which has been altogether overlooked by organ designers; in this direction it is on an equality with the LIEBLICH-GEDECKT family.

TONE AND REGISTRATION.—The compound tone of the QUIN-TATEN, when produced from pipes correctly scaled, and artistically voiced on wind of proper pressure, is extremely valuable in combination and artistic registration.   As before stated, the tone yielded by a QUINTATEN pipe is a compound of the prime and its second upper partial tone,—the first harmonic produced by a covered pipe,— and it is from this acoustical phenomenon that the stop derives its special value, enabling the Octave-quint or Twelfth to be introduced in registration in a degree of softness and refinement impossible to be imparted by an independent fifth-sounding stop.   The relative strength of the Twelfth varies in different stops.   In some it is subdued, while in others it is almost as prominent as the prime tone. In a really fine QUINTATEN, 8 FT., the prime tone should be firmly

*"On the Sensations of Tone," by Hermann L. F. Helmholtz, M.D.   Translated by A. J. Ellis, B.A., 1875.

established as the pitch of the stop; but as regards the relative strength of the upper partial, much will depend on the general stop apportionment in which the QUINTATEN is inserted: it should, however, in all cases be distinctly pronounced, otherwise the stop will lose much of its value.

An artistically voiced QUINTATEN forms an effective solo stop, notwithstanding the argument advanced against its use on account of the production of consecutive fifths. But this objection is of no real value, for it must be recognized that the natural fifths, produced as harmonic upper partial tones, have a widely different tonal effect from the independent consecutive fifths condemned in musical theory and composition. The fifth-sounding stops and ranks in compound stops, introduced in the Organ as harmonic-corroborators if properly apportioned and scientifically graduated in strength of tone, produce no objectionable tonal effects: on the contrary, they are demanded in the tonal structure of the Organ, and are absolutely necessary for the creation of many desirable qualities of compound tone; and, accordingly, have very important offices in artistic registration.

The QUINTATEN, 16 FT., although by no means so valuable in manual divisions as the unison stop, is greatly to be preferred to a BOURDON, 16 FT., of the ordinary class. Its subordinate upper partial, sufficiently representing the $5\frac{1}{3}$ ft. tone, gives great fulness and richness to all combinations in which the stop is introduced. The stop imparts great solidity and dignity to the tones of lingual stops of 16 ft. pitch. Voiced with the harmonic-bridge, the QUINTATEN, 16 FT., can be made an imitative DOUBLE BASS suitable for a small Organ.

The QUINTATEN, 4 FT., is comparatively of little value unless in association with the 16 ft. and 8 ft. stops—completing the family: but certain organ-builders have introduced it as the only octave stop in a manual division, rendering a TWELFTH, $2\frac{2}{3}$ FT., unnecessary, but the presence of a SUPER-OCTAVE, 2 FT., is imperative to cover the prominent upper partial of the QUINTATEN.

QUINTENBASS, Ger.—The name used by German organ-builders to designate the mutation or harmonic-corroborating stop, of $10\frac{2}{3}$ ft., pitch belonging to the 32 ft. harmonic series, and properly introduced in the Pedal Organ along with the DOUBLE DIAPASON, 32 FT.; or, in the absence of that important stop, with the view of producing in combination with the DIAPASON, 16 FT., the differential tone of 32 ft. pitch, sometimes designated "acoustic bass." The stop has been made of wood and metal, and of both open and covered pipes; but open pipes are to be desired in all cases. An example of the stop exists in the Pedal of the Organ in the Cathedral of Bremen; another, under the name QUINTBASS, exists in the Pedal of the Organ in the Cathedral of Riga; and one labeled MAJOR-QUINTE, $10\frac{2}{3}$ FT., is inserted in the Pedal of the Organ in the Marienkirche, Lübeck. Under the name GROSSQUINTENBASS, $21\frac{1}{3}$ FT., a stop exists in the Pedal of the Organ in the Cathedral of Bremen. See QUINT.

QUINT FLUTE.—Ger., QUINTFLÖTE.—An unimitative flute-toned stop of $5\frac{1}{3}$ ft. and $2\frac{2}{3}$ ft. pitch. Examples of the QUINT-FLÖTE, $5\frac{1}{3}$ FT., exist on the Second Manuals of the Walcker Organs in the Cathedral of Ulm and St. Paulskirche, Frankfurt a. M. A QUINTFLÖTE, $2\frac{2}{3}$ FT., is inserted in the Choir of the Organ in the Music Hall, Cincinnati. This stop is of open metal pipes, yielding a flute-tone which combines well, as a harmonic-corroborator and timbre-creator, with the unison and octave flute-work of the divison.

A compound QUINT FLUTE, 8 FT., has recently been introduced by Mr. George W. Till, of Philadelphia, Pa., and inserted in the so-called Etherial Organ of the large Concert instrument in the Wanamaker Store, in Philadelphia. So far as our knowledge extends, this is the most noteworthy dual stop of 8 ft. pitch ever constructed; and one that could only be inserted, under favorable conditions, in Concert-room Organs of the first magnitude. Its compound voice is of considerable grandeur, its tonality surpassing in depth and richness of color that of any other flute-toned stop known to have been produced up to the present time (1920).

The principal rank is a CLEAR FLUTE, 8 FT., formed of open wood pipes from CC to c^4, to which are added twelve open metal pipes for octave coupling. The scale is large, the CC pipe measuring, internally, 8 inches in width by $10\frac{1}{2}$ inches in depth. The subordinate rank is a QUINT, $5\frac{1}{3}$ FT., formed of covered wood pipes from CC to f♯²—43 notes, and open metal pipes from g² to c⁵—30 notes, all yielding a normal tone. The stop speaks on wind of 25 inches pressure.*

QUINTVIOLE.—The name given by Zöllner to a string-toned stop, of 8 ft. pitch, introduced by him in the Organ of the Stadtkirche, Wittenberg.†

---

* Full particulars of formation and scales of this QUINT FLUTE are given in our work, "The Organ of the Twentieth Century," pp. 102–4.

†"QUINTVIOLE 8' ist eine Stimme, welche im Hauptwerke der Jahre 1814 vom Orgelbaumeister Zöllner aus Hubertusburg erbauten Orgel der Stadtkirche zu Wittenberg steht. Die

R

RANKET, RACKET.—An old and now obsolete lingual stop, of 16 ft. and 8 ft. pitch, the resonators of which were short, and closed with exception of a few small perforations near their lower ends, necessary for the egress of wind and sound, after the fashion of certain REGALS. Under such treatment, the tone was necessarily muffled and probably humming or buzzing in character. When the stop was first introduced is not known; but Prætorius, in his "Theatrum Instrumentorum seu Sciagraphia" (1618), mentions it along with other lingual stops of a similar character. See REGAL.

RAUSCHFLÖTE, RAUSCHPFEIFE, Ger.—Literally, *Rustling Flute.* A dual stop commonly formed, according to Wolfram (1815), of two ranks of open metal pipes, of 2 ft. and 1⅓ ft. pitch, respectively. A RAUSCHPFEIFE of three ranks,—probably 2⅔ ft., 2 ft., and 1⅓ ft.,—was inserted in the Brustwerk of the Organ built by Hildebrand, in 1762, for St. Michaeliskirche, Hamburg. The name seems to have disappeared from German stop nomenclature now in use.

RAUSCHQUINTE, Ger.—Literally, *Rustling Quint.* The stop found in German Organs, usually formed of two ranks of open metal pipes, of 2⅔ ft. and 2 ft. pitch respectively, standing at the interval of a fourth apart. An example exists in the Hauptwerk of the Organ in the Church of St. Mary Magdalen, Breslau. The RAUSCHQUINTE of high pitch consists of two ranks, of 1⅓ ft. and 1 ft. pitch respectively, as in the stop in the Hauptwerk of the Organ in the Christ Church, Hirschberg. As the interval between the pitches of the ranks of the RAUSCHQUINTE is a fourth, the name QUARTE, or QUARTA, has been given it by old German organ-builders.

While the value of such a dual stop in harmonic-corroboration is unquestionable; yet, in its usual tonality, its ranks would be still more useful as separate stops. Dual stops are only really desirable when they are so formed as to produce new compound tones of exceptional beauty and value; which could not be created, under ordinary conditions, by the combination of stops of the usual or standard tonalities. Dual stop formation opens up a field for invention and skill, only just touched by the plow of the artistic pipe-maker and voicer.

Eigenschaften dieses Registers sind dem Verf. nicht bekannt;—soll es vielleicht eine Quintatön die eine, der Viola ähnliche Intonation hat, sein?"—Seidel-Kothe.

RECORDER.—A rare term in old organ-stop nomenclature, but one not difficult to understand and account for. The employment of the term by the early English organ-builders is shown in the following extracts: In an Agreement entered into by John Loosemore, in 1665, for the building of a Chamber Organ, we find, among the wood stops, "One Recorde" specified. And in the "Articles of Agreement" between the Dean and Chapter of York Cathedral and Robert Dallam, organ-builder, of London, in 1632, for an Organ to be erected in the cathedral, we find specified for the Great Organ: "Itm one Recorder unison to the said Principall. vi *li*."; and for the Chaire Organ: "Itm one Recorder of tynn, unison with the voice, viij *li*. Accordingly, these stops were respectively of 4 ft. and 8 ft. pitch. The instrument called Recorder was in all essentials similar to the Flûte Douce, belonging to the Whistle Flute or Flûte à Bec family. It is therefore very probable that the old organ RECORDER was simply a flute-toned stop, imitating the voice of the old instrument.

REGAL, Ger.—Fr., RÉGALE. Ital., REGALE.—The generic name for a large family of ancient lingual stops, which in their original forms have long ceased to be used in the stop appointments of Organs. The name, however, still lingers in some old German Organs, as in those in certain Lübeck churches. A REGAL, 8 FT., occupies a place in the Choir of the great Haarlem Organ; and there are in the Choir of the Organ in the Church of St. Dominick, Prague, a REGAL, 8 FT., and a JUNGFERNREGAL, 16 FT.

The term "Regal" was originally used to designate a portable reed organ, or "Portative," used in court ceremonies; from which fact it is understood to have derived its name. Subsequently the term was extended to certain lingual stops, introduced in large Organs, or "Positives," which in their voices more or less closely resembled those of stops in the earlier Regal. Widely different names have been employed to designate the various REGAL stops; some of which refer directly to the character of the tones they produce, while others refer to the peculiar forms of the resonators used.

The old organ-builders certainly exercised their inventive powers and fancy in devising curious shapes for the resonators of their lingual pipes termed REGALS. In the accompanying illustration, Fig. 30, are given the forms of REGAL pipes which have been preserved on the pages of old treatises. No. 1 is the SORDUNREGAL, having a capped resonator pierced with four holes for the emission of sound. As the name implies, its tone was very subdued. No. 2

is the KNOPFREGAL, deriving its name from its pear-shaped head, cut after the fashion of a sleigh-bell. No. 3 is the APFELREGAL, deriving its name from the form of its head, which is spherical and pierced with numerous small holes for the emission of sound. No. 4 is the KRUMMHORNREGAL, the tone of which is said to have resembled that of the old Krummhorn (see CROMORNE). No. 5 is the SCHALMEI, a stop of the REGAL family, the tone of which imitated that of the old instrument called Schalmei or Shawm. Other forms have been given to the pipes of the SCHALMEI (see CHALUMEAU). No. 6 is the BÄRPFEIFE, also a stop of the REGAL family, which yielded a low growling tone (See BÄRPFEIFE). No. 7 is the MESSINGREGAL, the tone of which had a brazen clang, probably resembling that of a Trumpet. No. 8 is the RANKET, the resonator

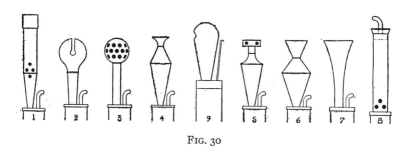

FIG. 30

of which is cylindrical, furnished with a tuning stopper, and pierced, in the neighborhood of the reed, with sound-holes (see RANKET). Fig. 9 is a REGAL which received the name JEU ÉRARD, after its inventor (see JEU ÉRARD). Other REGALS have been introduced in old Organs, of which the following are the names and probable tonalities: CYMBELREGAL, the tone of which was singularly bright and ringing. GEDÄMPFTREGAL, the tone of which was subdued or muffled. GEIGENREGAL, the tone of which somewhat resembled that of the Geige or Violin. HARFENREGAL, the tones of which bore the character of the sounds of roughly-plucked harp strings. JUNGFERNREGAL, the tones of which were of so refined a character as to resemble, to some degree, the youthful female voice—"La Voix ou Régale virginale." KÄLBERREGAL, the voice of which was of a soft and lowing character, like that of a calf (Kalb). KLEINREGAL, an octave or 4 ft. lingual stop of soft intonation. SCHARFREGAL, yielding a keen and cutting tone. SINGENDREGAL, the voice of which was of a singing tonality. SUBTILREGAL, the tone of which was subdued in character. TRICHTERREGAL, which derived its name from its funnelshaped resonators, probably yielded a bright horn-like tone. The term REGAL has now entirely disappeared from organ-stop nomenclature.

REGULA MINIMA, Lat.—The usual open metal SUPEROCTAVE or FIFTEENTH, 2 FT., belonging to the foundation-work, and corroborating the third upper partial tone of the foundation unison or prime 8 ft. tone. Yielding pure organ-tone. See FIFTEENTH.

REGULA MINOR, Lat.—The ordinary open metal OCTAVE, 4 FT., yielding pure organ-tone; belonging to the foundation-work, and corroborating the first upper partial tone of the prime 8 ft. tone yielded by the PRINCIPAL or DIAPASON, 8 FT. See OCTAVE.

REGULA MIXTA, Lat.—A compound harmonic-corroborating stop formed of several ranks of high-pitched pipes. See MIXTURE.

REGULA PRIMARIA, Lat.—An open metal stop, of full scale, and unison pitch, yielding pure organ-tone. It forms the foundation of the tonal structure of the manual department of the Organ, being identical with the PRINCIPAL or DIAPASON, 8 FT.

REIM, Ger.—The name given to a lingual stop, of 16 ft. pitch, the voice of which is of medium strength and good mixing quality. An example is to be found in the Pedal of the Organ in the Cathedral of Bremen, constructed by Schulze, the celebrated organ-builder, of Paulinzelle.

Lingual stops of comparatively soft intonation have been greatly neglected by organ-builders and organ-designers in the stop apportionment of modern Pedal Organs; yet the value of a unison lingual stop, that could be used alone or in combination with such stops as the LIEBLICHGEDECKT or DULCIANA, 16 FT., could not well be overrated.

REINFORZA A LIGNE, Ital.—A stop, of 16 ft. pitch, formed of free-reeds without the addition of resonant tubes, resembling in this respect the PHYSHARMONIKA in the Organ in the Cathedral of Lucerne. Italian organ-builders have introduced the REINFORZA A LIGNE only in cases where space was too limited for the accommodation of a proper lingual stop of 16 ft. pitch. An example exists in the largest Organ in the Basilica of St. Peter, Rome. See PHYSHARMONIKA.

RIPIENFLÖTE, FÜLLFLÖTE, Ger.—A stop, of 8 ft. pitch, yielding an unimitative flute-tone, of considerable volume without being unduly assertive or penetrating, used for filling up or imparting firmness and body to combinations of unison or foundation tone in a manual division, chiefly in the Hauptwerk or Great Organ. The term might be applied, with propriety, to such stops as the CLARABELLA or OFFENEFLÖTE; also to the DOPPELFLÖTE, which possesses remarkable filling-up properties in all combinations in which it is introduced.

REGISTRATION.—Stops of the RIPIENFLÖTE tonality are of great importance in artistic registration; forming backgrounds for the production of numerous tonal colorings which otherwise might lack firmness or richness; as is notably the case with lingual stops of thin quality and medium tone.

RIPIENO, Ital.—The name used by Italian organ-builders to designate a MIXTURE. As the term *Ripieno* signifies *filling-up*, it is appropriately applied to a compound harmonic-corroborating stop of the Organ. MIXTURES of two, three, four, and five ranks are respectively labeled RIPIENO DI DUE, RIPIENO DI TRE, RIPIENO DI QUATTRO, and RIPIENO DI CINQUE.

ROHRBORDUN, Ger.—The name that has been given to a full-scale labial stop, of 16 ft. pitch, the lower octaves of which are formed of covered pipes, and the higher octaves of half-covered ROHRFLÖTE pipes of large scale. The stop is properly made of wood throughout, but the two higher octaves are occasionally made of metal, capped and tubed, or fitted with perforated wooden stoppers.

ROHRFLÖTE, ROHRSCHELLE, Ger.—Dtch., ROERFLUIT. Fr., FLÛTE À CHEMINÉE.—The names given to a half-covered stop of metal or wood, or partly of both, usually of 8 ft. and 4 ft. pitch. When as a Pedal Organ stop of 16 ft. pitch, it is appropriately named ROHRFLÖTENBASS. Other names are employed by German organ-builders to designate certain members of the ROHRFLÖTE family.* The stops of both 8 ft. and 4 ft. pitch have been held in high estimation—and justly so—by all the great German organ-builders. It is

* "ROHRFLÖTE ist ein sehr angenehmes und wohl anwendbares Flötenwerk von Zinn, Metall und Holz, welches zwar gedeckt ist, aber in dem Hut oder Deckel eine Röhre hat, wodurch der Klang heller wird als bei gewöhnlichen Gedaeckten. Die Pfeifen werden der besseren Intonation wegen mit Seitenund Querbärten versehen und haben weitere Mensur als die Quintatön. Die Rohrflöte kommt zu 16, 8, 4, 2 und 1 Fusston (mit letzterer Grösse unter dem Namen Rohrschelle) sowohl im Manual als Pedal vor. Im Pedal heisst sie Rohrflötenbass. Als Quintregister trifft man diese Stimme zu 10⅔, 5⅓ und 1⅓ Fusston an, wo sie Rohrflautquinte oder Rohrquinte genannt wird. Es giebt Rohrflöten, welche nach Art der Doppelflöte mit doppelten Labien versehen sind und daher noch einen helleren Klang als die gewöhnlichen Rohrflöten haben, diese heissen Doppelrohrflöten. Die Namen: Gross-, Klein-, und Superflöte sind Benennungen, welche die Grösse des Registers näher bezeichnen."—Seidel-Kothe.

usual to find the ROHRFLÖTE, in one form or another, inserted in their Organs of any pretensions. Of 8 ft. pitch, it is inserted on the Second Manual and, of 4 ft. pitch, on the First Manual of the Organ in the Cathedral of Riga; and it appears, of 8 ft. pitch, on the First Manual of the Organ in the Cathedral of Vienna. Of 8 ft. pitch, and made of tin, it is inserted in the second division of the Second Manual of the Organ in Schwerin Cathedral. It exists, of 8 ft. pitch, in the Great and, of 4 ft. pitch, in the Swell of the Organ in the Centennial Hall, Sydney, N. S. W. It is remarkable that this beautiful and valuable stop should have been, and still is, so systematically neglected by French, English, and American organ-builders. It calls for too much labor and skill in its formation we suppose.

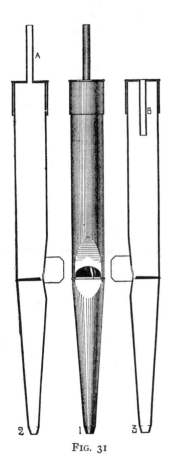

FORMATION.—ROHRFLÖTE pipes are made of both wood and metal, the latter being preferred. The wood pipes are quadrangular in form, the only radical difference between them and the pipes of the wood GEDECKT or BOURDON lying in the longitudinal perforation of their stoppers. The distinctive feature of the metal ROHRFLÖTE pipe is its peculiar cap, to which is attached an open tube communicating directly with the interior of the pipe and prolonging its air-column, in the manner shown at A, Section 2, in the accompanying illustration, Fig. 31. As the relative diameter and length of the tube, or so-called chimney, in proportion to the scale and length of the body of the pipe, affect the tone in a marked manner, its dimensions vary considerably in examples made by different builders.*

FIG. 31

The internal diameter of the tube varies in ordinary examples from one-sixth to one-third of the internal diameter of the body, while its length varies from one-

* " De tous les bourdons métalliques, il est facile de faire une *Rohrflœte* en perçant la calotte et y dressant une cheminée du calibre tracé par le trou qu'on vient d'y faire. 'Elle doit être,'dit Dom Bedos, 'd'autant plus haute qu'on la fait grosse; et plus elle est menue, plus elle doit être courte.' Il est juste, en effet, de proportionner la taille à la hauteur. 'Les plus grosses, ajoute-t-il, ont la moitié du diamètre du corps de tuyau. En ce cas, elles doivent être presque aussi hautes

fourth to one-half the speaking length of the body of the pipe. In the fine illustration given by Dom Bedos, the tube is exactly one-third the diameter and one-half the length of the body of the pipe. In all cases, the changes in the proportions of the tube not only affect the pitch but also the quality of the tone produced, due to the creation of certain inharmonic upper partial tones. The acoustical problem involved is somewhat obscure, and is complicated by the strange fact that the tone of the pipe is in no way affected by the tube being turned downward into the body of the pipe, in the manner indicated at B, in Section 3, Fig. 31. The central drawing, 1, shows the complete pipe and the most approved form of mouth. The rough tuning is done by moving the cap, and the fine tuning is done by bending the large flexible ears to or from the mouth. In a ROHRFLÖTE, 8 FT., it is neither usual nor necessary to carry the pipes with tubed caps below tenor C. The bass octave may be formed of covered pipes of wood or metal, preferably the latter. Large scales have been adopted by both German and French builders, but it is questionable if they are desirable in modern Organs. A scale, in the ratio 1 : 2.66, giving the tenor C pipe an internal diameter of 2.62 inches, would be generally suitable.

TONE AND REGISTRATION.—The exact tone of a fine ROHRFLÖTE is difficult to describe. It is an unimitative flute-tone of a liquid, bright, and singing quality, created by the presence of a special combination of harmonic upper partials. Professor Helmholtz treats of the question very slightly. He only remarks: "Narrow stopped pipes let the Twelfth be very distinctly heard at the same time with the prime tone, and have hence been called *Quintaten* (*quintam tenentes*). When these pipes are strongly blown, they also give the fifth partial [fourth upper partial], or higher major Third, very distinctly. Another variety of quality is produced by the ROHRFLÖTE, here a tube, open at both ends, is inserted in the cover of a stopped pipe, and in the examples I examined its length was that of an open pipe giving the fifth partial tone of the stopped pipe. The fifth partial tone is thus proportionately stronger than the rather weak third partial on these pipes, and the quality of tone becomes peculiarly bright." This is doubtless correct so far as it goes, but it does not go far enough to account for the refined and beautiful tones of certain ROHRFLÖTES, voiced on winds of low pressures.

The peculiar liquid and singing quality of the properly proportioned and artistically voiced ROHRFLÖTE, 8 FT., renders it highly suitable for insertion in the chief accompanimental division of the

que le corps de leurs tuyaux.' Les plus petites ont le quart et même le demi-quart du diamètre. Le timbre donc tient à la fois du tuyau ouvert et du bourdon; mais il tient d'autant plus du tuyau ouvert, que la cheminée est plus grande et grosse; et d'autant plus du bourdon, que la cheminée est plus mince et basse. La douceur des *Rohrflœten* est toujours mélangée de finesse, et c'est avec raison que souvent les facteurs les préfèrent aux bourdons dans une grande masse de fonds de grosse taille, parce qu'elles en relèvent la rondeur."—Regnier.

Church Organ. There it would be associated with stops of a similarly refined character, and would lend itself to highly effective combinations. As, tonally, it stands midway between covered and open unimitative flute-tones, its medium voice, combining body and brightness, is invaluable in artistic registration, especially with such lingual stops as the OBOE, CLARINET, FAGOTTO, and VOX HUMANA.

ROHRFLÖTENQUINTE, Ger.—The name given to the ROHRFLÖTE of 5⅓ ft. pitch, an example of which exists on the First Manual of the Organ in St. Nicolaikirche, Leipzig, built by Ladegast in 1862.

ROHRQUINTE, Ger.—The name commonly employed by German organ-builders to designate the half-covered stop, of 2⅔ ft. pitch, belonging to the ROHRFLÖTE family. The stop does not appear a common one in German Organs, but it exists on both the Second and Third Manuals of the Organ in St. Nicolaikirche, Leipzig. A ROHRQUINTE, 5⅓ FT., is inserted in the second division of the First Manual of the Organ in the Cathedral of Schwerin. The name ROHRNASAT has been given to the stop of 2⅔ ft. pitch.

S

SACKBUT, SAKBUT.—The original wind instrument of this name was a species of Trombone in use during the Middle Ages: and the name was applied by Hill, of London, to a lingual stop, of 32 ft. pitch, inserted by him in the Pedal of the Organ he erected in York Cathedral in 1833. This was the first lingual stop of that grave pitch introduced in an English Organ; and it remained in use until removed by Walker, when he reconstructed the Organ in 1903, and inserted, in its stead, the combined Contra-Trombone and Trombone in the north aisle Pedal Organ.

SADT.—In the "Schedule," prepared by Bernard Smith for the stop-appointment of the Organ he built for Temple Church, London, dated 1688, we find in the Choir list the following: "A SADT of mettle—61 pipes—06 foote tone." This is the only instance of the use of the term we have been able to find. While the exact nature and tonality of the stop are not known, it is believed to have resembled the stop now named GEMSHORN. The meaning of the term has not been determined.

SALAMINE.—This is one of the fancy names that organ-builders have introduced for reasons only known to themselves. It is always desirable that a stop name should have some meaning, and should convey either some idea of the tone or the characteristic form of the pipes forming the stop. The present name is meaningless from a constructional or a musical point of view. Meyer, organbuilder, of Hanover, gave the name to certain stops he inserted in Organs he constructed for churches in that city. The name was also used by Foster & Andrews, of Hull, in an Organ they built for the Church of All Souls, Halifax. The SALAMINE in this Organ (now removed) is stated to have been of 8 ft. pitch, formed of small-scale, open metal pipes, yielding a delicate tone slightly inclining to stringiness. This would point to a stop that would have been more expressively labeled ECHO SALICIONAL. Meaningless stop-names should be condemned by every organ-lover.

SALICETBASS, Ger.—The name given by Ladegast to an open wood stop, of 16 ft. pitch, inserted in the Piano-Pedal of his Organ in the Cathedral of Schwerin. The stop is of small scale, constructed of pine, and voiced to carry down the tone of the SALICIONAL, 8 FT., on the Third Manual. The value of a soft Pedal stop of this tonality is unquestionable.

SALICIONAL, SALICET.—The names given to open labial stops formed of cylindrical metal pipes of medium or small scales, belonging to the VIOL family. The stops are frequently introduced in German, French, English, and American Organs; usually of 8 ft. pitch, but other pitches are occasionally adopted, chiefly by German builders. Seidel says the SALICIONAL is "on the Manuals of four, eight, or sixteen feet pitch; and in the Pedal Organ, of eight or sixteen feet pitch, called SALICETBASS." A SALICIONAL, 8 FT., is inserted on the First Manual, and one, of 16 ft., on the Second Manual, of the Walcker Organ in the Cathedral of Vienna. In the Organ in the Cathedral of Riga, SALICIONALS, of 16 ft. and 8 ft. are placed on the Third Manual; a SALICET, 4 FT., is inserted on the Second Manual; and a SALICET, 2 FT., is placed on the Fourth Manual. The last stop is very rarely introduced. In French Organs, only the SALICIONAL, 8 FT., seems to have been introduced; and it is usually inserted in the Positif, as in the Organ in the Cathedral of Notre-Dame. It appears, however, in the Bombarde of the Organ in the Church of St. Eustache; and in the Grand-Orgue of the instrument in the Madeleine, Paris. In English and American Organs, the SALICIONAL, 8 FT., occupies its usual place in the Swell; but it cannot be said to be held in the estimation it deserves, for it is, by no means of general introduction. The omission of so valuable a stop from the tonal appointment of several very important Organs shows little thought on the part of their designers. There is no SALICIONAL, 8 FT., in the Organ in St. George's Hall, Liverpool, nor in one of the most important Concert-room Organs recently constructed in this country: but there is a SALICIONAL, 16 FT., in the Pedal of the St. George's Hall Organ, the only one of that grave pitch known to us in England. The name of the stop has been rendered in different spellings, but that followed in this article is clearly the most correct and desirable.* It is also desirable to adopt Walker's mode, as shown in the Riga Organ, applying the term SALICIONAL to the stops of 8 ft. and 16 ft., and the term SALICET to the stops of 4 ft. and 2 ft.

SCALE AND FORMATION.—The pipes forming the SALICIONAL, when of metal, are invariably cylindrical, varying in scale according to the ideas of the organ-builder regarding the most desirable tone. A satisfactory medium scale for the stop, speaking on a wind of from 3 to 4 inches, is that adopted by F. Haas, the distinguished organ-builder, of Lucerne. This scale, in the ratio 1 : 2.66, gives the CC pipe a diameter of 3.21 inches; the tenor C pipe a diameter of 1.97 inches; and the middle c¹ pipe a diameter of 1.20 inches. A slightly larger scale was favored by T. C. Lewis, of London: this scale, in the same ratio, gives the CC pipe a diameter of 3.34 inches; the C pipe a diameter of 2.05 inches; and the c¹ pipe a diameter of 1.25 inches. Roosevelt, of New York, used a similar scale for his beautiful SALICIONALS. Various widths of mouths have been adopted and their heights have rarely exceeded one-third their widths. The finer stops have been voiced with harmonic-bridges, or some form of beard attached to the lower lip. Some examples of the stop are slotted and others have plain pipes, their tones being affected accordingly. The German and French stops have usually been made of tin, or what is described by German organ-builders as " 14 löthig Zinn "—that is, an alloy composed of 14 parts pure tin and 2 parts pure lead. We are of opinion that for this and similar stops not requiring thick walls, the hard-rolled Hoyt two-ply pipe metal will be found in every way satisfactory and economical.

TONE AND REGISTRATION.—The tone of the SALICIONAL varies considerably in different examples of the stop: the difference being greater between the tones of those made by the Continental organ-builders of the latter half of the last century and those usually made by the English and American builders of to-day, than the difference between the tonalities of purely modern examples, which are usually characterized by too pungent and cutting voices. A broad survey of the subject inclines one to ask: What is the proper tone for the

---

* " Le *Salcional, Solcional* (on dit aussi *Salicional* et *Solicional*), ou *Salicet*, est un jeu de flûte ouverte dont les tuyaux sont fort étroits et dont les sons ont quelque analogie avec ceux de violoncelle. Ce jeu, qui se trouvait dans beaucoup d'orgues allemandes s'est introduit depuis peu de temps dans celles de France. "—Orgue de l'église royale de Saint-Denis: Rapport par J. Adrien de La Fage, 1844.

true SALICIONAL? A question, perhaps, not easily answered, because the tone of such a stop, if artistically conceived, should be dictated by the position the stop occupies in the Organ, and the nature and tonalities of the stops with which it is directly associated, and with which it will have, chiefly, to be combined in artistic registration. The late T. C. Lewis, of London, who was recognized as the greatest authority on matters of organ-tone among English organ-builders, places the SALICIONAL third in importance in his list of manual stops. After describing the tones of the DIAPASONS as "full, mellow, brilliant, and powerful; and the string-tone of the GEIGENPRINCIPAL as "next in power to the Great DIAPASONS, and of a bright and telling quality," he says the SALICIONAL is "another description of small reedy and quiet DIAPASON, but still retaining the clear, lifelike quality of the preceding stops. It can be made with various widths of mouths, and therefore of various strengths of tone, according to the place it occupies with regard to other stops." This description points to a rounder and richer voice than that commonly given to the SALICIONAL made to-day. The most desirable tone for the stop would seem to be a combination of that of the true English DULCIANA and the delicate singing string-tone of the VIOLA D'AMORE (q. v.). Anything approaching a keen, thin, and cutting string-tone is to be avoided; for not only is this quality furnished by the pronounced and imitative string-toned stops; but because the SALICIONAL has a valuable office to fulfil in artistic registration in which such a pronounced tone would prove undesirable. The SALICIONAL when artistically voiced, with just the proper proportion of pure organ-tone and string-tone, is a beautiful solo stop; while, as a body-giver and timbre-creator, it is extremely valuable in effective registration with both open and covered flute-toned stops, and also with the more delicately-voiced lingual stops, producing many very charming and refined compound tones, very seldom heard in these days of hurriedly-voiced and over-blown work.

SANFTGEDECKT, SANFTFLÖTE, Ger.—The names that have been given to covered stops of wood or metal, and commonly of 8 ft. pitch, yielding a quiet unimitative flute-tone. They properly belong to the LIEBLICHGEDECKT family, but are softer in tone. Stops of this quality would be admirably suited for insertion in the true Chamber Organ or the Echo Organ of larger instruments.

SAXOPHONE.—The name which has been given, in some few instances, to stops made in both lingual and labial forms. Several essays have been made by ingenious pipe-makers and voicers to

construct an organ-stop which shall imitate in a satisfactory manner
the peculiar compound tones of the single-reed instruments of the
Saxophone family.   All attempts hitherto made in the direction of
lingual stops have fallen short of being satisfactory, for it has been
found difficult, by the employment of either striking- or free-reeds
to produce the rich compound tones of the brass Saxophones.   While
the Saxophone strictly belongs to the Clarinet family, and is fitted
with the single reed of the Clarinet, its tone is decidedly *sui generis*.
On carefully studying the tone, one finds it to be a remarkable compound of orchestral reed- and string-tone, with a slight admixture of
flute-tone,—a remarkable combination and one difficult, if not impossible, to imitate in a single lingual stop.   Dr. W. H. Stone, speaking of the instrument, says: "The Saxophone, though inferior in
compass, quality, and power of articulation to the Clarinet, and
Bassethorn, and especially to the Bassoon, has great value in military combinations.   It reproduces on a magnified scale something
of the Violoncello quality, and gives great sustaining power to the
full chorus of brass instruments, by introducing a mass of harmonic
overtones."   It would seem highly probable that the SAXOPHONE
of the Organ will in its most satisfactory form be dual, constructed of
lingual and labial pipes of CORNO DI BASSETTO and VIOL tonalities.
The very few stops which have appeared in English Organs, under
the name SAXOPHONE, have been merely full-tone CLARINETS, and,
accordingly, by no means satisfactory.

Up to this point we have alluded to lingual stops only.   We have
now to speak of the wonderfully imitative labial SAXOPHONE, invented by W. E. Haskell, America's most distinguished artist in
labial pipe formation and voicing; and first introduced, in 1897,
in the Organ in the Church of the Holy Trinity, Philadelphia,
Pa.   This remarkable stop is of 8 ft. pitch and extends throughout
the compass of the clavier.   It is formed entirely of straight, quadrangular wood pipes, of small scale, the CC pipe measuring inter-
nally $3\frac{5}{16}$ inches in width by $4\frac{3}{16}$ inches in depth; the ratio of the
scale apparently being 1 : 2.66.   The pipes have sunk blocks, in-
verted mouths, beveled caps, and are fitted with cylindrical harmonic-bridges.*

Voiced on wind of $3\frac{1}{2}$ inches, this fine stop yields a compound
tone so closely imitative of that of the true Saxophones as to be positively deceptive to the ear.   The tones of the Saxophones are thus

* Further details of formation, accompanied by illustrations of the sound-producing portion
of a pipe, are given in "The Art of Organ-Building," Vol. II., p. 485; and in "The Organ of the
Twentieth Century," pp. 450-1.

described by Berlioz as possessing "most rare and precious qualities. Soft and penetrating in the higher part, full and rich in the lower part, their medium has something profoundly expressive. It is, in short, a quality of tone *sui generis*, presenting vague analogies with the sounds of the Violoncello, of the Clarinet, and Corno Inglese, and invested with a brazen tinge which imparts a quite peculiar accent." We were naturally very doubtful regarding the possibility of producing so complex a tonality from wood labial pipes: but all doubts were put to rest, on our being afforded the means of judging by direct comparison of the tones of the stop with those of the true Saxophone, performed upon within the Organ immediately alongside the stop. The imitation was practically perfect; while in certain parts of the compass the SAXOPHONE of the Organ was more even and pleasing than the reed instrument. This is only one of the inventor's notable achievements in wood pipe formation and voicing as these pages show.

SCHALMEI, Ger.—Ital., SCIALUMÒ,—A lingual stop, of 8 ft. pitch, the tone of which is supposed to imitate the voice of the old Schalmei or Shawm, the precursor of the Clarinet, and an instrument commonly used during the Middle Ages. See CHALUMEAU.

SCHARF, Ger.—Dtch., SCHERP.—A compound harmonic-corroborating stop, composed of three or more ranks of metal pipes, of high pitch and moderate scale, voiced to yield a bright and sharp tone, hence its name. Alluding to the old stop, Wolfram says it was usually of three ranks, starting with a 15th, 19th, and 22nd. Seidel, on the other hand, says the SCHARF differs from the ordinary MIXTURE by having one of its ranks third-sounding; and gives the starting composition for the three-rank stop, 15th, 17th, and 19th; for the four-ranked stop, 15th, 17th, 19th, and 22nd; and for the five-ranked stop, 12th, 15th, 17th, and 22nd. The introduction of the third-sounding rank adds greatly to the sharp intonation of the stop, especially under the somewhat crude system of voicing of compound stops followed by the German organ-builders, who made the SCHARF of pipes of too large scales, and voiced it too loud and piercing in tone. It seems strange that the old German builders either misunderstood or systematically ignored the true and scientific office of the compound stops. And it seems equally strange that the organ-builders of to-day are omitting, or discouraging the introduction of, the compound harmonic-corroborating stops in modern Organs. Is it through ignorance of their invaluable office in the tonal structure of the Organ? Or is it the narrow trade desire to avoid having to make such stops, requiring both scientific knowledge and high artistic skill in their proper formation? It unquestionably must be one or the other, and neither is creditable to the organ-builders of the twentieth century. See ACUTA.

SCHARFFLÖTE, Ger.—A metal labial stop, of 4 ft. pitch, voiced to yield a bright and piercing flute-tone. It is valuable, in the absence of a COMPENSATING MIXTURE, for imparting brightness to the Pedal Organ. A SCHARFFLÖTE, 4 FT., exists in the Pedal of the Organ in the Cathedral of Merseburg.

SCHARFREGAL, Ger.—An old and obsolete lingual stop, of 4 ft. pitch, and very keen intonation, as its name implies. See REGAL.

SCHLANGENROHR, Ger.—An old and now disused name for the lingual stop, of 16 ft. pitch, commonly inserted in the Pedal Organ, which is better known as the SERPENT (q. v.).

SCHÖNGEDECKT, Ger.—The name that has sometimes been used to designate a small-scaled covered stop, yielding a beautiful tone. The name is practically synonymous with LIEBLICHGEDECKT. The prefix Schön—signifying *beautiful*—has been applied to other names of labial stops.

SCHREIER, SCHREIERPFEIFE, Ger.—The names given by old German organ-builders to compound labial stops yielding, as the name implies, screaming tones; and also to a labial stop of a shrill and penetrating flute-tone, an example of which is said to exist in the Organ of the Bärfusskirche, at Erfurt. The stop was usually of three ranks, and was simply a large-scaled and loudly-voiced ACUTA (q. v.).* Stops of this noisy class are very objectionable, and have too often been introduced by inartistic organ-builders.

SCHUFFLET, Ger.—An old name given to the mutation harmonic-corroborating stop, of 1⅓ ft. pitch, representing the fifth upper partial tone of the fundamental manual unison, 8 ft. pitch. A stop of this name existed in the old Organ in the Church of St. Lambert, Münster.

SCHWEIZERFLÖTE, SCHWEIZERPFEIFE, Ger.—Liter-

* "SCHREIER, SCHREIERPFEIFE, Schryari, ist eine veraltete, gewöhnlich 3 fache Mixtur, welche aus Oktavchören zu 1', ½' und ¼' besteht. Sie würde, also disponiert, mit der Cymbel ein und dasselbe Register sein, wenn nicht vielleicht eine Verschiedenheit in der Mensur und namentlich in der Intonation obwaltet. Auch 2 fach soll diese Stimme gefunden werden, wo sie aus 2' und 1' besteht. Der Ton dieses Registers muss, dem Namen nach, sehr grell sein."—Seidel-Kothe.

ally *Swiss Flute*. An open labial stop of 8 ft., 4 ft., 2 ft., and rarely 1 ft. pitch; the pipes of which are cylindrical, of small scale, and have low mouths, yielding a voice between a flute- and string-tone, of a refined and pleasing character. In good work, the pipes are made of tin. Seidel says: "Dieses Register findet man sowohl im Manual als im Pedal, wo es alsdann SCHWEIZERPFEIFBASS oder SCHWEIZERBASS heisst. Im Manual trifft man diese Stimme zuweilen nur in den oberen Octaven an, wo sie unter dem Namen SCHWEIZERPFEIFDISKANT vorkommt." Locher says there is no foundation for the name SCHWEIZERFLÖTE, any more than for the name WIENERFLÖTE; and "in spite of its name it belongs to the string family, as for example in the Great Organ of the instrument in Magdeburg Cathedral, where it assumes the form of a full-toned GAMBA."

SCHWIEGEL, SCHWÄGEL, Ger.—The term that has been employed by old German organ-builders to designate metal labial stops of different formation and intonation. According to Schlimbach, the stop belongs to the Flute-work, and is of the scale of the QUERPFEIFE, with the intonation of the BAUERFLÖTE. Seidel, on the other hand, describes the stop as formed of pipes having cylindrical bodies surmounted by truncated cones; resembling those of the FLACHFLÖTE or SPILLFLÖTE. Respecting the tone, he remarks: "Der Klang dieser Stimme ist angenehm und dem Klang der Querflöte ähnlich, aber er soll noch etwas sanfter als der Ton der Spillflöte sein." The stop was made of 8 ft., 4 ft., 2 ft., and 1 ft. pitch; that of 4 ft. pitch being termed SCHWIEGELDISKANT or DISKANTSCHWIEGEL. An example, of 8 ft. pitch, was introduced in the Echo of the Organ built by Jagermann, of Dresden, for the Kreuzkirche in that city.

SEPTADECIMA, Lat.—Eng. SEVENTEENTH.—The mutation stop, of $1\frac{3}{5}$ ft. pitch, corroborating the fifth upper partial tone of the manual unison prime, 8 ft. See SEVENTEENTH.

SEPTIÈME, Fr.—The mutation harmonic-corroborating stop, of $4\frac{4}{7}$ ft. pitch in the Pedal Organ, and $2\frac{2}{7}$ ft. and $1\frac{1}{7}$ ft. pitch in the manual divisions. The pipes forming the stops are of open metal, cylindrical in form, of medium scale, and voiced to yield soft pure organ-tone. The SEPTIÈME represents the sixth upper partial tone of the prime tone, produced by seven times the number of vibrations that belong to the prime tone. Thus, if the CC prime tone is of 64 vibrations per second, the sixth upper partial tone, lying between a$\sharp^1$ and b$\flat^1$ (of the physical scale), is yielded by a pipe of say $1^1/_7$ feet speaking length, having 448 vibrations per second. Although very much higher partial tones are corroborated by stops in the Organ, the sixth upper partial tone has been very seldom corroborated by the introduction of the SEPTIÈME. The only example, in complete form, in an English Organ, known to us, is to be found, under the name "SHARP TWENTIETH," in the instrument in the Collegiate Institution of Liverpool, built by Jackson, of that city, in 1850. We know of no example in an American or German Organ. The only Organ in which the SEPTIÈME has been systematically and scientifically introduced is that built by Cavaillé-Coll, in 1868, for the Cathedral of Notre-Dame, Paris. In the Pedal Organ the stop is inserted, of $4^4/_7$ ft. pitch, belonging to the 32 ft. harmonic series. In the Clavier des Bombardes it appears, of $2^2/_7$ ft. pitch, belonging to the 16 ft. harmonic series: and in the Grand Chœur it is introduced, of $1^1/_7$ ft. pitch, belonging to the 8 ft. harmonic series.

This systematic introduction of the SEPTIÈME in all the harmonic series was due to Aristide Cavaillé-Coll's scientific knowledge and researches in tone production; and it is to be regretted that we do not see evidences of a similar knowledge and investigation in even the more important Organs built to-day. It is, however, hardly to be expected that such a stop as the SEPTIÈME should appear in Organs in which very little attention is paid to the provision of even a reasonably adequate harmonic structure. In the foundation-work of an important Organ the SEPTIÈME should certainly be introduced, preferably as a rank in a through compound stop in which it can be correctly adjusted tonally. The following four-rank CORNET would be a favorable stop for its introduction:

CORNET—IV. RANKS.

I.	SEVENTEENTH	.	.	.	.	Metal.	$1^3/_5$ Feet
II.	NINETEENTH	.	.	.	.	Metal.	$1^1/_3$ "
III.	SEPTIÈME	.	.	.	.	Metal.	$1^1/_7$ "
IV.	TWENTY-SECOND	.	.	.	.	Metal.	1 "

The pipes forming the stop to be of medium scale, and voiced to yield pure organ-tone. Ranks II. and IV. to be the most pronounced in strength of voice; rank I. to be softer; and rank III. to be regulated so as not to be unduly assertive. It is in the voicing and regulating of such an important stop that the artist can show himself.

SERAPHONFLÖTE, Ger.—The name given to a flute-toned

stop, of 8 ft. pitch, and very powerful voice; invented by W. F. Weigle, of Stuttgart. An example exists in the Organ of St. Sebalduskirche, Nürnberg. Under the name SERAPHONPFEIFE, a similar stop was, for the first time, introduced in the Organ constructed by Steinmeyer for the City Church of Wertheim, Baden.

The pipes forming these stops are of metal, cylindrical in form and of large scale. They have two mouths, formed in the usual manner, and placed as close to each other as practicable.* The large lineal measurement of the combined mouths—about four-tenths of the circumference of the pipe—affords the opportunity for the production of a remarkable volume of tone. The stop so formed is practically a metal DOPPELFLÖTE.

TONE AND REGISTRATION.—A powerful stop of this class, producing a pronounced unimitative flute-tone, would be of considerable value in two manual expressive divisions of the Concert-room Organ; namely, the Solo Organ and the expressive portion of the First or Great Organ, where its voice would be under control. In the former it would impart great body, solidity, and color to the more powerful lingual stops, while it would give great dignity to the Flute-work. A powerful normal flute-tone is absolutely necessary for the production of broad effects and tone-coloring in a properly stop-apportioned Solo Organ. In the expressive subdivision of the First Organ, a fine SERAPHONFLÖTE would be extremely valuable, as it would, under control as to its strength of voice, combine perfectly with the pure organ-tones of the PRINCIPALS or DIAPASONS; increasing their volume, and infusing into their somewhat monotonous voices an agreeable coloring by the introduction of certain of the lower harmonic upper partial tones. The stop would also prove highly effective in registration with the lingual stops which are enclosed along with it; and, generally, in all full-toned combinations.

SERPENT.—Ital., SERPENTINO.—A lingual stop, of 16 ft. pitch, the tone of which is between those of the BASSOON and the TROMBONE stops of the Organ. It is supposed to imitate in its voice the old instrument invented by Edmé Guillaume, a Priest of Auxerre, France, in the year 1590. The instrument was an improvement on the older Bass Zinken. It was a conical tube of wood, covered with leather, and bent into the form of a serpent, hence its name. It was played with a mouthpiece, not with a reed. Examples of the stop,

---

* Further particulars respecting this stop, accompanied by illustrations, as patented by G. F. Weigle, are given in "The Art of Organ-Building," Vol. II., pp. 534–6.

of 16 ft. pitch, exist in the Pedal of the Organ in the Cathedral of Ulm; and in the Schwell-Pedal of the Organ in the Cathedral of Riga. In the latter it would seem to be a species of DOUBLE CORNO DI BASSETTO. Under the name SERPENTINO, a similar stop exists in the Organ in the Church of Sanctissimo Crucifisso, at Como. An artistically-voiced CORNO DI BASSETTO, 16 FT., would be a valuable addition to the tonal forces of the Pedal Organ of the Twentieth Century. The name SERPENT might be retained for such a stop.

SESQUIALTERA, SEXQUIALTERA.—The compound harmonic-corroborating stop, formed of two or more ranks of open metal pipes of medium scales, yielding, in the foundation-work, pure organ-tone. The true SESQUIALTERA consists of two ranks of pipes only, carried throughout the compass of the clavier without a break; the ranks standing at the interval of a major sixth apart. This interval is secured by placing a fifth-sounding rank below a third-sounding one; as, in the eight feet harmonic series, a TWELFTH 2⅔ FT., and a SEVENTEENTH, 1⅗ FT., sounding G—e¹ on the CC key. On the First Manual of the Organ in the Cathedral of Riga there is a SEXQUIALTERA, belonging to the sixteen feet harmonic series, formed of a QUINT, 5⅓ FT., and a TIERCE, 3⅕ FT.; while on the same manual there are, in addition, independent stops of the same pitches, but of different tonality—a unique apportionment, so far as our knowledge extends. As independent stops, the QUINT, 5⅓ FT., and TIERCE, 3⅕ FT., are inserted on the First Manual of the Organ in the Cathedral of Ulm; and they appear in other Walcker Organs. A QUINT, 2⅔ FT., and a TIERCE, 1⅗ FT., as independent stops, are inserted on the Second Manual of the Riga Organ. When a SESQUIALTERA, belonging to either the eight feet or sixteen feet harmonic series, is placed in any manual division, its ranks should be made to draw separately.

The SESQUIALTERA belonging to the thirty-two feet harmonic series is necessarily rare; but one, formed of a QUINT, 10⅔ FT., and a TIERCE, 6²/₅ FT., exists in the Pedal of the Riga Organ; and in addition there is a QUINTBASS, 10⅔ FT., and a TERZBASS, 6²/₅ FT. This grand Pedal Organ has a remarkable harmonic structure; and in this direction affords a valuable lesson to organ-designers of to-day.

The so-called SESQUIALTERAS, of the old English organ-builders, were invariably harmonic-corroborating stops, formed of several ranks of open metal pipes, requiring two or more breaks in their compass. In these stops, the sexts did not invariably obtain in every break; those omitted being formed by the addition of an independent TWELFTH, 2⅔ FT. An example of this incomplete form of SESQUIALTERA is furnished by the stop inserted by John Snetzler in the Organ he constructed, in the latter part of the eighteenth century, for St. Mary's Church, Nottingham. The composition of the stop is here given:

SESQUIALTERA—IV. RANKS.

CC to G	. . . . .	15 —17 —19 —22.
G♯ to g¹	. . . . .	12*—15 —17*—19.
g♯¹ to top	. . . . .	8 —12*—15 —17*.

The following example of a five-rank SESQUIALTERA, in which sexts of different pitches obtain in the two breaks, gives the composition of the stop inserted in the Great of the Organ constructed by Harris and Byfield, of London, in 1740, for the old Parish Church of Doncaster.

SESQUIALTERA—V. RANKS.

CC to c¹	. . .	19*—22 —24*—26 —29.
c♯¹ to top	. . .	8 —12*—15 —17*—19.

The sexts are indicated by the asterisks. This SESQUIALTERA is here given in modern compass: the original stop in the Harris-Byfield Organ had the old compass of GGG to d³. It is interesting to note that in this Organ the SESQUIALTERA was accompanied by a TWELFTH, 2⅔ FT., and a TIERCE, 1⅗ FT., both complete and independent stops. A good four-rank SESQUIALTERA can be formed by omitting the acute fifth-sounding rank in both breaks.

TONE AND REGISTRATION.—The tone of the SESQUIALTERA may properly vary with the stop-apportionment of the division of the Organ in which it is inserted. When associated with the foundation-work, in the First or Great Organ, it should, as essentially a harmonic-corroborating stop, yield pure organ-tone: but when inserted in any other manual division, its tone may properly be dictated by the stop-apportionment with which it is associated. When considered desirable, the SESQUIALTERA may be formed of through ranks of pipes of special and different tonalities, becoming a timbre-creating stop. In all cases it is desirable that, in its voicing and regulating, the third-sounding rank should be made subordinate in tone to the fifth-sounding rank, so as to avoid undue assertiveness.

The value of harmonic-corroborating stops of the SESQUIALTERA class in the production of distinct tonal coloring deserves to be better known. The neglect of such stops in the tonal appointment of modern Organs is a mistake; and seriously cripples the means of producing compound tones of great variety and beauty. The registration of unison, octave, and super-octave stops alone, whatever their tonal character may be, must fail to satisfy the cultivated ear of the musician seeking to paint his tone-pictures in rich musical chiaroscuro. It is the tradesman, not the artist, who is to-day omitting such stops from the Organ.

SEVENTEENTH.—Fr., TIERCE.   Ger., TERZ, TERTIE   Ital., DECIMA SETTIMA.—A third-sounding mutation stop, formed of open metal pipes of medium scale, of 1⅗ ft. pitch in the manual divisions, standing at the interval of a seventeenth above the unison, 8 ft., and a major third above the SUPER-OCTAVE, 2 FT.* The SEVENTEENTH represents and corroborates the fourth upper partial tone of the prime or unison tone   In the Pedal Organ, the SEVENTEENTH is of 3⅕ ft. pitch, belonging to the 16 ft. harmonic series. When a stop of 3⅕ ft. pitch is introduced in a manual division, it is termed by French organ-builders GROSSE TIERCE,† as in the Clavier des Bombardes of the Cavaillé-Coll Organ in the Church of Saint-Sulpice, Paris. A GROSSE TIERCE, 6⅖ FT., exists in the Pedal of the Organ in the Cathedral of Notre-Dame. A TERZ, 3⅕ FT., is placed on the First Manual, and a TERZBASS, 6⅖ FT., in the Haupt Pedal of the Walcker Organ in the Cathedral of Riga. A SEVENTEENTH, 6⅖ FT., under the name TERTIA, exists in the Pedal of the Church at Perleberg: this stop is formed of wood pipes.

The SEVENTEENTH, 6⅖ FT., made either of open metal or wood pipes, is of considerable value in the Pedal Organ, brightening and enlivening its normal foundation tone: here it may be more pronounced in tone than is desirable for third-sounding stops in the manual divisions. This SEVENTEENTH belongs to the 32 ft. harmonic series.

---

* "La TIERCE, jadis nommée par certains auteurs *Sesqui-Octava* et mieux *Sesqui-Quarta*, est un jeu ouvert de dix-neuf pouces, ou cinquante-un centimètres, de grosse taille, d'étain ou d'étoffe, selon qu'on veut lui donner ou lui ôter du tranchant. Il parle à la *Tierce* de la *Doublette*, par conséquent à la dixième du *Prestant;* c'est pourquoi les Italiens l'appellent quelquefois *Decima*. Au positif, on la désigne par le nom de *Petite-Tierce*, en opposition avec celle du grand orgue qui est de taille plus forte, mais de même degré. Les Allemands l'appellent *Terz* et *Tertia*, et encore *Dez*, abrégé de *Decima.*"—Régnier.

† "La GROSSE-TIERCE parle à l'octave inférieure de la *Tierce* ordinaire, c'est-à-dire à la *Tierce* du *Prestant*, et à la dixième du huit-pieds. Elle est grosse taille, tout ouverte et d'étoffe, l'étain serait trop mordant. Pour que ce régistre fasse bon effet, il lui faut associer une grande masse de fonds, surtout en huit-pieds; un bourdon de seize ne nuira point. Le plus grand tuyau de la *Grosse-Tierce* a trois-pieds deux pouces, lorsqu'elle se trouve aux claviers de la main. En Allemagne, on la trouve en pédale de six-pieds, sous le nom de *Decem-Bass.*"—Régnier.

SHARP MIXTURE.—The term that has been used to designate a compound harmonic-corroborating stop formed of four or more ranks of open metal pipes, of high pitch, and penetrating tone. The SHARP MIXTURES of the old English organ-builders appear to have been invariably formed of octave- and fifth-sounding ranks; third-sounding ranks being confined to their SESQUIALTERAS.

Properly scaled, voiced, and regulated, a SHARP MIXTURE would be a useful stop, in either the wood-wind or brass-wind division of the artistically appointed Concert-room Organ, for the production of ringing qualities of compound tone. But as MIXTURES are made to-day by the generality of organ-builders, without regard to the dictates of science or art, the SHARP MIXTURE had much better be omitted altogether from the Organ.

SIFFLÖTE, SIEFFLÖT, Ger.—Fr., SIFFLET.—A small open metal stop, of medium scale, and 2 ft. and 1 ft. pitch, yielding a clear unimitative flute-tone. In some rare instances it has been introduced of $1\frac{1}{3}$ ft. pitch. The stop, of 2 ft. pitch, exists on the Second Manual of the Organ in the Protestant Church, Mülhausen; and, of 1 ft. pitch, in the Oberwerk of the Organ in the Cathedral of Merseburg.

SINGENDREGAL, Ger.—An old lingual stop, of 8 ft. pitch, which received its appellation on account of the singing character of its voice. Both the stop and name are obsolete. See REGAL.

SOAVE, Ital.—The name given to an open labial stop, of 8 ft. pitch, yielding an unimitative flute-tone of great softness and beauty.* It is to be regretted that unison stops of this refined tonality are so greatly neglected in the appointment of modern Organs.

SORDUN, Ger.—Fr., SOURDINE. Ital., SORDINI.—The name given by old Continental organ-builders to a covered labial stop, of 16 ft. and 8 ft. pitch, the pipes of which were commonly made of wood, and so treated as to produce a subdued or muffled tone; considered desirable before the swell was invented.†

* "SOAVE (ou *suabile*), huit-pieds, de grosse taille, lent à parler, mais très-doux et gracieux, comme l'indique son nom italien. On le désigne aussi sous le nom d'*englische Flœte*, flûte-angéli-que, qu'il ne faut pas confondre avec le jeu d'anche, qui porte à peu près le nom de *angelica vox*."—Regnier.

† "SORDINI (ital.), *Sordun* (all.), Sourdine. C'est un ancien bourdon de huit, ou de seize, selon qu'il se trouvait à la main ou à la pédale. Les tuyaux étaient cachés chacun dans une boite, pour rendre un son plus étient."—Regnier.

SORDUNREGAL, Ger.—An old lingual stop of the REGAL family, of 8 ft. pitch, softly voiced, and probably muted by being inclosed in some form of box. Both the stop and its name are now obsolete. See REGAL.

SPILLFLÖTE, SPINDELFLÖTE, Ger.—Eng., SPINDLE FLUTE. —A half-covered labial stop, of 8 ft., 4 ft., and 2 ft. pitch. The name is expressive of the peculiar form of its pipes, the bodies of which are cylindrical surmounted by long conical portions, truncated, leaving small openings at top. The form of the pipe, including its tapering foot, somewhat resembles that of a covered spindle, and has suggested the name. The form is shown in the accompanying illustration, Fig. 32. As it is not possible to tune the pipe by any manipulation of its small top orifice, without altering its tone, the fine tuning is done by means of large projecting ears, bent toward or from the mouth. As its name implies, the SPILLFLÖTE belongs to the Flute-work; but its tone is bright and without any distinctive flute quality, lying between the tones of the ROHRFLÖTE and the SPITZFLÖTE. Seidel compares it with the SCHWIEGEL (q.v.). Under the hands of a skillful and artistic voicer, and probably with the addition of the harmonic-bridge, there is little doubt but the SPILLFLÖTE pipe could be made to yield both a characteristic and a beautiful compound tone. The stop seems to have been introduced during the second quarter of the sixteenth century; but has become practically a curiosity in organ-building, doubtless due to the time and trouble involved in its construction.

SPITZFLÖTE, Ger.—Fr., FLÛTE À POINT, FLÛTE À FUSEAU. Eng., SPIRE FLUTE.—A metal labial stop, of 8 ft., 4 ft., and 2 ft. pitch; which derives its names from the form of its pipes, which is that of a slender truncated cone, open at top; closely resembling the form of the GEMSHORN pipe (See Fig. 19, Plate III). The stop is justly held in high estimation by German organ-builders, being introduced, usually of 8 ft. and 4 ft. pitch, in all their more important Organs. In Walcker's Organ in the Cathedral of Vienna, it is inserted, of 8 ft. and 4 ft. pitch, on the Second Manual. In the Organ in the Cathedral of Riga, it is inserted, of 4 ft. pitch, on the Third Manual.

FIG. 32

SCALE AND FORMATION.—The scale of the SPITZFLÖTE varies in different examples and according to the character and strength of the tone desired; and the proportion of the diameters at the mouth line and at the top of the pipe also varies slightly. The dimensions given by Töpfer, and apparently adopted by Friedrich Haas, the rebuilder of the Lucerne Organ, are practically as follows: For the CC 8 ft. pipe, 4.60 inches diameter at the mouth line, and 1.50 inches diameter at the open top. The diameter at top is, accordingly, a trifle under one-third of the diameter at the mouth line, approaching closely the proportion recommended for the GEMSHORN pipe. But Seidel says the SPITZFLÖTE pipes are more pointed than those of the GEMSHORN; and this would seem desirable for the production of the characteristic tone of the stop. The diameter at top should, however, never be less than one-fourth of that at the mouth. The width of the mouth may be one-fourth or two-ninths of the larger circumference; and its height may range from one-fourth to one-third of its width, according to the wind-pressure and the tone desired. As in certain half-covered stops, the upper lip of the mouth may be slightly arched, and the lower lip and languid nicked moderately fine. As the pipes must not be slotted at top, or coned in tuning, fine tuning must be done at the mouth by means of flexible ears. While the 4 ft. and 2 ft. stops have invariably been made of metal throughout, the bass octave of the 8 ft. stop has been made of pyramidal pipes of wood. This practice is not to be recommended.

TONE AND REGISTRATION.—The voice of the true SPITZFLÖTE is compound, which, owing to its delicate harmonics, partakes of both flute- and string-tone; inclining to either one or the other according to the manner in which the pipes are voiced, and, to some extent, according to their scales. This variable compound tone is a valuable property of the stop, as the artist voicer can adapt it to suit the tonal apportionment of which it is to form a part. We know that such refinement in tonal adjustment is paid very little attention to in this age of commercial organ-building; but it is, nevertheless, just such refinement, carried consistently throughout the stop-work of an Organ, that marks the artist-craftsman and makes the Organ a work of art.

It must be obvious to everyone conversant with compound tone production, that such a stop as the SPITZFLÖTE, standing midway in voice between the flute-toned and string-toned stops, must lend itself to the production of refined colorings in registration with the softer-voiced stops, both labial and lingual. With the latter especially, to which it will impart a desirable body and richness without destroying their characteristic tonalities. The true SPITZFLÖTE, 8 FT., combines perfectly with the CLARINET, CORNO DI BASSETTO, FAGOTTO, and COR ANGLAIS, producing beautiful compound tones. It also adds richness and body to the imitative string-toned stops; and, in both 8 ft. and 4 ft. pitch, a certain crisp fullness to the imitative flute-toned stops. The SPITZFLÖTE should find a place in the Choir of the Church Organ; and in the Second or accompanimental

Organ of the properly stop-apportioned Concert-room Organ.

SPITZQUINTE, QUINTSPITZ, Ger.—A SPITZFLÖTE, of 2⅔ ft. and 1⅓ ft. pitch, the pipes of which are formed in all respects similar to those of the unison SPITZFLÖTE (*q. v.*). As a harmonic-corroborating and timbre-creating stop, the SPITZQUINTE may be found valuable in special stop-apportionments: and, of 2⅔ ft. pitch, it may, with advantage, take the place of the ordinary TWELFTH, 2⅔ FT., in Organs of small size; lending itself more effectively to artistic registration, and proving more generally useful in combination.

STENTORFLÖTE, Ger.—The name given by Herr Weigle to a loudly-voiced, high-pressure, labial stop, of 8 ft. pitch, the pipes of which are constructed in accordance with his patented system.* An example exists on the First Manual of the Walcker Organ in the Synagogue, Strasbourg.

STENTORGAMBA.—The name used by Walcker to designate a loudly-voiced, string-toned, labial stop, of 8 ft. pitch, the pipes of which are constructed in accordance with the high-pressure, Weigle system. An example exists on the Second Manual of the Organ in the Synagogue, Strasbourg. Under the name SOLO-GAMBE, a similar stop exists on the Second Manual of the Weigle Organ in the Grand Hall of the Liederhalle, Stuttgart.

STENTORPHONE.—The name, derived from the Greek Στέντωρ—Stentor, and φωνή—voice or sound, and employed to designate a large-scaled metal labial stop, of 8 ft. pitch, the pipes of which are cylindrical in form and made of thick metal, so as to withstand the powerful pulsations of the columns of air within them, generated by the high pressures employed in the voicing. Properly this wind-pressure should range between seven and ten inches; but during the present prevailing craze for high wind-pressures and loud voicing, such reasonable pressures will be considered insufficient. Properly voiced, the STENTORPHONE yields a tone of great breadth, richness, and dignity. True to its name, it should be the most stentorian labial stop introduced in the Organ. Its large scale and its tonality places it, strictly considered, in the Flute-work of the Organ. This position is shown by the fact that the best substitute for the true STENTORPHONE, at present known, is a large-scaled

* Royal Letters Patent, Great Britain, No. 17718. United States Patents, Nos. 457686 and 520344.

open wood flute-toned stop, to which the name TIBIA PLENA has been given.

The powerful voice of the STENTORPHONE naturally points to the only two manual divisions in which it could be properly introduced; namely, the First or Great Organ and the Solo Organ. In its full tonality it is of most value in the latter, imparting a remarkable breadth and grandeur to the tones of the powerful lingual stops properly inserted there; and that without unduly increasing their assertiveness. In the First Organ, it should be inserted in the expressive subdivision, where its dominating voice will be under control. There it will lend itself to the production of impressive *crescendoes*, and impart great dignity to the TRUMPETS.

Examples of the metal STENTORPHONE, 8 FT., appear in several American Organs, notably in those by Roosevelt. He inserted it in the Solos of the Organs in the Auditorium, Chicago; and the Cathedral of the Incarnation, Garden City, L. I. A fine STENTORPHONE is inserted in the Solo of the Organ in the Cincinnati Music Hall. We inserted one in the Fourth Organ of our scheme for the Grand Concert Organ installed in the Festival Hall of the Louisiana Purchase Exposition (1904); now in the Wanamaker Store, Philadelphia, Pa. The STENTORPHONE has been introduced in certain German Organs. An example exists in the Organ in the great Concert Hall in Mannheim; and Walcker has inserted one, under the name STENTORFLÖTE, 8 FT., on the First Manual of the Organ in the Synagogue, Strasbourg. The STENTORPHONE is one of the large-mouthed, high-pressure, objectionable stops introduced and patented by Weigle, an example of which exists in the Organ he constructed, in 1895, for the Liederhalle, Stuttgart. The STENTORPHONE has not commended itself to either French or English organ-builders. We known of no example in a French Organ; and of only one in an English Organ, and that, strange to relate, in a Chamber Organ.

STARKGEDECKT, Ger.—A large-scaled covered stop, of 16 ft. pitch, the pipes of which are of wood, copiously blown with wind of moderate pressure, and voiced to yield a full and round tone of good mixing quality. Of this stop, Regnier says: "Grand bourdon de seize fortement embouché et donnant aux flûtes ouvertes de huit un velouté et une profondeur remarquables."

STILLGEDECKT, Ger.—This name, which signifies a *quiet-toned covered stop*, is employed by German organ-builders to designate stops which are softer in their intonation than the LIEBLICH-GEDECKTS. The STILLGEDECKT is usually made of wood, and of 8 ft.

and 4 ft. pitch.   The pipes are of a small scale, and speak on low-
pressure wind.   The stop is highly suitable for insertion in the softer
toned manual divisions of the Concert-room Organ, and in the chief
accompanimental division of the Church Organ; it is also an ideal
stop for the true Chamber Organ.   An example, of 8 ft. pitch, exists
in the Choir of the Organ in the Town Church of Fulda; and one, of
4 ft. pitch, is inserted in the Echo of the Organ in the Church of
Waltershausen.

STOPPED DIAPASON, Eng.—Ger., GEDECKT.   Fr., BOURDON.
Span., TAPADO, TAPADILLO.—A covered labial stop, of 8 ft. pitch in
the manual divisions, and of 16 ft. pitch in the Pedal Organ.   The
English name, though time-honored, is neither correct nor desirable,
for the stop has no resemblance to a true DIAPASON in form or tonality.   The stop yields an unimitative flute-tone, and belongs to the
Flute-work of the Organ.   The proper English equivalent is STOPPED
FLUTE.   The English practice is to make the pipes of the stop entirely of wood, but in some late examples metal pipes have been
used in the higher treble octaves.   The so-called STOPPED DIAPASON,
16 FT., is invariably constructed of wood throughout: the stop is only
a medium-scaled BOURDON, voiced to be as free from the second
upper partial as possible.   The old builders in England, and notably
Bernard Smith, made their STOPPED DIAPASONS of oak, and no
better material could be used for the purpose.   In the "Schedule"
of the Organ constructed by Smith for the Temple Church, London,
are mentioned two "GEDACKTS of wainescott"—a superior quality
of straight-grained oak grown abroad.   The German organ-builders
have made their GEDECKTS of both wood and metal; while the
French builders have preferred metal for their manual unison BOUR-
DONS.   See BOURDON and GEDECKT.

SUABE FLUTE.—The name given to a quadrangular wood
stop, of 4 ft. pitch, invented by William Hill, organ-builder, of London.   The stop is of medium scale; the pipes of which are open, have
sunk blocks and inverted mouths, and yield a soft and clear unimitative flute-tone which lies between the tones of the CLARABELLA and
the WALDFLÖTE, but is softer than either.   It is difficult to understand the signification of the name SUABE, for it seems to have no
appropriate derivation; it certainly cannot be derived from the law
term *suable*.   The term SUABILE certainly obtains in Seidel-Kothe's
list of stops, applied to a flute-toned stop of 8 ft. pitch.*

* "*Suabile* ist ein Flötenwerk zu 8', von angenehmer Intonation, welches sich zum sanften und
langsamen Vortrage besonders eignet.   Diese Stimme wird auch englische Flöte genannt."

SUAVE FLUTE.—A name, suggested by the Latin *suavis*—sweet, pleasant; and which we have considered appropriate for a flute-toned stop of peculiar formation, and of singularly smooth and agreeable intonation. The pipes of the stop are of wood, open, and of medium scale; their peculiarity obtaining in the formation of the mouth, the upper lip of which has a cylindrical piece of polished hard wood attached to it, in the manner shown in Fig. 33. This form of

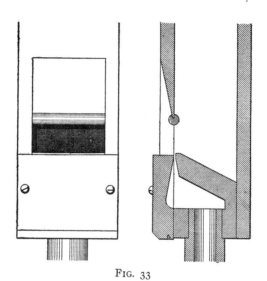

FIG. 33

mouth clearly demonstrates the value of the thick and rounded upper lip in the production of smooth and full flute-tone. Organbuilders of to-day have resorted to the easy, objectionable, and perishable expedient of covering the upper lip with leather in both metal and wood pipes. It is a cheap expedient to save labor and care in voicing; otherwise, it would never have been so readily adopted by organ-builders.

SUAVIAL.—According to Locher, a name given to a soft-toned stop of the GEIGENPRINCIPAL class, found in old Organs; usually of 8 ft. pitch, and of short compass, beginning at C. An example of which exists in the Organ in the French Church, at Berne.

SUB-BASS.—Ger., SUBBASS. Fr., SOUBASSE, SOUS-BASSE.—According to Wolfram (1815), the old German organ-builders used the name to designate Pedal Organ GEDECKTS, of 32 ft. and 16 ft. pitch, constructed of wood: and the practice has been followed by the French builders, as is shown by the Pedals of the Organs built by Cavaillé-Coll for the Cathedral of Orléans and the Church of Saint-Ouen, Rouen, in which we find a Sous-Basse, 32 ft., and a Sous-Basse, 16 ft., inserted. It also appears as a manual stop, of 16 ft. pitch, in the Bombarde of the Organ in the Cathedral of Notre-Dame, Paris; and in the Positif of the Organ in the Cathedral of Albi. The Subbass, 32 ft., exists in the Pedal of the Organ in the Church of St. Michael, Hamburg; and, of 16 ft. pitch, in the Pedals of the Organs in the Cathedrals of Riga and Ulm. In English instruments, we find the term Sub-Bass applied to both open and covered stops of 32 ft. pitch. In the Pedal of the Organ in the Temple Church, London, the Sub-Bass, 32 ft., is a covered stop of wood; while the Sub-Bass, 32 ft., in the same department of the Organ in the Town Hall of Leeds is an open stop of metal. It would seem very desirable, in the stop nomenclature of to-day, to confine the term Sub-Bass to the Pedal Organ covered wood stop of 32 ft. pitch. See Contra-Bourdon and Sub-Bourdon.

SUB-BOURDON.—A covered wood stop, of large scale, and of 32 ft. pitch, commonly introduced in the Pedal Organ when there is no accommodation for an open stop of 32 ft. A Sub-Bourdon, 32 ft., was introduced in the Pedal of the Organ constructed by Willis for the Alexandra Palace, Muswell Hill, near London. A Sub-Bourdon, 32 ft., is inserted in the Great of the Organ in the Parish Church of Doncaster; and another, of wood and metal, of tenor C compass, is inserted in the Great of the Organ in the Parish Church of Leeds, Yorkshire. For other names used to designate stops of this class, see Contra-Bourdon.

SUBPRINZIPAL, GROSSPRINZIPALBASS, Ger.—Fr., Principal Basse.—The names employed to designate the open labial stop, of wood or metal, and 32 ft. pitch, belonging to the Pedal Organ. Its usual name in English Organs is Double Open Diapason, 32 ft. Under that name, metal and wood stops exist in the Pedal of the Willis Organ in St. George's Hall, Liverpool. A Principal Basse, 32 ft. exists in the Pédale of the Concert Organ in the Salle des Fêtes, Palais du Trocadéro, Paris. A Sub-Principal, 32 ft., is inserted in the Pedal of the Organ in the Cathedral of Haarlem. The pipes of this fine stop are of pure Cornish tin, burnished, and displayed in the case. The CCCC pipe, which stands in the left tower, is nearly forty feet long and is fifteen inches in diameter. Under the name Principalbass, 32 ft., the stop exists in the Pedals of the Organs in the Cathedrals of Riga, Vienna, and Ulm. Under the simple term FLÛTE, 32 FT., this important stop exists in the Organ in the Basilique du Sacré-Cœur, Montmartre, Paris. For further particulars see DOUBLE DIAPASON.

SUBTILREGAL, Ger.—The name given to an old lingual stop, of 8 ft. pitch, the tone of which was of a soft and agreeable quality, probably differing slightly from that of the GEDÄMPFTREGAL (q. v.). Both stop and name are obsolete. See REGAL.

SUPER-OCTAVE.—The open, metal, labial stop, sounding two octaves above the foundation unison tones of the manual and pedal departments of the Organ, being of 2 ft. pitch in the former and of 4 ft. pitch in the latter. The term, unqualified, signifies that the stop is harmonic-corroborating and belongs to the Foundation-work, and yields pure organ-tone. The term SUPEROCTAV is commonly used by German organ-builders. In both the Riga and Ulm Organs, built by Walcker, the term is incorrectly applied to stops of 1 ft. pitch. The French builders commonly use the name DOUBLETTE, 2 FT. See FIFTEENTH.

T

TAPADILLO, TAPADO, Span.—The names given by Spanish organ-builders to covered labial stops, in all essentials similar to the English so-called STOPPED DIAPASON and the German GEDECKT. Under the name TAPADILLO, the stop exists in the Organs in the Cathedrals of Burgos and Valladolid; and under the name TAPADO, in the Organ in the Cathedral of Orense. A stop named FLAUTADO TAPADO exists in the Organ on the south side of the Coro in Burgos Cathedral, built in 1706.

TENOROON.—The name given by certain English organ-builders during the middle years of the last century, when incomplete stops were more in favor than they happily are now, to a covered stop, of 16 ft. pitch, which was carried downward only to tenor C on the manual clavier. The term is now obsolete, and it is to be hoped the incomplete stop it designated is equally so.

The term Tenoroon was originally employed to designate the Tenor Bassoon or Alto Fagotto in F; and it is, accordingly, evident that the name given to the organ-stop had no reference to the orchestral Tenoroon. Should it, however, be considered desirable to introduce in the Organ a FAGOTTO, of 4 ft. pitch, the name TENOROON could be given, appropriately, to it. Such a stop would complete the FAGOTTO family, and be of great value in artistic registration. At present the Organ is sadly deficient in soft octave reed-tone.

TENTH.—Ital., DECIMA. Fr., GROSSE TIERCE. Ger., TERZ.— A third-sounding mutation stop, introducing and corroborating the fourth upper partial tone in the 16 ft. harmonic series, introduced on the manuals, of $3\frac{1}{5}$ ft. pitch; and corroborating the fourth upper partial tone in the 32 ft. harmonic series, introduced in the Pedal Organ, of $6\frac{2}{5}$ ft. pitch. The unscientific English organ-builders have seriously failed to realize the value of this stop, for it appears in only one of their Organs known to us.. On the other hand, both the French and German builders have thoroughly realized its value in both the manual and pedal departments. The GROSSE TIERCE, $3\frac{1}{5}$ FT., exists in the Solo of the Organ in the Church of Saint-Sulpice, and in the Bombarde of the Organ in the Cathedral of Notre-Dame, Paris. The GROSSE TIERCE, $6\frac{2}{5}$ FT., is introduced in the Pédal of the Notre-Dame Organ. The TERZ, $3\frac{1}{5}$ FT., exists on the First Manuals of the Organs in the Cathedrals of Riga, Vienna, and Ulm. The TERZ, $6\frac{2}{5}$ FT., exists in the Pedal of the Riga Organ; and, under the term TERZBASS, $6\frac{2}{5}$ FT., it exists in the Pedals of the Riga and Vienna Organs. We agree with Töpfer that BASSTERZ would be the better name. The extended term TERZENBASS, $6\frac{2}{5}$ FT., has also been used by German organ-builders. Under the names GREAT TIERCE, $6\frac{2}{5}$ FT., and TIERCE, $3\frac{1}{5}$ FT., both stops exist in the Pedal of the Organ in the Parish Church of Doncaster, Yorkshire, built by Edmund Schulze, of Paulinzelle, in 1862. The term TIERCE, $3\frac{1}{5}$ FT., is, in our opinion, more expressive and desirable than the term TENTH.

The manual stop is formed of open metal pipes; and, as it belongs to the 16 ft. series, its scale should be derived from that of the DOUBLE DIAPASON, 16 FT., which is, properly, smaller than that of the principal DIAPASON, 8 FT. All third-sounding stops, wherever they are introduced, should be softer in tone than the unison, octave, and fifth-sounding stops with which they are associated. For artistic registration, this regulation of tone will be found of great importance. The Pedal Organ TENTH, $6\frac{2}{5}$ FT., should be formed of open pipes of wood or metal, preferably yielding a bright tone, imparting a desirable life to this grave department of the Organ. See SEVENTEENTH.

TERPODION.—The term derived from the Greek words τέρπειν—to delight, and ὠδή—a song. The musical instrument which gave this name to an organ-stop was invented by David Buschmann, of Berlin, in 1816. It was a clavier instrument, variously described as frictional and percussive, in form resembling a Pianoforte: its sounds were produced from sonorous wood in a manner not clearly described by writers on old instruments.

The stop to which the name was originally given was invented by J. Friedrich Schulze, of Paulinzelle, and inserted, for the first time, in the Organ he constructed, in 1838, for the Cathedral of Halberstadt. Other examples of the TERPODION, 8 FT., exist in the Oberwerk of the Schulze Organ in the Cathedral of Bremen; on the Third Manual of the Organ in the Marienkirche, Lübeck; and in the Swell of the Organ in the Parish Church of Doncaster, Yorkshire, built by Edmund Schulze, of Paulinzelle. As made by this master, the stop is formed of open cylindrical metal pipes, which have wide and low mouths, yielding a tone of a pronounced reedy quality. The stop, even at its best, seems to be of little tonal value. According to Schlimbach-Becker (1843), the TERPODION in the Halberstadt Organ, when combined with the LIEBLICHGEDECKTS, of 16 ft. and 8 ft. pitch, and the HARMONIKA, 8 FT., produced a tone resembling that of the instrument invented by Buschmann. What must the tone of this wooden instrument have been?

TERPOMELE.—The term, derived from the Greek words τέρπειν—to delight, and μέλος—melody or song; and first used to designate a free-reed stop, of 8 ft. pitch, which was inserted, about the year 1828, in the Organ in the Cathedral of Beauvais. The reeds were furnished with slender resonators, introducing the proper construction of free-reed stops. Availing himself of the fact that free-reeds can produce varied strengths of tone under different pressures of wind without alteration of pitch, the organ-builder arranged to impart powers of expression to the TERPOMELE by means of a contrivance placed under the control of the organist.

TERTIAN, TERZIAN, Ger.—A compound harmonic-corroborating stop, formed of two ranks of open metal pipes, properly of medium scales, which stand at the interval of a major third apart. The position is, accordingly, an inversion of that of the SESQUIALTERA, the third-sounding being larger, and lower in pitch, than the fifth-sounding one. The TERTIAN is composed of ranks of $1\frac{3}{5}$ ft. and $1\frac{1}{3}$ ft. pitch when it belongs to the 8 ft. harmonic series; of ranks of $3\frac{1}{5}$ ft. and $2\frac{2}{3}$ ft. when it belongs to the 16 ft. harmonic series; and of ranks of $6\frac{2}{5}$ ft. and $5\frac{1}{3}$ ft. when it belongs to the 32 feet harmonic series. Seidel tells us that in certain old Organs it comprised three ranks; namely, of 4 ft., 3⅕ ft., and 2⅔ ft. pitch.

When the two relative ranks are introduced as separate stops in any division of the Organ, it is not necessary to contemplate the addition of a TERTIAN, unless on special grounds directly relating to the very important matter of artistic and varied registration. In this case, the stop should be of small scale and carefully voiced, giving slight prominence in tone to the third-sounding rank. The stop may also, and very properly, be made timbre-creating, its ranks having contrasting tonalities. Only those who have made a special study of compound-tone production can realize the value of such a TERTIAN in imparting color in refined and artistic registration.

THIRTY-FIRST.—Ital., TRIGESIMA PRIMA.—A third-sounding MIXTURE rank, of open metal pipes, corroborating the fourth upper partial tone of the super-octave (2 ft. pitch) stops; its extremely acute pitch preventing its being considered, in anything save a purely philosophical sense, as belonging to a lower harmonic series. Owing to the smallness of the pipes forming this rank, it can only be introduced in the two lower octaves of a manual MIXTURE. While it appears to have been used, in some way, by the Italian organ-builders, as in one of the Organs in the Cathedral of Milan, we have been unable to find an instance of the insertion of this extremely acute third-sounding rank in a MIXTURE made by any known organ-builder. It may, however, exist in the ninety-five ranks of MIXTURE which are inserted in the Organ in the Monastic Church, Weingarten.

THIRTY-SIXTH.—Ital., TRIGESIMA SESTA.—An octave-sounding MIXTURE rank, of open metal pipes, corroborating the seventh upper partial tone of the super-octave (2 ft. pitch) stops; its extremely acute pitch preventing its being considered, in anything save a purely philosophical sense, as belonging to a lower harmonic series. Owing to the very small size of the pipes forming this rank, it can only be introduced in the bass octave of a manual MIXTURE. It appears, as in the case of the THIRTY-FIRST (q. v.), in one of the Organs in the Cathedral of Milan; but we have not been able to find the THIRTY-SIXTH introduced in any MIXTURE of English, French, or German origin. The only instance of its introduction known to us, is afforded by the seven-rank CYMBALE in the Great of the Organ in the Music Hall, Cincinnati; in this compound stop, the THIRTY-SIXTH is confined to the bass octave.

THIRTY-THIRD.—Ital., TRIGESIMA TERZA.—A fifth-sounding MIXTURE rank, of open metal pipes, corroborating the fifth upper partial tone of the super-octave (2 ft. pitch) stops; its extremely acute pitch preventing its being considered, in anything save a philosophical sense, as belonging to a lower harmonic series. The THIRTY-THIRD was introduced by the old English builders in their compound harmonic-corroborating stops. Harris inserted it, in conjunction with the TWENTY-NINTH, in the bass octave of the two-rank MIXTURE in the Organ erected by him, during the closing years of the seventeenth century, in the Church of St. Peter Mancroft, Norwich. It appears, in conjunction with the THIRTY-SIXTH, in the North Organ in the Cathedral of Milan. The THIRTY-THIRD is inserted in the bass and tenor octaves of the CYMBALE in the Organ in the Music Hall, Cincinnati.

TIBIA ANGUSTA.—(Lat. *Tibia*—a pipe; *Angustus*—narrow). —The term that has been employed by German organ-builders to designate a flute-toned stop, of small scale, and 8 ft. pitch. It resembles in formation and tone the DOLZFLÖTE (*q. v.*).

TIBIA BIFARA.—(Lat. *Tibia*—a pipe; *Bifarius*, double).— The stop, commonly named BIFARA (without the prefix), is formed in two ways; both with the view of imparting a tremulous or wavy effect to its voice. For full particulars of this stop, see BIFARA.

TIBIA CLAUSA.—(Lat. *Tibia*—a pipe; *Clausus*—closed).— The name given to a large-scaled covered stop, of 8 ft. pitch, the pipes of which are of wood. The mouths of the pipes are cut up about half their widths; their upper lips being thick, and very smoothly rounded and polished with black-lead. To save trouble and labor, the rounding and polishing are omitted, and the lips are covered with leather—a perishable expedient. When properly voiced, on a copious supply of wind of moderate pressure, the stop yields a beautiful and singularly pure quality of tone. A full scale for this stop, in the ratio $1 : \sqrt{8}$, gives the CC pipe a width of 5.56 and a depth of 7.52 inches; the C pipe a width of 3.30, and a depth of 4.46 inches; and the middle c^1 pipe a width of 1.96, and a depth of 2.66 inches. The name and modern treatment of this large-scaled GEDECKT were introduced by Hope-Jones.

TONE AND REGISTRATION.—The tone of the TIBIA CLAUSA, when artistically produced, is freer from harmonic over-tones than the voices of the generality of covered stops, and especially those of the BOURDONS; hence its peculiar value. In this respect it approaches the voice of the true LIEBLICHGEDECKT; but, on account of its large scale, the TIBIA CLAUSA yields a much greater volume of sound, and, accordingly, lends itself more effectively to the building-up of a valuable series of highly-colored compound tones. Its proper place is in the expressive divisions of the Organ, in which a firm ground-work of unison tone is required to balance and carry the assertive string-, reed-, and brass-tones of the orchestral stops: such as the so-called Swell in the Church Organ; and the wood-wind, brass-wind, and string-toned divisions of the properly stop-apportioned Concert-room Organ. In registration with the octave, mutation, and softly-voiced compound harmonic-corroborating stops, the TIBIA CLAUSA, 8 FT., produces a family of very beautiful tones.

TIBIA DURA.—(Lat. *Tibia*—a pipe; *Durus*—hard).—The name given to an open wood stop, of 4 ft. pitch, introduced by Hope-Jones; the tone of which is cold and penetrating; hence the name. The approved form of the pipes is quadrangular and inverted pyramidal, and wider than deep, so as to allow of a large mouth, which is of the inverted form. The tone of the stop has no special character to render it valuable in artistic registration. Examples exist in several Organs constructed under the superintendence of Hope-Jones.

TIBIA MAJOR.—(Lat., *Tibia*—a pipe; *Major*—greater).— The term employed by German organ-builders to designate a manual, covered labial stop, of the BOURDON class, and of 16 ft. pitch. It is commonly of large scale and of a full tone. Examples exist on the First Manuals of the Walcker Organs in the Cathedrals of Ulm and Vienna. Another exists in the Echo of the Schulze Organ in the Parish Church of Doncaster; in this instance the stop is of a comparatively soft tone. All the Echo Organs made by this builder being characterized by extreme delicacy and beauty of tone, as all Echo Organs should be.

TIBIA MINOR.—(Lat., *Tibia*—a pipe; *Minor*—smaller).— German organ-builders have, in some instances, given the name to a large-scaled covered stop, of 8 ft. pitch, which is practically the Octave of the TIBIA MAJOR, 16 FT. (*q. v.*). An example of the stop, under the simple name TIBIA, 8 FT., exists on the First Manual of the Organ in St. Paulskirche, Frankfurt. We are not certain, however, if this stop is covered. The name TIBIA MINOR has been given by John H. Compton, of Nottingham, England, to covered stops, introduced by him in certain of his Organs, the pipes of which are of large scale, and of wood and metal. The wood stop differs only slightly in treatment and tone from the TIBIA CLAUSA (*q. v.*). The metal TIBIA MINOR, 8 FT., as made by Compton, is a fine and valuable contribution to the flute-tone of the Organ of the Twentieth Century; and deserves the attention of every progressive organ-builder. The chief characteristics of its pipes are their very large scale and their very narrow mouths. The CC pipe has a diameter equal to that of a medium-scaled CC DIAPASON pipe. The mouths are cut high, arched, and leathered.

TONE AND REGISTRATION.—The tone of the Compton metal TIBIA MINOR, 8 FT., is *sui generis;* differing widely from that of the ordinary large-scaled GEDECKT; and therein lies much of its value. The Organ of to-day calls loudly for new voices of a refined, building-up, and timbre-creating character; not old voices coarsened by the use of inordinate pressures of pipe-wind, which seems to be the chief aim of the generality of voicers at the present time. The tone of the stop under consideration is thus clearly described by J. I. Wedgwood, who has had ample opportunity of forming an accurate estimate of its character: "The tone of the TIBIA MINOR is extraordinarily effective. In the bass it is round and velvety with a suspicion of smooth French Horn quality. In the treble the tone becomes very clear and full. The top notes of the stop, indeed, bear in them some resemblance to the full liquid notes of the Ocarina, though free, of course, from the undesirable features of that instrument. Whilst entirely devoid of the objectionable hooting quality sometimes displayed by powerful FLUTES, it forms a solo stop of remarkably fine effect, and in combination serves to add much clearness and fullness of tone to the treble, and, in general, exercises to the fullest extent the beneficial characteristics of the TIBIA class of stop." In registration, this stop lends itself to the creation of many beautiful compound tones and artistic colorings. See TIBIA CLAUSA.

TIBIA MOLLIS.—(Lat., *Tibia*—a pipe; *Mollis*—soft).—The name given by Hope-Jones to an open wood stop, of a soft flute-tone; the pipes of which have their mouths cut parallel to their sides, and the caps so placed as to direct the wind-stream transversely, in a manner similar to that from the mouth while playing the orchestral Flute. An example exists in the Organ in St. George's Church, Blackheath, London. The name is equally appropriate for any very soft flute-toned stop.

TIBIA PLENA.—(Lat., *Tibia*—a pipe; *Plenus*—full).—The name given to an open wood stop of 8 ft. pitch; the pipes of which are of greater depth than width, of very large scale, and have mouths cut moderately high, their upper lips being thick and carefully rounded and polished when properly finished. Leathering the lips has been adopted to produce sufficient smoothness. Lips carefully rounded and burnished with black-lead are to be preferred, as leather is certain to change and decay in a few years. The Tibia Plena is the most powerful of the wood stops of unimitative flute-tone; and should find a prominent place in every important Organ, preferably on the First or Great Manual and in its expressive sub-division. The stop has been made of several different scales, all of which are necessarily large. For instance, that stated for the stop in the Organ in the Cathedral of Worcester, gives the CC (8 ft.) pipe a measurement of $7\frac{13}{16}$ inches by 9 inches, and middle c^1 (2 ft.) pipe $2\frac{13}{16}$ inches by $3\frac{1}{4}$ inches. This is an extreme and unnecessarily large scale. Examples of the stop exist in several Organs in England and the United States.

Tone and Registration.—The tone of the Tibia Plena when artistically voiced, is singularly full and dignified; the presence of certain low harmonics imparting to it considerable richness, and rendering it of the greatest value in registration with the Diapasons, to the voices of which it imparts a remarkable color and grandeur. It is also of the greatest value in combination with such lingual stops as the Double Trumpet and unison Trumpet of the First or Great Organ, to which division it properly belongs. To be of maximum value it should be rendered expressive and flexible, so as to be largely available throughout the other more important divisions of the Organ. In a very large Concert-room instrument, a Tibia Plena may with the greatest advantage be inserted, as a tone-builder, in either the Solo Organ or that devoted to the brass-wind division; or, indeed, in both.

TIBIA PROFUNDA.—(Lat., *Tibia*—a pipe; *Profundis*—deep). —The name given to the Pedal Organ stop, of 16 ft. pitch, the pipes of which are similar in formation and quality of tone to those of the Tibia Plena (*q. v.*). An example exists in the Pedal of the Organ in the Church of St. Mary, Warwick, England.

TIBIA RURESTRIS, FISTULA RURESTRIS.—(Lat., *Fistula, Tibia*—a pipe; *Ruralis*—rural).—Names that have been used by the early organ-builders to designate a flute-toned stop in all essentials similar to the Bauerflöte (*q. v.*).

TIBIA SILVESTRIS.—(Lat., *Tibia*—a pipe; *Silvestris*—of a wood).—The term that has been used to designate an open wood,

flute-toned stop, identical with that commonly named WALDFLÖTE
(q. v.).   Seidel and Wolfram render the name TIBIA SYLVESTRIS.

TIBIA TRANSVERSA, TIBIA TRAVERSA.—(Lat., *Tibia*—
a pipe; *Transversus, Traversus*—across).—The names given by old
builders to the open labial stop, yielding imitative flute-tone, which
is now commonly designated FLAUTO TRAVERSO (q. v.) or ORCHES-
TRAL FLUTE.

TIBIA VULGARIS.—(Lat., *Tibia*—a pipe; *Vularis*—common).
—The name given in early times to the unimitative flute-toned stop,
now commonly termed BLOCKFLÖTE (q. v.).

TIERCE, Fr.—Ger., TERZ.   Eng., SEVENTEENTH.—A muta-
tion harmonic-corroborating stop, of $1\frac{3}{5}$ ft. pitch in the manual
divisions, where it belongs to the 8 ft. harmonic series; and $3\frac{1}{5}$ ft.
pitch in the Pedal Organ, where it belongs to the 16 ft. harmonic
series. See SEVENTEENTH.

TIERCINA.—The name given to a metal labial stop, of 8 ft.
pitch, the pipes of which are of small scale, covered, and voiced to
yield a tone in which the fourth upper partial tone (the Seventeenth)
is strongly in evidence; hence the name. This compound tonality is
enriched by the presence, in a subordinate degree, of the second
upper partial, the Twelfth. To enrich the harmonic structure, we
inserted a TIERCINA, 8 FT., in the Second Subdivision (String) of the
Third Organ of the instrument installed in the Festival Hall of the
Louisiana Purchase Exposition (1904).

TIERCE FLUTE.—The name given by its introducer, George
W. Till, of Philadelphia, Pa. to a labial dual stop, formed of a metal
HARMONIC FLUTE, 8 FT., having the compass of CC to c^5, and a
metal TIERCE, $3\frac{1}{5}$ FT., of the same compass, yielding pure organ-
tone, and belonging to the 16 ft. harmonic series. In this instance,
however, the TIERCE is a timbre-creating rather than a harmonic-
corroborating stop or rank. In combination with the HARMONIC
FLUTE it produces a compound solo voice of an absolutely new and
remarkable tone-color, impossible to be produced from a single-
ranked FLUTE, however made and voiced.
This dual stop is inserted in the Choir of the Organ in the Wanamaker Store, in Philadelphia, where it speaks on wind of 15 inches.
The stop is unique; and it is safe to say that such a dual stop has
never been even contemplated in the preparation of the tonal scheme
for any other Organ hitherto constructed. We know of no Organ

in which the component parts of the stop exist in any single manual division. The tone of the TIERCE FLUTE must be heard; it cannot be described. It is especially a solo stop.*

TRAVERSFLÖTE, Ger.—Ital., FLAUTO TRAVERSO.—The labial stop, properly formed of cylindrical or quadrangular wood pipes voiced to yield a tone as closely imitating that of the orchestral Flute as possible. Fine examples, of 8 ft. and 4 ft. pitch, voiced by Edmund Schulze, exist in the Choir and Echo of the Organ in the Parish Church of Doncaster, England. See FLAUTO TRAVERSO and ORCHESTRAL FLUTE.

TRAVERSENBASS, Ger.—The name given to a labial metal stop, of 16 ft. pitch, the higher notes of which produce tones similar to those of the TRAVERSFLÖTE, 8 FT. According to Wolfram (1815), an example exists in the Pedal of the Organ in the Church of St. Bonifacii, Langensalza. A clear flute-toned stop, of this class, and of medium strength of tone, would be extremely valuable in the Pedal of a Concert-room Organ.

TRICHTERREGAL, Ger.—Literally, *Funnel Regal.*—An old lingual stop of the REGAL class furnished with funnel-shaped resonators; hence its name. A TRICHTERREGAL, 8 FT., was inserted by Schnittker in the Organ he built for the Church of St. Jacobi, Hamburg. See REGAL.

TRINONA.—The name given by the builder of the Organ in the Church of St. Vincent, Breslau, to stops, of 8 ft. and 4 ft. pitch, inserted on the Second or Upper Manual. These stops are said to be of wood and of a soft viol quality of tone. The name would seem to imply the presence, in some prominence, of the fourth upper partial tone—the Seventeenth—in the voices of the stops, quite compatible with good viol-tone.

TRIPLETTE.—The term employed to designate a compound harmonic-corroborating stop formed of three unbroken ranks of open metal pipes, similar in treatment to the DOUBLETTE of the German organ-builders. The TRIPLETTE furnishes a favorable opportunity for the formation of a valuable timbre-creating stop. Its ranks may be of metal, or of wood and metal, open or covered, pipes, voiced to yield any desirable tones. Its ranks may be of $2\frac{2}{3}$ ft., 2 ft., and $1\frac{3}{5}$ ft.; 2 ft., $1\frac{3}{5}$ ft., and $1\frac{1}{3}$ ft.; or $1\frac{3}{5}$ ft., $1\frac{1}{3}$ ft., and 1 ft.

* Full particulars of the formation and scales of this stop are given in "The Organ of the Twentieth Century." Page 104.

pitch; all the ranks representing and corroborating upper partial tones of the 8 ft. harmonic series. Unless designed as a strictly timbre-creating stop, the TRIPLETTE has nothing to specially recommend its adoption: its ranks would be more useful as separate stops.

A finely-voiced timbre-creating TRIPLETTE would unquestionably be of great value in artistic registration; producing compound tones of great variety and beauty, unknown in the Organs hitherto constructed. It should be so placed as to be available on any manual clavier.

TROMBA, Ital.—Italian organ-builders have employed this term to designate lingual stops of the TRUMPET class, of both 8 ft. and 16 ft. pitch, as in the Organ in the Church of St. Allessandro, Milan. We find the term applied to a stop, of 32 ft. pitch, in the Great of the Organ in the Church of Sta. Maria di Carignano, Genoa; reconstructed by C. G. Bianchi, in 1863. Spanish and Portuguese organ-builders have applied the name, commonly with the addition of certain qualifying terms, to their TRUMPETS of powerful and special intonation. In the Organ on the north side of the *Coro* in Burgos Cathedral there are two lingual stops, labeled, respectively, TROMBA REAL (Royal Trumpet) and TROMBA BATALHA (Battle Trumpet). We find stops in the Organ in the Church of the Martyros, Lisbon, labeled TROMBA REAL, TROMBA BATALHA, and TROMBA MAGNA (Great Trumpet).

The TROMBAS, of 8 ft. and 16 ft. pitch, as made by German and English organ-builders, differ widely in tonality from those of the old Spanish builders: they are TRUMPETS yielding a full and smooth, unimitative brass-tone, more powerful than that of the ORCHESTRAL TRUMPET, but less assertive than the tones of the TUBAS. A TROMBA, 8 FT., made by Walcker, exists on the First Manual of the Organ in the Accademia di Sta. Cecilia, Rome. An example, by Norman & Beard, exists in the Organ in the Church of All Saints, Notting Hill, London. The late Edmund Schulze of Paulinzelle invented a labial TROMBA, 16 FT., the pipes of which were of wood, square and inverted pyramidal in form, and of medium scale, and voiced with the harmonic-bridge.

TONE AND REGISTRATION.—Given that the tone of the TROMBA, 8 FT., is distinct in strength and quality from the tones of the HARMONIC and ORCHESTRAL TRUMPETS, on the one hand; and from the tones of the TROMBONE, OPHICLEIDE, and TUBA, on the other hand, there can be no question as to the great value of the stop in the appointment of a large Church Organ or a Concert-room instrument. Like all lingual stops, its place is in an expressive manual division. In a properly stop-apportioned Concert-room Organ, its proper place is in the division devoted to the representatives of the "brass-wind" forces of the orchestra.* Its presence there will be of the greatest service in artistic registration, furnishing a rich and full lingual tone, of a neutral and good mixing quality, combining perfectly with any pure organ-tones, flute-tones, and viol-tones.

TROMBA CLARION.—The appropriate name for a TROMBA, of 4 ft. pitch, voiced considerably softer than the unison TROMBA (*q. v.*). Softly voiced octave lingual stops have been too much neglected in the stop-appointments of modern Organs; yet their value in artistic registration cannot well be overrated. They effectively enrich, brighten, and impart life to volumes of unison and double tones; which, without them, would be dull, heavy, and unmusical.

TROMBONE, Ital., Eng., Fr.—A lingual stop of 8 ft. pitch in the manual divisions and of 16 ft. pitch in the Pedal Organ. The stop belongs to the TRUMPET family; and its pipes are similar in form to, but of larger scale than, those of the ordinary TRUMPET, 8 FT., only having tongues and reeds yielding a distinctive and more powerful intonation. The stop is properly voiced to closely imitate the tones of the orchestral Trombones when played *forte*, but not *fortissimo*. The more powerful intonation being desirable in the POSAUNE (*q. v.*).

FORMATION.—The manual TROMBONE, 8 FT., is constructed of metal throughout; its resonators being of the inverted conical form, of large scale, and either of good pipe-metal or zinc; the latter being commonly used at the present time. The Hoyt Two-ply Pipe-metal is strongly to be recommend for high-class work. The Pedal Organ TROMBONE, 16 FT., is made either entirely of metal or of wood and metal. When of metal, it differs in no essential, save in dimensions, from the TROMBONE, 8 FT. When chiefly of wood, the pipes are necessarily different in form and construction. The resonators are quadrangular and of inverted pyramidal shape. The boots, when of wood, are square and of ample dimensions to receive the feet of the resonators, the reed-blocks, and all fittings. The reeds or *échalotes* are of the open class; and the tongues or *languettes* are of hard-rolled brass, of medium thickness, and finely curved so as to produce a bright quality of tone.

TONE AND REGISTRATION.—The proper tone of the manual TROMBONE, 8 FT., should resemble as closely as possible the tones of the orchestral Trombones when played without the production of

---

* See stop-apportionment of the Fourth Organ, in our scheme for the Concert-room Organ, given on page 311 of "The Organ of the Twentieth Century."

their extreme brazen clang. Fine examples of this stop, voiced by the masterly hand of the late George Willis, exist in the Great and Solo of the Organ in St. George's Hall, Liverpool. The value of this unison stop seems to be overlooked by the organ-builders and organ-designers of to-day, but its introduction in important instruments is strongly to be recommended. So firmly convinced are we of the value of its distinctive tone, that in our suggestive tonal scheme for the Concert-room Organ of the Twentieth Century, we have inserted in the First Organ (Great) a TROMBONE, 8 FT., and in the Fourth Organ (Brass-wind) the complete TROMBONE family; namely, a CONTRA-TROMBONE, 16 FT., TROMBONE, 8 FT., TROMBONE QUINT, 5⅓ FT., and TROMBONE OCTAVE, 4 FT.* It would be difficult to over-rate the importance of such a combination of lingual stops at the disposal of the organist; yet it has never appeared in any executed Organ. The neglect of the manual TROMBONE, 8 FT., is as remark-able as it is unwise, yet it is the only one which can properly repre-sent the orchestral Trombone. In a large collection of stop-lists of Organs, designed in this country, which lie before us, we fail to find a single TROMBONE, 8 FT., mentioned. Indeed, in the list of an im-mense divided Organ, embracing 283 speaking stops, there is only one TROMBONE given, and that, of 16 ft. pitch, in one of the Pedal Organs. In the Fourth or Solo Organ of the large instrument we designed, and which was installed in the Festival Hall of the Louis-iana Purchase Exposition, St. Louis, 1904, there was a TROMBONE, 8 FT., and a BASS TROMBONE, 16 FT.; both of metal.

TROMPETTE EN CHAMADE, Fr.—The term employed by French organ-builders to designate a TRUMPET, the pipes of which are projected horizontally and fanwise from the front of the case, as in the Organ in the Church of Saint-Ouen, Rouen (See Frontispiece). This treatment is common in important and noisy Spanish Organs. On both artistic and common-sense grounds the treatment is to be condemned. No lingual stop should be without expression.

TROMPETTE HARMONIQUE, Fr.—This important lingual stop was invented by Cavaillé-Coll, and introduced, for the first time, in the Organ of the Royal Church of Saint-Denis, constructed in 1841. In this remarkable instrument there were inserted no fewer than five examples of the stop of 8 ft. pitch; one in the Positif, two in the Grand-Orgue; and two in the Récit-Écho Expressif. In his "Rapport" on the Organ, J. Adrien de la Fage remarks:

* See "The Organ of the Twentieth Century," page 311.

"La *trompette harmonique* du clavier de récit est, par sa puissance et par l'excellence des sons qu'elle produit, incomparablement supérieure à tout ce que l'on connaît en ce genre. Le caractère tout-à-fait particulier de ses basses, lorsqu'on l'emploie comme partie chantante accompagnée des jeux de fond, est d'un effet admirable. On ne peut dire autant des séries de jeux de *flûtes harmoniques* qui donnent à l'ensemble de l'orgue tant de rondeur et de puissance."

For further particulars respecting the TROMPETTE HARMONIQUE, see HARMONIC TRUMPET.

TRUMPET.—Fr., TROMPETTE. Ger., TROMPETE. Ital., TROMBA. Dtch., TROMPET. Span., TROMPETA.—The manual lingual stop, of 8 ft. pitch, to which these names are given by the organ-builders of different countries, may reasonably, and under usual conditions, be considered the most generally useful, if not the most important lingual stop in the Organ. So much so is this the case, that no Organ of any pretension is constructed without one, commonly occupying a place in the Great or foundation division of the instrument. Unless when it is strictly of the solo or orchestral tonality, the TRUMPET is a chorus-reed of the first importance. Realizing this fact, the German organ-builders place the stop on different manuals. In the Organ in the Cathedral of Ulm the TROMPETE, 8 FT., is inserted on the Second and Third Manuals only, and also in the Pedal Organ. It commonly occupies a place in the Pedal Organ of Walcker's important instruments. In the Cavaillé-Coll Organ in the Church of Saint-Sulpice, Paris, there are two TROMPETTES in the Grand-Chœur, one in the Positif, one in the Récit, one in the Solo, and one in the Pédale—six TROMPETTES, of 8 ft. pitch (none harmonic), in an Organ of 100 speaking stops. The builder of this Organ fully realized the value of the chorus TRUMPET.* In English

---

* "La TROMPETTE est le registre d'anches le plus pur, le plus rond, le plus fin d'harmonie et de sonorité, quand il est bien fait; le plus désagréable, quand il est manqué. Chose singulière il réussit moins souvent en Allemagne qu'en France; j'ai déjà cherché la raison de cette différence dans la différence d'allures des deux nations: le bruit guerrier, l'éclat, tout ce qui tend à accentuer la musique, et à mieux marquer son rhythme, semble être de notre domaine. De leur côté, les facteurs allemands se vengent de la maigreur de leurs *Trompettes* par la variété, la finesse mélancolique de leurs jeux de fonds.

"Une bonne *Trompette* doit avoir le tuyau un peu plus long que de rigueur, de grosse taille et de solide épaisseur, en étain fin et bien battu, posé sur un-pied inébranlable et bien proportionné en hauteur et en embouchure. La languette, de laiton fortement écroui, médiocrement recourbée à l'entrée de l'anche, s'y posera bien également sans dévier, et sera comme cette anche de largeur et d'épaisseur proportionnées à la vigueur du courant d'air contre lequel elle combat. Le tuyau trop long ferait octavier; trop court, il pourrait donner un son plus tranchant, mais criard. Trop d'épaisseur serait inutile, et la minceur ferait grincer le tuyau. La languette trop lâche fait râler le son, trop ferme ou déviée de son aplomb, courbée trop haut ou trop bas, elle devient capricieuse, raide jusqu'au mutisme. Les justes proportions du tuyau de *Trompette* combinées avec celles du vent doivent donner un son égal, brillant sans trop d'éclat, mais mâle et doux à la fois. C'est cette dernière qualité, si rare que les bons accordeurs distinguent au bourdon qui ressort toujours d'une *Trompette* arrivée à sa juste harmonie. Toutes ces perfections

Organs of the usual Church type a single TRUMPET, 8 FT., is commonly introduced, inserted almost invariably in the Great. Even in the important Organ, of 70 speaking stops, in the Cathedral of York, there are only two TRUMPETS, one in the Great and the other in the Swell. In the Concert Organ in St. George's Hall, Liverpool, there is a TRUMPET, 8 FT., in the following manual divisions, Great, Choir, Swell, and Solo; and also one in the Pedal Organ. Judging from a survey of the tonal-appointments of American Organs, it would seem that organ-builders here have failed, as a rule, to realize the great value of the TRUMPET. An example of this neglect may be given: in an important College Organ, of 46 speaking stops (exclusive of 13 borrowed stops), built by a distinguished firm, there is not a single TRUMPET, or any lingual stop that can take its place in registration. Surely this is a step in the wrong direction. In another Organ, of 52 speaking stops, there is not a single TRUMPET or any stop of its tonal character. Further comment is unnecessary.

FORMATION.—The pipes of the TRUMPET are invariably made of metal; their resonators being of the inverted conical shape and of medium scale, formed of a good alloy of tin and lead (spotted-metal) or zinc. The Hoyt Two-ply Pipe-metal is to be recommended. The resonators are of about the same lengths as open labial metal pipes of the corresponding pitch, and are entirely open at top: they should be accurately cut to length and not slotted. The form of the complete TRUMPET pipe is shown in the accompanying illustration, Fig. 34. The scale of the resonators varies according to character and strength of the tone desired. The reeds or échalotes are properly of the open class; but in the case of the ECHO TRUMPET, or a stop suitable for a true Chamber Organ, the reeds may properly be of the closed variety. The tongues or languettes must in all cases be such as to impart a true Trumpet tonality: this should be pronounced in the case of the ORCHESTRAL TRUMPET.

TONE AND REGISTRATION.—The tone of the ordinary chorus TRUMPET, while of a true Trumpet character, should not too closely resemble that of the orchestral instrument played forte. A certain amount of brazen clang is desirable to give individuality to the stop; but it should not be such as to prevent its free use in general registration with stops of organ-tone. When of this tonality, the stop is

doivent se trouver dans chaque tuyau séparément, et dans tous comparés l'un à l'autre. Il faut y joindre enfin celle d'une grande promptitude et netteté de langage.

"La taille des Trompettes doit être en rapport avec leur place; ainsi, la pédale de Trompette sera de plus forte taille que celle qui chante à la main; celle du récit, plus délicate que celle du grand orgue. Quoiqu'on joue avantageusement la Trompette seule, l'alliance de ces octaves extrêmes avec celles du Clairon lui donne une grande vigueur, surtout à la pédale; l'habitude de certains facteurs de loger sur un seul clavier deux Trompettes de moyenne taille ne vaut rien, parce qu'elles sont rarement d'accord, et qu'il vaut mieux un seul instrument de forte taille, dont les vibrations aient l'avantage de la clarté et de l'unité."—Regnier.

most valuable in the First or Great Organ, where it can enter into combination with the DIAPASONS and the entire foundation-work, producing compound tones of great richness and dignity; this is due to the great number of upper partial tones its voice comprises. When enclosed and rendered flexible and expressive, as it should be in every artistically appointed Great Organ, the value of the TRUMPET is increased ten-fold. The solo stop, properly designated ORCHESTRAL TRUMPET, 8 FT., should be voiced to imitate as closely as possible the characteristic tones of the orchestral instrument. Its voice will, accordingly be singularly bright, silvery, and jubilant; differing, in these desirable qualities, from every other lingual stop of the Organ. It will be used in registration for the production of rich orchestral effects, in which its brilliant voice will prove invaluable. It properly belongs to the brass-wind division of the Concert-room Organ; where it will be found to be of the utmost service both in solo and combinational effects.*

TUBA, TUBA MIRABILIS.—Known by both names, this stop, of the TRUMPET class, is the most assertive lingual stop in the modern Organ, having a voice of great sonority and grandeur. The stop is of 8 ft. pitch, and has been placed in different divisions of important Organs; but its most desirable place is in the manual division containing the principal solo stops. In this position it exists in the Concert Organs in the Centennial Hall, Sydney, N. S. W., the Auditorium, Chicago, and the Music Hall, Cincinnati. It also exists in the Solos of the Organs in Westminster Abbey, the Cathedral of York, and the Cathedral of the Incarnation, Garden City, L. I. It exists on the First Manual of the Organ in the Cathedral of Riga, and in the Dome Organ in St. Paul's Cathedral, London.

FORMATION.—The pipes of the TUBA are, like those of the TRUMPET (Fig. 34) of inverted conical form, of large scale, and of thick and firm metal. Its reeds or *échalotes* are properly of the open class, and its tongues or *languettes* are wide, thick, and boldly curved. The TUBAS of different organ-builders have been voiced on, winds ranging from eight to twenty-five inches: the higher octaves of the stop in the Dome Organ in St. Paul's Cathedral speak on the latter pressure. The scale of the resonators varies in different examples; but the maximum may be

FIG. 34

* See "The Organ of the Twentieth Century," page 311.

accepted as seven inches diameter at top for the resonator of the CC (8 ft.) pipe.

A remarkable labial stop, designated TUBA MIRABILIS, has recently been invented by the distinguished artist in stop formation, W. E. Haskell, of Brattleboro, Vt. This is an open wood stop of very peculiar form and general treatment, in which the harmonic-bridge holds a prominent position. The form and construction of the pipes of this unique stop are fully shown on Plate IV. All the details given deserve the careful study of those interested in pipe formation. The stop speaks on a very copious supply of wind of fifteen inches pressure; yielding a tone of great volume and dignity, and of a most valuable quality. It may be said to open an entirely new chapter in the history of wood pipe development, and points the way to further achievements.

TONE AND REGISTRATION.—The Tuba of the modern orchestra, favored by Wagner on account of its majestic and impressive bass tones, belongs to the Saxhorn family; and its voice should, properly, be imitated by that of the TUBA of the Organ; but such a desirable imitation seems to have been completely neglected in the desire to produce the greatest volume and dominance of tone possible from lingual pipes and high-pressure voicing. This aim has certainly been reached in the HARMONIC TUBA (*q. v.*). A truly imitative TUBA, 8 FT., similar in power to the pure and unstrained voice of the orchestral instrument in B♭, would be an invaluable addition to the brass-tone forces of the Concert-room Organ. The extremely powerful tone of the TUBA, as it usually obtains in English and American Organs, is of very limited use in registration; but in full organ effects and *fortissimo* climaxes it is most impressive, dominating all other tonalities. Its presence is of most value in the Fifth or Solo Organ of the properly stop-apportioned Concert-room Organ.

TUBA CLARION.—A TUBA of octave or 4 ft. pitch, the pipes of which are formed in all respects similar to those of the unison TUBA, 8 FT. As this stop will accompany the unison stop, in whatever division of the Organ it is inserted, it should be subordinate in scale and strength of voice.

TUBA MAGNA.—The name given either to the TUBA MIRABILIS or the HARMONIC TUBA when voiced to yield a tone of great volume and assertiveness.

TUBA MAJOR.—The name employed in some instances to designate the CONTRA-TUBA, 16 FT., but more commonly applied to such a stop as the TUBA MAGNA (*q. v.*).

TUBA MINOR.—The name appropriately given to a TUBA, 8 FT., of small scale, yielding a softer voice than that of the other TUBAS. This stop may be introduced in the Swell or in the expres-

PLATE IV

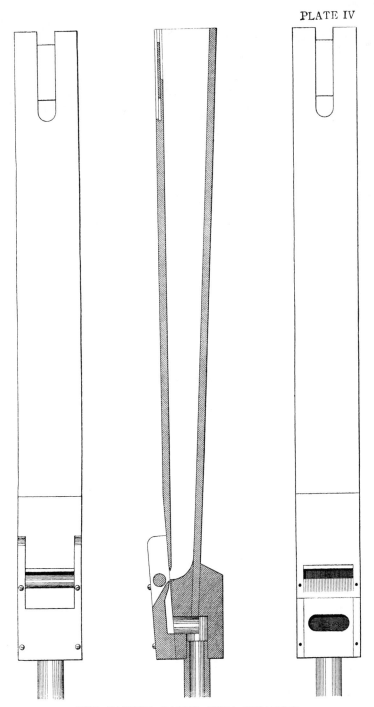

THE HASKELL LABIAL TUBA MIRABILIS

sive subdivision of the Great Organ; its subdued voice rendering it of considerable value in full combinations, especially with the DIA-PASONS, of 8 ft. and 16 ft. pitch. Good examples of this useful stop exist in several English Organs.

TUBA PROFUNDA.—The term employed to designate a stop of the TUBA class and of 16 ft. pitch, properly belonging to the Pedal Organ. When introduced in a manual Organ, the stop is commonly and appropriately named CONTRA-TUBA (*q. v.*). An example exists in the Solo of the Organ in the Centennial Hall, Sydney, N. S. W.

TUBA QUINT.—A mutation stop of the TUBA class, of 5⅓ ft. pitch, voiced to yield a tone considerably softer than that of the unison TUBA (8 ft.) in the same division. As it strictly belongs to the 16 ft. harmonic series, it can only be properly introduced in association with the CONTRA-TUBA, 16 FT. The complete family will accordingly comprise the CONTRA TUBA, 16 FT.; TUBA, 8 FT.; TUBA QUINT, 5⅓ FT.; and TUBA CLARION, 4 FT.;—a series of powerful lingual stops capable of producing compound tones of surpassing grandeur. The four stops alone admit, in registration, of eight perfectly satisfactory combinations, each of which would have a distinctive coloring. We know of no Organ in which the complete family is introduced.*

TUBA SONORA.—The name given by Robert Hope-Jones to a TUBA, 8 FT., voiced to yield a peculiarly full and pure tone, largely free from the clang due, in other stops of the TRUMPET class, to the prominence of high upper partial tones. A stop of this tonality is much more generally useful in artistic registration than the ordinary dominating TUBA. A fine example of the TUBA SONORA, 8 FT., voiced on wind of twenty inches pressure, exists in the Solo of the Organ in the Cathedral of Worcester, England.

TUBASSON, Fr.—The name that has been used by French and Belgian organ-builders to designate a Pedal Organ lingual stop of the TROMBONE class, of 16 ft. pitch, and softer in tone than the ordinary TROMBONE, 16 FT., as made by English and American organ-builders.

TWELFTH.—A fifth-sounding mutation stop, belonging to the 8 ft. harmonic series in the manual divisions, where it is of 2⅔ ft. pitch; and to the 16 ft. harmonic series in the Pedal Organ, where it

---

* We have inserted the four stops in the tonal-apportionment of the Fifth Organ in our scheme for the Concert-room Organ. See "The Organ of the Twentieth Century," page 315.

is of 5⅓ ft. pitch. In both cases it corroborates the second upper partial tone of the prime tone, as yielded by the DIAPASON, 8 FT., of the manual divisions, and the DIAPASON, 16 FT., of the Pedal Organ. The TWELFTH is properly formed of open cylindrical metal pipes, of a smaller scale than those of the OCTAVE, 4 FT., and voiced to yield pure organ-tone, softer than that of the OCTAVE. In old Organs, the TWELFTH, 2⅔ FT., was almost invariably made of too large a scale and voiced too loudly. The practice of making the TWELFTH of the same scale as the DIAPASON is strongly to be condemned, for with so large a scale it is not possible to obtain a scientific adjustment of power or the refined singing tone so desirable in this harmonic-corroborating stop.

The TWELFTH, 2⅔ FT., frequently enters into the composition of compound harmonic-corroborating stops; and as it requires to be covered by the SUPER-OCTAVE, 2 FT., it is sometimes associated with that stop as a two-rank MIXTURE, as in the RAUSCHQUINTE (q. v.). For further particulars, see NAZARD.

TWENTY-FOURTH.—Ital., VIGESIMA QUARTA.—A third-sounding MIXTURE rank, corroborating the ninth upper partial tone in the 8 ft. harmonic series, and the fourth upper partial tone in the 4 ft. harmonic series. The TWENTY-FOURTH does not often appear in modern MIXTURES, but it should always be introduced in those in which a third-sounding rank is used. The old English builders introduced it along with the SEVENTEENTH, in many of their MIXTURES. When properly scaled and proportioned in tone, the TWENTY-FOURTH has a very good effect in the bass and tenor octaves. It appears, associated with the SEVENTEENTH (DECIMA SETTIMA), in the North Organ in Milan Cathedral.

TWENTY-NINTH.—Ital., VIGESIMA NONA.—An octave-sounding MIXTURE rank, corroborating the seventh upper partial tone in the 4 ft. harmonic series, and, philosophically considered, the fifteenth upper partial tone in the 8 ft. harmonic series. The TWENTY-NINTH was commonly introduced in the acute MIXTURES of the old builders. It appears, associated with the TWENTY-SIXTH (VIGESIMA SESTA), in both the Organs in the Cathedral of Milan.

TWENTY-SECOND.—Ital., VIGESIMA SECONDA.—An octave-sounding harmonic-corroborating rank, of 1 ft. pitch, commonly found in MIXTURE work, but sometimes as an independent stop, as in the Grand Chœur of the Organ in the Cathedral of Notre-Dame, and the Positif of the Organ in the Church of Saint-Sulpice, Paris.

In both these noted instruments it appears as a PICCOLO, 1 FT. The extremely small size of the pipes forming the TWENTY-SECOND renders it almost impossible to carry the stop throughout the manual compass without a break. In MIXTURE work it is very seldom carried above the tenor octave. Associated with the NINETEENTH (DECIMA NONA) it appears in the North Organ, and separately in the South Organ, in the Cathedral of Milan.

TWENTY-SIXTH.—Ital., VIGESIMA SESTA.—A fifth-sounding MIXTURE rank, corroborating the eleventh upper partial tone in the 8 ft. harmonic series, and the fifth upper partial tone in the 4 ft. harmonic series. The TWENTY-SIXTH appears in the majority of high-pitched MIXTURES, but never above middle c♯¹, and rarely going so high as that note. Associated with the TWENTY-NINTH (VIGESIMA NONA) it appears in the North Organ in Milan Cathedral.

U

UNDA MARIS, Lat.—Literally *Wave of the Sea*. A name used to designate a single or a dual stop, of 8 ft. pitch, the pipes of which are usually open and made of metal, though occasionally of wood. In old Organs, the stop was formed of either open or covered flute-toned pipes, having soft intonation, and tuned slightly flat, so as to produce, when drawn with a unison stop of correct pitch, an undulating or wave-like effect. When in its best dual form, the stop produces slow undulations that may be counted; and not the objectionable fluttering tones which characterize it in Organs constructed by inartistic builders. This slow undulation, coupled with a soft flute-tone, properly distinguishes the UNDA MARIS from the VOIX CÉLESTE.* There seems, however, to be no recognized standard of tonality for the UNDA MARIS at the present time. In France it has been formed successfully of two ranks of pipes of a QUINTATEN tonality, tuned flat and sharp. In England and Germany the stop varies but slightly, if any, from the recognized character of the VOIX CÉLESTE (*q. v.*). The UNDA MARIS is to be found in numerous

---

* "UNDA-MARIS. Flûte de huit, en bois ou en étoffe. Elle s'accorde une idée plus haut que la montre, avec laquelle ce désaccord doit faire constamment une légère oscillation, un *battement* comme disent les accordeurs. Les ondulations que produit ce battment sont traduites par son nom latin d'*unda-maris*. Son effet, assez bizarre, est plus sensible avec des jeux moins accentués que la montre; et quand ce dernier régistre est fortement embouché, il parle trop haut pour laisser entendre son auxiliaire. Quelquefois, l'*unda-maris* est composée de manière à se passer de ses voisins; alors, comme la flûte double, appelée *bifara*, elle a deux bouches à chaque tuyau, mais sa puissance est d'autant moindre que les deux bouches sont alimentées par un seul pied."—Regnier.

Organs constructed by French and German builders, as on the Fourth Manual of the Walcker Organ in Riga Cathedral, and in the Positifs of the Cavaillé-Coll Organs in the Cathedral of Notre-Dame, the Church of Saint-Sulpice, and the Palais du Trocadéro, Paris. Good examples by English builders, formed of two ranks of pipes, exist in the Organs in Norwich Cathedral and the Centennial Hall, Sydney, N. S. W. An example exists in the Echo of the Roosevelt Organ in the Auditorium, Chicago. A dual stop of unusual formation, named UNDA MARIS by its inventor, George W. Till, of Philadelphia, Pa., has recently been inserted in the Choir of the Organ in the Wanamaker Store in that city. It consists of a GEMSHORN, 8 FT., of wood and metal, and a GAMBA, 8 FT., of tin. The former is tuned flat so as to produce about three undulations at tenor C, increasing to about double the number in the top octave.* How far it is desirable to introduce stops of the UNDA MARIS class in an Organ is open to question; but it is quite certain it is not required in dignified organ music.

UNTERSATZ, Ger.—Eng., CONTRA-BOURDON, SUB-BOURDON. Fr., SOUSBASSE.—A large-scaled covered wood stop, of 32 ft. pitch. It is inserted in both the manual and pedal departments of large Organs. When in a manual division it is usually labeled MANUAL-UNTERSATZ, 32 FT., as on the First Manuals of the Walcker Organs in the Cathedrals of Ulm and Vienna, and the Church of St. Paul, Frankfurt a. M. It appears, labeled UNTERSATZ, 32 FT., in the Pedal Organs of the Ladegast instruments in the Nicolaikirche, Leipzig, and the Cathedrals of Merseburg and Schwerin. See CONTRA-BOURDON.

V

VIOL.—Fr. and Ger., VIOLE.—A name that may be accepted as generic of all labial stops of unimitative string-tone, commonly known by the inappropriate name GAMBA; which, signifying *leg*, has no possible relation to tone. The term VIOL is, accordingly, to be strongly recommended for adoption in all appropriate cases; confining the term GAMBA to the only one stop to which it can be properly applied. The term Viol or Viole was originally applied to a family of string instruments commonly used in the sixteenth and seventeenth centuries. The Chest of Viols, mentioned by old

* Full particulars of the formation of this unique stop are given in " The Organ of the Twentieth Century," pages 106-107.

writers, consisted, in its complete form, of two Bass Viols, two Tenor Viols, and two Treble Viols: but a smaller Chest, which was much more common, comprised one Bass, one Tenor, and two Treble Viols. These instruments were severally strung with seven, six, and five strings; and had not the powerful tones of the perfected instruments of the Violin family. The term VIOL may be variously qualified, indicating tonal character; such terms as GRAND VIOL, MAJOR VIOL, MINOR VIOL suggesting themselves.

VIOLA, Ital.—The name properly given to an open labial stop, of 8 ft. and 4 ft. pitch, formed of metal or wood pipes, of small scale, voiced to yield an imitative string-tone of a fuller and richer quality than that of the stop known as the VIOLE D'ORCHESTRE or ORCHESTRAL VIOLIN, 8 FT. The following names are to be found in important Organs. On the Second Manual of the Organ in the Cathedral of Riga, there is a VIOLA DI ALTA, 8 FT.; on the Fourth Manual, a VIOLA TREMOLO, 8 FT.; and in the Schwell-Pedal, a VIOLA, 4 FT. On the First Manual of the Organ in the Cathedral of Vienna, there is a VIOLA MAJOR, 16 FT. In the Organ in the Monastic Church, Weingarten, there is a VIOLA DOUCE, 8 FT.

FORMATION.—The pipes of the VIOLA are usually made of metal, preferably tin, although fine examples have been formed of spotted-metal. The scale should be somewhat larger than that proper for the VIOLIN, 8 FT. The mouths are of medium width, low, and furnished with the harmonic-bridge. The pipes are slotted, and tuned by slides, in preference to coiled or bent tongues. VIOLAS of beautiful quality of tone have been made of wood. A fine example, made by Edmund Schulze, exists in the Choir of the Organ in the Church of St. Peter, Hindley, England. Its scale gives the CC (8 ft.) pipe an internal width of 2⅝ inches and a depth of 3⅝ inches: the mouth is 13/16 inch in height, and furnished with a harmonic-bridge of unusual form, attached immediately above a sunk cap, without the usual supporting ears. The stop speaks on wind of about 2 inches pressure, and its tone is imitative and remarkably effective.

TONE AND REGISTRATION.—It must be obvious to everyone interested in correct and expressive stop nomenclature, that the name VIOLA should be given only to the stop which yields tones imitative of those of the orchestral Viola. But the fact is, that in the large majority of cases the stops to which the name VIOLA has hitherto been given yield no imitative tones, many being less effective in this direction than ordinary SALICIONALS. It is, accordingly, most desirable that in the stop nomenclature of the Organ of the Twentieth Century the name VIOLA should be confined to the stop representing, in the tonal appointment of the Concert-room Organ, the Viola of the orchestra; and that its tone should be as closely imitative as the pipe-maker's and voicer's skill can reach.

In artistic registration, the tones of the VIOLA will be found much more valuable and of wider range in combination than the thinner and more cutting tones of the VIOLIN, especially as that stop has lately been made and voiced. The full and rich tones of the VIOLA, 8 FT., will impart strength and peculiar color to every combination into which they enter. With pure organ-tones and flute-tones, unimitative and imitative, they will produce very beautiful compound tonalities; while they will combine perfectly with the voices of all the softer lingual stops, creating singular and valuable tonal colorings. The VIOLA properly belongs to the String Division of the Concert-room Organ; but it may, with considerable advantage, find a place in other manual divisions, and in any expressive division of the Church Organ.

VIOLA DA GAMBA, Ital.—Fr., VIOLE DE GAMBE.—The only stop in the Organ in the name of which the word *Gamba* can be properly introduced. The name of the stop is derived from the old Viola da Gamba, a large string instrument, and the precursor of the Violoncello; which, like the latter, was supported by the legs of the player, hence the peculiar name. The stop is of 8 ft. pitch, and is formed of open metal pipes of small scale, usually cylindrical in form, but have frequently been made conical, surmounted by a long and slender bell. Owing to the trouble and expense of making pipes of this compound form, they now rarely, if ever, appear in the Organ. See BELL GAMBA. The VIOLA DA GAMBA is to be found in nearly all important German Organs; but it is very seldom of an imitative or refined quality of tone. It exists, of 8 ft. pitch, in most of Walcker's larger instruments, and placed invariably on the First Manual (Great). On that of the Organ in the Cathedral of Riga, the stop is inserted of 16 ft. and 8 ft. pitch. The VIOLE DE GAMBE, 8 FT., appears, often duplicated, in almost all of Cavaillé-Coll's important instruments. In the Organ in the Cathedral of Notre-Dame, it is inserted in both the Grande-Orgue and the Récit. The stop is to be found in numerous English Organs, though rarely in those of recent construction. It has usually been inserted of tenor C compass, as in the Organ in the Foundling Hospital, London, in which it is placed in both the Choir and Swell. The VIOLA DA GAMBA, 8 FT., is inserted in the Choir, Swell, and Solo of the Organ in St. George's Hall, Liverpool; furnishing the only unison string-tone in those divisions of the instrument. Name incorrectly rendered VIOLA DI GAMBA.

TONE AND REGISTRATION.—Properly formed and artistically

voiced, the stop should yield a tone imitating, as closely as practicable, that of the old Viola da Gamba; the tone of which was of a lighter and less expressive quality than that of the Violoncello, to the construction of which it led the way, and before the superiority of which it ultimately fell into disuse. The Viola da Gamba, or Bass Viol, had seven strings tuned in fourths, with a major third between the third and fourth strings. From these facts it will be realized that the voice of the VIOLA DA GAMBA of the Organ should be distinctly subordinate to that of the VIOLONCELLO, 8 FT.; and on account of this tonal subordination it will be of considerable value in artistic registration. Imitative string stops of a powerful and penetrating tonality are of very limited use in registration, save in that of a pronounced orchestral character, or for the production of assertive solo effects. With the DOPPELFLÖTE, ROHRFLÖTE, QUINTATEN, 8 FT., CLARABELA, and other flute-toned stops, the VIOLA DA GAMBA produces compound tones of great beauty and fine color, suitable for both accompanimental and melodic passages.

VIOLA D'AMORE, Ital.—Fr., VIOLE D'AMOUR.—The name given to an open labial stop, of 8 ft. and 4 ft. pitch; formed of very small-scaled pipes of metal (preferably tin), or partly of wood and metal when of 8 ft. pitch. The stop derives its name from the beautiful old instrument called the Viola d'Amore; which is a Tenor Viol, having seven strings played with the bow, and underneath which, passing through the bridge and under the finger-board, are stretched and tuned slender metal strings (from ten to fourteen in number) which sound sympathetically with the bowed strings.

The VIOLA D'AMORE of the Organ is the softest and sweetest of the imitative string-toned stops, and deserves a prominent place in every true Chamber Organ, in which refinement and delicacy of tone is preferred to musical noise. It also should find a place in the Choir or Echo of the properly appointed Church Organ. When formed of metal, the pipes are cylindrical, and are voiced with the harmonic-bridge, or the appliance called the *frein harmonique*. Wood pipes may be used, in the unison stop, from CC to tenor F♯, made either straight or pyramidal, having thin sides of choice spruce and fronts of a close-grained hard wood. The scale of the CC pipe should not exceed 2 inches square. All to be voiced with the harmonic-bridge. The VIOLA D'AMORE is by no means a common stop, preference being given to string-toned stops of more assertive tonality. German examples exist, incorrectly labeled VIOLA D'AMOUR, in the Organs in the Cathedrals of Riga and Lübeck, and St. Petrikirche, Hamburg. A VIOLE D'AMOUR, 4 FT., is inserted in the Récit of the Organ in the Church of Saint-Ouen, Rouen, where it is associated with two unison soft-toned stops, the VOIX ÉOLIENNE and VOIX CÉLESTE. A VIOLE D'AMOUR, 8 FT., and another of 4 ft. pitch exist in the Echo of the Organ in the Centennial Hall, Sydney, N. S. W.

TONE AND REGISTRATION.— When carefully made and voiced by a master-hand, the tone of the stop should closely resemble that of the old Viola d'Amore, thus described by Berlioz: "The quality of the Viole d'Amour is faint and sweet; there is something *seraphic* in it—partaking at once of the Viola and the harmonics of the Violin. It is peculiarly suitable to the legato style, to dreamy melodies, and to the expression of ecstatic or religious feelings." Though it does scant justice to the appealing voice of this unique and beautiful instrument, it is, perhaps, sufficient to convey a fair idea of the peculiar singing tone of the Viola d'Amore to those who have not enjoyed the privilege of hearing the instrument played upon, and studying its complex tonality—the privilege that has been enjoyed, under varied and favorable conditions, by the writer.

It cannot be difficult for the organist, who has given some special attention to the subject of tone creation, to realize the important rôle the VIOLA D'AMORE, with its soft, singing, and sympathetic voice, can play in the production of numerous delicate and beautiful tone-colors, based on foundations of pure organ-tone, produced by such stops as the ECHO DIAPASON and DULCIANA; of flute-tone, produced by the MELODIA, FLAUTO DOLCE and FLAUTO D'AMORE; and of reed-tone, produced by the CHALUMEAU and OBOE D' AMORE. The VIOLA D'AMORE, 8 FT., should be introduced in the String-Organ—Ancillary or otherwise—of every properly appointed Concert-room instrument; and in the Choir of every large Church Organ, where its sympathetic voice will be of the greatest value in accompanimental music.

VIOLA SORDA, Ital.—A stop, of 8 ft. pitch similar in form to, but smaller in scale than, the VIOLA. Its voice is intended to imitate the tone of the muted Viola of the orchestra. If a very subdued intonation, combined with a slight modification of timbre, is desired, the pipes forming the stop may be conical in form: the scale giving the CC (8 ft.) pipe the diameter of 2 inches at the mouth line, and of ⅞ inch at top. Artistically voiced, the tone of this MUTED VIOLA will be found extremely valuable in refined registration. Its proper place is in the String Ancillary of the Concert-room Organ.

VIOLE À PAVILLON, Fr.—The name that has been employed by French organ-builders to designate a string-toned labial stop, of 8 ft. pitch, the pipes of which have conical bodies surmounted by bells (*pavillons*), similar to those of the BELL GAMBA (*q. v.*); and, like them, tuned by means of large flexible ears. The pipes were usually made of tin; and voiced to yield a soft and agreeable string-tone. The stop has fallen into disuse.

VIOLE CÉLESTE, Fr.—The name given to a stop of the VIOL class, of 8 ft. pitch, the pipes of which are tuned sharp so as to produce a bright undulatory effect in combination with another unison stop (preferably of string tone) correctly tuned. As a dual stop, it is properly formed of two softly-voiced VIOLS, of 8 ft. pitch, one of which is tuned a few beats sharp, sufficient to create an agreeable *tremolo*, but not sufficient to produce an objectionable out-of-tune effect. See VOIX CÉLESTE.

VIOLE D'ORCHESTRE, Fr.—Eng., ORCHESTRAL VIOLIN.— The appropriate name given by William Thynne, organ-builder of London, to a stop constructed by him; the tone of which is, in our opinion, the most satisfactory imitation of that of the orchestral Violin which has been produced by organ-pipes up to the present time (1920).* In the construction and voicing, Thynne followed the teaching of Edmund Schulze, but surpassed him in the production of Violin tone from metal pipes. Fine examples of the VIOLE D'OR-CHESTRE exist in Organs built by William Thynne. For further particulars, see VIOLIN.

VIOLE SOURDINE, Fr.—The name given by William Thynne, organ-builder, of London, to a delicately voiced string-toned, open metal stop, the tone of which is imitative of that of the muted Violin. It was first introduced, by its inventor, in the Organ now in Tewkesbury Abbey. The stop is formed of slender cylindrical pipes, smaller in scale than those of the Thynne VIOLE D'ORCHESTRE, but voiced in a similar manner with the harmonic-bridge. The tone of the stop is extremely refined and beautiful; and, on account of its subdued and perfect mixing quality, it may be recognized as the most generally useful of the imitative string-toned stops in artistic registration with stops of contrasting tonalities.

---

* We have had pipes of the Thynne VIOLE D'ORCHESTRE tested, by being sounded with corresponding notes of a fine Violin, under conditions which prevented the hearers from positively knowing which was speaking. It was found impossible to decide which instrument was producing the notes; or, when both were sounded together in unison, which one became silent. No severer test could well be instituted. How many of the stops bearing the name, made by other organ-builders, would stand so exacting a comparison?

Modifications of the Thynne stop, subsequently introduced and appropriately named MUTED VIOLS, are formed of very small-scaled pipes, conical in shape, seldom exceeding, in the CC pipe (8 ft.), 1½ inches in diameter at the mouth line and tapering to about half that diameter at top; having mouths rarely exceeding one-sixth of the circumference, furnished with the harmonic-bridge. Like the original VIOLE SOURDINE, these MUTED VIOLS yield tones of great beauty and value.

VIOLETTA, Ital.—Literally *Small Viol.* The name appropriately given by Italian organ-builders to a string-toned stop, of 4 ft. pitch, the pipes of which are open, cylindrical, of small scale, and made of tin. The stop is properly voiced to yield an imitative tone of medium strength, which is very valuable in combination with the unison stops of imitative string-tone; brilliantly corroborating their first and most important upper partial tones, while enriching them with its own series of less pronounced harmonics. As an Octave, the VIOLETTA, 4 FT., is extremely valuable in artistic registration, imparting a bright and special coloring to all unison tones with which it may be combined. The Organs of to-day are very deficient in stops of 4 ft. pitch; far too much reliance being placed on the crude expedient of octave coupling, which, in its best form, interferes with the desirable independence of the claviers. This is a matter deserving careful consideration.

VIOLIN.—Ital., VIOLINO. Fr., VIOLON. Ger., VIOLINE.—An open, metal labial stop, of 8 ft. pitch, the tone of which imitates, as closely as practicable in organ-pipes, that of the orchestral Violin. This name appears at an early date in stop nomenclature; for in Bernard Smith's "Schedule" of the Organ he erected in the Temple Church, London, in 1688, we find mentioned "A VIOLL and VIOLIN of mettle, 61 pipes, 12 foote tone." The compass being GGG to g³. Notwithstanding the early use of the name, it seems very improbable that the builders of the seventeenth century knew anything of a highly imitative stop, such as we would now consider worthy of representing the Violin in the stop-appointment of the Organ. The modern use of the name appears to be extremely free and meaningless. On one hand, we find in the Pedal Organ of the Schulze instrument in the Church of St. Bartholomew, Armley, a VIOLIN, 16 FT., and, on the other hand, turning to American organ-building, we find in the Choir of the Organ in the Music Hall, Cincinnati a VIOLIN, 4 FT. In fact, neither of these stops can be correctly called a VIOLIN for neither is of proper pitch or imitative in tonality. To prevent confusion, the practice should be adopted of labeling the strictly imitative stop either ORCHESTRAL VIOLIN or VIOLON D'ORCHESTRE, 8 FT. The single terms are not in common use; but we find a VIOLINE, 8 FT., on the First Manual of the Organ in the Cathedral of Ulm, and a VIOLIN, 8 FT., in the Pedal of the Organ in Paulskirche, Frankfurt a. M. Neither of these stops is likely to be strongly imitative.

SCALE AND FORMATION. The variation of the scales which have been adopted in the formation of stops of imitative string-tone is greater than that shown in any other class of labial stops. This statement is supported by the fact that the scales used by William Thynne and other eminent labial pipe voicers for the CC (8 ft.) pipes of their VIOLINS, range from a diameter of 3.13 inches to the small diameter of 1.08 inches; the former scale being developed on the ratio of 1 : 2.519, halving on the nineteenth pipe; and the latter mainly on the ratio 1 : 2, halving on the twenty-fifth pipe. Thynne did not highly favor the adoption of very small scales, and our

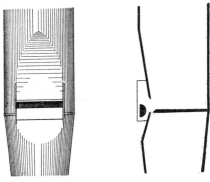

FIG. 35

experience leads us to agree with his practice; for we have never heard VIOLINS equal in fullness, richness, and imitativeness to those voiced by his master-hand. The thin, scratchy, and penetrating tones of the over-blown, small-scaled VIOLINS of certain makers are offensive to the cultivated ear, and of little value in artistic registration.

The pipes of the VIOLIN are invariably cylindrical; and, chiefly on account of their extremely small scale, should be made of tin or very high-grade alloy of tin and lead. They are usually slotted, and tuned by a metal slide in good work. It is very questionable if slotting is favorable to the tone, for it has a tendency to impart a horn-like timbre. The mouths of the pipes vary slightly in their widths. In the largest scale adopted by Thynne, the mouth of the CC pipe is two-ninths its circumference; this width being graduated to one-third the circumference at treble c^2, that proportion being carried to the top note. The heights of the mouths vary between one-fourth and one-third their widths, according to the wind-pressure used, and the character of the tone desired. The VIOLIN has been artistically voiced on pressures varying from $2\frac{1}{2}$ inches to 15 inches. The VIOLIN is invariably, and of necessity, voiced with the harmonic-bridge. In the accompanying illustration, Fig. 35, is shown the mouth of a Thynne C pipe, accurately drawn from one presented to us by its distinguished voicer and long a valued friend. The harmonic-bridge is semi-cylindrical in form, and of hard alloy, is shown in the Section, as carried between the ears, and in its position with regard to the mouth. This position is a matter of extreme nicety. Cylindrical bridges, formed of aluminium tubing or some hard wood, are commonly used by voicers.

TONE AND REGISTRATION.—Accepting the tone of the VIOLIN, 8 FT., to be as close as practicable to that of the Violin of the orchestra, as we have found it to be in certain examples (see VIOLE D'ORCHESTRE), its value in registration will be found in some directions to be considerable, while in others it will be questionable. The distinctive tonality of the stop—so assertive and penetrating—renders it unsuitable for general combinational purposes. With certain labial stops, notably the FLUTES, it will not fully combine; always dominating and asserting its individuality. With other and unimitative string-toned stops it unites agreeably, imparting richness, brightness, and force; creating volumes of string-tone very necessary in orchestral effects: accordingly, its proper place is in the special or Ancillary String Organ, where it joins in producing the volume of orchestral string-tone required in the adequate and artistic rendition of orchestral compositions. On this subject we have some right to speak, having been the first, in the history of organ-building, to introduce a complete and independent String Organ into the tonal appointment of the Organ. The VIOLIN combines well with most of the full-toned lingual stops; largely losing its identity in their somewhat kindred voices, so far as their harmonic structure obtains, which it improves in effectiveness and expressive force. A really fine imitative VIOLIN, 8 FT., is *par excellence* a solo stop, especially valuable in its compass from fiddle G to c^3; above that its imitativeness falls short of what is desirable. The bass and tenor notes from CC to F♯ will never be used in a correctly rendered Violin solo, for these belong to the Viola and Violoncello, but their necessity and utility cannot be denied. Besides, stops of short compass, or formed of pipes of different tonalities in different portions of their compass, are to be condemned from every artistic point of view, whatever argument may be advanced in their favor.

VIOLINA.—The name given by certain organ-builders to a string-toned stop of 4 ft. pitch, similar to that called VIOLETTA, 4 FT. (*q. v.*). Examples exist in the Swell of the Organ in the Music Hall Cincinnati, and in the Swell of the Organ in the Cathedral of the Incarnation, Garden City, Long Island.

VIOLIN DIAPASON.—The term that has been used by English organ-builders to designate an open labial stop, of 8 ft. pitch, similar in all essentials to that more commonly known as the GEIGENPRINCIPAL (*q. v.*).

VIOLINO SORDO, Ital.—Literally *Muted Violin.* A stop, of 8 ft. pitch, similar in form to, but voiced softer than, the VIOLIN. Its voice is intended to imitate the tone of the muted Violin of the orchestra. Under the name VIOLE SOURDINE (*q. v.*)., the stop was first introduced by W. Thynne, of London. As the imitative tone of the VIOLINO SORDO is much less assertive and penetrating than that of the VIOLIN, 8 FT., it is accordingly much more generally useful in registration. It will be found a valuable stop in the soft accompanimental division of the Church Organ, and should find a place in the special or String Ancillary of the Concert-room Organ, where it will be valuable in combinational and delicate solo effects.

VIOLINO VIBRATO, Ital.—A stop of 8 ft. pitch similar in the form and scale of its pipes to the VIOLIN (*q. v.*), but slightly softer in tone; occupying, in this respect, an intermediate place between the VIOLIN and the VIOLINO SORDO (*q. v.*). The distinctive peculiarity of this stop lies in its being tuned a few beats sharp, so as to produce a wavering effect when sounded in combination with a correctly tuned unison string-toned stop. As the VIOLINO VIBRATO occupies a similar place in the tonal scheme of the Organ to the VIOLONCELLO VIBRATO, its offices in the stop-apportionment of the Ancillary String Organ may be considered identical. Such being the case, reference may properly be made to what is said under VIOLONCELLO VIBRATO.

VIOLONCELLO, Ital.—Fr., VIOLONCELLE.—An open labial stop, of 8 ft. pitch, the pipes of which are cylindrical when of metal and square when of wood, voiced to imitate, as closely as practicable in organ-pipes, the tone of the orchestral Violoncello. When made of metal, the pipes are cylindrical and of small scale, but somewhat larger than the scales commonly adopted for the VIOLIN; and are properly voiced to yield a fuller and richer tone than that produced by either the VIOLA or VIOLIN. It is obviously desirable, as it is essential, that these three important unison imitative string-toned stops should have their voices clearly distinct both in volume and quality; otherwise, it would be undesirable to introduce them all in any one Organ. The VIOLONCELLO is the only one of the three which is imitative down to the CC note; and this fact gives it special value both in solo and combinational effects. A very fine VIOLONCELLO, 8 FT., voiced by William Thynne, exists in the Organ built under his directions, now in Tewkesbury Abbey.* This is one of the two finest VIOLONCELLOES we have ever heard in Organs. The most beautiful VIOLONCELLO formed of wood pipes, known to us, is that in the Solo of the Concert-room Organ in the Battersea Polytechnic, London, the work of John W. Whiteley, one of England's most celebrated labial pipe voicers. The pipes of this interesting and unique stop present several novel features deserving the attention of all interested in the formation of imitative string-toned stops.† A VIOLONCELLO, 8 FT., of the ordinary type exists in the Great of the Organ in St. George's Hall, Liverpool.

TONE AND REGISTRATION.—The tone of the VIOLONCELLO being imitative of that of the orchestral Violoncello, it is obvious that its utility in the tonal appointment of the Organ, and especially of the Concert-room Organ, does not admit of question. It is valuable both in solo effects and in registration. As a solo stop, it is to be desired in the Pedal and Solo of the Concert-room Organ; while in the Ancillary String Organ it is indispensable. It has, in some form or other, been usually inserted in the Pedal Organ, and invariably, hitherto, without being given powers of expression, seriously limiting its usefulness. It is remarkable how seldom this beautiful and valuable stop has been introduced on the manual claviers of even large Organs. The tone of a properly formed and voiced VIOLONCELLO is much more valuable in artistic registration than the thinner and more penetrating tone of the VIOLIN; and this fact should not be overlooked in scheming the tonal appointment of an Organ.

VIOLONCELLO SORDO, Ital.—Literally *Muted Violoncello.* A stop, of 8 ft. pitch, similar in form to, but voiced softer than, the VIOLONCELLO. Its tone is intended to imitate that of the muted Violoncello of the orchestra. As the imitative tone of the VIOLONCELLO SORDO is less assertive than that of the VIOLONCELLO, it will be found more generally useful in registration with the softer-toned stops, with which it will form numerous combinations of fine and varied colorings. Drawn with the VIOLONCELLO VIBRATO (*q. v.*),

---

* During the Recital at the Dedication of this Organ, at which we were present, the most beautiful number was a Sacred Song, accompanied by that stop only. The effect produced by the pure soprano voice and the sympathetic and expressive SOLO VIOLONCELLO was one we have never forgotten.

† Full particulars and dimensioned drawings of the formation of the pipes of this stop are given in "The Art of Organ-Building," Vol. II., pp. 475-6; and in "The Organ of the Twentieth Century," pages 447-8, Plate XXIX.

it will produce a beautiful VIOLONCELLE CÉLESTE, 8 FT. The most important place for the VIOLONCELLO SORDO is in the Ancillary String Organ; but, when such a tonal division does not exist, it may be properly inserted in the chief accompanimental division of the Church Organ, or the softest-toned division of the Concert-room Instrument, where it will be valuable in combinational and delicate solo effects.

VIOLONCELLO VIBRATO, Ital.—A stop, of 8 ft. pitch, similar in the form and scale of its pipes to the VIOLONCELLO (q. v.), but slightly softer in tone; properly occupying, in this respect, an intermediate place between the VIOLONCELLO and the VIOLONCELLO SORDO (q. v.). The distinctive peculiarity of the stop under consideration lies in its being so tuned slightly sharp as to produce a wavering effect when sounded in combination with a correctly tuned unison string-toned stop, preferably the VIOLONCELLO SORDO, imitating as closely as possible, under the conditions, the effect of the *vibrato* on the orchestral Violoncello. Drawn with such stops as the VIOLA SORDA, VIOLE SOURDINE, or VIOLA D'AMORE, it forms an effective VIOLONCELLE CÉLESTE. In full combinations of imitative unison and harmonic-corroborating octave, mutation, and compound stops, such as are provided in the proper stop-apportioned Ancillary String Organ, the VIOLONCELLO VIBRATO imparts to the volume of string-tone the nervous force which characterizes the full string effects of the grand orchestra—a forcefulness much to be desired in the adequate and truly artistic rendition of important orchestral compositions, or improvisations of an orchestral character and coloring.

VIOLONE, Ital.—Fr., VIOLON-BASSE.—An open labial stop, of 16 ft. pitch, the pipes of which are of small scale and formed of either metal or wood. It has almost invariably been confined to the Pedal Organ, and when artistically voiced is accepted as the organ equivalent to the Contrabasso of the orchestra; and its excellence is judged in proportion to the closeness of its imitation of the tone of that instrument. Artistic voicers, accordingly, endeavor to impart to their VIOLONES as much of the harmonic richness of the Contrabass as their expedients in formation and skill in voicing can accomplish; aiming also to secure that peculiar rasping effect which imitates the attack of the bow on the string, and which is only heard in the finer specimens of the stop. Although hitherto the VIOLONE, in its proper form and tonality, has been practically confined to the Pedal Organ, it is most desirable that it should find its proper place in the manual

Organs, especially in those of the Concert-room Instrument. As its pipes admit of mitering, it can be accommodated in swell-boxes of the size proper in Organs of large dimensions. When necessary, its lowest octave may be of covered pipes; or, indeed, the stop may be formed of covered pipes throughout.

The ordinary metal VIOLONES, such as exist in important English Organs, are not strongly imitative, and are slightly slow in speech, their notes sounding with more or less of a preparatory rasp. Representative examples exist in the Willis Organ in the Royal Albert Hall, London, and the Hill Organ in Centennial Hall, Sydney, N. S. W. As a rule the VIOLONES of the German builders, commonly named VIOLONBASS, 16 FT., are somewhat tardy in speaking their full tones, and on that account have frequently to be drawn with another and prompt-speaking stop or "helper," such as a softly-toned FLUTE, 8 FT. In the Pedal of the Organ in the Stiftskirche, Stuttgart, the stop, labeled VIOLON, 16 FT., is of two ranks of pipes—the stop proper of 16 ft. and its helper of 8 ft. Under the name VIOLONBASS, 16 FT., the stop exists in the Pedals of the Organs in the Cathedrals of Riga, Ulm, Lübeck, and Frankfurt, and in almost all the important Church Organs built by Walcker. The VIOLON-BASSE, 16 FT., is not a common stop in French Organs, but examples exist in the Pedals of the Organs in the Palais du Trocadéro and the Basilique du Sacré-Cœur, Paris.

The finest and most thoroughly imitative VIOLONE, 16 FT., that we have ever heard, is that in the Pedal of the Organ in the Church of St. Peter, Hindley, Lancashire. The stop is labeled VIOLONBASS; and its pipes are of wood and of small scale, the CCC (16 ft.) pipe measuring, internally, only $5\frac{1}{2}$ inches square.* Another fine example, labeled VIOLON, 16 FT., exists in the Pedal of the large Organ (94 speaking stops) in the Parish Church of Doncaster, Yorkshire, England. Both these Organs were constructed by Edmund Schulze, of Paulinzelle, and the stops alluded to were voiced by him.† In the Organ in the Marienkirche, Lübeck, is another representative example by the same artist.

---

* A full description of the formation of this stop, accompanied by accurate drawings, is given in "The Art of Organ-Building," Vol. II., pp. 470–1; and in "The Organ of the Twentieth Century," pages 443–5.

† In a description of the Doncaster Organ, from the pen of an authority, the following pertinent remarks obtain: "The individuality of the stops is remarkable, and must be ascribed to the artistic feeling possessed by all genuine organ-builders who perform that particular part of the work—the voicing—themselves, and do not delegate so important a branch of the art to workmen who, however skillful, will not on occasions devote the care necessary.

"The wood pipes of this instrument are very solid, clear, and firm in tone; and the muddiness often heard in many Organs from wooden stops, is not perceptible in this. Professor Tœpfer,

VIRGINREGAL.—Ger., Jungfernregal.—An old lingual stop, of 8 ft. and 4 ft. pitch, the tone of which was, in the best examples, soft and pleasing. The origin of the name has not been decided; but it is supposed that the stop was originally in a Portative, and was commonly played by young maidens. An example, of 4 ft. pitch, was inserted in the Pedal of the Organ in the Church of SS. Peter and Paul, Goerlitz, built by Eugenius Casparini & Son, and finished in 1703. Under the name Jungfernregal, the stop appears in the Choir of the Organ, of 71 speaking stops, in the Church of St. Dominico, Prague. According to Hopkins, this stop is of 16 ft. pitch. See Regal.

VOCE FLEBILE, Ital.—Literally *Mournful Voice*. The name given to stops, of 16 ft. pitch, inserted in the Swell of the Organ, of 49 speaking stops, in the Church of St. Alessandro, Milan. The name is expressive of the subdued and colorless character of their tones. We have not found the name in any other Italian Organ.

VOGELFLÖTE, Ger.—Literally *Bird-Flute*. The name given to a flute-toned stop, of 4 ft. pitch, voiced to yield a clear sound, somewhat resembling that of a bird's song. The stop was inserted on the First Manual of the Organ in the Church of Quittelsdorf, constructed by Andreas Schulze, of Paulinzelle, in the year 1791

VOGELGESANG, Ger.—Lat., Avicinium. Port., Passarinhos.—A stop which has been introduced in some old Organs, and which may be classed amongst the curiosities of organ-building. It was devised to imitate the warbling of birds. It was formed of three or more small metal pipes, of different tones, bent, and partly immersed in water.* The stop labeled Passarinhos in the Organ in the Church of the Martyros, Lisbon, built in 1785, is formed of six pipes so disposed. Stops of the class were introduced in several old German Organs.

VOIX CÉLESTE, Fr.—Lat., Vox Cœlestis. Span., Voz Celeste.—The name employed to designate an open labial stop, of 8 ft. pitch, formed of one, two, or three ranks of small-scaled pipes, one or two of the ranks being tuned slightly sharp or flat to the

the author of elaborate works on organ-building, says, 'that wooden pipes in their lower octaves as voiced by Herr Schulze, are as good as, or even superior to, metal pipes.' "

*"Vogelgesang. Unter allen läppischen Spielereien die grösste, indem das Gezwitscher der Vögel nachgeahmt werden sollte!—Welch ein Einfall!! Diess wird auf folgende Art bewerkstelligt: In einem blechernen Kästchen, das mit Wasser gefüllt wird, ragen 3—6 kleine Pfeifchen mit ihrem obern Ende in das Wasser, und geben dann einen gurgelnden, zwitschernden Ton."— W. Schneider (Merseburg, 1835).

correct unison pitch of the Organ in which the stop is inserted. In the large majority of examples, the stop is of one rank only, of either string-toned or pure organ-toned metal pipes, tuned a few beats sharp; which, when combined with another unison stop of correct pitch, produces a peculiar tremulous effect; and which, by a wonderful stretch of the imagination, has been likened to a celestial voice, whatever that may be. In some instances, the single-rank VOIX CÉLESTE has been tuned flat, but its effect is not so satisfactory as in the case of the sharp stop. In our opinion, the flat tuning should be confined to the UNDA MARIS (q. v.). The most important single-rank stops, tuned sharp, are those designed to impart to the volume of sound produced by the massing of imitative string-toned stops the nervous force which characterizes the full string effects of the grand orchestra. See VIOLINO VIBRATO and VIOLONCELLO VIBRATO.

The most satisfactory VOIX CÉLESTE is that formed of two ranks of pipes of special tonality, carefully voiced to produce a pleasing and refined effect, one of which is voiced just sufficiently sharp to create an artistic *tremolo*, not too pronounced. To avoid having to tune one rank too discordant with the correct pitch of the Organ, the discordancy has been divided by tuning one rank very slightly flat and the other rank equally sharp. This variety of the stop is to be preferred. In the Organ in St. Paul's Cathedral, London, reconstructed by Willis, in 1901, there is a VOIX CÉLESTE of three ranks, tuned flat, correct, and sharp. A stop of this formation could be made a valuable timbre-creator.

VOIX ÉOLIENNE, Fr.—The name given by Cavaillé-Coll to a labial stop, of 8 ft. pitch, inserted in the Récit Expressif of the Organ in the beautiful Church of St. Ouen, Rouen. The stop is tuned sharp and according to Philbert was designed to produce undulations of tone when drawn along with the FLÛTE HARMONIQUE, 8 FT.* This seems worthy of notice from the fact that the FLÛTE alluded to is placed in the Grand-Orgue. Such a disposition of the two stops

---

*Alluding to this stop, M. Philbert remarks: "À Saint-Ouen, on rencontre encore un troisième jeu ondulant, la VOIX ÉOLIENNE, destiné à produire l'ondulation avec la FLÛTE HARMONIQUE. Il consiste en une rangée de tuyaux bouchés accordés à battements, et l'effet m'en a paru médiocrement satisfaisant, parce qu'il est un peu lourd. Ce que j'ai vu de mieux comme jeu ondulant destiné à agir sur une FLÛTE ou un BOURDON, c'est le suavial de la Suisse allemande, formé de tuyaux ouverts, de taille à peu près identique à celle du SALICIONAL, mais dont le pied n'admet absolument qu'un filet d'air, de façon que le son propre en est extrêmement faible et se perd pour ainsi dire dans celui du jeu auquel on l'associe. La différence d'accord est en même temps très légère, au point que l'ondulation est à peine perceptible comme battement et ne fait qu'imprimer au timbre de la FLÛTE et surtout du BOURDON comme une teinte cristalline un peu vague réellement suave et empreinte de recueillement. Vogt aimait assez ce jeu et s'en servait habilement."—Causerie sur le Grand Orgue à Saint-Ouen de Rouen, p. 30.

deserves consideration, for it opens a nice question in artistic registration. Doubtless Cavaillé-Coll, the most scientific organ-builder
of his time, realized the possibility of beautiful effects being produced
by the combination of the uniform flute-tone and the changing and
expressive tone of the Voix Éolienne.

VOX ANGELICA, Lat.—Fr., Voix Angélique. Ital., Flauto
Angelico. Ger., Engelstimme.—These names appear to have been
employed to designate stops of any description which yielded some
specially beautiful and refined quality of tone. They have, accordingly, been applied to both labial and lingual stops. When applied
to the former, the term Vox Angelica properly indicates an open
metal labial stop, of 8 ft. pitch, the pipes of which are cylindrical
and of very small scale, voiced to yield the softest unison tone in
the manual department of the Organ. Fine examples of this form,
voiced, on very light wind, by Edmund Schulze, exist in the Echos
of the Organs in the Parish Church of Doncaster and the Church of
St. Bartholomew, Armley, Yorkshire, England. We have been able
to find one example in Walcker's Organs; the Vox Angelica, 4 ft.,
on the Fourth Manual of the Organ in Riga Cathedral. Soft-toned
stops have not been favored by German organ-builders to any note-
worthy extent. The labial Vox Angelica, 8 ft. may be either
organ-toned or string-toned, according as it is voiced to approach
the Dulciana or the Salicional or Viol.

Both Wolfram and Seidel describe the Vox Angelica as a lingual
stop, of 8 ft. pitch, but do not give any particulars respecting its
formation. The former writer, alluding to its tone, says its name is
the best part of it, which, when one thinks of what the lingual stops
were in his day and country, may be readily accepted as a just statement. Clarke, in his "Outline of the Structure of the Pipe-Organ,"
describes the stop as formed of "Free-reed pipes of the most delicate
voicing," giving no further information. In this form it was inserted in the Solo of the Roosevelt Organ erected in the Church of
St. Thomas, New York City. In the same form it exists in the Choir
of the Organ in the Church of St. Paul, Antwerp.*

VOX GRAVISSIMA, Lat.—The appropriate name to designate
the acoustical tone or effect which is produced by the simultaneous
sounding of stops of 32 ft. and 21⅓ ft. pitch, standing at the interval of a perfect fifth apart. It is the differential tone generated by

---

* "L'Angelica (Vox) est la première manière de *Voix humaine;* elle avait sur la nouvelle
l'avantage d'avoir été construite d'après une pensée sinon *angélique,* du moins religieuse et non
purement *humaine.*"—Regnier.

the combination that is the Vox Gravissima, 64 ft. For full particulars see Gravissima.

VOX HUMANA, Lat.—Fr., Voix Humaine. Ital., Voce Umana. Ger., Menschenstimme.—A lingual stop, of 8 ft. pitch, the pipes of which, in the most satisfactory examples, have resonators of cylindrical form, covered at top, and slotted for the emission of wind and sound, and much shorter than the standard lengths of open pipes. Other forms of resonators have been employed with varying and, generally, very unsatisfactory results. The most common form is cylindrical, very short, and entirely open at top; the tones of pipes of this form are generally objectionable. The stop is voiced with the view of producing tones, rich in harmonics, in imitation of the human singing voice; hence the name Vox Humana: but even the best results that have been obtained up to the present time fall far short of what is to be desired. The Vox Humana requires the aid of the Tremolant to impart the characteristic intonation to its voice; and that is greatly improved by the addition of a soft unison, unimitative flute-toned stop, such as the Melodia, 8 ft., which would impart desirable body to the usually thin and nasal voice of the stop. In high-class work, the solo Vox Humana should be a dual stop, permanently formed of the lingual rank, associated with a properly voiced, body-giving, labial rank of unison pitch. If the Vox Humana is properly made and artistically voiced it forms, when drawn without the Tremolant, a valuable stop in registration, imparting a distinctive coloring to soft combinations of contrasting tonalities. The tonal and imitative effects of the Vox Humana depend to a considerable extent on the position it occupies, and the manner in which it is treated in the Organ; and its imitative quality is also greatly affected by the acoustical properties of the building in which the Organ is placed. Of all the stops in the Organ, the Vox Humana is the one to which distance lends the greatest charm. Speaking of this stop, Max Allihn remarks: "The Vox Humana is intended to imitate the human voice, which will only be possible when the stop occupies a distant and covered place within a large instrument in a large room." Alluding to the formation of the stop, he adds: "The blocks and tongues correspond to those proper for an 8 ft. stop of large scale and delicate intonation, but the bodies of the Vox Humana pipes are of quite different proportions and form. Definite measurements or forms do not exist. Every organ-builder follows his own predilection and experience. Some use short cylindrical bodies, closed at top with the exception of a small opening; others make larger bodies with larger openings; while others prefer conical bodies closed with the exception of a small lateral opening. All treatments are alike in that the bodies are more or less covered."

TONE AND REGISTRATION.—There can be no question that the only desirable tone for the VOX HUMANA is that which, when combined with the *tremolo*, is as satisfactory as possible in its imitation of a human voice; and, when used without the *tremolo*, is perfectly suited for combination and artistic registration. That such a stop can be produced we have had ample proof. We inserted in our own Chamber Organ a VOCE UMANA, 8 FT., made by a most skillful and artistic voicer—E. Franklin Lloyd, of Liverpool—which was eminently satisfactory under both conditions. Mr. Clarence Eddy, the distinguished organist, in a written criticism of our Organ, says: " The reeds are exceptionally fine; and it would be difficult to find so satisfactory a VOX HUMANA; while its accessory, the Tremolo, is absolutely perfect." Mr. Eddy judged the stop while seated at the claviers, not ten feet distant from its pipes and the TREMOLANT. Apart from the TREMOLANT, the stop proved in combination as useful as any of the other four lingual stops Mr. Eddy has alluded to; while as a timbre-creator and color-giver it occupied the first place in registration. Played, alone, in full chords its tones were rich and beautiful. Such, in our opinion, the artistically voiced VOX HUMANA should be in every Organ.

The VOX HUMANA, of the tonality alluded to, enters into effective combination with all the softer-voiced labial and lingual stops of unison pitch; giving a special coloring to the tones of stops more assertive than itself, and intensity and fullness to the tones of stops of its own value. It combines perfectly with such lingual stops as the OBOE, CLARINET, COR ANGLAIS, and FAGOTTO, warming and enriching their voices; with string-toned stops it produces refined and effective compound tones rich in harmonics; and with open, half-covered, and covered flute-toned stops it produces a family of compound tones of beautiful colorings. Considering its value in artistic registration, the VOX HUMANA should find a place in all Organs of any pretensions. Its position on the claviers may vary; but it is imperative that it be placed in an expressive division. In the properly stop-apportioned Concert-room Organ, it should certainly find a place in the wood-wind division, and also in one of the soft-toned accompanimental divisions.*

* See " The Organ of the Twentieth Century," pages 307, 329, 334, 483, 505, and 506.

VOX MYSTICA.—The name given to a lingual stop, of 8 ft. pitch, the pipes of which have cylindrical resonators surmounted by a bell which is slotted. The tone of the stop is a modification of that of a Vox Humana. The stop exists in the Echo of the Concert-room Organ in the Colston Hall, Bristol, constructed by Norman & Beard in 1905.

VOX RETUSA, Lat.—Literally *Dull Voice*. The name given to a labial covered stop of subdued tone which exists in the Organ in the Cathedral of Lund, Sweden.*

VOX VINOLATA, Lat.—A very remarkable name given to a labial stop, of 8 ft. pitch, the pipes of which are of metal and conical in form, resembling the Spitzflöte. The apparently unique example of the stop exists in the Organ in the Cathedral of Lund, Sweden.†

W

WALDFLÖTE, FELDFLÖTE, Ger.—Lat., Tibia Sylvestris. Fr., Flûte des Bois. Dtch., Woudfluit.—Literally *Forest Flute*. An open labial stop, of 8 ft., 4 ft., and, rarely, of 2 ft., and 1 ft. pitch, the pipes of which are of large scale, and of either wood or metal, preferably of the former material. The Waldflöte (under its mixed name Wald Flute) appears in numerous English Organs, of 8 ft. or 4 ft. pitch, but very rarely of both pitches in the same Organ. An instance, however, obtains of the insertion of both stops, in the Great of the Organ in the Church of St. Matthew, Northampton. As a rule, English organ-builders prefer the stop of 4 ft. pitch, commonly inserting it in the Choir Organ. In the instruments made by Walker & Sons, of London, the Waldflöte, 8 ft., is almost invariably inserted in their Great divisions. In several important German Organs, the stop of 2 ft. pitch is to be found, as on the Second Manual of the Organ in the Cathedral of Riga, and on the First Manual of the Organ in the Cathedral of Ulm. We have not been able to find an instance of the insertion of the stop of 1 ft. pitch, although Seidel and others say that it is made of that high pitch.

---

* "Vox Retusa, 8' von Zinn ist ein Flötenregister, welches im obersten Manual der Domor-gel zu Lund in Schweden vorhanden ist. Retusa ist eine veraltete Benennung welche eine ge-dämpfte Stimme anzeigt. Ein ähnlicher, aber richtiger Ausdruck ist das schon erwähnte Ob-tusa."—Seidel.

† "Vox Vinolata, 8' von Metall, spitz aufwärts, von enger Mensur und schwacher Intona-tion, ist ein Flötenwerk im 3 (Ober-) Manual der Domorgel zu Lund. Wie der Ausdruck vi-nolata zu einem Orgelregister passt, dürfte schwer zu enträtseln sein."—Seidel.

SCALE AND FORMATION.—The WALDFLÖTE is not only made of different pitches but also of different forms and materials, and, necessarily, of different scales. Both German and French authorities describe it of large scale.* In German and French Organs the stop is to be found either of metal or wood; and, when of the former, of either a cylindrical or conical form. An example of the latter form exists on the Third Manual of the Schulze Organ in the Marienkirche, Lübeck. It is of tin and of 2 ft. pitch. In English Organs, the WALDFLÖTE, of 8 ft. or 4 ft. pitch, is invariably of wood and of the usual quadrangular form, deeper than wide. It is understood to have been first made in England by William Hill, of London, in 1841, and since then has been commonly made by all English organ-builders, its tonal value having been fully recognized. In the 8 ft. stop, the bass and tenor octaves were commonly of covered pipes; but in later and better examples the covered pipes are confined to the bass octave. In the 4 ft. stop no covered pipes should be introduced. The mouth of the English WALDFLÖTE pipe is inverted, placed on the narrow side, and usually cut up about one-third its width in height. In some examples the upper lip is cut thin, while in others it is somewhat thick, and carefully rounded and burnished, preferably with plumbago. In the best examples the block is depressed below the lower lip, the distance being equal to one-third the width of the mouth; this distance varies and influences the tonality to some extent. The front of the pipe, in which the inverted mouth is cut, should be of either close-grained mahogany or maple. The pipe is tuned by a metal shade at top, but it should be so accurately cut to length as to require fine tuning only by means of the shade. The entire stop must be very carefully regulated.

TONE AND REGISTRATION.—As the WALDFLÖTE is made of different forms and materials, it naturally follows that there are considerable differences in its tonality. These differences are marked between the stops of German and English formation and voicing. Seidel describes the tone as nothing peculiar, being rather broad, woody, and hollow. This is not descriptive of the voice of the proper English WALDFLÖTE, which is of unimitative flute-tone, peculiarly sweet, and inclining, in some fine examples, to a horn-like coloring. It is this compound tonality which renders the stop so valuable in combination and artistic registration. When artistically voiced, the stop, in both its 8 ft. and 4 ft. pitches, is valuable in solo passages if they are not too lengthy. In combination with the softer-toned lingual and the string-toned stops it produces beautiful and varied colorings of great artistic value and expression. Such being the case, it would seem very desirable to insert the stop in some soft and expressive division of the Organ: yet it is strange to find it inserted,

*"WALDFLÖTE, WALDPFEIFE, Tibia sylvestris, ist ein offenes weit mensuriertes Flötenwerk von Zinn, Metall, zuweilen auch von Holz, 8, 4, 2 und 1'. Die Intonation dieser Stimme is nicht sonderlich, denn sie ist breit-, hölzern-, und hohl-klingend."—Seidel.
"La FLÛTE DES BOIS (Waldflæte), de grosse taille, en étoffe, quelquefois même en bois, se fait depuis huit-pieds jusqu'à un pied. Elle ne se distingue guère de la Hohlflæte ni de la Holzflæte, dont elle a tour à tour et parfois tout ensemble la double caractère. C'est peut-être parce qu'elle n'a rien d'assez tranché qu'elle devient chaque jour plus rare."—Regnier.

apparently without exception, in the unexpressive Greats of Walker & Sons' important Organs, including that in York Minster, reconstructed in 1903. In the Concert-room Organ, WALDFLÖTES, of 8 ft. and 4 ft. pitch, would prove of great value in the expressive division chiefly devoted to the stops representing the brass-wind forces of the grand orchestra. In such a situation they would have to be of large scale and full intonation, voiced on wind of not less than 6 inches' pressure. To the voice of the HORN that of the WALDFLÖTE will impart richness, smoothness, and an increase of orchestral character: while, in registration with the other necessary labial stops of the division, it will create numerous valuable compound tonalities and colorings with or without the impressive lingual stops properly apportioned to the division.

WALDHORN, Ger.—The name given to a lingual stop, the voice of which is intended to imitate in its tonality that of the old Hunting Horn. It seems to have been made of 8 ft., 4 ft., and 2 ft. pitch;* but it appears that the imitative quality was confined to the 8 ft. stop or only the lower portion of its compass. On the Third Manual of the Organ in the Cathedral of Lund, Sweden, we find the stop labeled WALDHORN, BASS—CLARINETTE, DISCANT, 8 FT. This would clearly indicate that in this stop the WALDHORN portion is of a Bass Clarinet tonality: accordingly, the voice of the stop can have no relation to that of the Hunting Horn or Cor de Chasse. Whatever the tonal value of the Lund Organ stop may be; it may be safely said that a strictly imitative WALDHORN would not be desirable in the Organ of to-day.

WALDQUINTE, Ger.—This stop is mentioned by Seidel, Regnier, and Schlimbach. It has been made of 5⅓ ft., 2⅔ ft., and 1⅓ ft. pitch; but Seidel says that in Organs constructed in his time it was very seldom inserted. This would appear to have been the case, for we have failed to find a single record of the insertion of a WALDQUINTE in any Organ. Wolfram (1815) and Schlimbach describe the stop as similar in form and tonality to the WALDFLÖTE.

WEIDENFLÖTE, WEIDENPFEIFE, Ger.—Literally *Willow*

---

*"WALDHORN, Cornetto di Caccia, Cornu par force, C. sylvestre, Cors de chasse, sind Benennungen eines seltenen Rohrwerkes, welches zu 8, 4 und 2' im Pedal und Manual vorkommt und den Ton des gleichnamigen Blasinstruments nachahmen soll. Bis jetzt dürfte diese Stimme wohl noch keinem Orgelbauer gelungen sein. Musikdirektor Wilke ist der Meinung, dass der Charakter des Waldhorns eher durch Labialpfeifen als durch Zungenstimmen zu erzielen sei und zwar durch die, in der Pfarrkirche zu Neu-Ruppin stehende Stimme FLUTTUAN, deren Klang dem Waldhornton sehr nahe kommt."—Seidel-Kothe.

Flute. The name that has been used to designate a metal labial stop of extremely small scale and soft intonation. Its name would imply a flute-tone, which was probably somewhat indeterminate in its character. Such a stop would be suitable for a true Chamber Organ, or for insertion in an Echo or Ancillary Aërial Organ.

WIENERFLÖTE, Ger.—Literally *Vienna Flute.* Locher says this stop "is one of the most charming wood flutes, intonated rather brighter than the FLAUTO DOLCE. As a rule, it occurs on one of the upper manuals as an 8 ft. or 4 ft. solo stop, more particularly in Swiss Organs. . . . The denomination 'WIENERFLÖTE' lacks all etymological or historical foundation. In the new [1888] Votiv Organ, although this stands in Vienna itself, there is not a single WIENERFLÖTE amongst its sixty-one speaking stops." On the Third Manual of the Walcker Organ in the Cathedral of Vienna there is a WIENERFLÖTE, 8 FT. Another example exists on the Third Manual of the Organ in the Cathedral of Riga.

Carl Locher, Chief Organist of the Catholic Church, at Berne, who had favorable opportunities of judging the tonal value of the stop, remarks: "WIENERFLÖTE is one of the most useful stops on the upper manuals, not only as a solo, but also for combination with any other stop. I found it particularly beautiful in combination with the OBOE and FLAUTO TRAVERSO." It has been generally understood that the tone of the WIENERFLÖTE closely resembled the imitative tone of the FLAUTO TRAVERSO; but Locher's example of effective combination would seem to indicate a different tonality; unless the combination of the labial stops merely increased the imitative flute-tone.

The pipes of the WIENERFLÖTE are open, quadrangular, and have inverted circular or semicircular mouths, partly over or against which are adjusted sloping caps. Such a formation would point to the production of an imitative quality of flute-tone, but not so pronounced as that of the harmonic FLAUTO TRAVERSO, nor so valuable in solo effects or registration.

X

XYLOPHONE.—A percussion musical instrument recently introduced as a stop in certain Organs. Fine examples are made in this country by the Kohler-Liebich Co., and by J. C. Deagan, both of Chicago. The XYLOPHONE, made by the former firm, is constructed of four octaves, chromatic, of Rosewood bars, graduated

in size, and adjusted over properly tuned cylindrical metal resonators. The percussion action is electrically operated from the clavier
of any Organ in which the stop is placed. Stops of this class are
not suited for the dignified Church Organ.

Z

ZARTFLÖTE, Ger.—The stop bearing this name was, according
to Seidel, invented by the organ-builder Friedr. Turley, who first
called it a GAMBA; but as its tone was of a soft and refined fluty
quality rather than of a string character, Musikdirektor Wilke ad-
vised its inventor to adopt the more expressive name ZARTFLÖTE.
The stop is formed of small-scaled open pipes, usually of wood,
voiced to yield an extremely tender flute-tone; hence its name. It
has been made of both 8 ft. and 4 ft. pitch. As a stop of 8 ft. pitch
it is inserted in the Swell of the Organ in the Marienkirche, Wismar;
and as a wood stop, of 4 ft. pitch, it is to be found in the Echo of
the Schulze Organ in the Marienkirche, Lübeck. In the Echo of the
fine Organ in the Church of St. Bartholomew, Armley, Yorkshire,
built by Edmund Schulze, there is a ZARTFLÖTE, 4 FT., formed of
conical metal pipes from tenor C to c⁴. The bass octave is of small-
scaled wood pipes. This stop speaks on wind of 1½ inches, and has
a voice of an extremely soft and refined flute-tone. We do not find
the ZARTFLÖTE in any of Walcker's important Organs. A ZART-
FLÖTE, 8 FT., the pipes of which are of pine and pear-tree, exists on
the Fourth Manual of the Ladegast Organ in the Cathedral of
Schwerin. The stop is to be found in some English Organs; usually
of 4 ft. pitch, and inserted in the Choir or Swell.

The name ZARTFLÖTE has been used by John W. Whitely to
designate a beautiful stop invented by him in 1896. This stop, of
8 ft. and 4 ft. pitch, is formed of covered metal pipes with projecting ears carrying cylindrical aluminium harmonic-bridges. The
stop is a modification of the QUINTATEN, with every trace of coarseness removed.* Its voice is a light, bright, flute-tone, with sufficient
reedy quality to impart to it a distinctive tonal coloring. A stop of
this beautiful tonality would be of the greatest value in the soft
divisions of the Organ; contributing largely to refined and artistic
registration.

ZARTGEDECKT, Ger.—The name that has been used to designate a covered stop of wood or metal, of 8 ft. pitch, yielding an unimi-

---

* Full particulars, with illustration, of this stop are given in "The Art of Organ-Building,"
Vol. II., p. 549; and in "The Organ of the Twentieth Century," pages 391-2.

tative flute-tone softer and sweeter than that of the LIEBLICH-
GEDECKT, 8 FT. The stop requires, for the production of its characteristic voice— free of any pronounced harmonic—to be voiced on
wind of very low pressure, preferably 1½ inches. This stop is in all
essentials similar to the STILLGEDECKT (*q. v.*).

ZAUBERFLÖTE, Ger.—Literally *Magic Flute.* A covered
harmonic stop, invented by William Thynne, of London, and first
introduced by him in the Organ installed in the Inventions Exhibition, at South Kensington, London; and which was afterwards
erected in Tewkesbury Abbey. It is of 4 ft. pitch, and is inserted in
the Choir of the Organ. In the ZAUBERFLÖTE, 4 FT., in the Organ
in the Church of St. John, Richmond, Surrey, the harmonic pipes
commence at tenor C; and, as they are covered, they speak their
first harmonic, or the second upper partial tone—the Twelfth. To
prevent its speaking the prime tone, or that proper to its length,
each pipe is pierced with a small hole, as in the case of the open pipes
of the FLÛTE HARMONIQUE. The ZAUBERFLÖTE was made of both
8 ft. and 4 ft. pitch. When of the former pitch, the bass octave was
formed of covered wood pipes, voiced to carry down the characteristic tone of the harmonic portion of the stop as closely as possible,
but by no means satisfactorily, as can be supposed.*

TONE AND REGISTRATION.—The tone of the ZAUBERFLÖTE, as
voiced by its inventor, is *sui generis* and of a very refined and sympathetic character, highly appreciated by those endowed with ears
sensitive to tonal values. In artistic registration it is of great value;
and as an OCTAVE, it lends itself to the production of a series of
effective tonal colorings in combination with the softer string-toned
labial and reed-toned lingual stops; imparting a distinctive harmonic
structure to all dual combinations in which it is introduced, and to
which it gives a special brilliancy and vivid coloring. The stop is,
accordingly, of the greatest value in its 4 ft. pitch; and this fact its
inventor realized, as we know. He was for several years our valued
friend.

ZINK, ZINKEN, Ger.—A lingual stop made by the old German
organ-builders, and intended to imitate the tone of the obsolete
wind instrument known as the Zinken, or by the Italian name Cornetto Curvo and the French name Cornet-á-Bouquin. Describing

---

* Full particulars, with illustration, of the formation of this stop are given in "The Art of
Organ-Building," Vol. II., pp. 546–7; and in "The Organ of the Twentieth Century," pages
389–90.

the instrument, Carl Engel says: " Although the *Zinken* is blown through a mouth-tube somewhat similar to that of a trumpet, it has finger-holes like a flute. Its sound is harsh, and would be unpleasant in a room, but the *Zinken* was intended for the open air, and for performing chorales on the towers of churches, so that all the people in the town could hear the solemn music. They were, in fact, compelled to hear, for it vibrated through the air over their heads like the church bells themselves. Thus the *Zinken* may have served its purpose well in olden time, notwithstanding its harshness of sound." The organ ZINKEN was, apparently, a lingual stop, of 2 ft. pitch, having a strident voice, and finding its place in the Pedal Organ. Under the Dutch term, CINQ, 2 FT., stops of the class exist in the Pedals of the Organs in the Cathedral of St. Bavon, Haarlem, the Cathedral of St. Lawrence, Rotterdam, and other important Churches in Holland. In the Pedal of the Organ in the principal Protestant Church in Utrecht, built in 1826, there is, in addition to the CINQ, 2 FT., a CLARION, I FT.

A CATALOG OF SELECTED
DOVER BOOKS
IN ALL FIELDS OF INTEREST

A CATALOG OF SELECTED DOVER
BOOKS IN ALL FIELDS OF INTEREST

CONCERNING THE SPIRITUAL IN ART, Wassily Kandinsky. Pioneering work by father of abstract art. Thoughts on color theory, nature of art. Analysis of earlier masters. 12 illustrations. 80pp. of text. 5⅜ x 8½.   0-486-23411-8

CELTIC ART: The Methods of Construction, George Bain. Simple geometric techniques for making Celtic interlacements, spirals, Kells-type initials, animals, humans, etc. Over 500 illustrations. 160pp. 9 x 12. (Available in U.S. only.)   0-486-22923-8

AN ATLAS OF ANATOMY FOR ARTISTS, Fritz Schider. Most thorough reference work on art anatomy in the world. Hundreds of illustrations, including selections from works by Vesalius, Leonardo, Goya, Ingres, Michelangelo, others. 593 illustrations. 192pp. 7⅛ x 10¼.   0-486-20241-0

CELTIC HAND STROKE-BY-STROKE (Irish Half-Uncial from "The Book of Kells"): An Arthur Baker Calligraphy Manual, Arthur Baker. Complete guide to creating each letter of the alphabet in distinctive Celtic manner. Covers hand position, strokes, pens, inks, paper, more. Illustrated. 48pp. 8¼ x 11.   0-486-24336-2

EASY ORIGAMI, John Montroll. Charming collection of 32 projects (hat, cup, pelican, piano, swan, many more) specially designed for the novice origami hobbyist. Clearly illustrated easy-to-follow instructions insure that even beginning papercrafters will achieve successful results. 48pp. 8¼ x 11.   0-486-27298-2

BLOOMINGDALE'S ILLUSTRATED 1886 CATALOG: Fashions, Dry Goods and Housewares, Bloomingdale Brothers. Famed merchants' extremely rare catalog depicting about 1,700 products: clothing, housewares, firearms, dry goods, jewelry, more. Invaluable for dating, identifying vintage items. Also, copyright-free graphics for artists, designers. Co-published with Henry Ford Museum & Greenfield Village. 160pp. 8¼ x 11.   0-486-25780-0

THE ART OF WORLDLY WISDOM, Baltasar Gracian. "Think with the few and speak with the many," "Friends are a second existence," and "Be able to forget" are among this 1637 volume's 300 pithy maxims. A perfect source of mental and spiritual refreshment, it can be opened at random and appreciated either in brief or at length. 128pp. 5⅜ x 8½.   0-486-44034-6

JOHNSON'S DICTIONARY: A Modern Selection, Samuel Johnson (E. L. McAdam and George Milne, eds.). This modern version reduces the original 1755 edition's 2,300 pages of definitions and literary examples to a more manageable length, retaining the verbal pleasure and historical curiosity of the original. 480pp. 5³⁄₁₆ x 8¼.   0-486-44089-3

ADVENTURES OF HUCKLEBERRY FINN, Mark Twain, Illustrated by E. W. Kemble. A work of eternal richness and complexity, a source of ongoing critical debate, and a literary landmark, Twain's 1885 masterpiece about a barefoot boy's journey of self-discovery has enthralled readers around the world. This handsome clothbound reproduction of the first edition features all 174 of the original black-and-white illustrations. 368pp. 5⅜ x 8½.   0-486-44322-1

STICKLEY CRAFTSMAN FURNITURE CATALOGS, Gustav Stickley and L. & J. G. Stickley. Beautiful, functional furniture in two authentic catalogs from 1910. 594 illustrations, including 277 photos, show settles, rockers, armchairs, reclining chairs, bookcases, desks, tables. 183pp. 6½ x 9¼. 0-486-23838-5

AMERICAN LOCOMOTIVES IN HISTORIC PHOTOGRAPHS: 1858 to 1949, Ron Ziel (ed.). A rare collection of 126 meticulously detailed official photographs, called "builder portraits," of American locomotives that majestically chronicle the rise of steam locomotive power in America. Introduction. Detailed captions. xi+ 129pp. 9 x 12. 0-486-27393-8

AMERICA'S LIGHTHOUSES: An Illustrated History, Francis Ross Holland, Jr. Delightfully written, profusely illustrated fact-filled survey of over 200 American lighthouses since 1716. History, anecdotes, technological advances, more. 240pp. 8 x 10¾. 0-486-25576-X

TOWARDS A NEW ARCHITECTURE, Le Corbusier. Pioneering manifesto by founder of "International School." Technical and aesthetic theories, views of industry, economics, relation of form to function, "mass-production split" and much more. Profusely illustrated. 320pp. 6⅛ x 9¼. (Available in U.S. only.) 0-486-25023-7

HOW THE OTHER HALF LIVES, Jacob Riis. Famous journalistic record, exposing poverty and degradation of New York slums around 1900, by major social reformer. 100 striking and influential photographs. 233pp. 10 x 7⅞. 0-486-22012-5

FRUIT KEY AND TWIG KEY TO TREES AND SHRUBS, William M. Harlow. One of the handiest and most widely used identification aids. Fruit key covers 120 deciduous and evergreen species; twig key 160 deciduous species. Easily used. Over 300 photographs. 126pp. 5⅜ x 8½. 0-486-20511-8

COMMON BIRD SONGS, Dr. Donald J. Borror. Songs of 60 most common U.S. birds: robins, sparrows, cardinals, bluejays, finches, more–arranged in order of increasing complexity. Up to 9 variations of songs of each species.
Cassette and manual 0-486-99911-4

ORCHIDS AS HOUSE PLANTS, Rebecca Tyson Northen. Grow cattleyas and many other kinds of orchids–in a window, in a case, or under artificial light. 63 illustrations. 148pp. 5⅜ x 8½. 0-486-23261-1

MONSTER MAZES, Dave Phillips. Masterful mazes at four levels of difficulty. Avoid deadly perils and evil creatures to find magical treasures. Solutions for all 32 exciting illustrated puzzles. 48pp. 8¼ x 11. 0-486-26005-4

MOZART'S DON GIOVANNI (DOVER OPERA LIBRETTO SERIES), Wolfgang Amadeus Mozart. Introduced and translated by Ellen H. Bleiler. Standard Italian libretto, with complete English translation. Convenient and thoroughly portable–an ideal companion for reading along with a recording or the performance itself. Introduction. List of characters. Plot summary. 121pp. 5¼ x 8½. 0-486-24944-1

FRANK LLOYD WRIGHT'S DANA HOUSE, Donald Hoffmann. Pictorial essay of residential masterpiece with over 160 interior and exterior photos, plans, elevations, sketches and studies. 128pp. 9¼ x 10¾. 0-486-29120-0

THE CLARINET AND CLARINET PLAYING, David Pino. Lively, comprehensive work features suggestions about technique, musicianship, and musical interpretation, as well as guidelines for teaching, making your own reeds, and preparing for public performance. Includes an intriguing look at clarinet history. "A godsend," *The Clarinet*, Journal of the International Clarinet Society. Appendixes. 7 illus. 320pp. 5⅜ x 8½.
0-486-40270-3

HOLLYWOOD GLAMOR PORTRAITS, John Kobal (ed.). 145 photos from 1926-49. Harlow, Gable, Bogart, Bacall; 94 stars in all. Full background on photographers, technical aspects. 160pp. 8⅜ x 11¼.
0-486-23352-9

THE RAVEN AND OTHER FAVORITE POEMS, Edgar Allan Poe. Over 40 of the author's most memorable poems: "The Bells," "Ulalume," "Israfel," "To Helen," "The Conqueror Worm," "Eldorado," "Annabel Lee," many more. Alphabetic lists of titles and first lines. 64pp. 5$^{3}/_{16}$ x 8¼.
0-486-26685-0

PERSONAL MEMOIRS OF U. S. GRANT, Ulysses Simpson Grant. Intelligent, deeply moving firsthand account of Civil War campaigns, considered by many the finest military memoirs ever written. Includes letters, historic photographs, maps and more. 528pp. 6⅛ x 9¼.
0-486-28587-1

ANCIENT EGYPTIAN MATERIALS AND INDUSTRIES, A. Lucas and J. Harris. Fascinating, comprehensive, thoroughly documented text describes this ancient civilization's vast resources and the processes that incorporated them in daily life, including the use of animal products, building materials, cosmetics, perfumes and incense, fibers, glazed ware, glass and its manufacture, materials used in the mummification process, and much more. 544pp. 6⅛ x 9¼. (Available in U.S. only.)
0-486-40446-3

RUSSIAN STORIES/RUSSKIE RASSKAZY: A Dual-Language Book, edited by Gleb Struve. Twelve tales by such masters as Chekhov, Tolstoy, Dostoevsky, Pushkin, others. Excellent word-for-word English translations on facing pages, plus teaching and study aids, Russian/English vocabulary, biographical/critical introductions, more. 416pp. 5⅜ x 8½.
0-486-26244-8

PHILADELPHIA THEN AND NOW: 60 Sites Photographed in the Past and Present, Kenneth Finkel and Susan Oyama. Rare photographs of City Hall, Logan Square, Independence Hall, Betsy Ross House, other landmarks juxtaposed with contemporary views. Captures changing face of historic city. Introduction. Captions. 128pp. 8¼ x 11.
0-486-25790-8

NORTH AMERICAN INDIAN LIFE: Customs and Traditions of 23 Tribes, Elsie Clews Parsons (ed.). 27 fictionalized essays by noted anthropologists examine religion, customs, government, additional facets of life among the Winnebago, Crow, Zuni, Eskimo, other tribes. 480pp. 6⅛ x 9¼.
0-486-27377-6

TECHNICAL MANUAL AND DICTIONARY OF CLASSICAL BALLET, Gail Grant. Defines, explains, comments on steps, movements, poses and concepts. 15-page pictorial section. Basic book for student, viewer. 127pp. 5⅜ x 8½.
0-486-21843-0

THE MALE AND FEMALE FIGURE IN MOTION: 60 Classic Photographic Sequences, Eadweard Muybridge. 60 true-action photographs of men and women walking, running, climbing, bending, turning, etc., reproduced from rare 19th-century masterpiece. vi + 121pp. 9 x 12.
0-486-24745-7

ANIMALS: 1,419 Copyright-Free Illustrations of Mammals, Birds, Fish, Insects, etc., Jim Harter (ed.). Clear wood engravings present, in extremely lifelike poses, over 1,000 species of animals. One of the most extensive pictorial sourcebooks of its kind. Captions. Index. 284pp. 9 x 12. 0-486-23766-4

1001 QUESTIONS ANSWERED ABOUT THE SEASHORE, N. J. Berrill and Jacquelyn Berrill. Queries answered about dolphins, sea snails, sponges, starfish, fishes, shore birds, many others. Covers appearance, breeding, growth, feeding, much more. 305pp. 5¼ x 8¼. 0-486-23366-9

ATTRACTING BIRDS TO YOUR YARD, William J. Weber. Easy-to-follow guide offers advice on how to attract the greatest diversity of birds: birdhouses, feeders, water and waterers, much more. 96pp. 5³⁄₁₆ x 8¼. 0-486-28927-3

MEDICINAL AND OTHER USES OF NORTH AMERICAN PLANTS: A Historical Survey with Special Reference to the Eastern Indian Tribes, Charlotte Erichsen-Brown. Chronological historical citations document 500 years of usage of plants, trees, shrubs native to eastern Canada, northeastern U.S. Also complete identifying information. 343 illustrations. 544pp. 6½ x 9¼. 0-486-25951-X

STORYBOOK MAZES, Dave Phillips. 23 stories and mazes on two-page spreads: Wizard of Oz, Treasure Island, Robin Hood, etc. Solutions. 64pp. 8¼ x 11. 0-486-23628-5

AMERICAN NEGRO SONGS: 230 Folk Songs and Spirituals, Religious and Secular, John W. Work. This authoritative study traces the African influences of songs sung and played by black Americans at work, in church, and as entertainment. The author discusses the lyric significance of such songs as "Swing Low, Sweet Chariot," "John Henry," and others and offers the words and music for 230 songs. Bibliography. Index of Song Titles. 272pp. 6½ x 9¼. 0-486-40271-1

MOVIE-STAR PORTRAITS OF THE FORTIES, John Kobal (ed.). 163 glamor, studio photos of 106 stars of the 1940s: Rita Hayworth, Ava Gardner, Marlon Brando, Clark Gable, many more. 176pp. 8⅜ x 11¼. 0-486-23546-7

YEKL and THE IMPORTED BRIDEGROOM AND OTHER STORIES OF YIDDISH NEW YORK, Abraham Cahan. Film Hester Street based on *Yekl* (1896). Novel, other stories among first about Jewish immigrants on N.Y.'s East Side. 240pp. 5⅜ x 8½. 0-486-22427-9

SELECTED POEMS, Walt Whitman. Generous sampling from *Leaves of Grass*. Twenty-four poems include "I Hear America Singing," "Song of the Open Road," "I Sing the Body Electric," "When Lilacs Last in the Dooryard Bloom'd," "O Captain! My Captain!"–all reprinted from an authoritative edition. Lists of titles and first lines. 128pp. 5³⁄₁₆ x 8¼. 0-486-26878-0

SONGS OF EXPERIENCE: Facsimile Reproduction with 26 Plates in Full Color, William Blake. 26 full-color plates from a rare 1826 edition. Includes "The Tyger," "London," "Holy Thursday," and other poems. Printed text of poems. 48pp. 5¼ x 7. 0-486-24636-1

THE BEST TALES OF HOFFMANN, E. T. A. Hoffmann. 10 of Hoffmann's most important stories: "Nutcracker and the King of Mice," "The Golden Flowerpot," etc. 458pp. 5⅜ x 8½. 0-486-21793-0

THE BOOK OF TEA, Kakuzo Okakura. Minor classic of the Orient: entertaining, charming explanation, interpretation of traditional Japanese culture in terms of tea ceremony. 94pp. 5⅜ x 8½. 0-486-20070-1

FRENCH STORIES/CONTES FRANÇAIS: A Dual-Language Book, Wallace Fowlie. Ten stories by French masters, Voltaire to Camus: "Micromegas" by Voltaire; "The Atheist's Mass" by Balzac; "Minuet" by de Maupassant; "The Guest" by Camus, six more. Excellent English translations on facing pages. Also French-English vocabulary list, exercises, more. 352pp. 5⅜ x 8½. 0-486-26443-2

CHICAGO AT THE TURN OF THE CENTURY IN PHOTOGRAPHS: 122 Historic Views from the Collections of the Chicago Historical Society, Larry A. Viskochil. Rare large-format prints offer detailed views of City Hall, State Street, the Loop, Hull House, Union Station, many other landmarks, circa 1904-1913. Introduction. Captions. Maps. 144pp. 9⅜ x 12¼. 0-486-24656-6

OLD BROOKLYN IN EARLY PHOTOGRAPHS, 1865-1929, William Lee Younger. Luna Park, Gravesend race track, construction of Grand Army Plaza, moving of Hotel Brighton, etc. 157 previously unpublished photographs. 165pp. 8⅞ x 11¾. 0-486-23587-4

THE MYTHS OF THE NORTH AMERICAN INDIANS, Lewis Spence. Rich anthology of the myths and legends of the Algonquins, Iroquois, Pawnees and Sioux, prefaced by an extensive historical and ethnological commentary. 36 illustrations. 480pp. 5⅜ x 8½. 0-486-25967-6

AN ENCYCLOPEDIA OF BATTLES: Accounts of Over 1,560 Battles from 1479 B.C. to the Present, David Eggenberger. Essential details of every major battle in recorded history from the first battle of Megiddo in 1479 B.C. to Grenada in 1984. List of Battle Maps. New Appendix covering the years 1967-1984. Index. 99 illustrations. 544pp. 6½ x 9¼. 0-486-24913-1

SAILING ALONE AROUND THE WORLD, Captain Joshua Slocum. First man to sail around the world, alone, in small boat. One of great feats of seamanship told in delightful manner. 67 illustrations. 294pp. 5⅜ x 8½. 0-486-20326-3

ANARCHISM AND OTHER ESSAYS, Emma Goldman. Powerful, penetrating, prophetic essays on direct action, role of minorities, prison reform, puritan hypocrisy, violence, etc. 271pp. 5⅜ x 8½. 0-486-22484-8

MYTHS OF THE HINDUS AND BUDDHISTS, Ananda K. Coomaraswamy and Sister Nivedita. Great stories of the epics; deeds of Krishna, Shiva, taken from puranas, Vedas, folk tales; etc. 32 illustrations. 400pp. 5⅜ x 8½. 0-486-21759-0

MY BONDAGE AND MY FREEDOM, Frederick Douglass. Born a slave, Douglass became outspoken force in antislavery movement. The best of Douglass' autobiographies. Graphic description of slave life. 464pp. 5⅜ x 8½. 0-486-22457-0

FOLLOWING THE EQUATOR: A Journey Around the World, Mark Twain. Fascinating humorous account of 1897 voyage to Hawaii, Australia, India, New Zealand, etc. Ironic, bemused reports on peoples, customs, climate, flora and fauna, politics, much more. 197 illustrations. 720pp. 5⅜ x 8½. 0-486-26113-1

THE PEOPLE CALLED SHAKERS, Edward D. Andrews. Definitive study of Shakers: origins, beliefs, practices, dances, social organization, furniture and crafts, etc. 33 illustrations. 351pp. 5⅜ x 8½. 0-486-21081-2

THE MYTHS OF GREECE AND ROME, H. A. Guerber. A classic of mythology, generously illustrated, long prized for its simple, graphic, accurate retelling of the principal myths of Greece and Rome, and for its commentary on their origins and significance. With 64 illustrations by Michelangelo, Raphael, Titian, Rubens, Canova, Bernini and others. 480pp. 5⅜ x 8½. 0-486-27584-1

PSYCHOLOGY OF MUSIC, Carl E. Seashore. Classic work discusses music as a medium from psychological viewpoint. Clear treatment of physical acoustics, auditory apparatus, sound perception, development of musical skills, nature of musical feeling, host of other topics. 88 figures. 408pp. 5⅜ x 8½.   0-486-21851-1

LIFE IN ANCIENT EGYPT, Adolf Erman. Fullest, most thorough, detailed older account with much not in more recent books, domestic life, religion, magic, medicine, commerce, much more. Many illustrations reproduce tomb paintings, carvings, hieroglyphs, etc. 597pp. 5⅜ x 8½.   0-486-22632-8

SUNDIALS, Their Theory and Construction, Albert Waugh. Far and away the best, most thorough coverage of ideas, mathematics concerned, types, construction, adjusting anywhere. Simple, nontechnical treatment allows even children to build several of these dials. Over 100 illustrations. 230pp. 5⅜ x 8½.   0-486-22947-5

THEORETICAL HYDRODYNAMICS, L. M. Milne-Thomson. Classic exposition of the mathematical theory of fluid motion, applicable to both hydrodynamics and aerodynamics. Over 600 exercises. 768pp. 6⅛ x 9¼.   0-486-68970-0

OLD-TIME VIGNETTES IN FULL COLOR, Carol Belanger Grafton (ed.). Over 390 charming, often sentimental illustrations, selected from archives of Victorian graphics—pretty women posing, children playing, food, flowers, kittens and puppies, smiling cherubs, birds and butterflies, much more. All copyright-free. 48pp. 9¼ x 12¼.   0-486-27269-9

PERSPECTIVE FOR ARTISTS, Rex Vicat Cole. Depth, perspective of sky and sea, shadows, much more, not usually covered. 391 diagrams, 81 reproductions of drawings and paintings. 279pp. 5⅜ x 8½.   0-486-22487-2

DRAWING THE LIVING FIGURE, Joseph Sheppard. Innovative approach to artistic anatomy focuses on specifics of surface anatomy, rather than muscles and bones. Over 170 drawings of live models in front, back and side views, and in widely varying poses. Accompanying diagrams. 177 illustrations. Introduction. Index. 144pp. 8⅜ x11¼.   0-486-26723-7

GOTHIC AND OLD ENGLISH ALPHABETS: 100 Complete Fonts, Dan X. Solo. Add power, elegance to posters, signs, other graphics with 100 stunning copyright-free alphabets: Blackstone, Dolbey, Germania, 97 more—including many lower-case, numerals, punctuation marks. 104pp. 8⅛ x 11.   0-486-24695-7

THE BOOK OF WOOD CARVING, Charles Marshall Sayers. Finest book for beginners discusses fundamentals and offers 34 designs. "Absolutely first rate . . . well thought out and well executed."–E. J. Tangerman. 118pp. 7¾ x 10⅝.   0-486-23654-4

ILLUSTRATED CATALOG OF CIVIL WAR MILITARY GOODS: Union Army Weapons, Insignia, Uniform Accessories, and Other Equipment, Schuyler, Hartley, and Graham. Rare, profusely illustrated 1846 catalog includes Union Army uniform and dress regulations, arms and ammunition, coats, insignia, flags, swords, rifles, etc. 226 illustrations. 160pp. 9 x 12.   0-486-24939-5

WOMEN'S FASHIONS OF THE EARLY 1900s: An Unabridged Republication of "New York Fashions, 1909," National Cloak & Suit Co. Rare catalog of mail-order fashions documents women's and children's clothing styles shortly after the turn of the century. Captions offer full descriptions, prices. Invaluable resource for fashion, costume historians. Approximately 725 illustrations. 128pp. 8⅜ x 11¼.   0-486-27276-1

CATALOG OF DOVER BOOKS

HOW TO DO BEADWORK, Mary White. Fundamental book on craft from simple projects to five-bead chains and woven works. 106 illustrations. 142pp. 5⅜ x 8.
0-486-20697-1

THE 1912 AND 1915 GUSTAV STICKLEY FURNITURE CATALOGS, Gustav Stickley. With over 200 detailed illustrations and descriptions, these two catalogs are essential reading and reference materials and identification guides for Stickley furniture. Captions cite materials, dimensions and prices. 112pp. 6½ x 9¼. 0-486-26676-1

EARLY AMERICAN LOCOMOTIVES, John H. White, Jr. Finest locomotive engravings from early 19th century: historical (1804–74), main-line (after 1870), special, foreign, etc. 147 plates. 142pp. 11⅜ x 8¼.
0-486-22772-3

LITTLE BOOK OF EARLY AMERICAN CRAFTS AND TRADES, Peter Stockham (ed.). 1807 children's book explains crafts and trades: baker, hatter, cooper, potter, and many others. 23 copperplate illustrations. 140pp. 4⁵/₈ x 6.
0-486-23336-7

VICTORIAN FASHIONS AND COSTUMES FROM HARPER'S BAZAR, 1867–1898, Stella Blum (ed.). Day costumes, evening wear, sports clothes, shoes, hats, other accessories in over 1,000 detailed engravings. 320pp. 9⅜ x 12¼.
0-486-22990-4

THE LONG ISLAND RAIL ROAD IN EARLY PHOTOGRAPHS, Ron Ziel. Over 220 rare photos, informative text document origin (1844) and development of rail service on Long Island. Vintage views of early trains, locomotives, stations, passengers, crews, much more. Captions. 8⅞ x 11¾.
0-486-26301-0

VOYAGE OF THE LIBERDADE, Joshua Slocum. Great 19th-century mariner's thrilling, first-hand account of the wreck of his ship off South America, the 35-foot boat he built from the wreckage, and its remarkable voyage home. 128pp. 5⅜ x 8½.
0-486-40022-0

TEN BOOKS ON ARCHITECTURE, Vitruvius. The most important book ever written on architecture. Early Roman aesthetics, technology, classical orders, site selection, all other aspects. Morgan translation. 331pp. 5⅜ x 8¼.   0-486-20645-9

THE HUMAN FIGURE IN MOTION, Eadweard Muybridge. More than 4,500 stopped-action photos, in action series, showing undraped men, women, children jumping, lying down, throwing, sitting, wrestling, carrying, etc. 390pp. 7⅞ x 10⅝.
0-486-20204-6 Clothbd.

TREES OF THE EASTERN AND CENTRAL UNITED STATES AND CANADA, William M. Harlow. Best one-volume guide to 140 trees. Full descriptions, woodlore, range, etc. Over 600 illustrations. Handy size. 288pp. 4½ x 6⅜.   0-486-20395-6

GROWING AND USING HERBS AND SPICES, Milo Miloradovich. Versatile handbook provides all the information needed for cultivation and use of all the herbs and spices available in North America. 4 illustrations. Index. Glossary. 236pp. 5⅜ x 8½.
0-486-25058-X

BIG BOOK OF MAZES AND LABYRINTHS, Walter Shepherd. 50 mazes and labyrinths in all–classical, solid, ripple, and more–in one great volume. Perfect inexpensive puzzler for clever youngsters. Full solutions. 112pp. 8¼ x 11. 0-486-22951-3

PIANO TUNING, J. Cree Fischer. Clearest, best book for beginner, amateur. Simple repairs, raising dropped notes, tuning by easy method of flattened fifths. No previous skills needed. 4 illustrations. 201pp. 5⅜ x 8½.   0-486-23267-0

HINTS TO SINGERS, Lillian Nordica. Selecting the right teacher, developing confidence, overcoming stage fright, and many other important skills receive thoughtful discussion in this indispensible guide, written by a world-famous diva of four decades' experience. 96pp. 5⅜ x 8½. 0-486-40094-8

THE COMPLETE NONSENSE OF EDWARD LEAR, Edward Lear. All nonsense limericks, zany alphabets, Owl and Pussycat, songs, nonsense botany, etc., illustrated by Lear. Total of 320pp. 5⅜ x 8½. (Available in U.S. only.) 0-486-20167-8

VICTORIAN PARLOUR POETRY: An Annotated Anthology, Michael R. Turner. 117 gems by Longfellow, Tennyson, Browning, many lesser-known poets. "The Village Blacksmith," "Curfew Must Not Ring Tonight," "Only a Baby Small," dozens more, often difficult to find elsewhere. Index of poets, titles, first lines. xxiii + 325pp. 5⅝ x 8¼. 0-486-27044-0

DUBLINERS, James Joyce. Fifteen stories offer vivid, tightly focused observations of the lives of Dublin's poorer classes. At least one, "The Dead," is considered a masterpiece. Reprinted complete and unabridged from standard edition. 160pp. 5³⁄₁₆ x 8¼. 0-486-26870-5

GREAT WEIRD TALES: 14 Stories by Lovecraft, Blackwood, Machen and Others, S. T. Joshi (ed.). 14 spellbinding tales, including "The Sin Eater," by Fiona McLeod, "The Eye Above the Mantel," by Frank Belknap Long, as well as renowned works by R. H. Barlow, Lord Dunsany, Arthur Machen, W. C. Morrow and eight other masters of the genre. 256pp. 5⅜ x 8½. (Available in U.S. only.) 0-486-40436-6

THE BOOK OF THE SACRED MAGIC OF ABRAMELIN THE MAGE, translated by S. MacGregor Mathers. Medieval manuscript of ceremonial magic. Basic document in Aleister Crowley, Golden Dawn groups. 268pp. 5⅜ x 8½. 0-486-23211-5

THE BATTLES THAT CHANGED HISTORY, Fletcher Pratt. Eminent historian profiles 16 crucial conflicts, ancient to modern, that changed the course of civilization. 352pp. 5⅜ x 8½. 0-486-41129-X

NEW RUSSIAN-ENGLISH AND ENGLISH-RUSSIAN DICTIONARY, M. A. O'Brien. This is a remarkably handy Russian dictionary, containing a surprising amount of information, including over 70,000 entries. 366pp. 4½ x 6⅛. 0-486-20208-9

NEW YORK IN THE FORTIES, Andreas Feininger. 162 brilliant photographs by the well-known photographer, formerly with *Life* magazine. Commuters, shoppers, Times Square at night, much else from city at its peak. Captions by John von Hartz. 181pp. 9¼ x 10¾. 0-486-23585-8

INDIAN SIGN LANGUAGE, William Tomkins. Over 525 signs developed by Sioux and other tribes. Written instructions and diagrams. Also 290 pictographs. 111pp. 6⅛ x 9¼. 0-486-22029-X

ANATOMY: A Complete Guide for Artists, Joseph Sheppard. A master of figure drawing shows artists how to render human anatomy convincingly. Over 460 illustrations. 224pp. 8⅜ x 11¼. 0-486-27279-6

MEDIEVAL CALLIGRAPHY: Its History and Technique, Marc Drogin. Spirited history, comprehensive instruction manual covers 13 styles (ca. 4th century through 15th). Excellent photographs; directions for duplicating medieval techniques with modern tools. 224pp. 8⅜ x 11¼. 0-486-26142-5

DRIED FLOWERS: How to Prepare Them, Sarah Whitlock and Martha Rankin. Complete instructions on how to use silica gel, meal and borax, perlite aggregate, sand and borax, glycerine and water to create attractive permanent flower arrangements. 12 illustrations. 32pp. 5⅜ x 8½. 0-486-21802-3

EASY-TO-MAKE BIRD FEEDERS FOR WOODWORKERS, Scott D. Campbell. Detailed, simple-to-use guide for designing, constructing, caring for and using feeders. Text, illustrations for 12 classic and contemporary designs. 96pp. 5⅜ x 8½. 0-486-25847-5

THE COMPLETE BOOK OF BIRDHOUSE CONSTRUCTION FOR WOODWORKERS, Scott D. Campbell. Detailed instructions, illustrations, tables. Also data on bird habitat and instinct patterns. Bibliography. 3 tables. 63 illustrations in 15 figures. 48pp. 5¼ x 8½. 0-486-24407-5

SCOTTISH WONDER TALES FROM MYTH AND LEGEND, Donald A. Mackenzie. 16 lively tales tell of giants rumbling down mountainsides, of a magic wand that turns stone pillars into warriors, of gods and goddesses, evil hags, powerful forces and more. 240pp. 5⅜ x 8½. 0-486-29677-6

THE HISTORY OF UNDERCLOTHES, C. Willett Cunnington and Phyllis Cunnington. Fascinating, well-documented survey covering six centuries of English undergarments, enhanced with over 100 illustrations: 12th-century laced-up bodice, footed long drawers (1795), 19th-century bustles, 19th-century corsets for men, Victorian "bust improvers," much more. 272pp. 5⅜ x 8¼. 0-486-27124-2

ARTS AND CRAFTS FURNITURE: The Complete Brooks Catalog of 1912, Brooks Manufacturing Co. Photos and detailed descriptions of more than 150 now very collectible furniture designs from the Arts and Crafts movement depict davenports, settees, buffets, desks, tables, chairs, bedsteads, dressers and more, all built of solid, quarter-sawed oak. Invaluable for students and enthusiasts of antiques, Americana and the decorative arts. 80pp. 6½ x 9¼. 0-486-27471-3

WILBUR AND ORVILLE: A Biography of the Wright Brothers, Fred Howard. Definitive, crisply written study tells the full story of the brothers' lives and work. A vividly written biography, unparalleled in scope and color, that also captures the spirit of an extraordinary era. 560pp. 6⅛ x 9¼. 0-486-40297-5

THE ARTS OF THE SAILOR: Knotting, Splicing and Ropework, Hervey Garrett Smith. Indispensable shipboard reference covers tools, basic knots and useful hitches; handsewing and canvas work, more. Over 100 illustrations. Delightful reading for sea lovers. 256pp. 5⅜ x 8½. 0-486-26440-8

FRANK LLOYD WRIGHT'S FALLINGWATER: The House and Its History, Second, Revised Edition, Donald Hoffmann. A total revision–both in text and illustrations–of the standard document on Fallingwater, the boldest, most personal architectural statement of Wright's mature years, updated with valuable new material from the recently opened Frank Lloyd Wright Archives. "Fascinating"–*The New York Times.* 116 illustrations. 128pp. 9¼ x 10¾. 0-486-27430-6

PHOTOGRAPHIC SKETCHBOOK OF THE CIVIL WAR, Alexander Gardner. 100 photos taken on field during the Civil War. Famous shots of Manassas Harper's Ferry, Lincoln, Richmond, slave pens, etc. 244pp. 10⅝ x 8¼. 0-486-22731-6

FIVE ACRES AND INDEPENDENCE, Maurice G. Kains. Great back-to-the-land classic explains basics of self-sufficient farming. The one book to get. 95 illustrations. 397pp. 5⅜ x 8½. 0-486-20974-1

A MODERN HERBAL, Margaret Grieve. Much the fullest, most exact, most useful compilation of herbal material. Gigantic alphabetical encyclopedia, from aconite to zedoary, gives botanical information, medical properties, folklore, economic uses, much else. Indispensable to serious reader. 161 illustrations. 888pp. 6½ x 9¼. 2-vol. set. (Available in U.S. only.)   Vol. I: 0-486-22798-7   Vol. II: 0-486-22799-5

HIDDEN TREASURE MAZE BOOK, Dave Phillips. Solve 34 challenging mazes accompanied by heroic tales of adventure. Evil dragons, people-eating plants, bloodthirsty giants, many more dangerous adversaries lurk at every twist and turn. 34 mazes, stories, solutions. 48pp. 8¼ x 11.   0-486-24566-7

LETTERS OF W. A. MOZART, Wolfgang A. Mozart. Remarkable letters show bawdy wit, humor, imagination, musical insights, contemporary musical world; includes some letters from Leopold Mozart. 276pp. 5⅜ x 8½.   0-486-22859-2

BASIC PRINCIPLES OF CLASSICAL BALLET, Agrippina Vaganova. Great Russian theoretician, teacher explains methods for teaching classical ballet. 118 illustrations. 175pp. 5⅜ x 8½.   0-486-22036-2

THE JUMPING FROG, Mark Twain. Revenge edition. The original story of The Celebrated Jumping Frog of Calaveras County, a hapless French translation, and Twain's hilarious "retranslation" from the French. 12 illustrations. 66pp. 5⅜ x 8½.
0-486-22686-7

BEST REMEMBERED POEMS, Martin Gardner (ed.). The 126 poems in this superb collection of 19th- and 20th-century British and American verse range from Shelley's "To a Skylark" to the impassioned "Renascence" of Edna St. Vincent Millay and to Edward Lear's whimsical "The Owl and the Pussycat." 224pp. 5⅜ x 8½.
0-486-27165-X

COMPLETE SONNETS, William Shakespeare. Over 150 exquisite poems deal with love, friendship, the tyranny of time, beauty's evanescence, death and other themes in language of remarkable power, precision and beauty. Glossary of archaic terms. 80pp. 5³⁄₁₆ x 8¼.   0-486-26686-9

HISTORIC HOMES OF THE AMERICAN PRESIDENTS, Second, Revised Edition, Irvin Haas. A traveler's guide to American Presidential homes, most open to the public, depicting and describing homes occupied by every American President from George Washington to George Bush. With visiting hours, admission charges, travel routes. 175 photographs. Index. 160pp. 8¼ x 11.   0-486-26751-2

THE WIT AND HUMOR OF OSCAR WILDE, Alvin Redman (ed.). More than 1,000 ripostes, paradoxes, wisecracks: Work is the curse of the drinking classes; I can resist everything except temptation; etc. 258pp. 5⅜ x 8½.   0-486-20602-5

SHAKESPEARE LEXICON AND QUOTATION DICTIONARY, Alexander Schmidt. Full definitions, locations, shades of meaning in every word in plays and poems. More than 50,000 exact quotations. 1,485pp. 6½ x 9¼. 2-vol. set.
Vol. 1: 0-486-22726-X   Vol. 2: 0-486-22727-8

SELECTED POEMS, Emily Dickinson. Over 100 best-known, best-loved poems by one of America's foremost poets, reprinted from authoritative early editions. No comparable edition at this price. Index of first lines. 64pp. 5³⁄₁₆ x 8¼. 0-486-26466-1

THE INSIDIOUS DR. FU-MANCHU, Sax Rohmer. The first of the popular mystery series introduces a pair of English detectives to their archnemesis, the diabolical Dr. Fu-Manchu. Flavorful atmosphere, fast-paced action, and colorful characters enliven this classic of the genre. 208pp. 5³⁄₁₆ x 8¼.   0-486-29898-1

THE MALLEUS MALEFICARUM OF KRAMER AND SPRENGER, translated by Montague Summers. Full text of most important witchhunter's "bible," used by both Catholics and Protestants. 278pp. 6⅝ x 10.
0-486-22802-9

SPANISH STORIES/CUENTOS ESPAÑOLES: A Dual-Language Book, Angel Flores (ed.). Unique format offers 13 great stories in Spanish by Cervantes, Borges, others. Faithful English translations on facing pages. 352pp. 5⅜ x 8½.
0-486-25399-6

GARDEN CITY, LONG ISLAND, IN EARLY PHOTOGRAPHS, 1869–1919, Mildred H. Smith. Handsome treasury of 118 vintage pictures, accompanied by carefully researched captions, document the Garden City Hotel fire (1899), the Vanderbilt Cup Race (1908), the first airmail flight departing from the Nassau Boulevard Aerodrome (1911), and much more. 96pp. 8⅞ x 11¾.
0-486-40669-5

OLD QUEENS, N.Y., IN EARLY PHOTOGRAPHS, Vincent F. Seyfried and William Asadorian. Over 160 rare photographs of Maspeth, Jamaica, Jackson Heights, and other areas. Vintage views of DeWitt Clinton mansion, 1939 World's Fair and more. Captions. 192pp. 8⅞ x 11.
0-486-26358-4

CAPTURED BY THE INDIANS: 15 Firsthand Accounts, 1750-1870, Frederick Drimmer. Astounding true historical accounts of grisly torture, bloody conflicts, relentless pursuits, miraculous escapes and more, by people who lived to tell the tale. 384pp. 5⅜ x 8½.
0-486-24901-8

THE WORLD'S GREAT SPEECHES (Fourth Enlarged Edition), Lewis Copeland, Lawrence W. Lamm, and Stephen J. McKenna. Nearly 300 speeches provide public speakers with a wealth of updated quotes and inspiration–from Pericles' funeral oration and William Jennings Bryan's "Cross of Gold Speech" to Malcolm X's powerful words on the Black Revolution and Earl of Spenser's tribute to his sister, Diana, Princess of Wales. 944pp. 5⅜ x 8⅜.
0-486-40903-1

THE BOOK OF THE SWORD, Sir Richard F. Burton. Great Victorian scholar/adventurer's eloquent, erudite history of the "queen of weapons"–from prehistory to early Roman Empire. Evolution and development of early swords, variations (sabre, broadsword, cutlass, scimitar, etc.), much more. 336pp. 6⅛ x 9¼.
0-486-25434-8

AUTOBIOGRAPHY: The Story of My Experiments with Truth, Mohandas K. Gandhi. Boyhood, legal studies, purification, the growth of the Satyagraha (nonviolent protest) movement. Critical, inspiring work of the man responsible for the freedom of India. 480pp. 5⅜ x 8½. (Available in U.S. only.)
0-486-24593-4

CELTIC MYTHS AND LEGENDS, T. W. Rolleston. Masterful retelling of Irish and Welsh stories and tales. Cuchulain, King Arthur, Deirdre, the Grail, many more. First paperback edition. 58 full-page illustrations. 512pp. 5⅜ x 8½.
0-486-26507-2

THE PRINCIPLES OF PSYCHOLOGY, William James. Famous long course complete, unabridged. Stream of thought, time perception, memory, experimental methods; great work decades ahead of its time. 94 figures. 1,391pp. 5⅜ x 8½. 2-vol. set
Vol. I: 0-486-20381-6   Vol. II: 0 486-20382-4

THE WORLD AS WILL AND REPRESENTATION, Arthur Schopenhauer. Definitive English translation of Schopenhauer's life work, correcting more than 1,000 errors, omissions in earlier translations. Translated by E. F. J. Payne. Total of 1,269pp. 5⅜ x 8½. 2-vol. set.   Vol. 1: 0-486-21761-2   Vol. 2: 0-486-21762-0

MAGIC AND MYSTERY IN TIBET, Madame Alexandra David-Neel. Experiences among lamas, magicians, sages, sorcerers, Bonpa wizards. A true psychic discovery. 32 illustrations. 321pp. 5⅜ x 8½. (Available in U.S. only.) 0-486-22682-4

THE EGYPTIAN BOOK OF THE DEAD, E. A. Wallis Budge. Complete reproduction of Ani's papyrus, finest ever found. Full hieroglyphic text, interlinear transliteration, word-for-word translation, smooth translation. 533pp. 6½ x 9¼. 0-486-21866-X

HISTORIC COSTUME IN PICTURES, Braun & Schneider. Over 1,450 costumed figures in clearly detailed engravings–from dawn of civilization to end of 19th century. Captions. Many folk costumes. 256pp. 8⅜ x 11¾. 0-486-23150-X

MATHEMATICS FOR THE NONMATHEMATICIAN, Morris Kline. Detailed, college-level treatment of mathematics in cultural and historical context, with numerous exercises. Recommended Reading Lists. Tables. Numerous figures. 641pp. 5⅜ x 8½. 0-486-24823-2

PROBABILISTIC METHODS IN THE THEORY OF STRUCTURES, Isaac Elishakoff. Well-written introduction covers the elements of the theory of probability from two or more random variables, the reliability of such multivariable structures, the theory of random function, Monte Carlo methods of treating problems incapable of exact solution, and more. Examples. 502pp. 5⅜ x 8½. 0-486-40691-1

THE RIME OF THE ANCIENT MARINER, Gustave Doré, S. T. Coleridge. Doré's finest work; 34 plates capture moods, subtleties of poem. Flawless full-size reproductions printed on facing pages with authoritative text of poem. "Beautiful. Simply beautiful."–*Publisher's Weekly.* 77pp. 9¼ x 12. 0-486-22305-1

SCULPTURE: Principles and Practice, Louis Slobodkin. Step-by-step approach to clay, plaster, metals, stone; classical and modern. 253 drawings, photos. 255pp. 8⅛ x 11. 0-486-22960-2

THE INFLUENCE OF SEA POWER UPON HISTORY, 1660–1783, A. T. Mahan. Influential classic of naval history and tactics still used as text in war colleges. First paperback edition. 4 maps. 24 battle plans. 640pp. 5⅜ x 8½. 0-486-25509-3

THE STORY OF THE TITANIC AS TOLD BY ITS SURVIVORS, Jack Winocour (ed.). What it was really like. Panic, despair, shocking inefficiency, and a little heroism. More thrilling than any fictional account. 26 illustrations. 320pp. 5⅜ x 8½. 0-486-20610-6

ONE TWO THREE . . . INFINITY: Facts and Speculations of Science, George Gamow. Great physicist's fascinating, readable overview of contemporary science: number theory, relativity, fourth dimension, entropy, genes, atomic structure, much more. 128 illustrations. Index. 352pp. 5⅜ x 8½. 0-486-25664-2

DALÍ ON MODERN ART: The Cuckolds of Antiquated Modern Art, Salvador Dalí. Influential painter skewers modern art and its practitioners. Outrageous evaluations of Picasso, Cézanne, Turner, more. 15 renderings of paintings discussed. 44 calligraphic decorations by Dalí. 96pp. 5⅜ x 8½. (Available in U.S. only.) 0-486-29220-7

ANTIQUE PLAYING CARDS: A Pictorial History, Henry René D'Allemagne. Over 900 elaborate, decorative images from rare playing cards (14th–20th centuries): Bacchus, death, dancing dogs, hunting scenes, royal coats of arms, players cheating, much more. 96pp. 9¼ x 12¼. 0-486-29265-7

CATALOG OF DOVER BOOKS

MAKING FURNITURE MASTERPIECES: 30 Projects with Measured Drawings, Franklin H. Gottshall. Step-by-step instructions, illustrations for constructing handsome, useful pieces, among them a Sheraton desk, Chippendale chair, Spanish desk, Queen Anne table and a William and Mary dressing mirror. 224pp. 8¼ x 11¼.
0-486-29338-6

NORTH AMERICAN INDIAN DESIGNS FOR ARTISTS AND CRAFTSPEOPLE, Eva Wilson. Over 360 authentic copyright-free designs adapted from Navajo blankets, Hopi pottery, Sioux buffalo hides, more. Geometrics, symbolic figures, plant and animal motifs, etc. 128pp. 8⅜ x 11. (Not for sale in the United Kingdom.) 0-486-25341-4

THE FOSSIL BOOK: A Record of Prehistoric Life, Patricia V. Rich et al. Profusely illustrated definitive guide covers everything from single-celled organisms and dinosaurs to birds and mammals and the interplay between climate and man. Over 1,500 illustrations. 760pp. 7½ x 10¼.
0-486-29371-8

VICTORIAN ARCHITECTURAL DETAILS: Designs for Over 700 Stairs, Mantels, Doors, Windows, Cornices, Porches, and Other Decorative Elements, A. J. Bicknell & Company. Everything from dormer windows and piazzas to balconies and gable ornaments. Also includes elevations and floor plans for handsome, private residences and commercial structures. 80pp. 9⅜ x 12¼.
0-486-44015-X

WESTERN ISLAMIC ARCHITECTURE: A Concise Introduction, John D. Hoag. Profusely illustrated critical appraisal compares and contrasts Islamic mosques and palaces–from Spain and Egypt to other areas in the Middle East. 139 illustrations. 128pp. 6 x 9.
0-486-43760-4

CHINESE ARCHITECTURE: A Pictorial History, Liang Ssu-ch'eng. More than 240 rare photographs and drawings depict temples, pagodas, tombs, bridges, and imperial palaces comprising much of China's architectural heritage. 152 halftones, 94 diagrams. 232pp. 10¾ x 9⅞.
0-486-43999-2

THE RENAISSANCE: Studies in Art and Poetry, Walter Pater. One of the most talked-about books of the 19th century, *The Renaissance* combines scholarship and philosophy in an innovative work of cultural criticism that examines the achievements of Botticelli, Leonardo, Michelangelo, and other artists. "The holy writ of beauty."–Oscar Wilde. 160pp. 5⅜ x 8½.
0-486-44025-7

A TREATISE ON PAINTING, Leonardo da Vinci. The great Renaissance artist's practical advice on drawing and painting techniques covers anatomy, perspective, composition, light and shadow, and color. A classic of art instruction, it features 48 drawings by Nicholas Poussin and Leon Battista Alberti. 192pp. 5⅜ x 8½.
0-486-44155-5

THE MIND OF LEONARDO DA VINCI, Edward McCurdy. More than just a biography, this classic study by a distinguished historian draws upon Leonardo's extensive writings to offer numerous demonstrations of the Renaissance master's achievements, not only in sculpture and painting, but also in music, engineering, and even experimental aviation. 384pp. 5⅜ x 8½.
0-486-44142-3

WASHINGTON IRVING'S RIP VAN WINKLE, Illustrated by Arthur Rackham. Lovely prints that established artist as a leading illustrator of the time and forever etched into the popular imagination a classic of Catskill lore. 51 full-color plates. 80pp. 8⅜ x 11.
0-486-44242-X

HENSCHE ON PAINTING, John W. Robichaux. Basic painting philosophy and methodology of a great teacher, as expounded in his famous classes and workshops on Cape Cod. 7 illustrations in color on covers. 80pp. 5⅜ x 8½. 0-486-43728-0

LIGHT AND SHADE: A Classic Approach to Three-Dimensional Drawing, Mrs. Mary P. Merrifield. Handy reference clearly demonstrates principles of light and shade by revealing effects of common daylight, sunshine, and candle or artificial light on geometrical solids. 13 plates. 64pp. 5⅜ x 8½. 0-486-44143-1

ASTROLOGY AND ASTRONOMY: A Pictorial Archive of Signs and Symbols, Ernst and Johanna Lehner. Treasure trove of stories, lore, and myth, accompanied by more than 300 rare illustrations of planets, the Milky Way, signs of the zodiac, comets, meteors, and other astronomical phenomena. 192pp. 8⅜ x 11. 0-486-43981-X

JEWELRY MAKING: Techniques for Metal, Tim McCreight. Easy-to-follow instructions and carefully executed illustrations describe tools and techniques, use of gems and enamels, wire inlay, casting, and other topics. 72 line illustrations and diagrams. 176pp. 8¼ x 10⅞. 0-486-44043-5

MAKING BIRDHOUSES: Easy and Advanced Projects, Gladstone Califf. Easy-to-follow instructions include diagrams for everything from a one-room house for bluebirds to a forty-two-room structure for purple martins. 56 plates; 4 figures. 80pp. 8¾ x 6⅜. 0-486-44183-0

LITTLE BOOK OF LOG CABINS: How to Build and Furnish Them, William S. Wicks. Handy how-to manual, with instructions and illustrations for building cabins in the Adirondack style, fireplaces, stairways, furniture, beamed ceilings, and more. 102 line drawings. 96pp. 8¾ x 6⅜. 0-486-44259-4

THE SEASONS OF AMERICA PAST, Eric Sloane. From "sugaring time" and strawberry picking to Indian summer and fall harvest, a whole year's activities described in charming prose and enhanced with 79 of the author's own illustrations. 160pp. 8¼ x 11. 0-486-44220-9

THE METROPOLIS OF TOMORROW, Hugh Ferriss. Generous, prophetic vision of the metropolis of the future, as perceived in 1929. Powerful illustrations of towering structures, wide avenues, and rooftop parks–all features in many of today's modern cities. 59 illustrations. 144pp. 8¼ x 11. 0-486-43727-2

THE PATH TO ROME, Hilaire Belloc. This 1902 memoir abounds in lively vignettes from a vanished time, recounting a pilgrimage on foot across the Alps and Apennines in order to "see all Europe which the Christian Faith has saved." 77 of the author's original line drawings complement his sparkling prose. 272pp. 5⅜ x 8½. 0-486-44001-X

THE HISTORY OF RASSELAS: Prince of Abissinia, Samuel Johnson. Distinguished English writer attacks eighteenth-century optimism and man's unrealistic estimates of what life has to offer. 112pp. 5⅜ x 8½. 0-486-44094-X

A VOYAGE TO ARCTURUS, David Lindsay. A brilliant flight of pure fancy, where wild creatures crowd the fantastic landscape and demented torturers dominate victims with their bizarre mental powers. 272pp. 5⅜ x 8½. 0-486-44198-9

Paperbound unless otherwise indicated. Available at your book dealer, online at **www.doverpublications.com**, or by writing to Dept. GI, Dover Publications, Inc., 31 East 2nd Street, Mineola, NY 11501. For current price information or for free catalogs (please indicate field of interest), write to Dover Publications or log on to **www.doverpublications.com** and see every Dover book in print. Dover publishes more than 500 books each year on science, elementary and advanced mathematics, biology, music, art, literary history, social sciences, and other areas.